The Winds of Revolution

Latin America Today—And Tomorrow

The Winds of Revolution

Latin America Today—And Tomorrow

REVISED EDITION

TAD SZULC

FREDERICK A. PRAEGER, *Publishers*
New York • Washington

BOOKS THAT MATTER

Published in the United States of America in 1963
by Frederick A. Praeger, Inc., Publishers
111 Fourth Avenue, New York 3, N.Y., U.S.A.

Revised Edition, 1965

Second Printing, 1965

© 1963, 1965 by Frederick A. Praeger, Inc.
Library of Congress Catalog Card Number: 65-13348

Printed in the United States of America

To
Nicole

Contents

The Winds of Revolution

Latin America Today—And Tomorrow

Preface to Revised Edition

THERE IS PERHAPS no better indication of the intensity, depth, and diversity of the Latin American revolution than the vast changes and far-reaching developments that have taken place in the Hemisphere in the short span of one year.

Since this book was completed, early in October, 1963, the march of events in Latin America—and of other events in the United States relating to the fate of Latin America—has made it virtually out of date. All these changes in the political landscape of the Hemisphere, some of them basic in character, have necessitated the present revision of THE WINDS OF REVOLUTION, to take into account the speed with which Latin America's revolutionary history, both subtly and obviously, is racing ahead.

In the course of these twelve months, the foundations of the whole relationship between the United States and Latin America were severely shaken by President Kennedy's assassination. It has taken more than half a year to guide this relationship back to where it stood on the day of the tragedy of November 22, and even now, as President Johnson and his new Latin American policy team have firmly grasped control, doubts and hesitations still linger in Latin America about the new Administration.

The Alliance for Progress, the program launched by President Kennedy as the United States response to the Cuban revolution, has entered its fourth year and a new phase. The creation of CIAP, a steering committee for the Alliance, may well lead to its revitalization after these difficult and tentative first years.

Cuba has remained the great unsolved problem of the Hemisphere, and the reverberations from Havana have continued to be felt in many parts of Latin America. Late in 1963, a Cuban-supported revolutionary attempt in Venezuela failed when Venezuelans turned their backs on pro-Communist guerrillas and went ahead with elections that greatly strengthened democratic institutions in their country. Cuba's involvement in Venezuela led the American Foreign Ministers in July, 1964, to declare her an aggressor and to apply sanctions against the Havana regime—an unprecedented act in Hemispheric dealings with the Cuban problem.

Violent riots in the Panama Canal Zone in January, 1964, resulted in a three-month interruption in U.S.–Panamanian relations and, subsequently, an agreement to renegotiate the Canal treaty. This was the Johnson Administration's first major experience of the volatility of Latin America.

In April, 1964, a civilian-military revolution ousted the government of President João Goulart in Brazil, in order to arrest the country's rapid drift toward utter chaos and the establishment of a radical, leftist regime. The long-term direction that Brazil will take under the provisional regime that is to serve until January, 1967, may become one of the crucial tests for the development of the Hemisphere.

Elections of immense political importance for all Latin America were held in Chile in September, 1964. The landslide victory of Senator Eduardo Frei Montalva, a Christian Democratic reformer, over a Communist-backed opponent was one of the most encouraging events of the decade, strengthening the trend toward democratic social reform.

The ouster of President Paz Estenssoro of Bolivia, by a military junta, in November, 1964, meant still another crisis for Hemispheric democracy, and a period of factional strife loomed ahead.

Thus, in a kaleidoscopic succession of developments, the face of Latin America has undergone all these and other changes, emphasizing the power and the momentum of the onrushing great revolution.

T. S.

Washington
November, 1964

1. The Stage and the Setting

The Spirit of Revolution

THE REVOLUTIONARY THEME—clarion-clear in some parts, still muted, uncertain, almost unconscious in others—is the dominant motif sounding amid the restless, poverty-plagued, disoriented, and explosively expanding populations of Latin America in this decisive decade.

It is a theme rich in variations, making itself heard in as many different tones as there are nationalities, cultures, ideologies, and special conditions in the twenty republics and the handful of colonies and foreign-controlled territories that make up the geographic and political concept known as Latin America.

Yet, all these variations do reflect a common theme: the demand for a better material life and, simultaneously, profound political and psychological changes that still remain largely undefined and only partially understood. The emphasis is on change, on experimentation, on adventure, and on a surging desire to upset the patterns of the old and to venture alone, if necessary, along the paths of the new.

This revolutionary spirit has reached an extreme stage—and a point of contagious inspiration—in Cuba under the Fidel Castro regime, which has chosen Communism as its ideological mantle, and an intimate alliance with the Soviet world as its instrument for bolstering the revolution economically and protecting it militarily from outside attack.

Cuba's choice of Communism thrust her own revolution and, subsequently, the notion of social revolution in Latin America as a whole into the context of the East-West Cold War. It led the United States to espouse, still haltingly, the idea of promoting a program of social evolution and basic reform—backed by more than $1 billion annually in loans and grants—to make certain that the irreversible new movements in Latin America were kept within the framework of representative democracy and allegiance to the West. As had been demonstrated in Cuba, the immediate alternative was that the mounting wave of protest would be absorbed into the sea of Communist influence, wild-eyed Jacobinism, and anti-Yankee ultranationalism. These forces, potentially in some places and actually in others, have made a considerable advance in Latin America in the years following the Cuban revolution.

The revolutionary trends elsewhere in the Hemisphere—at least late in 1964—are not yet so extreme and awesome as those that have arisen in Cuba. In many cases, they are developing more quietly and subtly—taking the form, for instance, of pronounced nationalism, neutralism, and opposition to the Western economic and political presence and influence. But, whatever their form, they represent the greatest challenge thus far to the position of the United States and the West in Latin America.

Therefore, when the United States finally realized that the now Communist-inspired siren song of the Cuban revolution might find avid listeners throughout Latin America—because until then no other alternative has been offered the neglected Hemisphere by the complacent West—it moved, belatedly but forcefully, toward recognition of the need to remake the entire structure through intensive economic development, land and tax reform, and other urgent measures.

Falling into the spirit—and the semantics—of the times, the United States announced its readiness to lead this erupting "revolution of rising expectations," hoping to draw on the traditions of its own revolutionary past. The moderate shift toward liberalism in the United States, symbolized by President Kennedy's election, seemingly promised to equip this nation with a new insight and a strengthened determination to go along with the revolution of the underdeveloped world.

The battle for the Latin American social revolution, now integrally a part of the East-West conflict, thus pits the general aims of the Alliance for Progress program—providing for local self-help and massive United States aid within the scope of democratic institutions—against the Communist-inspired radicalism urged in different forms by Havana, Moscow, and Peking. But Latin America's own ultimate response to this battle may well provide a third dimension of revolution.

President Kennedy's Alliance program, a refinement and expansion of ideas that the Eisenhower Administration began to formulate in its last nine months in office (after passively observing for seven years the unmistakable increase in economic and social tensions in the Americas), is the key mechanism in the reaction of the United States to the Jacobinist onslaught. On its success in the course of the decade of the 1960's—and success implies not only tangible physical results but, even more essential, the acceptance of the formula of the "democratic revolution" by the new generation of Latin American political leaders, the unsophisticated but increasingly conscious masses, and the still powerful and unprogressive conservative economic elite—hinges the entire future of Latin America. The chief question that arises as the Alliance, after its first three tentative years, begins to acquire a shape is whether there is enough time left to implement it in the face of the skepticism, the impatience, and the mounting revolutionary spirit in Latin America.

It is still too early, of course, to predict whether or how the Alliance will succeed in the broad sense. The results thus far are, however, quite inconclusive as it was not until 1964 that the Alliance began to demonstrate that it was not merely a somewhat sophisticated form of United States financial aid. To remake this distorted image and to fashion the program into the Hemisphere-wide "democratic social revolution" that President Kennedy had intended it to be, the Alliance was equipped with a strong steering committee—known as the CIAP (Comité Interamericano de la Alianza para el Progreso, or Inter-American Committee for the Alliance for Progress)—and hope arose that a new phase lay ahead.

But the outcome of the Latin American contest is bound to weigh heavily in the larger battle between Western democracy and Communism to decide which of them is to be the world's "way of the future."

A revolutionary Latin America that is anti-United States—or even outspokenly neutralist—and has active sympathies for the East, would obviously be a tremendous asset for the Communist camp, far more important than the control of, for example, Africa. It would be the dramatic transformation of our peaceful Hemispheric backyard—politically reliable, economically rewarding as an export market, and a source of raw materials, and so long and confidently taken for granted—into an enemy-infiltrated rebel zone.

The Rising Pressures

The signs that this could happen—ignored for years despite urgent warnings by our friends in Latin America—are becoming increasingly clear. Communist and Fidelista propaganda tirelessly beats the drums for its own version of social justice and for political and economic "independence" from the United States. The rising ultranationalism is being exploited to the hilt everywhere. The Communist world is accelerating its programs of economic, political, and cultural penetration. The Kremlin is propounding "wars of national liberation," and "popular front" policies, whichever seem to apply better in a specific instance. Revolutionary agitation, advocated by Cuba and Communist China, is spreading from the Caribbean to the Central American isthmus and the South American mainland. And all these appeals and influences are winning growing attention in Latin America's restless universities, in her urban slums, and in her miserable rural huts and villages.

To the people who are often hungry and diseased, unemployed or underemployed, these revolutionary calls do not represent ideological or political concepts—of Communism on the one hand or of representative democracy on the other. By and large, such notions remain essentially meaningless. All that really matters is the promise of food for the children, of decent housing for the family, of full employment twelve months of the year, of human and national dignity, and of a chance for a better life in every sense.

So deep is this awakening hunger for social improvement and the fulfillment of nationalistic desires that even politically sophisticated leaders and groups in Latin America refuse to see a Communist threat in the Cuban revolution or its repetition—even now that Cuba has been officially proclaimed a Marxist-Leninist state marching toward full-fledged Communism—and, instead, still prefer to view it solely as a pace-setting social upheaval.

The Cuban missile crisis of October, 1962—which abruptly brought the Soviet military presence and the immediacy of a nuclear war to the Western Hemisphere—was an immense shock to Latin America, its leaders, its thinkers, and its revolutionaries. It created, in the face of a clear and present danger, a sense of Hemispheric political unity that had not existed since the days of World War II. But while it served to an important extent to help emphasize the dangers involved when a Latin American revolution falls under the control or inspiration of an extracontinental power, the October crisis did not result in an all-out rejection of the Cuban revolutionary ideas—and of their political and nationalistic implications—on the part of many important Hemispheric statesmen.

Although the missile crisis did damage the Soviet position in

Latin American eyes and weakened still further Dr. Castro's position as a Hemispheric leader, the Western camp has failed to translate it immediately into an ideological victory for its camp or for representative democracy. Once again, the West has demonstrated its inability to follow up politically and ideologically its power advantage. If the crisis had any effect in Latin America, it was to stimulate the quest for some sort of "third position" in the terms of the world conflict and in the terms of its ultimate revolutionary definition. As an illustration of post-crisis sentiment, it may be useful to listen to Brazil's ex-President João Goulart as he discussed the Cuban problem in February, 1963, in an interview with the London *Economist:*

> Our purpose is to help to establish the understanding, so that Cuba may become re-integrated in her relations with all the American countries. . . . It is an essential point in the relations among nations that none of them should become the base for ideological or military aggression. What characterizes ideological aggression are the facts or conditions that could make it probable or even imminent. This is why we think that the withdrawal of nuclear weapons from Cuba was a gesture of wisdom. . . . There exists already in the world a co-existence between Communist and non-Communist countries; though this co-existence is developing in a context of the cold war, the fact is that it is moving ahead and that there is a general effort to make it more normal. I have the impression that the world tends to reconstruct its political patterns, so that, through contacts between different ideologies, there may be established new criteria of political and social stability. . . .

Although Goulart himself was overthrown by a civilian-military revolution on April 1, 1964, because of his attempt to set up a radical leftist state in Brazil, his remarks were, and still are, representative of a large segment of Latin American political thought. This was again demonstrated in July, 1964, when four influential countries opposed sanctions by the Organization of American States against Cuba for her intervention in Venezuela.

In relating President Goulart's statement to the present-day realities of Brazil or Latin America, it must be kept in mind that promises of agrarian reform and other basic changes, in a region where between 3 and 8 per cent of the landlords own between 60 and 80 per cent of the cultivable land, speak louder and more convincingly than the traditional democratic slogans or the fears of Communism in Cuba. And it is bound to be so—notwithstanding the chilling experience of the missiles—unless these democratic slogans are finally backed by far-reaching social measures and effective implementation of democratic ideology.

Hundreds of thousands of Latin American students, peasants, workers, and intellectuals still believe—or want to believe—the tales of the successes of land reform in Cuba, not bothering to inquire whether the propaganda claims are accurate and closing their eyes to other tales from Cuba describing overflowing prisons, the ubiquitous secret police, and the denial of all political freedom. Their enthusiasm often seems undeterred by the fact that strict food rationing had to be imposed on Castro's island three years after the victory of the revolution, that shoe and clothes rationing followed, that the 1962 and 1963 sugar crops were alarmingly below the previous years' crops, and that revolutionary planning has produced seemingly insoluble chaos. They are impressed when they hear about the Cuban literacy campaign, the end of graft and corruption, the elimination of racial discrimination, and the admission of the people to the once-private beaches. Even as late as July, 1964, when the Hemisphere Foreign Ministers met to invoke sanctions against Havana for promoting subversion in Venezuela, this sentiment of tolerance was seen in the refusal by Bolivia, Chile, Mexico, and Uruguay to vote for these measures.

Yet, on the positive or promising side of the ledger, Latin Americans do have a tradition of political freedom—though it has always been more an ideal than a reality in their lives. The same students and workers who now riot either because they favor a Cuban-type revolution or perhaps merely because they are impatient with the desperately slow march of democracy filled the streets of Argentine, Colombian, and Venezuelan cities only a few years ago to brave the soldiers and the policemen of the military dictatorships in the name of political democracy—just as Cubans did in the beginning against the Batista regime.

The reservoir of good will toward the United States has not yet been completely emptied, and many other thousands or millions of Latin Americans are still receptive, in principle, to American cooperation in solving their problems, though skepticism is again fast setting in, as the Alliance moves too slowly toward a breakthrough.

Perhaps much of the responsibility for the continued restiveness lies with the older generation of Latin America's democratic leaders, who knew how to conduct political revolutions against dictatorial oppression but stopped short of encouraging the social change so clearly needed. Surely, it was Fidel Castro's decision not to halt at the boundary of political and social revolutions, but to race ahead toward radical change, that has given him his strength and influence. The tragedy for both Cuba and Latin America was that before long Castro had to turn his social revolution into a Communist police regime.

With hindsight about Cuba's course, it is clear, then, that democracy's most urgent challenge in Latin America is to demonstrate that a free society can solve its basic social, human, and economic problems as well as or better than a Communist police state. And, indeed, this is the central philosophical problem of our time.

The refusal thus far of many Latin Americans, perhaps justifiably skeptical of the long unfulfilled promises of democracy, to believe that there is another way besides "Fidel's way," or its variations, makes them especially receptive to Communist-inspired revolutionary programs. And, conversely, warnings of Communist infiltration have far less impact than the mystique of a great social revolution unless democracy finally comes forth with its own mystique of equal or greater power.

But to compound the magnitude of these problems, democracy in Latin America still falls far short of offering a convincing philosophy to the impatient youth and the destitute masses.

This continuing failure was underlined once again in Argentina in March, 1962. There the military *coup d'état,* which ousted President Arturo Frondizi after the electoral victories of parties supporting former dictator Juan D. Perón, represented principally a blow against democracy and against the validity of its claims before Argentine and continental public opinion. It was a historically regressive movement threatening to weaken and compromise democracy at a time when all its spiritual strength needed to be demonstrated. If, indeed, the only defense of a democratic society against the inroads of radicalism is a military coup, then it is tantamount to a confession of democracy's weakness and helplessness.

Imitated elsewhere in Latin America—as it was in Peru four months later—the Argentine example could not fail to play into the hands of those who seek to discredit democracy. The argument of the Argentine generals and admirals that they overthrew Dr. Frondizi to prevent the spread of the totalitarian influences of Peronismo and Communism—and the even less convincing reasoning of the Peruvian military—can only have the long-range effect of aiding those whom the military ostensibly set out to smash.

The young people of Latin America cannot be expected to have faith in representative democracy as the cornerstone of their political systems if its fundamental principle of respect for free elections is violated in democracy's own name.

That elections were finally held in Peru and Argentina in the summer of 1963, and that the winners were allowed to take office, unquestionably represents a shot in the arm for the democratic cause. But the new Presidents of Peru and Argentina must now demonstrate, after the loss of a precious year, that political democracy is the road toward a social and economic breakthrough and not an obstacle to it, as has so often been the case in Latin America.

While Peru's President Fernando Belaúnde Terry has set in motion an exciting development program, President Arturo Illia of Argentina has been unable to end his country's long period of stagnancy. Military *coups d'état* in the autumn of 1963 ousted the constitutional regimes in the Dominican Republic and Honduras, and the new rulers have done little but fight to stay in power. In Brazil, the Goulart government fell in the spring of 1964 because the President had attempted to subvert the country's democracy. The case of Brazil does provide an example—highly controversial as it may be—of democracy's exercise of the right to defend itself from Communist- or right-wing subversion, or frontal attack. The final test of the validity of the Brazilian revolution as a means of preserving democracy is still to come.

In Venezuela late in 1961, the democratic government of President Rómulo Betancourt had to use all its power to break the Cuban-backed attempt by the "Armed Forces of National Liberation"—a hard core of guerrillas and urban terrorists—to set up a Castro-type regime. Ultimately, Betancourt became the first elected President of Venezuela to complete his term, and he turned the office over to his constitutional successor, Raúl Leoni. This was a dramatic instance of the triumph of democratic institutions.

Elsewhere in Latin America, democracy has not fared well since the Cuban revolution polarized political thinking. Besides the short-lived Argentine and Peruvian coups, there were the breakdown of the constitutional system in Brazil between the resignation of President Jânio Quadros in 1961 and the collapse of the Goulart regime in 1964; the successive ousters of Presidents José María Velasco Ibarra and Carlos Julio Arosemena in Ecuador; and the military takeovers in Guatemala and Bolivia. On another level, most of the countries were having difficulty in initiating the domestic structural reforms required under the Alliance for Progress.

Throughout the Latin American universities and among the younger politicians, responsive to the restiveness among the masses, the notion has begun to develop that the Western brand of representative democracy is little more than a rationale for the capitalistic system. So the very essence of democracy, upon which at least in theory Latin America's political tradition was built for 150 years, is being called into doubt. Consequently, the craving has begun for experimentation with new forms, with the unknown.

There has not yet been an overt repudiation of the idea of democracy in any of the republics aside from Cuba—Latin Americans admit they are grievous sinners against it but not out-and-out heretics—and its outward forms are respected. But there are sound reasons to fear that the heresy may spread. The Guatemalan regime, for example, will not even discuss elections; it hints that the country may need at least three years of Army rule to bring about economic and social changes.

The possibility that Senator Salvador Allende, the Socialist-Communist candidate, might win the Chilean Presidential elections in September, 1964, was another manifestation of the deep ferment in the Hemisphere. As it happened, Allende was roundly defeated by Senator Eduardo Frei Montalva, a Christian Democrat, but no election since the 1948 Italian elections had been as anxiously watched in Washington. At stake was the question of whether a nation would freely and democratically choose a Marxist-oriented regime. Frei's victory thus ranked as one of the most decisive events in the Hemisphere since the Cuban revolution. Developments in Venezuela, Brazil, and Chile in 1964 did encourage the feeling that after five years, the trend toward violent solutions had been reversed, but the fundamental Latin American revolution was not arrested—it merely took on another dimension. This might simply mean that democracy was being given another chance.

In the field of inter-American relations, United States diplomats, seeking to win the backing of the moderate Latin American governments for some form of collective action against the Communist beachhead in Cuba, have continuously met with a barrier created by the minimizing of the Communist problem. They have often been told that Americans worry only about Communism.

At the conference of American Foreign Ministers at San José,

Costa Rica, in 1960, the United States was unable to obtain a majority agreement to single out Cuba by name in a resolution deploring the acceptance of Sino-Soviet military aid by an American state. Eighteen months later, at Punta del Este, Uruguay, after Premier Castro had announced that he would be a Marxist-Leninist "until the last day of my life," a bare two-thirds majority of votes was marshaled in a tough diplomatic battle for a decision to "exclude" Cuba from the work of the Organization of American States. But five countries, including Argentina, Brazil, and Mexico, pointedly abstained, having first set forth their opposition to this action.

The reasons for the abstentions varied. The Brazilians—in a demonstration of their new "independent" foreign policy—argued coexistence with Cuba in the hope of bringing her back to the inter-American system. The Mexicans and the Argentines objected on juridical grounds that, in their eyes, transcended any political considerations. Bolivia, Chile, and Ecuador, though their governments may have privately sympathized with the United States stand, opposed the anti-Cuban measures primarily because they feared that public opinion at home would construe them as an assault on the social revolution. Reluctant to embark on effective social measures in their own countries, many of the governments stood paralyzed before the revolutionary menace from within and without and adopted the classic posture of the ostrich with its head buried in the sand.

In October, 1962, before the eruption of the missile crisis but after it had become known that the Soviets were shipping thousands of troops and masses of modern military matériel to Cuba, the United States could win from reluctant Latin Americans no more than an expression of condemnation of this vastly dangerous state of affairs. To obtain this condemnatory communiqué—even though it carried no powers of enforcement—required the most skillful diplomacy on the part of Secretary of State Dean Rusk at an "informal" conference of Hemisphere Foreign Ministers in Washington. The Administration's simultaneous and almost desperate attempts to penalize ships that carried Soviet supplies to Cuba evoked little Latin American sympathy, though it did bring a grudging acceptance, and antagonized Washington's NATO allies.

In a sense, however, the "informal" communiqué and the resolutions heroically won at Punta del Este ten months earlier, did provide the United States with a legal framework for demanding and obtaining instant Hemispheric action in support of its naval quarantine of Cuba after the presence of the Soviet missiles on the island was made known by President Kennedy on October 22.

Before as well as after the missile crisis, Soviet and Cuban propaganda scored considerable success in depicting the pressures on Premier Castro's totalitarian regime as an assault by United States "imperialism" and capitalism on the Cuban social revolution and the forces of social justice. The horror evoked by the missile crisis did recede in time, but the argument that Cuba's social revolution—and not the Soviet missiles—was the prime target of the United States has lived on in much of Latin America.

The abortive United States-backed invasion at the Bay of Pigs, in April, 1961, was also portrayed as an attack on the social revolution. In fact, the Bay of Pigs attack gave the Castro regime the moral right to cry wolf rather convincingly in the ensuing years, and many Latin Americans who normally entertain no pro-Communist sympathies did find in it a justification of sorts for Cuba's acceptance of additional Soviet weapons—even including the missiles.

The resulting confusion of political notions and juridical principles—and the talent for "double think" so brilliantly displayed by Communist and Fidelistas—has made it possible for the traditional, though clearly obsolete, Hemispheric doctrine of nonintervention to be used to thwart any action against the Havana regime. The fact that Cuba's interference in the affairs of her sister republics and her close military ties with the Soviet bloc violated other inter-American principles seemed to have no influence on Latin American opinion, for the most part.

Once the immediate danger of the Soviet missiles and bombers was removed, the voices advocating a continuing respect for nonintervention and a form of coexistence with Cuba were heard again. Neither the United States nor the other Hemispheric governments seemed able to formulate energetic and plausible policies to follow up the October successes.

By the middle of 1963, the impact of the missile crisis had subsided to such an extent that the United States could not muster support for a comprehensive system to combat Communist subversion in the Hemisphere. Although there was no doubt of Cuba's involvement in the Venezuelan terrorism—including smuggling arms to the rebels—seven months elapsed before a meeting of American Foreign Ministers could be convened to consider it. At the meeting, in July, 1964, sanctions were voted against Cuba, despite the opposition of Bolivia, Chile, Uruguay, and Mexico. Nevertheless, the first three acted quickly to abide by the decisions of the parley and broke relations with Cuba, leaving Mexico the only OAS nation to maintain diplomatic ties with Havana.

This, then, was the political landscape in Latin America in late 1964, as the battle for the continent—emotionally as well as economically and politically—went on in a somewhat different dimension, but always and principally on the grounds of social protest and of a quest for new revolutionary definitions. And with all these anxieties and cravings of long generations of Latin Americans now exploding into revolutionary pressures, the Hemisphere was quickly approaching the third major milestone of her history.

The Milestones

The first of these great milestones was the Age of Discovery, from the late fifteenth to the seventeenth century. The second was the Age of Political Emancipation, when, breaking their ties from France, Spain and Portugal, the Latin American nations one by one won their formal independence during the years after 1800. And, finally, the Age of Social Revolution is now emerging throughout the Hemisphere, from the Caribbean to Patagonia and from the Atlantic to the Pacific, to remake once more the face and the institutions of Latin America. Linked to the great currents of modern history, the Latin American social revolution has a close kinship with the revolutionary winds blowing in the Middle East, Africa, and Asia.

It should not be surprising that the new leaders of Latin America, men such as Fidel Castro and his would-be imitators, think of themselves as the contemporary Bolívars and San Martíns of the continent. They have visions of soaring into posterity as the economic and social emancipators of their republics, if not of the whole Hemisphere, just as Simón Bolívar became the political emancipator in leading Latin America to liberation from European colonial rule. It would do an injustice to Castro's historical instinct and appetite to doubt that he must still be dreaming of playing someday a role similar to that of Bolívar, but with greater success, in seeking to unite Latin America as one great confederation of his version of liberated nations. Indeed, in his historical musings, he may accept the idea of a triumphal meeting with some modern San Martín advancing from the south in a repetition of the Guayaquil encounter.

The sense of individual mission, real or false, has always loomed large in history, and, therefore, Castro's notion, born in the days of the Sierra Maestra, that he is a Latin American, not just a Cuban, revolutionary is an important element in the over-all picture of the developing social revolution. Aside from his Hemispheric and historical pretensions, Castro is sufficiently realistic to know that a revolution in Cuba could not prosper in the midst of a hostile Latin America, and it was not an accident that one of his earliest slogans described his island as the first "Free Territory of the Americas" and a subsequent slogan spoke of the Andes being the Sierra Maestra of the Hemisphere.

But that social revolutions, or a climate propitious to them, had to make their advent in Latin America was a matter of history and reality, not in the Marxist sense of determinism or of Castro's own revolutionary proclivities, but in terms of logic and the ability to discern facts and their meaning.

Modern Latin American history abounds with incidents and indications that social protest has long been fermenting under the deceptively quiet surface of the continent and its islands, exploding at irregular but significant intervals in local revolutions, riots, and periods of tension and unrest. A revolutionary has always existed within the hunched figure of the indolent Latin American of the popular cartoons, his frustrations and cravings hidden under his poncho and sombrero. It was most unfortunate that so many North Americans were willing for so long to accept this convenient stereotype served up in their newspapers.

The Mexican revolution of 1910, never quite understood, almost forgotten in the rest of the Hemisphere, and known in the United States mostly through the twisted, picturesque technicolor renditions of the *Viva Zapata!* variety of film, was the first major guidepost in the half-century-long, on-and-off march toward the acceptance of social protest as an inevitable Latin American reality.

In the years that followed the Mexican explosion, the revolutionary process, often dressed in a weird and deceptive mantle, progressed through the APRA (Alianza Popular Revolucionaria Americana) ideas in Peru that began in the late 1920's and are even more intensely alive in 1964—and a whole chain of related movements. APRA itself did lose the 1963 elections, but its original ideas of social equality for the Indian masses and of an Americas-wide revolutionary movement have lived for forty years.

There was the Brazilian revolution of Getúlio Vargas in 1930, which degenerated from social reformism into political fascism, and which is being reborn today in a new context. Then came the 1945 revolution of the Argentine *"descamisados"* ("the shirtless ones") of Colonel Perón, which likewise forsook its vague, chaotic, and corrupt *"Justicialismo"* for a mob-backed dictatorship of the right. The 2 million votes cast for the Peronistas in the March, 1962, elections and the ensuing crisis emphasized that the Perón revolution as a social movement is intensely alive in Argentina, even if a year later Perón himself lost much of his backing.

Also in 1945 occurred the left-wing *coup d'état* in Venezuela by the Acción Democrática, which was aided by the Army and three years later succumbed to it. But the social-reformist consciousness returned with President Rómulo Betancourt's election in 1958 and survives both in his "evolution" policies and the radical agitation of the extreme left.

In 1952, Bolivia went through a drastic social revolution that has not yet run its course. In 1954, Guatemala experienced the inept Communist-aided revolution that collapsed under United States pressure but is again ready to burst forth. Almost simultaneously with the Guatemalan affair, a Marxist regime emerged through free elections in British Guiana, riding the crest of social protest, and it took a landing by British troops to stamp it out for the time being. But the same regime was elected again in 1957, and Britain had to come to terms with it, despite the continuing concern that Guiana may turn into another Hemispheric stage for radical social revolution. In 1963, Cheddi B. Jagan, Guiana's Marxist Prime Minister, turned to Cuba and the Soviet Union for economic help during a political strike; Britain reacted to the explosive situation by postponing Guianan independence *sine die*.

Mixed as so many of these movements were with the political ambitions of groups and individuals and with semidigested ideologies, all of them shared the common denominator of responding, at least in the beginning, to social pressures and demands.

Along with all these events of the very recent past, there were the increasingly alarming and obvious danger signs of the present. Yet, incredibly, logic and the ability to observe and interpret history and a whole array of self-evident political and economic facts were almost never applied to the Latin American scene, either by the United States or by the supposedly enlightened elites in the various countries, who should have been alerted by their daily contacts with the problems at home. This analytical vacuum persisted until Castro's revolution in Cuba short-circuited the situation, and suddenly it seemed to be too late.

The basic facts themselves were simple and eloquent. The first fact was that Latin America, always subject to rapid demographic growth, hit the stage of a full-blown population explosion in the postwar years. In the decade between 1951 and 1961, the population of the 20 Latin American republics rose, according to conservative measurements, from 163 million to 206 million, an annual increase of more than 4 million persons to feed, house, and employ. Cautious projections anticipate a population of 265 million by 1970 and of more than 590 million at the turn of the century, but the reality could well be even more spectacular.

In Brazil, the largest of the republics, the population went from 52 to 66 million between 1945 and 1955, and exceeded 75 million in 1963. Venezuela, where one-half of the inhabitants are below the age of twenty-five, gained more than 1.5 million people in ten years, an increase of 30 per cent. Tiny El Salvador, with Latin America's second highest rate of population density, saw the number of its inhabitants grow by one-half.

While the Latin American human mass thus rose by 50 million in a decade, the United States, by contrast, had a population increase of only 26 million, and Canada had added 1.7 million inhabitants. The headlong ascent of the Latin American birth rate, now exceeding 3 per cent annually, compared to 1.7 per cent in the United States, not only underscores dramatically the material and social needs of the Hemisphere, but also suggests the extent to which the region is expanding in sheer human weight in relation to North America—a phenomenon alarmingly reminiscent of China or India, and rife with political implications.

The second fact was that, despite the vastness and general or potential fertility of its land mass, Latin America was not remotely prepared to feed, house, or care for this skyrocketing population. Except for islands of relative prosperity, like sections of Argentina and Uruguay or the booming industrial center of São Paulo in Brazil, Latin America was tightly held in the vise of poverty—or what economists elegantly term underdevelopment—and of extraordinary economic distortions that helped to deepen the gulf between the shrinking minority of the very rich and the growing masses of the very poor.

The expanding but still relatively small urban middle class, having attained a new status and emancipated itself from economic and cultural misery, saw its new resources sapped by inflation, as production could not satisfy the new demand.

Although a quick and superficial visit to Latin America affords exciting and spectacular examples of progress—the splendid skyscrapers, the asphalt highways, the humming industries—a longer look, aided by statistics, will reveal that, in fact, the over-all situation in the opening years of the decade of the 1960's was comparatively worse than ever before.

All these facts and projections were clearly visible long before Castro launched the Cuban revolution and so abruptly placed them in the new revolutionary context. For years, Latin American leaders had been calling attention to them, but the affluent and complacent West was not ready to look and listen.

The Revolutionary Conditions

Now, however, the winds of social revolution are blowing over Latin America. Her soil is fertile and ready to receive the seeds of rebellion and to nurture them into great movements of protest and deep change. Fidel Castro's call for new Sierras Maestras to erupt in the Andes as springboards of Latin American revolutions may not yet presage immediate outbreaks of guerrilla activities everywhere, but as a concept of insurgency and political warfare, this is infinitely more than just a rabble-rousing figure of speech. Castro's companion and master planner Ernesto ("Che") Guevara in his book on guerrilla warfare has even provided a detailed blueprint for the inception and execution of such undertakings—and this revolutionary handbook has become something of a clandestine best seller in many parts of Latin America.

In Marxist parlance, "objective" revolutionary conditions—like a nationwide movement of rebellion against a dictatorship, such as the classic case presented in Cuba by the Castro-led rebellion against Fulgencio Batista—are still lacking in most of the republics to provide the spark for a sweeping social revolution. The final rallying point may still be missing, but the growing agitation fed by the worsening economic and social problems is beginning to create such conditions, and most of the governments are experiencing the treadmill phenomenon: They have to move faster and faster just to stand still. In other words, such efforts as are made—and more often than not they are woefully inadequate—to stabilize internal conditions are at best only holding operations, despite the sizable injection of United States funds under the Alliance for Progress programs.

Against this backdrop of general inadequacy—though there are notable exceptions, such as the efforts of Colombia, Venezuela, and the new government of El Salvador under President Julio Rivera—the radical activists are relentlessly experimenting with Castro-type techniques. In all the cases thus far, they have been confined to the *coup de main* technique, recommended by Castro and the Chinese but frowned upon by the Moscow-directed Communist orthodoxy, or to small guerrilla and terroristic undertakings of an essentially romantic character that such outstanding technicians as Mao Tse-tung and Guevara would dismiss as "pre-first stage."

Yet, all these experiments contribute to a spreading sense of agitation, with the common denominator being the extremist social revolution. And the Cubans are not reluctant to provide the burgeoning movements with political advice, guerrilla handbooks, funds, and even weapons from their immense, Soviet-supplied arsenal. Thus, in 1962 and 1963, small guerrilla operations composed mainly of students were reported in Venezuela, Ecuador, and Guatemala. Small-scale training of pro-Cuban guerrillas was known to be taking place in Peru, Bolivia, and Brazil.

On another level, extreme leftist revolutionary attempts occurred in Bolivia in June, 1961, and in the Venezuelan ports of Carupano and Puerto Cabello in May and June, 1962. The Venezuelan uprisings were relatively serious, inasmuch as they involved garrisons of Marines and National Guardsmen. They were carried out against the background of steadily increasing Communist and Cuban-type student rioting and agitation in Caracas and mounting urban terrorism. The latter approach was designed to create instability, which would goad the military into taking over the government and providing the rallying point of an antidictatorial national struggle.

Though all of them were minority movements, partly because the masses tend to remain passive until a revolt shows signs of success, they cannot be shrugged off as unimportant or insignificant.

In this connection, it is useful to note that the Cuban revolutionary government has offered programs of political and guerrilla indoctrination to selected Latin American students under a system of academic fellowships. The students, averaging about 1,000 annually, spend six months in Cuba, where they are submitted to Marxist-Leninist indoctrination and are treated as the future leaders of the "Latin American liberating revolution." They receive guerrilla and related training in the Oriente Province camps of tough militia units, such as the Minas del Frío. Returning to their countries, they become, in the best Communist tradition, the cadres for future revolutions.

In the Brazilian Northeast, the revolution is nurtured in the classic surroundings of rebellious peasants, who for the last seven years have been organized into Peasant Leagues by Marxist leaders assisted by university students. The Leagues now demand a sweeping land reform and promise violence if they do not achieve it peacefully. Here, among the destitute peasants, neatly fitting the theory of Mao Tse-tung—adapted by Guevara for Latin American use—is the breeding ground of the peasant-based revolution. Interestingly, Francisco Julião, the most influential leader of the Leagues, who at first called himself a Marxist, announced that he, too, was a Communist within forty-eight hours of Castro's own ideological admission in December, 1961.

The April revolution in Brazil put a lid—at least temporarily— on the Northeast agitation, and Julião and his associates were imprisoned. But swift reforms by the new regime will be required if the Northeast movements are not to resume.

In the Peruvian highlands, where the conditions of the Indians have not changed noticeably in 300 years, landless peasants have been fighting government troops to keep possession of their rocky farms. These actual and potential guerrilla, revolutionary, and subversive activities have alarmed the United States and many of the Latin American governments to the extent of concentrating a large portion of the military aid to the region on antiguerrilla and antisubversive weapons and techniques. Special equipment for dealing with internal strife—from helicopters to radio-equipped jeeps and tear-gas grenades—is being supplied on a growing scale to Latin American security forces. Latin American officers are trained in antiguerrilla operations and in "civic action" at the Army's Special Forces Branch school at Fort Bragg, North Carolina, and at the Jungle Warfare School at Fort Gulick in the Panama Canal Zone. United States antiguerrilla advisers are attached to training missions throughout Latin America, with a special emphasis on Colombia where the fourteen-year-old backlands bandit wars could well turn into political revolutionary movements. A sizable unit of the Special Forces troops—the Seventh Group—was transferred to the Canal Zone, the site of the United States Caribbean Command, early in 1962 to act as a pool of antiguerrilla advisers to the Latin American armies and, if the need should ever arise, to be used in action on the request of a friendly government. A paratroop force was added to the Panama command early in 1963.

A "Special Consultative Committee on Security" of the Organization of American States was established by the Punta del Este Conference of Foreign Ministers in January, 1962, to collect information on subversion patterns and recommend remedial measures. Emphasizing the importance of the committee, the United States initially named General Thomas D. White, former Chief of Staff of the Air Force, as its representative, and the group has periodically submitted detailed reports on the subversion problems. Yet, strange as it may seem, most Latin American governments still shy away from any collective action against subversion—chiefly on grounds of protecting their sovereignty from any inter-American interference.

The Political Revolution

There is a natural tendency to see the threat of the Latin American revolutions as starting and ending with violent uprisings, guerrilla activities, and scattered rioting. But in this age, the great social revolutions—of which these outbreaks are but a symptom— are being fought and conducted as well in the political, ideological, psychological, and emotional realms. Indeed, the ultimate victory or defeat, not of the social revolution as a historical concept but of democracy in its revolutionary battle with Communist Jacobinism, is more likely to be settled in broad political combat, rather than in street scuffles or guerrilla skirmishes.

It is in this field, of course, that the positive forces of Latin American democracy and of reason—so often obscured by the more eye-catching incidents of violence, subversion, or extremist harangues—can assert themselves in the historic battle now being joined in the Hemisphere.

Despite democracy's frequent failings and the traditional disorganization of the democratic forces in Latin America, these positive elements do exist and, properly utilized, could yet play a decisive stabilizing role. Broadly speaking, they are the political parties of the old liberalism and of the anti-Communist left, the growing Christian Democratic movements, the enlightened young generation of businessmen and industrialists, and even the democratically minded military officers. The socially progressive segment of the Roman Catholic Church, slowly but steadily changing the old image of reactionary Latin American clericalism, is another important element in the equation of the democratic social revolution.

It is wrong to conclude, as one may be tempted to do after reading constantly about the riots, subversive movements, and anti-Yankeeism, that all Latin American students, workers, peasants, and intellectuals favor Cuban-type or Communist revolutions. This is the impression that, for obvious reasons, the Cubans and the Communists endeavor to spread and that, because of its tendency to oversimplify and sensationalize the issues, a part of the American press transmits.

But the fight against Communism and extremism is carried on every day in student and professional associations, in labor unions, and among peasants, though it rarely wins the headlines accorded the reports about the smashing of windows in a U.S. Embassy or about several hundred youths demonstrating against the government. Here again, as in Europe in the 1930's, the democratic forces, prey to near-suicidal disorganization, play down or pass in silence the counteractions of their forces against Jacobinism. By default, the democratic forces permit the enhancement of the activities of tightly organized radical minorities and thereby create the psychological conditions in which these minorities may someday triumph, with catastrophic results.

Yet there are some significant gains for the forces of democracy. Much of the power of the left-of-center democratic Venezuelan regime of President Raúl Leoni derives from the support of the strongly anti-Communist unions of the oil workers, and the peasant federations, and the Christian Democratic students of the Copei Party have scored notable successes in elections against the Communists and the Revolutionary Movement of the Left (MIR) extremists in the Central University in Caracas. A Latin American Student Congress at Natal, Brazil, in October, 1961, became the scene of a major battle between Communist and anti-Communist delegates. Elsewhere, the contest goes on constantly and the democratic forces are not always the losers. But Latin America's moderates, so often underestimated and neglected by the United States, must soon be given a direction and a real political alternative or they will be swept up by the winds of radicalism.

The outcome of the main struggle, then, will depend on the ability of Latin America, assisted by the United States, to make a democratic social revolution prevail against a radical or totalitarian social revolution. To be sure, the great Latin American social revolution is already on the march but the direction it ultimately takes will depend on the understanding of its immense complexities.

In its most simple definition, a social revolution is a movement designed to right the obvious social and economic wrongs in a society and to assure abundance and justice for all. But the true modern social revolution cannot be confined to these goals alone.

The very dynamics of a revolution require that it become, sooner or later, closely related to a political ideology—if not identified with it—or, at least, that it embark on a feverish search for such an ideology. In its vast complexity, a social revolution thus encompasses not only the social gains and a formal political ideology, but also the interplay of domestic politics of every kind, the country's foreign policy and its psychological state, and such hard-to-define and hard-to-control phenomena as the surge of nationalism. For this reason, a social revolution—even if its immediate origins seem to lie in land hunger, food hunger, or wider distortions in the social structure—is inseparable from the other elements, which act and react upon each other in the quickening succession of upheavals.

The modern social revolution thus means a breakthrough into a completely virgin territory of thoughts and attitudes, into a new institutional and human order, in short, into a national adventure.

In sum, then, the social revolution represents the change-over and restructuring of a whole society, of its institutions and of its relationship to the outside world. Latin America is today going through this revolutionary process, and whether this great transition is accomplished through violent or through peaceful and gradual means, she will fairly soon bear little resemblance to the Latin America we have known until now—just as the end of European colonialism transformed her so greatly during the nineteenth century.

But it does not follow from this proposition that Latin America must be transformed into a violently radical or Communist continent. Even if the concept is semantically objectionable, modern social revolution can develop peacefully and democratically, achieving through quick evolution objectives that are truly revolutionary. The belief that this can be achieved is the crux of the West's philosophical contest with Communism. As we shall see later, this evolutionary process of the "white revolution" is under way in several of the republics in defiance of the extremist pressures.

The Ideologies

To understand fully the depth of the epochal revolution currently gathering shape and momentum in Latin America—and to judge whether it has possibilities of being directed into democratic channels—it is necessary to see it in the broader context of the pressures and forces of attraction operating within it and around it.

The first context that must be analyzed is that of the Latin American revolution's relationship to political ideology in the context of the world struggle of ideas that is now reaching its crescendo. The Latin American revolution is not isolated from this global clash now sweeping all the underdeveloped regions. This clash has become particularly sharpened and pronounced now that Marxism-Leninism has advanced from its earlier socio-economic concepts to a full-blown political philosophy, while at the same time, traditional Western democracy has evolved to a point of blending its essentially political nature with a social and economic credo, shedding its old laissez-faire attitudes. This synthesis on both sides resulted from the hardening postures—and their implications—of the West and the Communist camp as the two main power centers in the world.

The Latin American revolutionary trends, therefore, must be situated within the framework of opposing political ideologies or their variations. Similarly, the political and psychological posture and background of the Latin American republics will be presently examined to provide some insight into the forces that go into the making of the revolutionary climate.

Although the Cold War has redefined all the relationships, the link between the social and political aspects of the great revolutions goes far back into history. The French Revolution was born from the political thinking of Voltaire, Condorcet, and the Encyclopedists as much as from the reaction to Marie Antoinette's insolent remark that if the starving people had no bread, they should eat cake. The

storming of the Bastille was an act of protest against the political
as well as the social system of Louis XVI's France. The Russian
revolution of 1917 started with the objective of wresting political
and social concessions from the Czarist system, but little time
elapsed before Lenin's Bolsheviks captured it, filling with Communism the ideological void left by the Petrograd rebels of the
July days. Vague notions of Western democracy proffered to a
collapsing nation that lacked democratic traditions and experience
were not sufficient to resist the assault by a well-organized and
ideologically conscious minority equipped with a specific and detailed program. In a sense, the Russian pattern was repeated in
Cuba after 1959, with the difference that Castro was not a Kerensky
(though many of his companions acted in that vein), and it could
conceivably be played out again elsewhere in Latin America if an
ideological void is allowed to exist.

The Chinese revolution had absorbed the political ideology of
Communism long before Mao Tse-tung left the caves of Yenan.
It was only through ignorance that many well-intentioned West-
erners who did not understand revolutions wanted to believe that
the Chinese Communists were simple agrarian reformers and that
Mao had suddenly forgotten his Marxist persuasion.

That a social revolution cannot exist within a political vacuum
thus is an established fact that should be clear even to the most
superficial student of history. But Western policy-makers, whose
high degree of political sophistication seems to have isolated them
from the quickly forgotten but now resurging science of revolutions,
have chosen to ignore the history books. This is particularly true of
the Washington-based planners of the Alliance for Progress, who
still labor under the impression that a democratic social revolution
can be carried out simply with a call for reforms in Latin America,
a massive investment of funds, and platitudes about democracy
recited in speeches and monotonously disseminated by the Voice of
America. A great social revolution implies unconventional warfare
—politically and otherwise—and it must be approached on an unconventional level.

Western thinkers have also overlooked the historical record (or
have failed to draw the proper conclusions from it), which demon-
strates that the great and lasting revolutions were the brain children and the product of men of the middle class, who, by definition,
were politically conscious and sophisticated. And when their move-

ments did not promptly embrace radical political forms, other men wrested the control of events away from them.

France's Mirabeau was a man of the middle class who helped to open the sluice gates and release one of the world's greatest revolutions. Because he and his companions of 1789 did not move quickly enough along the radical revolutionary lines, the French revolution eventually slipped into the hands of the Robespierres, the Dantons, and the Marats. Again, the parallel with Latin America suggests itself, and again, history emphasizes the danger of a political or ideological void in revolutionary times. But if the men of 1789 in France, Kerensky in Russia in 1917, and the Cuban moderates of 1959 did not have at hand a political ideology sufficiently strong and captivating to resist the radical blandishments, Latin America in the 1960's may draw on the traditions of freedom and of Western democracy—provided that they exhibit a new dynamism.

Kerensky, too, came from the middle classes, but his political weakness after Czar Nicholas' abdication forced him to make room for Lenin and Trotsky, both of them classic representatives of the Russian middle class.

Mao, who dabbled in poetry and haunted libraries, and was a self-made man of the Chinese middle class long before he became a Yenan *guerrillero,* was firmly committed to the Communist ideology and, therefore, it was unrealistic to expect him to settle for bucolic agrarian reformism.

Fidel Castro, the most recent but probably not the last of the long line of bourgeois revolutionaries, had no historical choice but to embrace, in the end, a political ideology, and it was a tragedy that external circumstances and the peculiar revolutionary dynamics of Cuba pushed him to select Communism. But until the last bitter moment, a great many of the West's political thinkers—and Europeans were just as misguided as Americans—refused to believe that Castro, too, had to subordinate himself to history and adjust his social revolution to the requirements of a political ideology. Because the West had ignored the lessons of history and had not learned to understand the dynamics and mechanics of social revolutions, nothing more attractive than Communism was offered to Castro. The moderates, still highly influential in the formative days of the Cuban revolution, had no workable alternative with which to oppose the Communist inroads.

But despite this formidable evidence, there still seems to be little realization in the politically mature West that the Latin American social revolution inherently has a political content and that it cannot be treated solely as a statistical problem of increasing production, distributing wealth more equitably, and providing educational and health services. Though these material needs must, of course, be filled, there also is an abysmal political and psychological void in Latin America that will invite other ideologies if democracy cannot make its influence felt. And it may be more urgent today to fill this vacuum than to offer another billion dollars or even to raise the annual per capita income by 2.5 per cent, as the Alliance for Progress unrealistically prescribes. For there is in Latin America a profound feeling of unrest, unfulfillment, and frustration among intellectuals, students, politicians, and the middle class. There is a hunger for a new orientation that sends Latin Americans in increasing numbers to the meccas of Havana, Peking, and Moscow—in that order—and makes so many of them challenge the meaning of Western representative democracy and raise the crucial question, "Why should we follow the United States?"

Almost four years after President Kennedy proposed the Alliance for Progress, this country has not yet provided an answer to this question in political terms fully satisfying to the Latin Americans. Although the Alliance is slowly beginning to be considered in terms of a political concept instead of merely an aid-and-self-help proposition, it has not yet been able to generate the political excitement and mystique that is vital for the success of the democratic social revolution President Kennedy invoked. Held in the uncreative grasp of the Washington bureaucracy, the Alliance is muddling through the third year of the "Decade of Progress" because its planners fear to tread with political courage—even though they may be preventing it from becoming a true alliance. It is an ironic contrast that at the meeting of the South American Communist parties in Montevideo in 1950, even Moscow granted the Latin American Communists the right to determine their own objectives and to suggest the strategy to be used in their own territories. Washington, however, has preferred to maintain the Alliance operation under its own control.

The Social Yearnings

The quest for a political ideology to accompany the yearnings for social reform cast a shadow across the contemporary history of

Latin America until the middle of the 1950's. Then, the shadow reversed its direction, and the urge for deep social and psychological change was superimposed upon the formal political democracy achieved in most of the republics after the fall of the mid-century dictators. In such a change, there was patently the danger of the political vacuum.

Vargas' revolution in Brazil in 1930 was at its outset a social movement, though it was born in part of nationwide protest against the corrupt political manipulations of the ruling elite, and it produced advanced labor and welfare legislation. But it had no clearly defined ideology until seven years later, when Vargas finally dressed it in the tropical fascist trappings of his *"Estado Novo"*—the "New State"—which responded to the Nazi-fascist political thinking of the day and drew most of its inspiration from Mussolini's Italy and Salazar's Portugal. In what was probably the first attempt in modern Latin American history to relate a domestic political phenomenon to a current world struggle, Vargas came close to allying Brazil with the Axis—until his sense of opportunism, as well as powerful internal and external pressures, led him to embrace the Allied cause instead.

Juan Perón's disorderly social revolution of 1945, carried out with the support of big-city workers, who still remain loyal to his ideas, was launched after Germany's defeat in the war had discredited the Nazi-fascist ideology and the appeal of Communism had not yet become widespread. Consequently, Perón stumbled into his concept of *"Justicialismo"*—a vague ideology mixing political, social, and personal notions—to provide a façade for his corrupt dictatorship. Perón's military imitators—General Marcos Pérez Jiménez in Venezuela, General Manuel A. Odría in Peru, and General Gustavo Rojas Pinilla in Colombia—likewise toyed with concepts of social content to streamline their regimes and put them more in tune with the spirit of the times.

But all four dictators were removed between 1955 and 1958 as the result of political movements, with considerable grass-roots backing, that were designed to restore formal democracy. Their departure from the scene marked the end of an era in Latin America, but unfortunately, it did not usher in a new era of social development under democratic auspices. At that point, what should have become the democratic social revolution—following the democratic political revolution—missed its first great chance to make a breakthrough. The political conditions were then propitious for the beginning of real social changes, eschewing radicalism, socialism, or Communism, but despite all the danger signs, the democratic leaders failed to display the necessary foresight. Today, they have to try for the same breakthrough under the gun of revolutionary threats and under incomparably more difficult circumstances.

Venezuela's President Betancourt, a veteran leftist, was the only Latin American liberal to comprehend the new social pressures to any significant degree. His gradual land-reform program, though bogged down in bureaucracy and inexperience, was the only one of its kind to be put in practice in the region (the earlier revolutionary land reforms of Mexico, Bolivia, and Guatemala must still be considered inadequate). But even President Betancourt was subjected to a continuous clamor for a radical social revolution, and there were repeated leftist and rightist conspiracies to oust him. In Peru, under the democratic regime that took power in 1956, the Congress has for years successfully blocked a land-reform bill. Colombia, liberated from dictatorship in 1957 and beset by backlands violence, finally approved a land-reform law late in 1961.

In other Latin American republics where formal democracy has reigned for long years, the governments and the ruling classes have practiced electoral democracy, but have overlooked social needs. Thus, the cycle of the democratic revolutions and adjustments of the 1950's has failed to bring about a marriage with the cause of social justice.

With the violent advent of the Cuban revolution on January 1, 1959, Latin American history made another swing around, though in its initial days, the pattern was not so clear. Fidel Castro started out with a makeshift private ideology of "Humanism," a combination of his social "Revolutionary Laws of the Sierra" and of his alleged devotion to liberal democracy. It was intended as an answer to capitalism, which, he said, "killed people with hunger," and to Communism, which threatened "the liberties which are so dear to men." For a year, his followers defiantly and self-consciously proclaimed that "We are Humanists and not Communists."

But inside of another year, he convinced himself, or allowed certain of his friends to convince him that, after all, his "Humanism" was not a satisfactory ideology. He then proceeded to place the strait jacket of Communism upon his sweeping social revolution—with the accompanying denial of the very liberties that were so dear to the Cubans that they had blindly followed him in his war against the Batista dictatorship.

In justice to Castro—accepting the assumption that his early and chaotic radicalism evolved only later into Communism—it should be recorded that his short-lived stab at "Humanism" may have initially been a serious attempt to find a compromise, or synthesis, between the traditional freedoms of Western democracy, which was so. remiss in providing social justice, and the Marxist doctrines that sacrificed freedom for a theoretical equality of opportunity. It may have been his way of seeking a solution for the historical imbalance between liberty and justice in nonaffluent societies. Whatever may be said of Castro's sincerity or political wisdom in expounding his "Humanism," the fact is that millions of his followers took it as gospel in those first intoxicating days of the revolution.

Perhaps because, deep down, he may be aware of his failure to be true to his own ideas and of his abdication before the pressures of Communism, Castro had a sheepish answer when I asked him, in the course of a lengthy conversation in June, 1961, why he had turned his back on his "Humanism." Visibly uncomfortable, Castro replied: "We all evolve politically, and I, too, have evolved." He subsequently expanded at great length on his "evolution" in his famous speech of December 1–2, 1961, in which he declared that he would be Marxist-Leninist until "the last day of my life."

Less important than the actual circumstances of Castro's conversion to Communism is the overriding fact that he has situated Cuba within the Communist system. As a result, the battle for the Latin American social revolution has become a contest between the Western concepts of democracy and Communism, which, according to Castro, is the only rational system for the development of backward Latin America. The Cold War has thus been introduced into the Western Hemisphere, turning it into still another East-West battleground.

Export of Revolutions

The present meaning of Cuba's activities in "exporting" her revolution to the rest of Latin America and the mounting local pro-Communist operations throughout the Hemisphere—taking advantage of the climate of social revolution—are a fundamental part of this Cold Warfare picture. In realistic political terms, therefore, the chief danger Cuba presents to the position of democracy and of the United States in the Hemisphere arises not from the Soviet MIG jet fighters in the Cuban skies, the Soviet military technicians, or the ground-to-air missile bases on Cuban territory, but from the Communist-oriented ideological campaign Havana beams toward Latin America. As a wise United States Senator remarked some time ago, Cuba is not a dagger poised against the heart of this country, but a painful thorn in its side. This estimate was briefly invalidated during the 1962 missile crisis, but its soundness remains.

Though Cuba is the fountainhead of Latin American revolutionary activities, operating through its indoctrinated student cadres, emissaries, diplomats, and radio broadcasts—and through its sheer example—the impact of the Cuban revolution has already been sufficiently great for the revolutionary momentum to roll ahead even if the Castro regime should vanish overnight. As Castro does not tire of repeating mischievously, "We are a bad example for Latin America."

Aside from the direct guerrilla raids and subversive uprisings and conspiracies, the Communist parties of Latin America, through an immense variety of front organizations and infiltrators, are actively spreading their version of the social revolution, with Cuba as the foremost slogan. Their aim is to weaken the existing institutions, capture the control of labor, student, and opinion-making sectors, and discredit domestic and international cooperative efforts for social and economic improvement, such as the Alliance for Progress and the Latin American Common Market.

It is a skillful and many-sided campaign to soften the fabric of the society before applying the big blow. In the words of the first report of the OAS Special Consultative Committee on Security, issued in May, 1962, the Communist parties operate on the basis of the four principles of the "maintenance of the objective, economy of forces, sustained action and the firm will to win."

"It is an undertaking without hurry but without pause," the Committee said. "It is sustained action, carried out with minute precision."

The Committee went on to underline that in this contest with Communism, democracy has "to travel a rougher road" because "the feelings of rebellion among the despairing and discouraged sectors of the countries' populations are frequently based on the prevailing indifference to national problems and on a lack of faith in the political, social and economic values of Western civilization."

The Committee then noted what has long been a highly disturbing phenomenon in Latin America in connection with Communist activities: that "citizens of free countries of the Hemisphere tolerate, or are inclined to tolerate and support, known Communists." It said that prominent persons in the Hemisphere underestimate, or persist in underestimating, the Communist danger, maintaining that it is easy to control since the number of Communists in the Hemisphere is still small. This tolerance, or support, of Communists and their movements by non-Communists is one of the striking political and psychological factors on the Latin American scene, dating back many decades.

In the purely political field, non-Communist politicians often seek or accept Communist support in elections. In return, in countries where the Communist parties are illegal, Communists may be allowed to run for elective office on the tickets of non-Communist parties, thereby gaining a foothold in the legislatures and a general aura of respectability. The price of Communist support frequently also is a tacit agreement by the democratic governments not to interfere with Communist operations.

A classic case in point is that of Brazil, where the illegal but highly active Communist Party supported Juscelino Kubitschek for President in 1955, and enjoyed for his entire term a comfortable tolerance of its maneuvers. The Brazilian Labor Party of João Goulart, the President who was deposed in 1964, opened its tickets to Communist candidates in congressional and local elections. When Kubitschek picked a quarrel with the International Monetary Fund in 1959, Communist Party Secretary Luiz Carlos Prestes stood next to him during a round of protest speeches in the gardens of the Presidential Palace in Rio de Janeiro. In the 1960 Presidential elections, Army Marshal Henrique Teixeira Lott, an extreme conservative and a practicing Catholic, allowed Prestes to campaign with him on the same rostrum. Prestes had traveled a long way toward political respectability since Vargas released him from prison fifteen years earlier to enlist him as an ally.

The psychological factor that permits latitude toward Communists stems from the curious patterns of political thinking in Latin America. It is simply unfashionable, or "reactionary," in many intellectual, high-society, and other circles to be vocally anti-Communist. It is, however, quite fashionable to be anti-

American, in the patronizing manner of some Europeans. One reason for this attitude is that Washington's tendency in the Republican years to concentrate on anti-Communism as a policy in itself created the impression that the United States equated every progressive and democratic movement with Communism. Contributing to this was the long-held policy of cordiality toward the military dictators, which has created such deep and lasting damage to United States prestige.

Another important reason for tolerating Communism is that many Latin Americans feel that they are thereby asserting a form of independence and nationalism. The third reason, highly peculiar to Latin America, is that because of personal, family, academic, professional, or political connections, Communist leaders and intellectuals are far from being treated as pariahs and are fully accepted in many quarters. That a great many outstanding intellectuals and artists in Latin America are Communists or extreme leftists evidently plays a role in the formation of this attitude. Among famous painters, Brazil's late Candido Portinari was a Communist, as is Mexico's David Alfaro Siqueiros. The list includes Chile's Nobel Prize-winning poet, Pablo Neruda; Brazil's foremost architect, Oscar Niemeyer, and its leading novelist, Jorge Amado; Mexico's top novelist, Carlos Fuentes; and a whole galaxy of lesser lights.

Hundreds of non-Communist but left-wing intellectuals, writers, artists, and politicians have accepted invitations to visit Communist China, the Soviet Union, and Cuba, and the great majority have returned with glowing reports of what they saw. Their reports have been made in books, newspaper articles and speeches, and the over-all impact has unquestionably been favorable to the Communist cause. Those returning from similar trips to the United States, on the other hand, are either uninspired or, because of the local climate of opinion, are reluctant to make positive observations about their experiences. This is one crucial field in which the United States is a frequent loser, but it may well be that if the programs for Latin American visitors were revised, and if some flexibility were introduced in the visa-granting procedures, these reactions could become more positive.

A notable example of how the pro-Communist machinery operates in Latin America, feeding directly on the local misery and the attraction of the social revolution, is offered by the situation in the poverty-stricken Brazilian Northeast. There, agitators of the Peasant Leagues lard their campaigns for land for the peasants with anti-United States, pro-Cuban, and pro-Communist slogans. Julião, the best-known leader of the Leagues, set the tone for his preachings in a "Letter to the Peasants," which was circulated all over the Northeast. It promised social justice and land reform "in the way of Fidel and Mao."

Wandering players of the *viola*—a two-stringed Brazilian guitar —who fulfill the bard-like or calypso-like function of human newspapers in that huge region where illiteracy reigns supreme, sing the glories of Julião, the Peasant Leagues, and "socialism," and protest against sending Brazilian sugar to Franco's Spain or Chiang Kai-shek's Taiwan. Brazilian sugar is not, in fact, exported there, but the protest happens to rhyme in that particular political jingle, and it serves the deliberate purpose of acquainting the unsophisticated peasant masses with the Communist international demonology. It is interesting to record here that when a United States propaganda official was recently apprised of the activities of the Brazilian *viola*-players, he suggested that a well-known United States labor-union folk singer be sent to the Northeast to counteract Julião's propaganda—in English.

Ironically, what prevents Julião and other extreme leftists of the Northeast from winning high offices in their region is the Brazilian law barring illiterates from voting. If this prohibition were lifted—and, obviously, obtaining the vote for illiterates is one of the top priority items of the left—chances are that the destitute peasants, who have few friends outside of the Leagues, would vote massively for these candidates. Thus, democracy has to hide behind a legal provision to protect itself from elected radicalism. But even so, Miguel Arraes, the Communist-supported Mayor of Recife (Pernambuco's and the Northeast's principal city), succeeded in October, 1962, in his bid to be elected State Governor.

Communist techniques among the Northeast peasants are stark in their simplicity. During a visit late in 1960 to a League-held rural estate near Recife, I asked one of Julião's colleagues what possible meaning indoctrination against such targets as "American imperialism" could hold for the half-starved peasants whose world ends on their plot of land. "It's very simple," he replied. "We tell them that it is 'American imperialism' that backs the cruel landlords who exploit them. They all understand what landlords are, so when we equate landlords with imperialism, we transfer the hatred against the landlord to hatred against imperialism. This way, the notion of 'American imperialism' as something to be hated acquires an intimate meaning." Communism, as an ideology, is never mentioned in the harangues to the peasants. As happened in Cuba, this comes much later—when it is too late for the nominally democratic society to react.

The candor of Communists—whether it is a "Che" Guevara openly proposing Marxist revolutions in Latin America, or a Peasant League agitator in the Brazilian Northeast explaining the mechanics of his work—is amazing. But equally amazing, as the OAS Security Committee has pointed out, is the fact that a great many people still refuse to take them seriously, just as Hitler's *Mein Kampf* was considered a piece of extravagance in the middle 1930's.

The Communists' quiet ideological work, adapted to different conditions and circumstances in different parts of Latin America, goes on apace in schools, universities, fields and factories, political parties, and professional and cultural organizations. It may take the shape of Communist control of a student association in a Caracas high school, of a neighborhood-improvement group in Lima, or of identification with nationalistic aspirations in Brazil.

Or it may be the fantastic story of Peruvian Indians who beat up a group of United States and Canadian engineers after someone had spread the tale that Americans were *pistacos* (devils), who were out to catch the Indians to boil out their body fat for use as an ingredient in atomic bombs. And so painstaking are the Communists about the details of their multilevel campaign in Latin America that in 1960, Moscow radio began beaming programs in the Quechua dialect of Peruvian, Ecuadorian, and Bolivian Indians on the off-chance that someone would listen to them. Subsequently, Havana inaugurated Quechua programs, and it seems to have won an audience.

Thus, the Communists in their "sustained action" never pause in the endeavor of fitting the erupting social revolution into their side of the ideological Cold War. Their tactics emphasize again that democracy—and the Alliance for Progress—must soon find a way to project its ideology through similar grass-roots techniques if the Latin American social revolution is not to be captured by Communism.

The Democratic Left

Credit must go to the Communists for always having remembered that social upheavals cannot be separated from political ideologies. The West, which organically and constitutionally does not seem to perceive the mechanics of great revolutions, ignored this historical fact.

Even when the realization began to grow, during the late 1950's, that the age of social revolution had dawned over Latin America, and the United States began to tailor new policies to meet this reality, Western leaders still ignored the urgent need to fill the ideological gap. Platitudes about Jeffersonian democracy, meaningful at home but meaningless in the Latin American social drama, were patronizingly passed out when what was desperately needed was a fresh and inspiring form of political leadership—particularly to complement the developmental ideas of the Alliance for Progress.

Little or no effort was made in the Eisenhower days—which overlapped the first two years of the Cuban revolution—to attract the restless but still uncommitted and fundamentally pro-American groups in the Hemisphere. Despite the evident and probably irrevocable trend in Latin America toward positions left of the center—but far from Communist-oriented—the United States through its government and business communities reacted with strong suspicion toward democratic leftist factions. The notion of the "non-Communist left" was held to be just a notch less subversive than the notion of Communism or "creeping socialism." What seemed to concern us was the danger of Communism rather than effective ways of combating its political appeal.

The attitude toward the Latin American "non-Communist left" has not really been altered in the Kennedy days, perhaps because of bureaucratic inertia, even though Administration spokesmen pay it increasing verbal encouragement. As Puerto Rico's Governor Luis Muñoz Marín warned in a speech in Chicago in May, 1962, "there is grim irony in the fact that, in many a country where the Alliance may be pouring in tens of millions of dollars, the ultimate political battle may be lost because the parties of the democratic left lack a few thousands of dollars for desperately needed, legitimate, democratic action."

With the deeply ingrained suspicion prevailing during the Republican era against the leftist phenomenon characteristic of the awakening underdeveloped countries, there was suspicion and hostility against the rising sentiments of nationalism and self-assertion. Little distinction was made between rabid ultranationalism, fanned by Communism, and legitimate nationalistic sentiments, spreading in the Hemisphere as in Asia and Africa. And above all, there was no desire to understand what was happening under our very noses, though there was no lack of well-intentioned advice from Latin America.

It was not just a refusal to come to terms with leftism or nationalism in Latin America, but a refusal to come to terms with history. As an affluent and somewhat less flexible society, we declined to see that behind this leftism and this nationalism—which we feared because we made no effort to understand it—there was the rising shadow of the social revolution in its fullest sense. This revolution could not be stopped by wishful thinking, patronizing advice, the Marines, or even money. But this revolution, with which we belatedly now wish to come to terms, could have also been a great opportunity for refashioning our relationship with Latin America and keeping it as a friendly partner in the Western corner.

The Communists, on the other hand, wasted no time in jumping aboard the bandwagon of the social revolution with the full arsenal of ideology and apparent sympathy for, and outward identification with, its cause. For them, the emergence of the social revolution in Latin America in the shape of the Cuban revolution of 1959 was, to use non-Marxist terminology, God-sent manna from heaven.

Where for decades the Latin American Communist parties had been fairly ineffective, generally not respected, and having really no following or goal, the Cuban revolution provided them with the first truly popular and spectacular cause to champion—and, subsequently, to take over. Just as they had earlier set out to monopolize the concept of peace through their Stockholm Peace Appeal, and then to steal and pervert the name of democracy, so they moved with alacrity in Latin America to declare their proprietorship of the social revolution. While the United States was still attempting to analyze the meaning of the Cuban revolution as a local Cuban event, instead of relating it at once to the whole Latin American picture, the Hemisphere's Communist parties were already busy exploiting it to the hilt and becoming the loudest defenders and propagators of the *Fidelista* faith. In fact, they outshouted us.

As early as May, 1959, while Washington was debating the possibilities of a workable relationship with Castro within the old framework—and wondering if he would turn out "all right"—the new Communist line in Latin America was ready to be unveiled. Returning from conferences in Moscow and Peking, Luis Corvalán, the General Secretary of the Chilean Communist Party, told the Party's Central Committee in Santiago that Communists must ally themselves with "progressive bourgeois movements," like that of Fidel Castro in Cuba. To the Communists, Castro thus still had the taint of a "bourgeois putschist"—despite the company of such Communist regulars as his brother Raúl and "Che" Guevara—but they had no hesitation in throwing their full support behind the Fidelista regime.

This unqualified support given Castro by the Communists in 1959, when he still seemed to hesitate about the course his revolution would take, was unquestionably a major factor in convincing him that Marxism-Leninism was a cure-all for Cuba and Latin America. By 1962, old-line Cuban Communists were loudly acclaiming Castro as the best Communist in the country, but the "Maximum Leader" complained publicly of the Party's hush-hush criticism of his "putschist" origins.

The Soviet Blueprint

The manner in which the Soviet Union actively began to relate the emergence of the social revolutions in the underdeveloped countries, and notably in Latin America, to its own world-wide program of propagating Communism can be perceived in clear and painstaking detail in the "Program of the Communist Party of the Soviet Union," published as a "draft" late in July, 1961, and adopted at the Twenty-second Congress, the following October. At the time, authorship of the Party Program was credited to Nikita Khrushchev, as Premier, and his successors have given no indication that they plan to revise his blueprint.

Starting from the Marxist-Leninist dogma that social and "anti-colonialist" revolutions are part of the inevitable process of the disintegration of "imperialism" and capitalism, Khrushchev tied these erupting social rebellions to the socialist (or Communist) ideology, proclaimed the justice of "wars of national liberation," and, in sum, offered a full-fledged political-ideological program for the capture of social protest movements by Communists.

The Khrushchev blueprint, in effect, claimed the proprietorship of all the social revolutions for Communism, just as the Communists had declared themselves the owners of the Cuban revolution. In fact, the Cuban experiment may well have inspired him to set forth so explicitly the grand Soviet design for using the social and "anticolonialist" revolutions in the underdeveloped countries as the principal vehicle for the spread of Communism in the current stage of its battle with the Western democracies.

To be sure, this notion was not novel to the Communist thinking. But it took the Cuban revolution and its subsequent Communization to provide the Soviet Union with a living example of her dogmas and theories. And it is this dogma, which may be Communism's weakness as well as its strength, that led Khrushchev to conclude that every social revolution—including those that may occur in Latin America in the future—is bound to follow the Cuban Communist pattern.

So confident did Khrushchev appear to be that his Communist interpretation of the world's destiny was correct that he chose to lay down in the Party Program what really amounts to a recipe for the conquest of backward countries, spelling it out with greater clarity than had ever been done in a public Soviet state paper. Again, it can be virtually taken for granted that the Cuban revolution, which at first developed classically along the lines of the Khrushchev blueprint, considerably influenced his general thinking. It seemingly convinced him that the Castro phenomenon may have been the turning point in the world's revolutionary development at a time when the anxieties and hopes of the former colonies and of the other backward countries were erupting.

In tune with this theory, Khrushchev announced in his Party Program that it is the "internationalist duty" of the Soviet Union to aid any and all promising "wars of national liberation" that may come along. This was reminiscent of a small boy's claim that after having deliberately smashed the cookie jar, he now has the obligation to eat the cookies. Although this announcement, couched in the usual righteous tones of Communist rhetoric, was tantamount to an open declaration of war against the West, it at first commanded surprisingly little attention outside of the small specialized circles in the United States that now take with utmost seriousness the threat of the Communist-inspired guerrilla and subversive activities in the underdeveloped nations. A "war of national liberation" in actual development, such as the full-scale guerrilla war in Vietnam, was rapidly recognized for what it was and brought about the present United States involvement there.

But the potential "national liberation wars" in Latin America, based on the Cuban example and springing out of the inherent local social and political conditions, fanned by Communist agitation techniques, are still seen as remote possibilities and evoke no serious prophylactic political actions. Curiously, the Pentagon finds itself a step ahead of the political planners in devoting special attention to antiguerrilla and antisubversion dangers in Latin America. It has long been advocating the use of Latin American armies in "civic action" programs, such as road building, water-well drilling, and literacy campaigns. The civilians still shy away from any notion of political warfare.

Khrushchev did, of course, realize that what the Marxists call "objective revolutionary conditions" do not exist at the present juncture in all the underdeveloped countries. Other tactics, therefore, must be used there.

Despite the long-standing tactical differences between the Soviets on the one hand, and the Cubans and the Chinese on the other, the international Communist movement had initially evolved a form of synthesis between the so-called Dimitrov thesis of popular fronts, now favored by Moscow, and the Chinese-Cuban insurrectional approach, which Dimitri Manuilsky championed in Russia in the Stalinist days. What it means is that the insurrectional technique is to be applied in countries where the "objective conditions" are ripe for it, and the popular-front strategy where the process has not yet been sufficiently advanced. But in 1963, the Chinese and the Cubans began increasingly to push for open insurgency everywhere, emphasizing the growing ideological split with Moscow.

In Cuba's "national liberation war," where Castro improvised rather than responding to doctrinaire theses of Moscow or Peking, the two approaches were initially combined on several levels and at different times. Thus, the armed insurrection against Batista led by the Sierra Maestra *guerrilleros* was backed by a popular-front-type alliance of the Cuban political movements, which the Communists joined toward the end, when they had picked the winner in Castro. Subsequently, the Communists took over the national front from within and proceeded to seize power peacefully. But in the later stages, the Fidelistas rebelled against their erstwhile allies and the still unresolved split—a reflection of the Moscow-Peking clash—strongly colors the Cuban political situation.

After Castro visited the Soviet Union in May, 1963, he accepted Khrushchev's thesis of "peaceful coexistence" in world politics. A joint communiqué issued after their meeting, however, emphasized their agreement that the road to "socialism" in Latin America could be either peaceful or violent, depending on local conditions in each country.

In countries like Argentina, Brazil, Uruguay, Chile, and Mexico, where, by Hemispheric standards, there is a comparatively high level of political sophistication and where living conditions have tended to improve spottily in recent years, the Communist strategy is still basically to cooperate with the "progressive bourgeoisie" through popular fronts or simply to encourage and exploit the rising sentiments of national independence.

In these cases, the Communists and their friends seek to ally themselves with non-Communist nationalistic groups in pressuring the established governments—usually the moderate democratic regimes that have succeeded the rightist military dictatorships—into domestic reforms, into stringent measures against foreign capital, and into opposition to the United States. The Communist slogans, which find a growing audience, speak of the struggle against "imperialism," the "preparation of imperialist wars," and "imperialist economic oppression" through the "trusts and monopolies." The example of the Cuban revolution is the counterpoint to this chorus of blandishments.

In the words of Khrushchev's Party Program, "the Communist parties favor cooperation with the social democratic parties not only in the struggle for peace, for better living conditions for the working people, and for the preservation and extension of their democratic rights and freedoms, but also in the struggle to win power and build a socialist society."

He wrote further on that "establishing and developing national democracies opens vast prospects for the peoples of the underdeveloped countries." The Party Program stated that "the political basis of a national democracy is a bloc of all the progressive, patriotic forces fighting to win complete national independence and broad democracy, and to consummate the anti-imperialist, antifeudal, democratic revolution."

At the same time, however, the Soviets and the Latin American Communists violently oppose what the Party Program calls "Right-socialist reformist illusions" and "social-reformist ideology." This spells out the policy of fighting tooth-and-nail such liberal, evolutionary programs as the Alliance for Progress on the Hemispheric scale, or local undertakings, such as President Betancourt's land reform in Venezuela and the Washington-directed operation for rehabilitating Bolivia's tin industry, under the tripartite sponsorship of the Inter-American Development Bank, the West German Government, and the U.S. Alliance. Earlier, the Communist targets included Brazil's "Operation Pan America" proposals and the efforts toward establishment of the Latin American Common Market.

The success of the collective and individual programs for social and economic improvement of Latin America's living standards would bring about a high degree of stability and thus loom as a threat to the revolutionary success of Communism confidently predicted by Khrushchev. The Chinese-Cuban advocacy of immediate revolutions is clearly a sign of impatience with the gradualism of the Soviet blueprint.

For Moscow, United States efforts to help the progress of the underdeveloped countries are part of a dark "imperialist" plot. The Program charged that "under the guise of 'aid' they are trying to retain their old positions in those countries and capture new ones, to extend their social basis, lure the national bourgeoisie to their side, implant military despotic regimes, and put obedient puppets in power." While Americans may tend to dismiss these statements as the straight Communist Party line, it is curious to observe how many Latin Americans, especially students—who may not be pro-Communist—are ready to accept the Kremlin's assertions and equate Western democracy with capitalism and "imperialism."

What the Moscow Communists seek in practice is the mobilization of political and public opinion in the Latin American republics in favor of close relations with the Soviet bloc—and trade with the "socialist camp" is constantly used as bait in this endeavor—coupled with the kind of political and economic "in-dependence" that would loosen or cut the Hemisphere's ties with the United States and lead to neutralism and, subsequently, pro-Communist policies.

In Moscow's estimate, the creation of such situations in the more developed Latin American countries can serve as the bridge toward future peasant-proletarian revolutions on a wide scale, obviating the direct guerrilla or insurrectional techniques recommended for the smaller, more backward, and tension-gripped nations. Should it be possible, however, to set off a broadly backed insurrection in an area like the Brazilian North-east—as Havana and Peking believe to be the case—the strategy in Brazil would obviously change, and chances are that efforts would be made to pit different sections of the country in a civil war, such as that in China in the 1940's.

In 1963, the talk of the country's entering the "prerevolutionary" stage became commonplace in Brazil. While unrest had been grow-ing among the peasant masses clamoring for land reform, the pre-revolutionary leaders, middle class to a man, were also calling for radical change, unaware that they might well be its first victims.

The peasant-proletarian revolutions propounded in Khrushchev's Program would, according to the pattern, calmly devour their first-born bourgeois-nationalist sons, just as the Castro revolution in Cuba disposed of all its founders, except the hard-core Com-munist faction.

In the Kremlin's explicit belief that the road to Communist revolutions in the relatively developed Latin American countries leads through the transition phase of anti-Yankee nationalism lies the explanation of the assiduous attentions that the Soviet Union has been directing in recent years to some of the big republics, notably Brazil.

In fact, a strong argument can be built for the theory that as early as 1961, Brazil—in every respect Latin America's most im-portant country—had become considerably more valuable and in-teresting in Moscow's eyes than Cuba. While Castro's island loomed as a completed conquest—and, incidentally, a sizable drain on Soviet economic resources—Brazil seemed to offer new long-run possibilities in terms of Soviet Communism's dogmatic interpretation of history.

Though the Moscow methodology, geared to the patient approach, did not anticipate the establishment of a "socialist" or Communist state in Brazil in the foreseeable future—barring lucky events such as a Northeastern insurrection—the Soviet Union stood ready to encourage by all the subtle and unsubtle means a Brazilian shift toward neutralism and ultranationalism. Aside from fulfilling the first-stage requirements of Communism for the march toward a proletarian state, the emergence of Brazil as a strongly neutralist power right in the heart of South America would constitute a major prize for Soviet policies in the Hemisphere.

In this light, the "independent" or neutralist direction given Brazilian foreign policy by ex-Presidents Quadros and Goulart constituted a major turning point in the history of Latin America's basic relationships with the United States—potentially more important than Cuba's entry into the Communist orbit and the presence there of dwindling numbers of Soviet troops.

Brazil's quasi neutralism between 1961 and 1964—evident at inter-American conferences as well as at the Geneva Disarmament Conference—was brusquely reversed by the April revolution. The government of President Humberto Castelo Branco, a retired Army marshal, broke diplomatic relations with Cuba and, at the Washington Foreign Ministers' Conference, in July of 1964, it supported sanctions against Havana, in sharp contrast to its attitude at the 1962 Punta del Este Conference, when Brazil opposed the exclusion of the Castro regime from the OAS and, instead, advocated coexistence.

The new policies have halted neutralist momentum in Brazil, but it should not necessarily be assumed that all these pressures have vanished and that they will not reassert themselves at a later time. The Latin American variety of neutralism, or "independence" in foreign policy, remains strong in Mexico, and it is certain to break out again in Chile now that the Presidential election is over.

It is evident that the trend toward these neutralist or "independent" attitudes here and there in Latin America cannot be chalked up as a Soviet achievement traceable directly to the attractions of Communism as an ideology or to Khrushchev's influence. It is, instead, a phenomenon with infinitely older historical roots— quite unrelated to Russia or Communism—that began coming to the fore in the early 1960's under the impact of a series of polarizing forces, including the Cuban revolution, which acted as the catalyst through its nationalistic rather than its Communistic aspects. This phenomenon is also an integral part of the social revolution as it is now developing, because the mounting feeling in Latin America is that it should preserve its meager resources for social and economic development instead of risking them—and its whole future—in an involvement in a cold or hot war. A selfish motive also emerges in this context, for by becoming nonaligned, the Latin American republics hope to benefit from the East-West rivalry and win aid and trade from both sides—as the new African nations have done.

This, then, is the stage and the setting for the rising Latin American social revolution in all its complexity, in its myriad aspects, and with all the forces tugging at it from opposing directions. The central question is whether this irreversible forward surge of a region of 220 million people can be channeled into the direction of a new form of democracy meeting all of Latin America's anxieties, or whether it must succumb to radicalism, and then to Communism, as Cuba did, or whether it will choose still another alternative, a system of military-directed authoritarianism operating in favor of basic reforms, and reminiscent of the Nasser rule in Egypt.

2. The Ingredients

The Exploding Populations

BUT WHY SHOULD THERE BE a social revolution in Latin America now? Have misery and death and disease not been the lot of Latin Americans since the Age of Discovery—and before it, when the Incas, the Mayas, and the Aztecs ruled the three Americas?

To these questions, there are obvious statistical and political answers.

The fantastic population explosion constitutes the first answer. It has raised the human pressures to a boiling point, and in the last twenty years, it has reshuffled all the traditional social patterns. Veritable invading hordes—swollen far beyond mere migrating bands—of landless rural populations are moving upon the cities, which cannot begin to absorb them and are rapidly being turned into festering pockets of misery under the thin veneer of urban modernization and face-lifting.

The rate of population increase, operating like an arithmetic progression from generation to generation, has made Latin America one of the world's fastest-growing regions; its annual rise now runs to 2.8 per cent. Central America has the top Latin American rate of 3.4 per cent annually, with Costa Rica hitting the world peak of 4 per cent, which is matched only by Ghana. Of the two former world leaders, India's population was increasing in the 1950's at a rate of between 2 and 2.4 per cent, and China was growing by 2.3 per cent annually.

Official statistics set Latin America's population in 1961 at 206 million people—43 million more than ten years earlier—and tentative figures for 1963 showed a total of at least 220 million inhabitants. A population of 270 million is anticipated in 1970. This means that the region will have 64 million additional people at the end of the decade of the Alliance for Progress.

In Brazil, the 1960 census disclosed that the country had a population of 74 million, 5 million more than had been estimated. In other words, the Brazilian population has quadrupled in the sixty years since the turn of the century. In 1964, the Brazilian population probably neared the 80-million mark, and the over-all Latin American figure edged toward 230 million people, though primitive statistical facilities could not turn out up-to-date tallies of the actual growth in population.

This tremendous human expansion daily augments the social pressures in the Hemisphere and, in itself, constitutes the most powerful reason for a social revolution, as the available resources under the existing antiquated economic and social structures cannot make even a dent in the needs of the runaway populations. A few of the countries were just a jump ahead of the break-even point, others were already falling behind as the increase in the gross national product failed to keep pace with the increase in inhabitants, much less surpassing it.

The Latin American drama was summed up in these figures of vast disparity: Over-all production in 1960 had risen over the 1959 levels by an infinitesimal 0.3 per cent, while the rate of the population growth for the year was that frightening 2.8 per cent.

In human terms, this meant that Latin America managed to raise its production—food, housing, and goods and services of every description—at a rate that met the requirements of only slightly more than one-tenth of the new populations emerging every year. And by Western standards, even these requirements were incredibly minimal—in the daily calorie intake, in health services, in education, in sanitary housing, or in any kind of housing.

But perhaps the most chilling of all statistics is the fact that in 1960, actual agricultural production fell 2 per cent below the 1959 levels, while the population had risen by 2.8 per cent. Put in other words, this meant that in 1960, Latin America was producing less food per inhabitant than it had in 1938, although 60 per cent of the total population is engaged in agriculture. A report of the Inter-American Development Bank for 1963 said that "per capita food production in 1962–1963 was 7 per cent lower than the pre-war level" and that "most farm families continue to live on incomes at the margin of subsistence."

If this trend is not arrested—and vast structural changes involving people and institutions are required if it is to be arrested—

then much of Latin America will inevitably plummet to real starvation from what today is merely nagging hunger, bare subsistence, and malnutrition. The region inside of ten or twenty years may well become a major famine problem on the Chinese or Indian model.

Latin America is a world of vicious circles turning within vicious circles. An inadequate and nightmarishly distorted economy breeds social problems. The social problems, in turn, block the development of an adequate economy.

For example, the lack or improper use of national resources prevented a supply of water in 1961 from reaching 100 million Latin Americans, or nearly one-half the population. The resulting diseases, the early mortality, and the weakening of individuals hamper agricultural and other production, and the low production, in turn, hampers the development of resources and a fair distribution of wealth. Latin America's chief asset, man, is thus being wasted to an extraordinary degree.

But where health standards have improved, such as in the areas where DDT campaigns have eradicated malaria, the populations are growing faster as mortality rates are being cut. Yet ironically, because society is so woefully disorganized, the blessings of better health breed new problems.

The vicious circle affecting man is meshed with the vicious circle of general production and population movements. The utter misery in many of the rural areas, where millions live outside the money economy and produce only the bare minimum they must have to subsist, sends a mounting wave of the peasant population migrating to the cities. Their presence in the urban centers creates an added demand for food that the countryside cannot satisfy, because those who remain behind do not produce enough to spare. Shelter and jobs are not available, either, to the migrating families in the cities. A parasite population of millions is thereby created, which offers superb breeding grounds for every type of political agitation. Yet Latin America is big enough and potentially rich enough to absorb usefully her population today and tomorrow, provided that her internal structure is refurbished and conditions are created for gainful and decent work.

But under the impact of the prevailing conditions and of the new ideas radiating from Cuba and elsewhere, the notion has begun to develop that a radical social revolution may be the only way of breaking the vicious circles imprisoning Latin America.

Hunger, poverty, and despair are the stuff from which revolutions are made, and there certainly is no lack of these ingredients in Latin America. Then leaders emerge to relate them to people's other aspirations and anxieties, or to manufacture hatreds and desires. This leadership is fast rising in the Hemisphere today, and the long-suffering people are told, over and over, that hunger, misery, and passivity are not ordained by God in the divine scheme of things and that they have the right and the duty to fight for a better life.

This is why, in the language of statistics and of their political interpretation, the social revolution has come to Latin America. But, starkly convincing as the statistics and their interpretation may be, they still have to be translated into human terms so that the full extent of the Latin American tragedy can be understood.

The Journey to Misery

To do so, take a journey to misery in Latin America, instead of making the usual enchanting trip to the romance of the sunsets, the beaches, the luxury hotels, and the mansions of those who today are the mighty and the wealthy. Then you will understand the social revolution.

Start with the cities. It does not matter which one. It can be Rio de Janeiro for a start. Climb the nearest hill—the city is dotted with them—and you are in the world of the *favela*. It is an ugly world of dirt, piles of garbage, waterless shacks with packing-case walls and corrugated-iron roofs, filthy and sick children playing in refuse, abandoned young mothers, and boys who become *malandros* before they mature to manhood. To be a *malandro* is often to take refuge in the only social pattern that offers protection in the human jungle of the *favela,* because it is aggressive. The *malandro* is the wise guy, the owner of a knife or a switch blade, which he uses with ballet-like grace on an opponent; the master of the *capoeira,* which is the dance-like art of kicking the feet from under the enemy in mortal combat; the thief and the pickpocket. Or he is the smart operator and sharp dresser, like Pedro Mico in Antonio Callado's fine play about the *favelas,* or maybe the pimp.

The Rio hills have names that almost tell their own stories; the Hill of the Pig, the Hill of the Dog, the Hill of the Skeleton.

They are like sovereign states within the city, and strangers and policemen seldom venture up the steep cliffsides to see what goes on in these private worlds or to claim criminals who hide there. Periodically, police trucks pull up at the bottom of the *favelas,* and troopers with submachine guns comb the labyrinth of the shacks that may then yield some of their *malandros*—or dead bodies.

The weird world of the Rio *favela*—home to at least a quarter million of the city's total population of 3.5 million and growing fast as new contingents of rural migrants pour in, has its own economic and social rules. The *favela* dweller is not a squatter. He pays rent for his miserable *baracão,* and a steep rent it is, to the landlord, who often is a respected citizen of that other Rio that the tourist knows so well. Those who cannot bring their own water up the hill from the municipal hydrant below (and the telltale sign of a *favela* is the continuous parade of women with five-gallon water cans poised on their heads), have to pay for it in cash. Those among the *favelados* who earn a little extra money are not very interested in improving their conditions; they prefer to buy Sunday clothes, save for the annual Carnival costume, or buy a television set. So, etched against the Rio Bay or the blue South Atlantic—one of the world's most beautiful sights—the *favela* stands fermenting in the hot sun, incongruously topped by a forest of TV antennas. In the warm night, the beat of the drums and the singing of the hill people, practicing for the Carnival, descends upon the city.

Those who are better off in Rio and are not confined to the *favelas* face other pressures and irritations. The workers and white-collar employees who live in the remote and sprawling suburbs commute every day into the city, hanging on the outside of over-crowded trains like flies stuck to gummed paper. When the trains are late, which is all the time, the travelers periodically erupt into blind rages. Suburban stations and trains are stoned or burned until troops arrive to restore order. Other Rio commuters display the incredible patience required to wait in line every day, one hour in the morning and one hour in the evening, for the buses that take them to and from work.

But if the *favela* and commuting life seem bad in Rio, go elsewhere in Brazil to see what urban misery can be. In Brasília, the gleaming new capital in the central plateau, a belt of miserable shack villages has grown, like a horrible open wound, on the outskirts of the young city.

There, the migrants from the drought-plagued, overpopulated Northeast have met their new destiny. They were brought in open trucks over the long, dusty roads to find employment and high wages in building the capital. Often, enterprising truck-fleet owners sold them by the lot or the truckload, to the building contractors who, in the first feverish years of Brasília's construction, were eager for labor and for whom money was no object. Arriving near Brasília, the new workers were kept in corral-like enclosures until the contractors came to pick them up and pay the commissions to the truckers. But since 1960, the building boom has slowed down in Brasília, unemployment has emerged, and the Northeast workers have become another idle, diseased, and potentially rebellious mass.

But it is a matter of opinion whether they are worse off around Brasília than they were at home. You can go to Recife, the big Northeast city, and make up your own mind. Like every Brazilian town, Recife receives its daily influx of migrants from the countryside, especially when a long drought has killed the scrawny cattle, parched the poor land, and ushered in one of those periodic paroxysms of widespread hunger that regularly hit the Northeast.

Where Rio has its hilltop *favelas* and Brasília its belt of shack towns, Recife has the *mocambos*. They are tiny wooden shacks standing on stilts in the low-tide mud of the city's rivers. Sometimes the high tide sends the water up to their doorsteps. When it recedes, organic matter rots in the hot sun, giving off the ghastly smell of the *mocambo* world. At low tide, thousands and thousands of the *mocambo* dwellers, including women and children, go to work. Work is to stand knee-deep in the fetid water, picking up the *caranguejos,* or river crabs, from the bottom. The crabs are the main staple in the diet of the *mocambo* people, and what they do not eat, they sell to pay for their other meager necessities.

Standing on a bridge and looking at the lovely Recife skyline, the visitor sees, as the weird foreground, the river, crawling with thousands of human beings looking almost like river crabs themselves. Picking the crabs has become such a basic occupation in Recife that Dr. Josué de Castro, an outstanding Brazilian sociologist and nutrition expert, has called the "Cycle of the *Caranguejo*" a major social pattern of the Northeast. It may be mentioned in passing that Dr. Castro, who has been a Congressman and an Ambassador, is the recipient of a Stalin Prize. As was noted earlier, Recife's onetime Mayor, Miguel Arraes—later Pernambuco State Governor—is a pro-Communist and the city is a Communist stronghold. Though Arraes was ousted in the 1964 uprising, the problem of the social revolution speaks for itself.

But Brazil is not unique in its wealth of urban slums, which are fast becoming a pattern of modern Latin American civilization, suspended between the feudal subsistence of the countryside and the will-o'-the-wisp proximity of middle-class affluence. Every Latin American country has its plague of the slum, and the plague is worsening every day. With the backlog of housing deficiency so great that nobody really knows its dimensions, current estimates are that Latin America's *new* annual requirements are on the order of 1 million dwellings.

In Santiago, Chile, the *callampas* (mushrooms) gird the city with a belt of mushrooming misery. The traditionally strong Chilean leftist parties, including the Communists, have their stronghold in the *callampas*. This is one reason why the possibility of the election of a pro-Communist President in Chile in 1964 was not at all in the realm of fantasy. Again, the political aspect of the social revolution is clearly evident.

Up the West Coast, in Lima, Peru, the slums rising with an incredible speed on the black sands of the desert surrounding the city have become a major social and political problem. The vast slum, ironically called "Ciudad de Dios" ("City of God") is reminiscent of the North African *bidonvilles,* built from tin cans and packing cases. Garbage from the slums piles up high atop the nearby sand dunes, providing nourishment for the clouds of black vultures that are the ever-present symbol of the life in the *barriadas*. In the highland towns of Arequipa, Puno, and Cuzco, Indians fleeing from the Andean droughts have established their own slums, hurtling overnight from the medieval patterns of their villages into the slum civilization.

It is almost superfluous to say that Peruvian Communism and its peculiar derivations have their strongholds in these Andean slums. Even as a casual visitor spending two days in Lima, former Vice-President Richard M. Nixon remarked that Peru lives atop a social volcano—and this observation was not prompted merely by the student attacks on him. The statistical explanation for Peru's potential for social revolution lies in the fact, reported in

1961 by the government's housing institute, that with a population of 11 million, the country has an urban and rural housing deficiency of nearly 2 million units.

In neighboring Ecuador, the slum problem is alarming in the highland capital of Quito and even more severe in the hot Pacific port of Guayaquil. There, about 250,000 persons in a population of 300,000 live in what a report of the Inter-American Development Bank dryly describes as "substandard conditions of housing, sewerage, water supply, public transportation, and other essentials." This means that practically the entire population of the country's largest city lives in shacks or vermin-ridden, waterless, overcrowded old houses. It is pertinent to mention here that Guayaquil is the scene of frequent riots and violent demonstrations in which almost any excuse is seized to let off the gathering pressures.

In oil-rich Venezuela, the hilltop *ranchos* of Caracas are reminiscent of Rio's *favelas*. They, too, are little kingdoms of misery, and they feed the frequent extreme-leftist riots in the city's downtown sections with thousands who come down from the hills for rampages. With per capita income ten times as high in Caracas as in the countryside, there has been a rural exodus in Venezuela that has almost doubled the size of the cities in the last decade. Today, the urban population exceeds the rural population by 75 per cent, creating awesome unemployment in the cities and undermining food production in the countryside. Betancourt's land-reform program is designed to arrest this trend, but years will elapse before its impact is really felt.

No Latin American city has escaped the plague of the urban slum. In Panama City, 30 per cent of the population lives in city slums of the worst kind and in the neighboring shantytowns. In Colón, the proportion of slumdwellers is even higher. In Mexico City, the capital of a country that has already undergone one social revolution, the slums are growing alarmingly as the industrial development increased the city's population by 58 per cent between 1950 and 1960—to an amazing total of 5 million inhabitants. The country needs 1 million new dwelling units a year, for the most part in the cities, just to satisfy the backlog.

Argentina, an affluent nation, has developed *"villas miserias,"* which are just what the name indicates, around Buenos Aires and her other cities. To meet current needs in five of the main cities, 1 million new dwelling units are currently required. Today, hundreds of thousands live in slum tenements, infested by rats and vermin and lacking all sanitary facilities, that make New York's East Harlem look like a couch of luxury. Thus, in 1962, more than 2 million Argentines cast their votes for the Peronista parties, still responding to the call of social revolution, and in 1964, President Illia's chief opponents were Peronistas.

The earnings of urban workers in Latin America are generally inadequate, and inflation further reduces their real purchasing value. Theoretical minimum-wage levels are often disregarded. Unemployment runs very high. It is impossible to draw the line between employment and underemployment, for uncounted thousands, including women and children, are engaged in part-time occupations, such as street-peddling, lottery-ticket hawking, shoe-shining, running errands, and doing odd jobs. This accentuates the instability of the labor force, and of urban society as a whole.

The Feudal Order

The urban misery and overcrowding is, as we have seen, one of the results of the situation prevailing in Latin America's rural regions. The search for clues to the social revolution must, then, move from the cities to the countryside of the Hemisphere—its jungles, savannas, plains, swamps, plateaus, high mountains, and plantations.

The first general observation to be made about rural Latin America is that, except for favored areas of Argentina and Uruguay and some islands of relative prosperity developed elsewhere in recent years, not very much has changed since Spanish and Portuguese colonial days. In some instances, little fundamental change has occurred since the Inca era. This state of affairs is directly linked to the problem of food production and over-all economic conditions, but, for the time being, we are concerned with its human aspects.

In the relationship between man and the land, the dominating pattern is that of the ownership of immense tracts of territory—the *latifundios*—by a small group of landowners. Available statistics are not accurate, and the actual ratio varies from country to country, but it is probably safe to assume that 90 per cent of all land belongs to 10 per cent of the landowners. Most of the balance of Latin America's arable land is in the form of *minifundios,* or dwarf holdings, which are just as unsatisfactory humanly and economically as the vast *latifundios.*

In Paraguay, for example, 11 farms cover 35 per cent of the eastern region, the wealthier half of the country. In Chile, 63 per cent of the arable land is held by big estates, while only 0.3 per cent of it is devoted to small farms. The balance are unproductive dwarf holdings. In the Peruvian highlands, 1.3 per cent of the estates control more than 50 per cent of the land.

The first consequence of this tenure system is that the overwhelming majority of Latin American peasants are directly or indirectly employed by the landowners—if they are not virtually owned by them. The second consequence is that these land empires are not utilized with long-run effects in mind, because the landlord, as a rule, is interested only in the profit-making cash crops, primarily for export. However, he usually will not allow the land-hungry peasants to work the farm acreage. If the peasants move in as squatters, which is increasingly the new phenomenon, the landlord will remove them forcibly with his own henchmen or call in the local authorities—whom he probably controls—or even appeal to national authorities to see his rights are protected. But lately, squatters have been enjoying an increasing measure of success, which is an indication that the violent social revolution is penetrating the countryside.

It is simply to state the obvious to say that the perpetuation of this system of land tenure in this day and age is possible only because of an extraordinary degree of social, economic, and political irresponsibility on the part of the landowners and because of incredible blindness on the part of the politicians and the governments. But it is to the point to examine what this system does to the Latin American peasants, to say nothing of the national economy and political stability, before the *campesino* and his family finally flee to the cities to create another social problem.

In the first place, the system keeps uncounted millions of peasants entirely or almost entirely outside of the money economy. They are not producers and they are not consumers in the economic sense because they have nothing to sell to anybody and, therefore, have no money to buy anything. The proportion of the population thus vegetating at the margin of the economy differs from country to country and from region to region, but it engulfs most of the rural populations of the Andean highlands of Bolivia, Peru, Chile, Ecuador, and Colombia. It includes the inhabitants of the jungle regions, especially in the Amazon and Orinoco basins, which cover sections of five countries. Half of Ecuador's population falls into this category. Of the 25 million inhabitants of the Brazilian Northeast, as many as 10 million do not belong to the economy. Most of Haiti and much of Paraguay and Central America, including parts of Mexico, can also be thus classified.

Most of those who statistically are included in the economy might as well be considered outside it for all practical purposes. The following figures will explain why. The annual per capita income for a large segment of the Brazilian Northeast population is below $75. In Chile, more than one-half of all the *families* living on the land have an annual income of between $100 and $135, which, on a per capita basis, may amount to $20 or $25. In Ecuador, the national per capita income in 1959 was $160, but 66.7 per cent of the *families* earned $120 annually. Since most of the countries suffer from serious inflation, it is evident how far a family can stretch $120 in a year in terms of buying clothes, shoes, tools, and medicines. Obviously they buy virtually nothing.

Those employed by the big estates are day laborers, tenants, or sharecroppers (*colonos*). Their wages range from nothing to very little. In the Brazilian Northeast, the tenants are usually not allowed to plant anything, not even tiny garden plots, on the landlord's property. They may receive free housing or have it deducted from their wages, sometimes along with food. In practice, no money is paid out.

The institution of virtual bondage is widespread in many countries. In the Northeast of Brazil, there still exists today the system of the *cambão,* under which the peasant has to work one day a week free for the landlord for the privilege of employment or for the right to raise a subsistence crop. In Ecuador, the owners of the big *haciendas* receive free labor under the *huasipungo* system, providing for unpaid work in exchange for the *huasipungueros'* right to farm their own plots on the estate. The Ecuadorian *siembras* method allows the peasant to cultivate virgin land until it is brought into production, when it must be returned to the landlord, who then pays out a cash remuneration or lets the worker keep a part of the crop. Peru still tolerates the *yanaconaje* system, which requires free labor on the estate but permits the peasant to keep whatever he may grow himself on a tiny plot.

When the frequent droughts hit the Peruvian and Bolivian *altiplanos,* the sullen Indians descend upon the towns in the valleys, waiting for relief handouts so that their usual semistarvation will not be transformed into total starvation. Year round they chew the coca leaf, whose narcotic content compensates for the lack of normal nourishment.

On many estates where the owners actually live or often visit, a paternalistic system has developed whereby the workers receive free housing, special benefits, and considerable attention—especially during major holidays. But absentee ownership is the prevailing pattern, vesting in the administrator of a *hacienda* the power of life and death, to say nothing of employment, over his peasants. At his pleasure, the administrator can, and often does, evict a peasant family from the estate, which usually means it is deprived of its livelihood. There is no shortage of other peasants to take the place of the evicted family. For an administrator or his henchmen to kill a recalcitrant peasant is commonplace. Dispatches to *The New York Times* from the Brazilian Northeast early in 1962 related the case of a Peasant League organizer being shot dead by a landlord's *capangas* (henchmen) and that of an administrator who put up a sign in a workers' barracks proclaiming that even after death the men have to "shake a leg."

Some land is cultivated on a communal basis with families or the villages owning it, but most of the land in the hands of the peasants is probably worked individually in conditions not too different from those of the dawn of civilization. The pathetic sight of a man or woman pulling a wooden plow up a rocky Andean hill, picking his way among stones and boulders, is a common one in Peru and Ecuador. In Bolivia, the 1952 revolution and the subsequent land reform improved somewhat the lot of the peasants, but in many of the Andean areas, conditions and tenure systems remain unchanged since Inca days.

In most of the primitive rural areas, the first step in social improvement—getting the animals out of the house—has not yet been reached. Pigs and chickens still share the smoke-filled huts with the human dwellers. Windows are still unknown in many parts.

In the forests of Brazil, Paraguay, Colombia, and Venezuela, the peasant lives by burning the underbrush and the trees to clear out a plot where he can plant some rice, yucca, or bananas. If he cannot, the mandioca (manioc) root and bad coffee are the basis of his diet. When the soil is exhausted and eroded, he moves on with his family to burn more forest ahead. The acrid smoke from the burning underbrush clings to houses, clothes, and people, permeating everything. It is the smell of Latin America's rural misery, and the bluish haze seen from high-flying aircraft is the symbol of rural Latin America.

Despite the loud talk of land reform, modest progress in that direction in a handful of the republics, and plans being drawn for the changes, the land-tenure system remains largely as it was when the huge grants were made by the Spanish and the Portuguese crowns. If anything, it has worsened in proportion as land conquered from nature was added to the huge estates or formed new ones.

In reality, the land problem in Latin America is not insoluble. There is, by and large, enough old and new land to go around, provided that it is properly distributed and placed in production to open new sources of food, absorb the populations, and liberate them from man's and nature's bondage. But time is needed to accomplish the reforms, build roads to markets, irrigate the drought areas, and set Latin America's agriculture and its manpower on a new footing. Meanwhile, the once-resigned peasants are beginning to be reached by politicians and agitators who tell them of the riches social revolution offers. And they may well respond.

The Tragedy of Water

The fundamental social problem of the underprivileged urban and rural masses of Latin America makes them both the cause and the victims of fundamental deficiencies in basic services that affect the Hemisphere's republics in a way difficult to imagine in affluent Western societies.

Despite considerable efforts, often aided by outside sources, to improve the situation, Latin America suffers from the lack of waterworks and sewage systems and, consequently, from a very high incidence of fatal or extremely debilitating diseases. Other factors impair the general health of the people. There is a drastic shortage of doctors and nurses. Educational facilities—physical plants and teachers—are inadequate to handle the skyrocketing population. At least one-half of Latin America's population is illiterate, and the figure may be higher if the considerable percentage of regression from literacy is added. The universities graduate only a fraction of the doctors, engineers, economists, and agronomists needed to cope with the development problems of the region.

This shocking inability of Latin American society to provide for the needs of its members results in part from the traditional negligence of the governments and the elites in regard to social and health problems. It stems in part from the terrible material and human backwardness of the Hemisphere and, in part, of course, from the speed with which the populations are increasing.

It is, then, another of those vicious circles that revolve, one within another, in Latin America. In addition to the basic living problems of the poorest urban and rural populations, this social inadequacy that reaches into every corner of human endeavor is one of the chief ingredients of the revolutionary climate in Latin America. But, in terms of priorities and responsibilities, it is evidently hard to tell which problem is the most serious and which shortage begets which difficulty.

In a 1961 study on "Health in Relation to Social Improvement and Economic Development in the Americas," the Pan American Health Organization does suggest a priority:

> If a single program were chosen which would have the maximum health benefits, which would rapidly stimulate social and economic development, and which would materially improve the standard of living of people, that program would be water supply with provision for running water into or adjacent to the house.

The study reports that "in the 20 countries in Latin America, 33 million persons or 39 per cent of the urban population are without water from a community water supply in 1961." It adds that "smaller cities and rural populations had even more limited facilities" and that 70 per cent of the rural population had no water service at all. "An estimated 100 million persons in Latin America need water service at present," the study concluded.

The Pan American Health Organization further reported that while about 25 million additional persons have been supplied with water between 1950 and 1960, the population during the decade had grown in excess of that figure, creating a new deficit. "Unless there are substantial increases in rates of construction," it said, "by 1980 there may be some 150 million persons without water service."

Even where water service is available, the water is usually not potable. Rio de Janeiro is a case in point, and the same situation obtains in much of Brazil.

The problem of sewage and its disposal, the Pan American

Health Organization reports, "parallels in magnitude that of water service in Latin America." Entire cities lack a sewer system, in some it is highly inadequate, and in others the disposal problem has not been faced, with the result that sewage pollutes the water supply.

The following examples illustrate Latin America's water-shortage tragedy. In Rio de Janeiro, large sections of the city may go without a drop of water for weeks on end because of chronic shortages and the speed with which the city is growing. In Caracas, shortages are likewise commonplace, and 43 per cent of Venezuela's urban population has no water supply at all. In the Brazilian Northeast, the city of Salvador and the surrounding area has potable water in limited quantity for only 52 per cent of its 691,000 inhabitants. In Chile, 40 per cent of the inhabitants of the fast-growing Concepción-Talcahuano industrial area have no potable water at all. For the others, the supply is inadequate in quantity and quality. Of Chile's total urban population, 34 per cent receives no water. In Montevideo, which has 40 per cent of Uruguay's total population, the low-income groups have no sewer facilities; they are available for only 47 per cent of the urban area. Only 27 per cent of Colombia's urban population has potable water.

In Costa Rica, one-half of the rural population lacks water supply. Only 8 out of 65 Costa Rican towns have sewer facilities. In Ecuador, only 7 per cent of the urban population has sewer service, and 45 per cent of the population centers across the country lack water supply. In El Salvador, 70 per cent of the rural population has no water service. In Guatemala City, only 26 per cent of the houses have public sewer connections. In Haiti, there is inadequate water supply for 48 per cent of the urban population and virtually no supply in the countryside. Sewers are practically nonexistent. Only 10 per cent of the Honduran population has home water service, and only 9 per cent of the urban population has sewer service. Half of Mexico's population has no water supply. In Nicaragua, one-half of the urban population lacks water. Because it lacks adequate water or sewage service, 65 per cent of Panama's housing is considered unhealthful. In Paraguay, 85 per cent of the urban population and the entire rural population have no water system of any kind. Until 1959, Asunción's drinking water came from wells. The capital has sewers for one-third of its population, but the service does not exist elsewhere in the country.

All these statistics refer only to water for human use. They do not cover the shortages of water for irrigation purposes that constantly plague such areas as the Brazilian Northeast and the Andean regions. This is a separate problem of vast proportions.

The water and sewage inadequacy is directly responsible for Latin America's dire health standards. The Pan American Health Organization says in its report that "death rates in children under five years of age are very high in Latin America due to gastrointestinal diseases and communicable diseases of childhood" and that "a significant proportion of these deaths could be prevented by adequate water supplies." The Organization lists diarrheal disease and typhoid fever among the illnesses caused in Latin America by water problems, but there are a host of other gastric and parasital disorders caused by the intake of polluted water. Though there are no full statistics on the subject, it can be assumed that bad water is one of the chief causes of death, disease, and debilitation.

While in 1959 the Latin American infant mortality rate stood at 91.5 per 1,000 live births, or 9.2 per cent (Haiti has the highest rate, 17.1 per cent), in the Salvador area of the Brazilian Northeast, it was 16 per cent, attributable to bad water alone. In Paraguay, gastric diseases were the chief killer of infants. In Costa Rica, they were the principal cause of death in all age brackets. In Ecuador, gastric diseases attributed to the water problem accounted for 22 per cent of all deaths, and in Mexico 21.6 per cent of all diseases stemmed from the water supply. How the improvement of water supply can curtail deaths was shown in Mexico, where the installation of new facilities cut down the mortality rate from 457 to 205 per 100,000 inhabitants between 1942 and 1958.

Reports from the Brazilian Northeast tell of two villages where sometimes not a single infant has lived over the age of one because of esquimatosis, the local variety of gastroenteritis. In this region, the disease is transmitted by tiny snails in the rivers from which the population draws its drinking water. The disposal of untreated sewage in the rivers returns the bacteria to the carrier snails. Recently, the emptying into the rivers near Recife of industrial waste from the new factories there resulted in poisoning the fish, which used to absorb a certain amount of the polluted snails and thereby had made the water safer. Immediately, the incidence of esquimatosis soared. It was another of those incredible vicious circles haunting Latin America: The arrival of desperately needed industry was causing disease and mortality. When Northeastern migrants traveled to Brasília to help build the new capital, they took the infection with them.

Throughout Latin America, the frequent sight of sad-eyed children with grotesquely distended bellies is a shocking reminder of the human problem caused by the water. Not surprisingly, then, the Alliance for Progress and the Inter-American Development Bank have made water supply one of their top-priority targets—perhaps not a spectacular one, but nonetheless a vital one.

But Latin America's diseases are not all water-carried. Tuberculosis, according to the Pan American Health Organization, "remains one of the principal causes of death" in the continent. Although the incidence of tuberculosis has been decreasing due to massive BCG vaccination campaigns, the disease remains a threat to Latin America so long as its inhabitants are plagued by malnutrition, crowded living conditions, and other social ills.

While DDT campaigns and other measures have been successful in eradicating malaria fully or partially in large areas of Latin America—and thereby sending up the population rate—the disease is still extracting its toll in hundreds of thousands or even millions of wrecked persons whose ability to work is sharply curtailed. Official statistics show that by mid-1960, almost 78 million persons —more than one-third of Latin America's total population—lived in areas where malaria remained highly active, mostly in Eastern and Central Brazil, the northwestern section of South America, the Caribbean, and Central America.

Endemic goiter, caused by lack of iodine in food and water, affects 30 million persons, reaching an incidence of 90 per cent of the population in some areas. This disease results in lower mental efficiency, sometimes in cretinism.

Eye diseases, general malnutrition, venereal diseases, leprosy (of which there are 200,000 known cases and 10,000 new cases reported annually), tropical skin ailments, brucellosis, and scores of other forms of sickness also afflict Latin America. It is today an unhealthy region of unhealthy people whose energies are sapped by disease instead of being liberated for development work.

To conquer disease, Latin America has only 100,000 physicians. This averages to 1 doctor per 2,000 inhabitants—exactly one-half of the required minimum—but in practice there are wide areas where there is only 1 doctor for 4,000 or more persons. Only Argentina and Uruguay (and Cuba before the revolution) met the minimal requirements, and even so, the physicians there, like elsewhere, were concentrated in the large cities where practice is profitable. The ratio in Haiti is 1 doctor for 10,000 inhabitants, in El Salvador it is 1.4 doctors for 10,000 people, and in Bolivia it is 2.6 for 10,000 inhabitants.

The Pan American Health Organization estimates that by 1980, Latin America will need at least 350,000 doctors to meet the population growth. But all the 88 medical schools in Latin America together graduated only 6,722 doctors in 1957, an average recent year. The number of graduates must more than double immediately to reach the 1980 goal—and this does not make allowance for doctors practicing today who will have to be replaced because of death or retirement.

The outlook for accelerating the education of doctors is not very encouraging, despite the Alliance for Progress assistance plans to Latin American universities. Medical schools are not developed overnight, and at present, quite a few of them do not have full-time faculty members. There is a woeful lack of teaching materials, books and laboratories, and equipment. Compounding the problem of the doctor shortage is the lack of trained nurses in Latin America. In 1961, there were only 37,000 nurses for a population of more than 200 million.

The deficiency in doctors and nurses is accompanied by a highly inadequate hospital situation. While the United States has 4.5 beds in general hospitals for each 1,000 inhabitants (Canada has 6.5), in ten countries of Latin America, the ratio is less than 2 beds per 1,000 people. For each 1,000 persons, Chile has 3.7 beds and Argentina 3.6 beds, but Brazil has only 2 beds, Ecuador 1.7 beds, and Haiti 0.5 bed.

The Drama of Education

The problem of doctors and nurses is but one manifestation of the abysmal general picture of education in Latin America. With one-half of the population over the age of fifteen completely illiterate and at least 15 million children of school age without any schooling facilities, the region clearly lacks a base for the educational leap forward that is vital for any comprehensive program of economic and social development.

One of the emergency aims of the Alliance for Progress is to attack on the education front, and the task will be monumental. Where the Castro regime in Cuba claims to have eradicated illiteracy in one year through a massive program involving tens of thousands of volunteer teachers, it had to cope with an illiteracy rate of only 22 per cent in a population of fewer than 7 million inhabitants. But elsewhere in Latin America the problem is a hundredfold more complicated because of a vastly higher illiteracy index and the virtual isolation of great areas, rendering the mass-teaching approach impossible, even if it were deemed effective.

Thus, Brazil has a population that is 50 per cent illiterate, or more than 35 million people who have to be taught the alphabet. In Guatemala, the illiteracy rate is 70 per cent; in Ecuador, it is 43 per cent; and in Haiti, 90 per cent.

It should be recorded in passing that some of the highest illiteracy rates and the most neglected educational conditions are in evidence in the countries that have lived under dictatorships. When General Pérez Jiménez was ousted from power in Venezuela in 1958, he left behind 2 million illiterate adults out of a total population of 6.8 million, and 40 per cent of school-age children without schooling facilities. And this was in a country that enjoyed a billion-dollar annual income from oil. President Betancourt's government, facing reduced revenues and high debt payments, succeeded in two years in providing schools for 80 per cent of eligible children. Generalissimo Trujillo in the Dominican Republic countenanced a 58 per cent illiteracy rate despite his immense revenues. In Haiti, the never-ending succession of dictators has made no attempt to solve any of the social problems, including education, which is why 9 out of 10 Haitians cannot read or write.

But impoverished Bolivia managed to raise primary-school attendance in the rural areas from 17 per cent in 1951 to 50 per cent in 1961 through the efforts of the revolutionary government. Her illiteracy rate in 1953 was 68 per cent; now it is sharply lower.

Despite the formidable problem that has faced the region for so long, the average allocation for education in Latin America is the incredibly low 12.2 per cent of annual expenditures. (Costa Rica is an exception, with 20 per cent.) This is a fair example of the irresponsible attitude of the Latin American ruling classes toward today's social situation.

The first difficulty is the drastic shortage of schoolhouses, particularly in rural areas, which often have none at all. The second difficulty is that while primary education is in principle free and compulsory in most countries, millions of children either do not attend classes or drop out after the first few grades because they must work or because they do not have the strength to go to a far-away school. The extent to which the availability of food encourages school attendance was demonstrated in the Peruvian highlands late in 1961, when a school-lunch program from United States surplus stocks sent 50 per cent more children to their classrooms. The program was also a reminder of how much can be accomplished with very little in a well-planned social-assistance undertaking. The third difficulty involving primary education is the lack of qualified teachers—or, in some areas, of any teachers.

In the teaching field, only so much improvisation is advisable, but Bolivia more than doubled the number of rural teachers in ten years, and Venezuela increased her teaching force by 61 per cent in one year, between 1959 and 1960, after accelerating training courses and opening twenty-one new normal schools.

Though millions of Latin American children have been enrolled in primary schools, only about 10 per cent of them completed elementary education. The reasons are both social and economic, but one important factor is that an overwhelming number of youths saw no opportunities for themselves in terms of jobs if they stayed in school. So here is another of those maddening Latin American vicious circles: The region's rhythm of development is impaired by a lack of trained persons, but people are not becoming educated because of a shortage of schools and subsequent opportunities in what they see as excessively narrow societies.

The resulting difference between primary- and secondary-school enrollment is even more striking, running at a ratio of six to one. In the United States, on the other hand, about 45 per cent of primary-school students go on to high school.

Making the transition from high school to university in Latin America is even more unusual. Here, the ratio of those going on to college is one student out of every ten, compared with a rough ratio of one out of three in the United States. An exception is Mexico with almost one of every two high-school students enrolling in a university.

From a population of almost 70 million in 1960, there were only 95,691 university students in Brazil, but Argentina, with a total population less than one-third of Brazil's, sent 144,042 youths to college. Colombia, with a population of 15 million and high intellectual traditions, had only 19,212 university students in 1958. One of the main reasons for this situation is the shortage of facilities, especially in technical schools.

But another gulf exists between college enrollment and graduation, and herein lies Latin America's great tragedy at the threshold of her plunge into the "Decade of Progress." We have already seen that fewer than 7,000 doctors were graduated in 1957. Other figures are even more discouraging when one considers the Hemisphere's immense development tasks.

Fewer than 200 dentists graduate annually in all of Latin America. Only 100 sanitary engineers are graduated every year. In 1960, Brazil graduated 1,400 engineers, while 12,000 students applied for admission and only 2,400 could be accepted. In Panama, 27 architects and 52 engineers were graduated between 1957 and 1961.

Although the development of agriculture is Latin America's most pressing economic problem, the entire region has only 16,000 trained agronomists, while at least 43,000 are now required. The 60 agricultural colleges in what are essentially agricultural countries graduate only 2,000 agronomists annually. At the Central University in Caracas, only 1.5 per cent of the students—368 of them—studied agronomy in 1960, even though the land problem is one of the keys to Venezuela's future. At the University of Uruguay, 1.8 per cent of the students studied agriculture in 1957. In the light of this situation, one wonders how Latin Americans expect to carry out their land reforms—for which university students so loudly agitate at political rallies.

In a more general vein, it must be stressed that Latin American thinking in regard to higher education must urgently switch from the traditional emphasis on humanities and law—which are convenient gateways to politics—to technical and related subjects if the region really expects to develop. A social revolution will not by itself blueprint a new economy—and the shortage of professional economists is another Latin American problem—nor will it build roads, bridges, dams, and factories. Cuba is the best available example of how a social revolution can come close to derailing itself through the lack of a managerial and technical class, and it is highly doubtful that the Soviet bloc can spare enough technicians in every field to build up a whole continent.

The Legacy of Greed

While social and economic problems in Latin America are obviously closely interrelated, the situations discussed here suggest that in a large measure, the former are an effect of the latter. It can thus be argued that if Latin America's economy had not been allowed in the past centuries, and particularly in recent decades, to become so thoroughly distorted through lack of planning and thoughtlessness, today's social problems would not loom so large and menacing. Put another way, it may be said that the rising social revolution has its roots in the economic monstrosity that is Latin America.

And, as always, the roots are in the soil and in the land. At first, out of a sense of greed, the Latin American economic elites concentrated almost entirely on land and agriculture—when they should have become aware of the Industrial Revolution in the Western world—because it was the easiest, the quickest, and the safest way to a cash profit. Almost from the colonial days, the masters of Latin America were willing to go along with successive cycles of demands for commodities—sugar, natural rubber, coffee, wheat, cattle, or, from the bowels of their soil, gold, silver, copper, and, finally, oil.

The foreign capital that came into Latin America in the nineteenth century and subsequently encouraged this selfish and shortsighted policy because it suited its own shortsighted interests. Yet it was this foreign capital that built Latin America's railways, her public utilities, and her first industries. It did so because, again, it suited its interests and because the Latin Americans preferred to sell land, mineral, and utility concessions to the foreigners or borrow money from the London or New York money markets rather than invest their own capital. This capital, they reasoned, was better invested in buying more land to make more killings in the export of produce or in land speculation or in foreign banks. No effort, therefore, was made to diversify agriculture, to break away from the monoculture pattern, to improve the conditions of the peasants and with it their productivity, and to fix them firmly on the soil. This, then, was the sin of greed which has turned Latin America into the producer of raw materials for an outside world that was becoming rapidly industrialized—a role Latin America's economists, nationalists, politicians, and students bitterly bemoan today and for which they blame the United States.

To concentrate so exclusively and so wrongly on land was the first phase in the process of economic distortion, the phase that lasted until roughly the end of World War II. It was at that juncture that Latin America discovered industry and became imbued with a violent spirit of industrialization for economic, political, and nationalistic reasons.

The billions of dollars saved by Latin America's exporters during the war, when there was nothing to import from abroad, were squandered almost overnight on purchases of luxury goods and on harebrained industrial schemes. Brazil and Argentina, perhaps the most mature of the Latin American countries, led this parade of spendthrifts, and soon their favorable balances of payment became unfavorable and emissaries rushed to Washington to seek bailout loans.

But the headlong rush toward industrialization was on. It became a matter of national honor to create a steel industry, and following Brazil's example, Chile, Colombia, and Venezuela began shopping for this badge of distinction. There is no question that Latin America had reached the point where she urgently had to industrialize herself and she still needs industrialization today in an increasing degree. The falling prices of her commodities on the world markets could no longer finance the needed consumer-goods imports for the mushrooming populations, and there was no reason why Latin America should not develop industry of her own and cease being merely the supplier of raw materials. In fact, the population explosion and the start of the massive migrations from the countryside to the cities made it imperative that new sources of employment be provided. And the more industry was erected, the more migrants streamed into the cities in still another turn of the Latin American vicious circles.

Between 1948 and 1960, nearly $2 billion in foreign investments flowed into Latin America to help set up the new industry. Brazil gained an automotive industry that rapidly became Latin America's largest, and the São Paulo area became the region's biggest, wealthiest, and most booming industrial complex. Hundreds of millions of dollars went into manufactures of every kind, and after 1956, Brazil invested other hundreds of millions of her own dollars and cruzeiros in building the dreamlike new capital of Brasília. And on a lesser scale, the Brazilian industrial phenomenon was repeated elsewhere in Latin America—in Mexico, Venezuela, Colombia, Argentina, Chile, and Peru. Easy bank credit, stemming from the inevitable inflation, helped to finance more industry as well as real estate speculation as a hedge against further inflation. It was a dizzying and spectacular new era as the dream of industrialization finally began to come true.

This, then, was the second phase. And like the first one, it carried with it a fatal error in judgment, again concerning the land. This time the error was that in attempting to fashion the region into a patchwork of industrial islands, the Latin Americans forgot agriculture, and their farm lands became the impoverished step-children of the successive governments and of the economic elites. Even cattle- and wheat-rich Argentina succeeded in grievously damaging her agriculture under the Perón regime in favor of a graft-ridden state-run industry. The hurrying Hemisphere over-looked .what the United States had made a point of remembering during its own Industrial Revolution: that an industrial society, too, has to be fed and that it is suicidal to erect an economy without an agricultural base. It is also a point that the Soviet Union has been trying to make for its own benefit for forty-five years, one over which Communist China stumbled and fell in her attempted "great leap forward" in 1958, and one that is bedeviling revolutionary Cuba.

But the sin of greed was, as usual, present even in this neglect of the land. While governments and great landowners still did not think seriously of diversifying the monocultures and increasing the food production through improvement and extension of arable land and a fairer tenure system, all of them jumped into a demented round of overproduction of highly profitable export cash crops.

The excuse for this greed was that the coffee, cocoa, and sugar would finance imports of capital goods and thus give another shot in the arm to the scheme of rapid industrialization. By 1959, the predictable results of this madness were self-evident: The world markets were glutted with Latin America's tropical commodities, the prices collapsed, and the whole economic policy boomeranged against its authors. Local currency became greatly depreciated, particularly in the great coffee-producing countries, like Brazil and Colombia. The money presses worked overtime to turn out enough banknotes to pay for the coffee production for which there were no export markets. This, and the neglect of relatively unprofitable staple crops, such as rice and beans, set off a runaway inflation and food shortages in the cities. Social unrest followed immediately.

As Latin America entered the decade of the 1960's, and the revolutionary winds began to blow strong over the region, her economy, with very few exceptions, was in a shambles. Although in fast-developing countries like Brazil, the statistics showed an impressive upward curve in the rate of growth, much of it was illusory.

There was no relationship between industry and agriculture, and even less between different regions of the country. The Northeast and the rapidly rising South-Center were separate worlds. The increase in the growth rate and the per capita income applied mainly to the industrialized area and hardly touched the vast peripheries, where the population pressures were the greatest.

Almost everywhere domestic budgets were deep in deficits and new, inflation-breeding money was being printed to pay the bills. With a few exceptions, the international balances of payment were highly unfavorable. The corrupt and unwieldy machines of public administration were absorbing the bulk of the revenues. Unemployment and strikes mounted. But only palliatives were applied: Few governments had the political courage to strike at the root of their problems.

Food production, transportation, and distribution remained—and will remain for a long time—the key to these problems. Despite some recent changes in policy, though not always in practice, food production in most of Latin America is still regulated by factors that range from the weather to the conditions in world commodities' markets. Export crops still occupy most of the attention of landowners, and the needs of the expanding and destitute rural and urban masses are seldom taken seriously into consideration. The domestic private capital that could finance a change in the agricultural pattern is still either invested in industry, city real estate, and land purchases, or salted away abroad to escape taxation and the inroads of inflation. Though even the approximate figures are unknown, anywhere between $5 billion and $25 billion in Latin American private capital may be kept in foreign banks or foreign stock markets—perhaps as much as the United States plans to invest in Latin America during the ten years of the Alliance for Progress. This is money that could be used to build roads, finance land reforms, and perhaps even to hold back a violent social revolution. But the vicious circle of greed still holds Latin America in its grip.

To relate the human situation to Latin American food production in another dimension, let us take the story of rice, the main staple in the region's diet. It is as good an introduction as any to the strange economic distortion ruling Latin America.

Between 1955 and 1958, Brazil increased its rice production by only 9 per cent, while the population grew by about 14 per cent. Tiny El Salvador, where the population expanded by 50 per cent in ten years, to create the second greatest density of inhabitants in Latin America, maintained a stationary rice production between 1955 and 1958. Ecuador, which has good rice land on the coast and nightmarish hunger among the highland Indians, produced considerably less rice in 1958 than in 1955.

These statistics throw light on one of the most important aspects of Latin America's rural economy and its relationship to the human problem. To be most profitable, rice must be produced on large tracts of land, because adequate fertilization, irrigation, and harvesting are not practicable on tiny family plots or *minifundios*. But the current pattern—unless it is broken by an efficient land reform—in most of Latin America is for the big landowners to shy away from low-profit products like rice. At the same time, the rate of population growth results in a dramatic overcrowding of the *minifundios,* which cannot produce even remotely enough to feed their owners. Not only do the *minifundistas* lack land for large-scale production, but their rock-bottom incomes prevent them from acquiring fertilizer and from irrigating the soil—to say nothing of purchasing harvesting and threshing machinery.

The case of El Salvador, where, as was mentioned above, rice production remains stationary while the population skyrockets, makes this point convincingly in terms of human pressures and the land-tenure system. In that immensely overpopulated republic, slightly more than 1 per cent of the *fincas* occupy one-half of all farm land; 80 per cent of the farms have less than 5 hectares (12 acres), and 94 per cent have less than 20 hectares (48 acres). Of the 5-hectare plots, 56 per cent are worked by tenant farmers and settlers and their unceasingly growing families. The big estates are given over mostly to coffee growing, which produces 72 per cent of the country's export revenues, but some lie idle. Meanwhile, the 200,000 or so peasant families on the *minifundios* live on the verge of hunger. President Rivera's social-minded new government has its work cut out in trying to change this pattern peacefully.

But if the example of El Salvador's rice production is shocking, the situation in Venezuela was almost unbelievable during the dictatorship of Pérez Jiménez, whose wild malpractices truly ushered in the age of social revolution in that country. In 1958, the year the dictator was ousted, Venezuela grew only one-fourth of the rice produced three years earlier, while the population had risen 10 per cent since 1955. In general, as well as in the particular case of rice, the policies of the Pérez Jiménez regime tended toward an outright abandonment of agriculture in favor of oil-financed billion-dollar megalomaniacal schemes, like the never-completed complex of steel and petrochemical industries greatly exceeding Venezuela's needs, like the luxury hotels and the aerial trains.

The accompanying trend toward more and bigger *latifundios* and the rising concentration of population in the dwarf holdings created in Venezuela the same problem of the relationship of the people to the land and food as in El Salvador, but on a greatly magnified scale. Nearly 82 per cent of the total agricultural area was held in estates larger than 500 hectares (1,200 acres). In the words of the 1961 report of the Social Progress Trust Fund of the Inter-American Development Bank, "the increase in the rural population, without a change in the number of direct owners . . . shows a clear tendency toward intensification of the social problem of land tenure." It is also responsible for the tremendous exodus of rural populations to the cities, and the development there of a pre-revolutionary social situation. But the efforts of the Betancourt regime since 1959 have begun to make a dent in the over-all situation, notably in increasing food production.

In the area of rice, Mexico and a few other countries did succeed, however, in sharply raising production. It is one of the top—but still unfulfilled—targets of revolutionary Cuba, which in 1961 grew less rice than in 1958.

Moving along the gallery of horrors of Latin American farm economics, we come upon the next example—that of black beans. Along with rice, the *frijoles* (*feijão*, in Brazil) are the foundation and often the sum total of the daily nourishment of scores of millions of people.

Here, again, Brazil offers a good case history. While the population rose at the rate of 1.4 million annually, black-bean production went up imperceptibly between 1955 and 1958, the last year for which complete data are available. Similar instances of production of staples lagging far behind population expansion are reported in a number of the other republics.

But the obverse of this dramatic neglect of food production is the tale of Latin America's coffee adventure in the 1950's. Acting under the stimulus of artificially high prices and official subsidies, Brazil, the world's largest producer, increased its coffee production by 25 per cent between 1955 and 1958, while the acreage of its coffee plantations rose by 17 per cent in the same period. Between 1954 and 1956, coffee was fetching as much as

90 cents a pound for the top Colombian grades and nearly that amount for Brazilian coffee on the New York commodity market. It was a bonanza for the coffee planters and, temporarily, for the Brazilian dollar balance. Speculators bought land wherever coffee could be grown and feverishly cleared the ground to plant the precious trees.

Latin America's fourteen other coffee growers joined the parade. Following Brazil's madcap example, Costa Rica doubled her coffee production and so did Panama. Paraguay also became a coffee producer. Diversification of agriculture, religiously preached everywhere but seldom practiced, was laid completely aside. It was the dance of the millions, like the sugar bonanza in the Caribbean thirty years earlier, and everybody profited from it—except the Latin American masses.

As had to happen, the bubble finally burst about 1958. Africa, encouraged by the spectacle of the Latin American killings in the world markets, stepped up its coffee production. The cheaply produced African coffee began to undercut the Latin American product, whose cost was higher because of antiquated methods, more expensive labor, and higher profits. As the Latin American trees planted around 1954 began to produce fruit four years later, surpluses started to pile up. By 1959, 50 million bags of excess coffee filled warehouses throughout the Hemisphere. The overblown prices collapsed and the Brazilian coffee that had fetched 85 cents a pound in 1954, brought only 32 or 33 cents in 1960.

At that point, the masses began to pay the bill for the coffee joyride. To bail out the overextended coffee growers, the Brazilian Government had to buy up—and store—the unsold beans, to the tune of $370 million in 1959 and 1960. To finance this operation, it had to unloose another cascade of freshly printed cruzeiros, thus worsening the inflation and, again, adding to the social ferment.

Between 1956 and 1960, Latin America lost billions of dollars in revenue, and in most cases, there were no alternate sources of income. It could be argued that these losses were on paper only, because they were the difference between the artificially high prices and their reasonable level. But since the economies of the fifteen Latin American producers became geared to the high coffee-price level, the loss was a real one in terms of the damage it caused. The producers calculated their losses on the basis of a formula that determined that a drop of 1 cent a pound in the price of green coffee meant an annual loss of $60 million to the region. Between 1954 and 1959, the drop was about 50 cents a pound.

The actual damage varied from country to country and was related to each country's dependence on its coffee exports. Brazil, battered as it was by the experience, was in a relatively better position to absorb the blow because of its broader economic base and the fact that by 1960 coffee provided only 59 per cent of her export income. Recently developed iron, manganese, and other exports had lessened the Brazilian reliance on coffee. But Colombia, 66 per cent of whose exports are in coffee, was hard hit. The Central American countries, where dependence on coffee ranges from 52 per cent of exports in the case of Costa Rica to 72 per cent for El Salvador and Guatemala, had received a body blow. Their already low living standards were dropped further, just as revolutionary agitation emanating from Cuba began to center on the isthmus.

After 1960, a Latin American coffee agreement was signed in an effort to stabilize prices, and in 1963, it was expanded into a world pact with the participation of consumer nations, including the United States. But, essentially, the farm and human structures remained unchanged in the coffee lands of the Hemisphere.

It may appear strange that the clues to revolutions or to stability should be found in rice, beans, coffee, or housing and health statistics. But in Latin America, the crazily rising and falling lines on production and price charts and the dull, impersonal figures spell out worsening economic distortions, deepening social pressures, and rising human protest and despair. This is why the story of rice and the story of black beans and the story of coffee—and their relationship to all the features of Latin American life—loom so importantly in the present and the future of the Hemisphere.

The Leap Forward

The ingredients of the Latin American social revolution lie, then, in every aspect of the huge region's human and physical and economic structure. The solution to Latin America's ills lies in the task, without parallel in human history, of building, almost from scratch, in forbidding surroundings and mostly in a tropical climate, an economic edifice and a whole new human society. It is an undertaking far exceeding the Marshall Plan, whose goal was only to reconstruct Western Europe, a relatively small war-ravaged area that had the advantage of industrial, production, and trade traditions and a fairly intact managerial class.

Reason suggests that if this extraordinary task is ever to be accomplished, it can be done only through peaceful and orderly procedures, with the cooperation of the entire Western world and aided by a new sense of responsibility on the part of Latin America's elites. There is nothing to indicate that a radical revolution—even with considerable Communist aid—can do the job better. In fact, chances are that a revolutionary breakdown would, instead, throw the region into convulsions and upheavals lasting years, perhaps worsening in the long run the lot of the suffering masses. Again, it is illuminating to consider the example of Cuba, whose economy goes on deteriorating four years after the Castro revolution, despite massive Soviet aid.

But reason does not necessarily prevail in such cases, particularly when the pressures are mounting as rapidly and powerfully as they now are in Latin America. And to complicate the problem, Latin America now, and in the foreseeable future, has to run fast just to stand still, even under the best and most orderly circumstances.

Thus, it appears from the projections of a formula worked out by Joseph Marion Jones in a recent population study published by the Center for International Economic Growth that Latin America has to make an almost impossible leap forward to meet the goals of the Alliance for Progress.

In order for her per capita income to rise by 2.5 per cent annually during ten years—which may mean an average of $75 in the decade—her national income must be increased in aggregate by 69 per cent. The calculation is made on the assumption that Latin America's population increase rate will average only 3 per cent annually for the decade, which may be wishful thinking.

But it is highly debatable, if not downright impossible, that an increase of 69 per cent in national income can be achieved in Latin America. Mr. Jones notes that "even with its vast capital resources and technology, the United States was able to increase its national income in the fifteen years, 1945–1959, by about forty per cent, and its per capita income by eleven per cent." In contrast, the Alliance's aggregate goal for the "Decade of Progress" calls for a 25 per cent increase in per capita income.

Aside from the loaded political question whether these widely heralded but seemingly insufficiently analyzed goals may not be dangerously delusive, there is little in Latin America's present rate of annual growth to indicate that the individual national incomes are likely to soar during the decade of the Alliance to the point where the promised increases in per capita income can become a reality.

However, there have been both encouraging and discouraging trends since 1961. Brazil, which had a 7 per cent annual growth rate in 1961, slowed to a rate of less than 3 per cent in 1963, leading to a drop in per capita income. Venezuela, Mexico, Guatemala, and five other countries surpassed the desired increase of 2.5 per cent in per capita income in 1962 and 1963, but Argentina, Haiti, Paraguay, and several others joined Brazil in losses in per capita income, thus keeping the regional average well below the Alliance's 2.5 per cent goal.

Certainly, the great infusion of outside funds under the Alliance and the hoped-for domestic reforms designed to increase productivity and production will accelerate the growth of national income. But even so, with the population explosion wiping out real increases in per capita income, it will be immensely difficult to bridge the gulf between Latin America's capabilities and the Alliance's hopes.

As Mr. Jones points out, a country with a per capita income of about $250 annually, which is the average for most Latin American republics, and a population growth rate of about 2.5 per cent must raise its present national income by 28 per cent at the end of ten years "in order merely to prevent a decline in per capita income over the ten years."

This statement illustrates the effort that Latin America must make just to avoid backsliding in her economic and human problems, and it raises the basic question of whether the restless populations are prepared to work hard and patiently for the future of the next generations—if not of their own.

But again, the answer to this question may be found in the political and psychological posture of the continent, especially in the light of the fortunes of democracy there. It thus is pertinent to review the situation as it existed in this field in the years before the revolutionary clarion call was sounded in Cuba.

3.   The Threshold

The Democratic Illusion

THE MODERN POLITICAL HISTORY OF LATIN AMERICA has revolved since the days of Simón Bolívar around the theoretical concept of democracy. Freeing themselves one after another from colonial rule, most of the Latin American republics adopted constitutions patterned after the United States constitution, incorporating the libertarian ideals of the Bill of Rights, while borrowing from France the jurisprudence of the Napoleonic Code. Elections and Presidential terms were defined, and the power was to be vested in the people, represented by Congress.

But, in practice, Latin American democracy in the last 150 years has been neither democratic nor representative, except for brief periods. Its concepts were proved by and large meaningless. Revolution followed revolution, civil wars were often a normal state of affairs in many countries, and what passed for the practice of democracy was restricted to a small echelon of the population drawn from the literate, the rich, and the powerful. The elite groups, despite their continuous shifts, maintained their own political machines designed to assure their perpetuation in power.

When Presidents and legislators were democratically chosen, it was generally done without the participation of the masses, who were disfranchised by various practices and by, more than anything else, their own indifference and isolation from the main stream of political life. Illiteracy and the extreme poverty of the masses, especially in the rural areas that until fairly recently were the overwhelming centers of the population, effectively kept them separated from their nation's body politic. The masses were brought into the picture only to be incited to riot in the streets or to form private political armies for reasons they never quite understood, except that they were responding to leadership of powerful personalities.

Political parties, when they existed, were also the intellectual and political property of small groups. From this situation grew the personalist tradition in Latin American politics and the system of *"partidos de etiqueta,"* parties that were merely a label for the personal ambitions of their leaders. The true idealists—and there were comparatively many of them in the Latin American Creole romantic tradition—inspired movements that either were quickly captured by predatory chieftains or were submerged in oblivion. After their deaths, many of their names were used to gild the political machinations of governments and rival parties. This was the posthumous destiny of Bolívar, San Martín, and Tiradentes, and later of José Martí and a whole legion of political idealists. Such practices, disguised with the mantle of democracy, prevailed throughout the nineteenth century and well into the twentieth. At best, Latin American democracy was a benign autocracy; at worst, it was dictatorship and unceasing upheaval.

Thus, in Ecuador, no President in this century served out his full term until the Galo Plaza period between 1948 and 1952. The new pattern was soon broken with the ouster of President Velasco Ibarra in 1961 and of President Arosemena in 1963. In Venezuela, dictatorships followed each other until, at the turn of the century, Juan Vicente Gómez took matters into his hands and held them until he died, in 1935. In Colombia, often called the Athens of Latin America, democracy was also something of a travesty despite the country's fame for constitutionality. Power alternated between the Conservative and the Liberal parties, which were not essentially different from each other, and if the masses had any opinions at all, it was not too important. Paraguay knew little besides dictatorships, particularly since the ascetic but formidable nineteenth-century reign of José Gaspar Rodríguez Francia, the *"Supremo."* From the 1910 revolution to this day, Mexico has been the political domain of the ruling Party of Revolutionary Institutions. Elsewhere, dictators came and went, there were shorter or longer interludes of formal democracy, but very few countries were developing sound democratic traditions and institutions.

When Latin American politics finally began to crystallize and stabilize after a fashion about 1930, it was for the most part in the mold of dictatorships. Some were the continuation of the old-fashioned tyrannies, others were more modern and streamlined.

Thus, Gómez still ruled Venezuela. In the early 1930's, Vargas took over Brazil under the pretense of a democratic social revolution, and Trujillo established his fief in the Dominican Republic without any pretense. General José Uriburu ousted the democratic Hipólito Irigoyen regime in Argentina. Anastasio Somoza captured Nicaragua to turn it into his private estate. Augusto Leguía experimented with dictatorship in Peru. General Carlos Ibáñez in Chile and José María Velasco Ibarra in Ecuador did likewise. Jorge Ubico had Guatemala and Tiburcio Carías Andino had Honduras. Fulgencio Batista ruled Cuba after the brief attempt at democracy that followed the ouster of Dictator Gerardo Machado. Although there were occasional flashes on the horizon, the decade of the 1930's was one long night of dictatorship in Latin America, and it remained so well into the 1940's, when much of the world was battling for freedom and democracy—and Latin America's autocrats, fattening on war profits, were paying easy lip service to it.

But, inevitably, the war and the consequent awareness of world affairs—and of their relationship to the situations at home—produced a new trend in political thinking in the region. In fact, it led to what may be described as the entrance of modern political thought into Latin America on a continental scale, affecting the masses as well as the elites. Though this modern political thought evidently had made some inroads before—even involving the masses, as in the APRA movement in Peru in the 1930's—it was not as articulate, widespread, and centered on the issues of democracy as in the new wave that came to Latin America's shores in the wake of the war. Deep sympathy for the Allied cause existed throughout the war—though many of the governments did not share it privately even if in the end they did declare war on the Axis—and the liberalizing influence of the victory of the democracies could not fail to be felt.

In October, 1945, not long after Brazilian troops had returned from the war in Italy, the Vargas dictatorship was overthrown by a bloodless *coup d'état* carried out by the Army under the influence of prodemocratic civilian elements. In Cuba, Batista tried to behave like a democrat. Democratic governments already existed in Chile and Peru, and it seemed for a while as if the hour of democracy had finally arrived in Latin America.

In 1948, the Charter of the Organization of American States was signed in Bogotá, Colombia, by the American Foreign Ministers, proclaiming representative democracy as the cornerstone of the Hemispheric system, but it was fated to be a myth for some time to come. The wild rioting during the conference touched off by the murder of a Colombian political leader was a strange backdrop for the deliberations on democracy.

The rising political consciousness in the Hemisphere also gave rise to social movements resulting in aberrations, monstrosities, or upheavals that, in turn, were to have catastrophic outcomes. In Argentina, it opened the way for the Perón revolution, which was presented as a social-justice movement, but which soon degenerated into a graft-ridden dictatorship. In Venezuela, Rómulo Betancourt's Acción Democrática allied itself with the military to stage a mixture of social and political revolution that, in the end, became an inviting target for the Army officers to take over and transform into a dictatorship. In Peru, agitation by the Apristas attracted the military back to the picture. In Brazil, democracy prevailed, but significantly, Vargas had no trouble being elected a Senator by two states on a platform of social justice.

The Dictatorial Cycle

The first experience in continental democracy was thus highly inconclusive and short-lived; even before the decade of the 1940's was over, Latin America slid back into the dictatorial twilight zone. Responding in their own way to the liberal political movements and to the nascent social pressures and economic difficulties, the military and their conservative civilian associates struck again.

In 1948, the Venezuelan Army ousted the Acción Democrática government and the country's elected President to set up a military junta. A month earlier, in Peru, General Manuel Odría led a revolution that overthrew the chaotic but democratic regime of José Luis Bustamante y Rivera. On March 10, 1952, Batista staged another revolution against a democratic government to return to power as Cuba's dictator. In June, 1953, General Gustavo Rojas Pinilla took over as dictator in Colombia. General Paul Magloire was in control in Haiti. General Alfredo Stroessner rose as Paraguay's dictator. Trujillo and Somoza continued as dictators of the Dominican Republic and Nicaragua. Perón was solidly entrenched in Argentina. As the decade of the 1950's approached its mid-point, the picture was indeed dismal almost everywhere in Latin America.

Three events occurred, however, during that period that should have alerted Latin America—and the West—to the fact that the contest of democracy versus dictatorship was not the only problem to be considered in the region. The first one was the Bolivian revolution of 1952, followed by a sweeping land reform and the attainment of considerable power by the tin miners. It was, in fact, the first major social revolution in Latin America since the Mexican upheaval of 1910. Rapidly, a revolutionary dictatorship emerged in Bolivia to put the new reforms into effect. The United States proceeded to aid the revolutionary regime—indeed, it kept it alive —but generally for the wrong reasons. The aid was not based on the understanding of the social revolution, as it should have been, but was motivated by the Eisenhower Administration's fear that Communism might be the only alternative. Yet, whatever the reasons, this significantly demonstrated that the United States could cooperate effectively with a social revolution.

In 1951, a regime that was a weird mixture of chaotic social revolution and pro-Communism emerged in Guatemala—along with Bolivia one of Latin America's poorest nations and likewise burdened by a socially oppressed Indian population—after a group of Army officers staged a bloody coup. As in Bolivia, the new regime in Guatemala immediately plunged into the land reform with equal or greater confusion. One of the differences, however, was that Colonel Jacobo Arbenz Guzmán, the new President, was solidly surrounded by Communists, and the Soviet bloc soon began acting as if it had already won a beachhead in Latin America. Another difference was that land owned by United States corporations was involved in the agrarian reform.

The United States, through the activities of the Central Intelligence Agency, helped Guatemalan rebels to overthrow the Arbenz regime in a pushover operation. But the fact that behind the Communist associations of the Arbenz regime, there existed the pressures of a social revolution was lost on Republican Washington. Carlos Castillo Armas, the new President installed with United States backing, turned out, predictably, to be a budding dictator, a political failure, a wastrel of American aid, a protector of corruption, and an unthinking defender of the prerevolutionary *status quo*.

The third event, finally, was the 1954 electoral victory in British Guiana of Cheddi B. Jagan, a young Marxist, whose People's Progressive Party became a point of attraction for the impoverished East Indian sugar-estate workers. Jagan's victory in itself was not a social revolution, but its seeds were obviously there. The British quickly disposed of Jagan, primarily because he had demonstrated too much enthusiasm for the Soviet bloc. American opinion saw in the Guianan episode, developing almost in conjunction with the Guatemalan affair, the danger signs of Communist influence in the Hemisphere, but again, the social revolutionary potential was generally ignored. Besides, Guiana was a British colony and London's responsibility, and it did not really have a place in any general thinking about Latin America.

Actually, a fourth event occurred during that period, on July 26, 1953, but it was so insignificant that it was lost in the rush of more important happenings. It involved the abortive attempt by a young Cuban named Fidel Castro Ruz and a pack of rebels to storm the Cuban Army barracks in Santiago and start a revolt against Batista, who had returned as dictator the year before. This was the week the Korean Armistice was signed, and the attention of the West was riveted on Panmunjom and not on a small Cuban city.

Besides all these revolutionary situations in widely separated spots of the Hemisphere, there were the continuing gyrations of Juan Perón in Argentina. Playing up heavily the social justice angle to satisfy his labor-union supporters, Perón had no hesitation in switching back and forth between ostentatious anti-Americanism, coupled with ostentatious flirtations with Moscow, and cordiality toward the Eisenhower Administration. It was a rather unsubtle form of political blackmail, but Washington allowed itself to be sucked into it with the lack of analysis that characterized its entire political relationship with Latin America.

This relationship was based on the acceptance by the United States of the dictatorial phenomenon in Latin America—because it was the line of least resistance and because Washington convinced itself that the dictatorships offered a firm guarantee against Communist inroads in the Hemisphere—and the ensuing unnecessary cordiality to them. Thus, the United States loans were given to the dictatorships with no less alacrity than to the democratic regimes, unmindful of the fact that the taxpayers' money often went to line the pockets of the dictators, their cronies, and the local wealthy classes, or was simply wasted, instead of bettering the lot of the populations through rational development projects.

At the same time, Washington's warmth for the dictators was displayed through the award of medals to such exemplars as Perón, Odría, and Pérez Jiménez. Although no Latin American liberals seriously expected the United States to oust the dictatorships forcibly, they bitterly resented the policies that resulted in political as well as economic strengthening of the dictatorships. The whole exercise, conducted by a nation that loudly preached democracy's superiority over totalitarianisms like Communism, did little to enhance the democratic cause or to awaken faith in it. Yet, common sense and a show of sympathy for the democratic forces, fully in line with the great American tradition, could have been a sound, practical investment for the immediate future.

American Attitudes at Mid-Century

Reconstructing the United States attitude toward Latin American politics in those days, it appears that, in its general outlines, it stemmed primarily from a comparatively limited interest in the Hemispheric doings. It has been said that Secretary of State John Foster Dulles was simply bored by Latin America, and there is little evidence that Dean Acheson, his Democratic predecessor, had much more interest in it. When Mr. Dulles had to attend the American Foreign Ministers' Conference in Caracas in 1954, he did so just long enough to make arrangements to secure inter-American political backing for the approaching operation against the Arbenz regime in Guatemala. In short, then, United States policy in Latin America was stamped by a very considerable lack of interest and imagination, as the real planning effort went into East-West relations and the affairs of Europe and Asia. Yet, a modicum of imagination might have suggested that before long, Latin America, too, could become a Cold War battlefield.

As it was, the United States earned political black eyes the length and the width of the Hemisphere. Its reactions to the problems of dictatorships, of rising nationalism, and of the economic needs of Latin America combined to stimulate the anti-American sentiments its enemies were busily encouraging.

The issue of dictatorship, however, was perhaps the foremost one in the minds of Latin Americans because of its immediacy and urgency, even though countries like Brazil, untroubled directly by dictatorship, were already turning their attentions to the great problems of economic growth and nationalism. The question of dictators thus easily developed into a political test of United States intentions and philosophies. Democracy as a system was being tested in Latin American eyes along with the whole posture of the United States.

One of the special features of the situation—and, perhaps, the underlying one—was that, in contrast with the past, Latin Amer-

icans were no longer resigned to the idea of dictatorship. The
world had changed since the days of the prewar dictatorships when
domestic events in Latin America were utterly isolated from the
world scene. But in the 1950's, travel, greater general and political
education, and the growing role of the press, radio, and television
were quickly modifying the Latin American political climate. Even
censorship under the dictatorships was no longer an effective obstacle to the flow of ideas. Unlike their role in the past, the enlightened affluent classes were now turning against the dictatorships, and plotting against them went on in the board rooms of the
big corporations as well as in student associations. Yet, Washington was still oblivious of the new trends. It went on ignoring the
warnings, repeated daily, that in these troubled days, governments
had a way of coming and going while the people, with their long
memories, remained.

Nationalism, a natural phenomenon in the underdeveloped countries, was also on the rise, and here again, the United States embroiled itself in endless misunderstandings. In the dictatorial countries, it opened itself to charges, unfair as they may have been, that
it favored the strong men to protect its investments. In countries
like Brazil, it picked unnecessary quarrels with the nationalists over
the issue of Petrobrás, the state oil monopoly, seeking through
subtle and unsubtle means to convince the Brazilians that they
should revise the law to allow the entry of private oil companies.
As far as it went, the United States argument was perfectly sound
from the economic viewpoint, because Petrobrás was growing into
a chaotic, ineffective bureaucratic giant as interested in playing
nationalistic politics as it was in finding oil. But politically, to
quarrel with the idea of Petrobrás was playing with fire as well as
playing into the hands of Communists, ultranationalists, and everybody else who had ambitions and needed a tried and true demagogic
cause. Underestimating the strength of Brazilian nationalism, ir-
respective of its wisdom, the United States Government and business
community were handing the cause to its enemies.

The basic argument of the Republican Administration that good
treatment of foreign private capital was the answer to all of Latin
America's development problems, along with a bonus of public
aid, was causing added resentments. How, Latin Americans asked,
were they to make private investors finance the building of highways, dams, schools, homes, hospitals, and other unprofitable but

vital ventures? Since, at the same time, United States official loans were generally restricted to industrial projects, Latin America saw little hope of a breakthrough in her fundamental problems. That her own efforts in that direction left much to be desired was added fuel in the controversy in which both sides were oversensitive and often unreasonable. Even Washington's dictatorial friends knew how to display bitter dissatisfaction with the United States when it suited them.

For all these reasons, then, the first really serious wave of modern anti-Americanism was gathering momentum in Latin America. For the time being, the Soviet Union was content to watch it with quiet though interested detachment. While it would have been ready to offer a helping hand in Guatemala or British Guiana, if it had been given time to act, the Soviet Union and the local Communist parties preferred to await tangible opportunities before moving. It was the patient policy of economy of forces. But while the Communists waited for the next big opening, they were by no means idle.

Locally, the incessant labor of infiltration went on through the political parties and labor, student, trade, intellectual, and civic groups, exploring dissatisfaction, with the Communists forming new alliances, espousing popular causes like nationalism, and criticizing dictatorships, though they often supported them quietly. The long-range objective was to give Communism a solid foothold in strategic centers of the society, while it acquired maximum respectability so that it would be ready when that next great opportunity came. Moscow talked enticingly of trade, cultural, and diplomatic relations and of world peace. She sent artistic groups and cultural delegations as well as a steady flow of propaganda materials through her embassies in Mexico, Argentina, and Uruguay.

This, then, was democracy's situation in Latin America, with all its pressures, problems, contradictions, and side shows, as the year 1955 rolled along. With its advent, a new phase in the Hemisphere's political history suddenly dawned and the entrenched dictatorships began collapsing one after another like a row of dominoes. It was a phase that unleashed immense ferment, both promising and dangerous, and that was to last until the end of the decade, when the Castro revolution in Cuba ushered in a completely new era in Latin America.

The Democratic Renaissance

The democratic renaissance in the Hemisphere was touched off by the revolution against Perón in Argentina in September, 1955. The dictatorial wave of the postwar years had reached its crest, and now it had to recede. Since political movements in Latin America always seem to come in cycles, the ouster of dictator Perón triggered a chain reaction that took more than three years to run its course.

Perón's fall had been in the making for some time. The opposition to him had been growing steadily among the students, the intellectuals and, most important, among the military of the three services. The opposition political parties, crushed as they were by the dictatorship's steamroller, provided a rank-and-file following for the rebels. But, after ten years of rule, Perón still commanded loyalty among his *"descamisado"* workers—the "shirtless ones"—because they were still deriving profit from certain illusory benefits offered by the regime and because they had a sense of participation in power through the leadership of the unions. The bosses of the Peronista unions, usually capable of calling out rowdy mobs into the streets, were part of the vast governmental apparatus, sharing in its immorality, its graft and corruption. In United States terms, it was as if the Teamsters' Union participated in the Administration and James Hoffa were the Secretary of Labor or special adviser to the President.

Essentially, then, the brewing revolt against Perón was a middle-class movement based on the three pillars of the military officers, the students and the white-collar workers, professionals, and other elements of the large Argentine bourgeoisie. The wealthy rural "aristocracy," hit hard by Perón, also supported the revolt. An important force in the emerging anti-Perón coalition was the Roman Catholic Church, which was goaded into active opposition by the dictator's legalization of divorce and the subsequent burning of churches in Buenos Aires. It was the first time in modern Latin American history that the Church stood up against a dictator, and it was the beginning of a new trend in the Church policies in the Hemisphere as it strove to identify itself with democratic and progressive forces. Perón's quarrel with the Church, which he could have avoided, was perhaps his greatest error, but curiously, it was repeated by all the other dictators as they neared ouster.

The line-up of forces on the eve of the 1955 revolution may have suggested that inasmuch as Perón claimed to represent a social revolution of sorts, his enemies were chiefly a right-wing coalition of the military, the Church, and the more or less wealthy —the traditional triangle of Latin American reaction.

But what Perón was directing in those closing days of his rule was a totally botched and monstrously distorted social revolution. In fact, the social-justice aspect of it was merely a shield of deceit intended to cover up the strict dictatorship, the corrupt greed of the regime, and Perón's own ambitions for spreading his influence, if not his hegemony, throughout Latin America. Ineptly, his agents and "labor attachés" in Latin American capitals sought to buy politicians, labor-union leaders, and newspapermen while his diplomats maneuvered for customs and economic unions with Argentina's neighbors in the hope of hammering together a Peronista sphere of influence in the southern part of South America that could later be spread to other areas of the continent. It was an idea with which Fidel Castro was to experiment more deftly and more lethally some years later.

Internally, the Perón dictatorship had abolished all political and civil liberties. Almost the entire press was in the hands of the government, dedicated to the building of a personality cult for the dictator, and the few newspapers that remained independent dared not speak out against the regime. The universities lost their autonomy and the faculties were loaded with Peronista hacks. The prisons were full of political prisoners and Perón's Federal Police even contributed the method of the *"picada"*—electric shock applied to testicles and other parts of the body—to the treasurehouse of modern torture.

Economically, the Peronista rule wrought damage so deep and extensive in Argentina that she is still far from recovery today. Agriculture, the country's main wealth, was put in the hands of a government export corporation, and promptly ruined. The dollar, pound-sterling, and gold reserves were lost through gigantic follies like the outright purchase of the British-owned railways and imports of millions of dollars' worth of industrial machinery and equipment that rotted at dockside because nobody knew what to do with them. Millions of pesos were drained by the Eva Perón Foundation, allegedly a social-works institution established by Perón's late wife, and channeled into the pockets of the top

Peronistas. It was one of the most efficient modern extortion-and-confidence rackets.

But, perhaps as much as anything else, the country and its articulate elements resented the awesome immorality into which Perón had plunged Argentina. It ranged from the dictator's own sordid love affair with a fifteen-year-old girl to a miasmatic corruption of every national institution.

By 1955, then, Argentina had had enough of Perón. Conspiracies spread among the military and among the students. In June, the Navy staged a frustrated rebellion when its aircraft bombed the Casa Rosada, the Presidential Palace, but fog on the River Plata prevented its ships from joining the action, and friendly Army troops somehow got their signals mixed up. The attempt failed and Perón promised blood and vengeance.

But the June experience served only to accelerate the plotting. The dictator's mounting feud with the Church and his other excesses strengthened the resolve of the rebels. On September 18, Army garrisons, supported by university and high-school students, rose in the province of Córdoba under the command of Eduardo Lonardi, a retired Army general. The next day, the powerful Army of the Cuyo, in the Western provinces, joined the movement. The Navy, which was Perón's most bitter foe, and units of the Air Force declared themselves in rebellion. The government still controlled the Army troops in and around Buenos Aires, but Perón's power was now quickly waning.

Within two days, the anti-Peronista troops and students won the control of Córdoba. A Navy task force steamed up from its base in Bahía Blanca and anchored off Buenos Aires, its guns aimed at the capital. An ultimatum was dispatched to what remained of the government. In the evening of September 21, Perón gave up and fled to asylum at the Paraguayan Embassy, to be transferred later to a Paraguayan gunboat undergoing repairs in the harbor. A clean-up battle was fought in Buenos Aires between Army tanks and a contingent of Peronista terrorists holed up in their downtown headquarters. Cannon fire gutted the building, and presently nothing was left of the Peronista dictatorship.

Significantly, public opinion in Argentina was convinced that the United States was ready to defend Perón and a wild rumor even spread that the United States Navy was speeding toward Buenos Aires. This was the fruit of the policy of friendship with

Perón conducted by Washington up to the last moment, and an ingredient of future troubles.

Meanwhile, General Lonardi was proclaimed Provisional President, and Argentina began to settle down to the immense task of political and economic reconstruction. In November, Lonardi, whose political views were too far to the right to suit most of the military, was quietly removed and General Pedro Eugenio Aramburu was sworn in as President.

For the next three years, a civilian government headed by General Aramburu prepared the country for the return to full-fledged democracy and order. Political parties and a free press were restored, and a tough austerity program was instituted to get the runaway economy back on the tracks. Peronista strikes and terrorism complicated these efforts, but the military and the civilians were united in their determination to restore democracy, and there was hope in Argentina.

In February, 1958, Arturo Frondizi, a leftist intellectual with nationalistic sympathies who headed a rebel wing of the Radical Party, was elected by an overwhelming majority to be Argentina's first constitutional President in more than fifteen years. His electoral supporters spanned political and ideological differences: democrats, Peronistas, extreme right-wingers and Communists. Though General Aramburu and the military would have preferred the victory of Ricardo Balbin, Señor Frondizi's chief opponent, they had no hesitation in handing power over to the elected President. After assuming office on May 1, 1958, in the presence of Vice-President Nixon, Frondizi inaugurated a policy of financial stabilization and economic development with the aid of foreign private capital, and, most difficult of all, of the restoration of political and social peace to Argentina. He succeeded fairly well in the first two undertakings but, as events were to prove four years later, he failed in the latter.

The Trend Sets In

Because nothing happens in a vacuum in Latin America, events in Argentina late in 1955 had immediate repercussions in Peru. There, General Odría, the military dictator, was approaching the end of the Presidential term to which he had been "elected" in 1950 without facing rival candidates. The election was designed to legitimize his 1948 seizure of power and it was in line with the desire of Latin American dictators to give an appearance of legality to everything they did, no matter how illegal. Since "elections" is a magical word in Latin America, even Trujillo went through the motions of being re-elected periodically or having his stooges elected. Vargas had given up this pretense in 1937, but his Latin American followers in the 1950's scrupulously observed the procedure. Perón did it twice—and, in fact, marshaled a majority of votes—and, as we shall see, Rojas Pinilla in Colombia and Pérez Jiménez in Venezuela brought about their own downfalls through such farcical travesties of democracy.

But the new element in Peru was that Odría appeared to have no desire to remain in office and, indeed, had promised free elections for June, 1956. It was a most unusual departure from the time-honored patterns, and Peruvians were extremely skeptical about his promise, particularly after Odría jailed a number of his prominent opponents early in 1956 after an abortive military coup against him. But the quiet, somewhat retiring general insisted that he had captured power only to restore political and economic order to Peru and that he felt that he had accomplished his objective.

Actually, Odría's claims were not wholly inaccurate. After the extensive political and economic chaos in the closing months of the Bustamante government in 1948, the unspectacular military dictatorship had quieted down the country, and long strides were made to repair the economy. Private foreign capital was attracted to Peru, and a sound if modest program of economic development got under way, focusing on the mining industry. In the political field, Odría banned the APRA, and jailed and exiled its leaders. When Víctor Raúl Haya de la Torre, APRA's chief, obtained asylum at the Colombian Embassy in Lima, Odría refused him a safe conduct for more than five years in what became the most celebrated case of this kind.

Although the Odría regime went through the motions of interesting itself in the social problem and inaugurating its share of schools and hospitals, it failed to touch the fundamental problems of land hunger and of the huge destitute Indian population. In short, the Peruvian dictatorship was mildly efficient but unimaginative in its general policies, except when it came to keeping the opposition down, and the country's affairs were just a notch above the level of orderly stagnation.

The extent to which the fall of Perón in Argentina had influenced

Odría to keep his word about free elections is a matter of conjecture. His promise had been made before the Argentine revolution, but there are reasons to believe that the Argentine events had impressed him with the fact that a new trend was in the making in Latin America. Possibly, he did not want to be its next victim.

Whatever his precise motivation, Odría let APRA return to political activity early in 1956, freeing its leaders from prison and allowing the return of all the exiled Apristas except Haya de la Torre. All the signs were that APRA remained a powerful force, and Odría held conferences with the Aprista leadership in a bid to secure their support for his hand-picked candidate, an obscure corporation lawyer named Hernándo de Lavalle, who also had the support of an important segment of Peru's affluent classes. In Latin America, alliances between the oppressors and those recently oppressed are not a novelty—Communists are experts in such arrangements—and APRA was shopping for a candidate to support. It did not wish, however, to go along with Lavalle who had refused to agree to APRA's basic condition: an iron-clad promise to legalize the party the moment he took office. Lavalle, aware of the traditional military hatred for APRA, was not prepared to risk such a promise.

Unable to present its own candidate, APRA had only one choice: Manuel Prado y Ugarteche, a vain and wealthy aristocrat who had served as President during the war and had a reasonably clean democratic record. Prado, nearly seventy years old, had returned from residence in Paris to run for President on the ticket of his hurriedly created "Pradista" movement, a typical Latin American personalist "label" party. The other candidate was Fernando Belaúnde Terry, a young architect who had quickly built liberal and leftist support for his Popular Action Party. Since APRA was a leftist mass party, it made no sense for it to support a rival leftist movement. When Prado agreed to promise to legalize the party upon his inauguration, APRA threw the support of its disciplined masses behind him and handed him a narrow victory over Belaúnde.

Until the last moment, there was some doubt whether Odría would bow out in the light of the smashing defeat of his candidate, Lavalle. But the general had broken a hip a few weeks before the elections and was flown to the United States for treatment. At one point, a group of generals attempted to stage a coup, but cooler heads prevailed and nothing came of it. Democracy had thus returned to Peru through the ballot box, but as the subsequent years were to demonstrate, only a superficial dent was made in the country's tremendous social problems. Prado, the old aristocrat, was not disposed to lead even a gradual social revolution, and APRA was reluctant to see it done on his time. Yet it is to Prado's great credit that in July, 1962, he preferred to let himself be deposed and arrested ten days before the expiration of his term, rather than submit to military demands that he annul the Presidential elections of the previous month, apparently won by APRA. The sequel to the 1962 election and the subsequent coup was the rerun of the same race a year later. This time, however, Haya de la Torre fared badly, and the Presidency was won by Fernando Belaúnde Terry, to whom the Army had no objections.

Colombia's May Rebellion

With Odría's quiet departure, the antidictatorial trend was in full swing in Latin America. History then turned its attention to the next dictator on the list, General Gustavo Rojas Pinilla in Colombia.

Rojas had captured power in 1953 when, to the applause of virtually the entire population, he led the Army in a coup to oust the government of the Conservative Party, which had five years earlier plunged Colombia in a backlands civil war with the Liberals. Rojas raised the slogan of "Motherland Above the Parties," an idea that was appealing to Colombians after the years of interparty carnage, and the nation was willing to forgo for a while its normal political life in order to see peace restored at last.

But it did not take long before Rojas demonstrated that he was just another general with great personal vanity and unbridled dictatorial appetites. In short order, Rojas began to devote his energies to the consolidation of his personal rule, aided by a civilian-military clique, while violence continued unabated in the provinces. The main excuse for his holding office thus vanished, and Colombians began to realize that Rojas was an error that had to be soon corrected.

It took almost four years to do it. Meanwhile, Rojas was weaving a crazy-quilt dictatorial pattern, borrowing ideas from Perón on how to exploit the labor unions and millions of underprivileged citizens for his own ends and imitating his strong-man colleagues elsewhere in ways of staying in power.

Classically, he banned the activities of the political parties—ostensibly to prevent continued Liberal-Conservative bloodshed—but went ahead with plans to form his own "social justice" party, the "Third Force," an inept and pathetic imitation of Perón's *"Justicialismo."* It never got off the ground because nobody took it seriously and because the Catholic Church, a power in Colombia, stepped in to intervene. Using Perón-invented tricks, Rojas penalized opposition newspapers by depriving them of newsprint and slapping astronomical tax penalties on them. Official censorship did the rest to prevent a free expression of opinion. Editors were jailed and released. The SIC (the military secret service) became something of a state within the state. These activities were accompanied by a steady deterioration in the Colombian economy, despite the bonanza of high coffee prices in those days. Graft and incompetence were rampant, money was spent on projects designed to glorify the dictator rather than to develop the country—such as the placing of his Caesar-like busts in the main squares of all the Colombian towns and villages.

Early in 1957, Rojas made the mistake of announcing his plans for re-election, even though his term did not expire until 1958. His greed cost him his power. Colombians, who had been prepared to wait until the end of his legal term before moving against him, were aroused.

Rojas hardly had time to steamroll his re-election through a rubber-stamp legislature in the first days of May, 1957, before the furious reaction came. High-school and university students began to riot in Bogotá, and the Rojas regime committed the additional error of arresting Guillermo León Valencia, the opposition's Presidential candidate. This set off nationwide riots, which troops and police quelled with gunfire and bayonets, killing scores of demonstrators. At this point, Colombia's politicians and aristocrats—the bankers, businessmen, and industrialists—moved in. Banks and businesses were closed in protest against the government, with the enthusiastic approval of the workers, and the nation's economic life came to a standstill. More riots followed, and Rojas made his final error. His police, under orders to restore peace at any cost, invaded a church where some of the demonstrators had taken refuge, and exploded tear-gas grenades. The same evening, two youths were killed in a riot following another church demonstration. That was all the provocation Colombia's old Cardinal Crisanto Luque needed to lower the boom on

Rojas. A pastoral letter was issued censuring Rojas, and for all practical purposes, the Church allied itself openly with the revolutionaries. After two more days of severe rioting, the military saw the writing on the wall and advised the dictator the time had come for him to quit. At dawn on May 10, 1957, Rojas fled to the Dominican Republic.

The same generals who had served Rojas and then ousted him, now formed a government junta that immediately restored all the democratic liberties. It presided over a referendum that changed Colombia's constitution to initiate a system under which the Liberals and the Conservatives were to alternate in office every four years for sixteen years in a "National Front" policy. Then they supervised the election of Alberto Lleras Camargo, head of the Liberal Party, to the Presidency and elegantly handed him the power. In 1962, the Conservatives succeeded to power, and Dr. Lleras was replaced by Dr. Valencia.

Thus, political democracy had returned to one more Latin American country. But, as in Argentina and Peru, it was not using its strength and popularity to face up to Colombia's desperate social problems. A new Latin American pattern was emerging, in which the ouster of dictators was followed by re-establishment of a political democracy that largely ignored its social responsibility.

Yet, in that year of 1957, the friends of democracy in Latin America were rejoicing. Argentina, Peru, and Colombia had turned their backs on military dictators and had restored democratic institutions. Ecuador was proud that two Presidents in a row had completed their terms and the third freely elected President was in office. In Brazil, the political crisis and the threats of military intervention had died down, and President Juscelino Kubitschek was practicing tolerance and democracy at their best. In Bolivia, a free election had been held under the revolutionary government.

The signs of the great social crisis were still being overlooked, and those that were noted were put down to temporary economic difficulties, such as inflation, that the democratic governments were pledged to solve rapidly. Almost unnoticed, the young Cuban revolutionary named Fidel Castro was holed up with a small band of companions in the mountains of Oriente Province, where he had landed in December, 1956, to launch a rebellion against the Batista dictatorship. Those in Latin America who were aware of him cheered him on as another romantic fighter for Hemispheric democracy, though few thought he had any chances of success.

The Battle of Venezuela

Then the spotlight of Latin American history switched to Venezuela and the nascent rebellion against the dictatorship of General Marcos Pérez Jiménez. This was to be the next prize in the Hemispheric battle against dictatorships, now that three of them had fallen and two more were shaken through the assassinations of Nicaragua's Somoza and Guatemala's Castillo Armas.

The vast damage the Pérez Jiménez dictatorship had caused the Venezuelan economy has already been described in some detail: Agriculture was desperately neglected, and Venezuela's great oil resources were geared to the construction of generally useless but spectacular projects and to the financing of the colossal graft that made the Pérez Jiménez regime outstanding in this field of competition among dictators.

The regime's official excuse for existing was that it represented the "New National Ideal," dedicated to the eradication of political life in Venezuela—because politics allegedly dispersed the national energies—and to economic development. With the aid of one of the Hemisphere's most brutally efficient secret police apparatuses—specializing in political murders, refined tortures, and wholesale imprisonments—the Pérez Jiménez clique was successful in its political endeavors. The second part of the "New National Ideal," economic development, was a fantastic hoax perpetrated on the people of Venezuela and the gullible United States Government.

While Venezuela had the highest per capita income in Latin America, in actuality, a handful of the very wealthy, including the friends of the dictator, enjoyed vast incomes, and a small urban managerial class was quite affluent. The rest of the population—probably 90 per cent—lived in abysmal poverty in the overcrowded *minifundios* or in the miserable huts of the Caracas *ranchos*. The high per capita income was, then, a bookkeeping mirage, as was the gleaming, *nouveau-riche* appearance of downtown Caracas and its wealthy suburbs. The city was a gigantic Potemkin Village.

Although anyone who devoted a few hours to close observation would have no trouble concluding that the Pérez Jiménez regime was a rotten enterprise politically, economically, and socially, the Eisenhower Administration was quite content with it. The right-wing military regime offered a sound guarantee that the strategic oil resources of Venezuela were safely protected against any Soviet inroads. The regime's assurances that it kept local Communists under severe controls pleased Washington, which was not informed that the dictatorship had a quiet deal with the Communists, using them as informers against the other political groups in return for a promise to leave them alone. Since Venezuela also was a haven for private capital, both the Eisenhower Administration and the American business community held the regime in high esteem, dismissing as relatively unimportant the stories of persecutions, murders, and denials of liberty. Pérez Jiménez was thus decorated with the Legion of Merit and a United States Navy submariner's medal, and the successive American Ambassadors maintained the most cordial personal relations with the dictator and his top officials. As events were to show before very long, this blind, complacent policy was fated to blow up in America's face.

Meanwhile, Pérez Jiménez hastened his own end in December, 1957, by arranging a plebiscite in which the voters were to say "Yes" or "No" to his re-election to another five-year term. This was a new twist in the dictatorial re-election techniques. Not surprisingly, the returns showed that he had received an overwhelming "Yes" vote after the Interior Ministry counted the ballots. So, Pérez Jiménez settled back confidently to what he thought would be another five years of operating his brutal gravy train.

To his immense surprise, however, the Venezuelans had decided that they had had enough of him and of the "New National Ideal." In the morning of January 1, 1958, as Pérez Jiménez recovered from a New Year's Eve celebration, Air Force jets led by his personal pilot struck at Caracas in dive-bombing attacks aimed at the Palace. Simultaneously, a tank regiment rose in rebellion. But the conspiracy was unlucky and poorly prepared, and Pérez Jiménez easily survived.

The rebel pilots, safe in Colombia after the failure of their uprising, wondered aloud why the United States was not supporting the revolution. They told of their training in the United States, where they were taught democracy along with flying, and said that their action against Pérez Jiménez had been inspired by these Stateside teachings about liberty. "And where are the Americans now?" they asked bitterly.

But the pilots' defiance had not been in vain. In Caracas, students rioted and fought the troops and the police. Then suddenly, the whole nation stood on the verge of rebellion. Tough workers and the unemployed from the showcase housing projects erected by the regime in Caracas and from the *rancho* slums joined in the fray, burning cars and buses. The intellectuals and big businessmen circulated manifestoes demanding the dictator's ouster. The Church actively supported the movement. Plans were made for a general strike. An underground "Patriotic Junta," whose existence hardly anyone suspected, coordinated the rebellion. Navy destroyers anchored at La Guaira stood ready to lob shells into Caracas over the Avila mountain range if the regime did not capitulate. Marines prepared to march on Caracas up the freeway from the coast. Late at night, several Naval commanders met with the Army chiefs at the Military School, and the decision was made by the armed forces that Pérez Jiménez must go. The Argentine and Colombian pattern was being repeated in almost every detail. At dawn on January 23, Pérez Jiménez flew to the Dominican Republic, following by a few days his recent guest, Juan Perón.

Later in the day, the populace and the troops fought a pitched battle with secret-service agents barricaded in their downtown headquarters building. When the building fell, the ransacking crowds found among the official papers a personal letter from a former United States Ambassador to the head of the secret police expressing hope that the New Year's Day rebellion would be put down. Inevitably, the letter found its way to the Communist Party's newspaper, which published it with relish. With their talent for playing both ends against the middle, the Communists had simultaneously cooperated with Pérez Jiménez through their secret deal and fought him through the Patriotic Junta. In the end, they emerged among the heroes of the antidictatorial battle.

A military-civilian junta headed by Admiral Wolfgang Larrazábal took power and immediately discovered that the dictatorship not only had wasted Venezuela's oil income but also had contracted short-term foreign debts running well over a billion dollars. Unemployment was rampant, and social protest was not long in asserting itself. In December, 1958, elections were held, and Rómulo Betancourt emerged as the constitutional President, defeating Larrazábal, who ran with Communist support and carried the restless Caracas area. Despite some reservations about Betancourt's own social-reformist background, the military passed the government to him in February, 1959—five weeks after Castro had won his revolution in Cuba. Democracy had scored a double victory on the shores of the Caribbean, or so it seemed.

Only Trujillo in the Dominican Republic, the last of the great Latin American dictators, remained unshaken in his insular domain. He played host to his ousted colleagues from all over the Hemisphere, convinced that as long as he lived, he would remain the ruler. As it developed, it was to be a singularly prophetic attitude, though not in the way he meant it. Paraguay's General Alfredo Stroessner and Haiti's François Duvalier also held fast in their backwater dictatorships.

The Lost Chance

But let us go back to the events of 1958 and take another look at what promised to be a period of hope for democracy, but one that also nurtured the seeds of grave new problems.

As we have seen in every instance, the democratic political revolutions of the 1950's halted at the line of social change. Perhaps because of a lack of vision and historical imagination; perhaps because the immediate problems of repairing the damage inflicted by the dictatorships loomed as the most urgent ones; perhaps, finally, because it did not seem politically feasible to do so at the time, the new democratic leadership in Latin America preferred not to experiment with any far-reaching reforms. Someone else could do that later, when the nation's economic foundations were strengthened, when the democratic institutions were consolidated, and when a more propitious time came.

Thus, the democratic revolutions lost their great chance and their great opportunity, letting the Jacobins reap later the harvest of the ideas of social reform. Although it was clear—or should have been clear—that the Latin American land-tenure system demanded modification for economic as well as social reasons, no democratic government in the Hemisphere felt impelled to do anything about it—except to discuss it in theoretical terms if someone raised the question. The presence or the influence of landlord elements in the national parliaments—and their political and financial power outside of them—discouraged any serious attempts at land reform. Though President Betancourt in Venezuela did undertake it in 1959, no other government felt that it was desirable or feasible to embark on a peaceful and legal land reform, however modest, merely to blaze the trail and deprive the left-wing radicals of their arguments that nothing was being done in the direction of social justice. Though the Hemisphere was facing profound structural problems that could not wait indefinitely for solutions, the democratic governments contented themselves with palliatives.

The principal concern—and it was surely commendable—was to protect and tend the flower of the young democracy, as delicate as the jungle orchid, ignoring the fact that it could not grow or survive without the nourishing soil of social justice. The reverse was evidently also true: that nominal or alleged social justice without freedom and democracy was bound to degenerate into a new form of dictatorship, as the Perón experience had shown. But the postdictatorial regimes had no time for such theories. Although they realized the acute need to improve the living conditions in their countries, their emphasis was on greater United States assistance to develop the national resources. But, for all these complex reasons, there was no readiness to match such aid with far-reaching internal reforms, and without them, American money could only ripple the surface.

While around Latin America democracy muddled through on hope and expediency, a new phenomenon that was soon to short-circuit all these situations was taking shape in Cuba. There, in the mountains of Sierra Maestra in Oriente Province, Fidel Castro's rebel band was gaining strength, stature, and political influence.

From the twelve survivors of the yacht *Granma,* which had brought them from Mexico in December, 1956, the Castro force had by 1958 grown into a regular guerrilla army controlling vast stretches of Oriente Province and enjoying the active support of the nationwide "26th of July Revolutionary Movement" and its arms-buying and money-raising branches in the United States. From a romantic adventure, the Castro rebellion had been transformed into a deadly threat to the Batista dictatorship, whose 40,000-man Army and several police organizations were unable to stamp out the spreading movement.

The regime fought back with brutality, tortures, murders, and imprisonments, but every day the rebellion gained more supporters and more power. Virtually the whole nation was now behind Castro and against Batista, as students and young professionals sneaked to the mountains to join the guerrilla force or formed urban sabotage and propaganda units. Wealthy businessmen and industrialists invested millions in financing the revolution. On the surface, it looked like a repetition of the Argentine, Colombian, and Venezuelan pattern of political democratic revolution led by the youth and the middle class. The pattern was identical, down to Washington's cordiality for the embattled dictatorship. In this case, it included the continuing training of Batista's Army by a United States military mission, the sale of weapons to him (until the State Department slapped on an embargo in March, 1958), and backing for a fraudulent election scheme through which a stooge was picked to continue the dictatorial rule.

But there was an important difference in the Cuban picture: It was the particular type of leadership offered by Castro and his top companions and the very unusual ideas they held. These ideas were summed up in their belief that a social revolution, preferably of a Marxist character, should follow the anticipated ouster of Batista. It is a matter of argument—and it probably will be so for years—whether Castro at that juncture was a believer in Communism or just a starry-eyed and politically confused Marxist or socialist. Some of his companions undoubtedly were Communists, while others very definitely were not. But there seemed to be general agreement among all of them that some sort of social change was needed in Cuba after the revolution. Perhaps because of their youth, or because they had no connections with traditional politics or with the established social and economic patterns, the Sierra revolutionaries could afford to be bolder and more forward-looking in their thinking than the older men who had taken over from the fallen dictators elsewhere in Latin America.

In his speech known as "History Will Absolve Me," delivered in 1953 to the Batista judges who tried him for the assault on the Moncada Army Barracks in Santiago, Castro made very clear his ideas about social changes. And of the four "revolutionary laws" he listed in this speech, which became something of a Magna Carta of the Cuban revolution, land reform was one. His "Laws of the Sierra," written in 1957 and 1958, emphasized the social-revolutionary thinking of the Rebel Army's leadership. The first draft of the Agrarian Reform Law was written in the Sierra. And, finally, Castro and his lieutenants wasted no time in putting reformist policies into practice in the areas of Oriente Province under their control. Peasants were told to take over plantation lands, and the Rebel Army set up schools for their children. As Ernesto ("Che") Guevara—Castro's Argentine-born companion and a participant in the Guatemalan adventure under Arbenz—explained later in detail in his handbook on guerrilla warfare, the rebels were establishing a political base for a social "peasant revolution" while simultaneously carrying on their military operations against Batista. What was being prepared in the Sierra Maestra, therefore, was quite different in character from the anti-dictatorial political revolution to which Latin America was becoming accustomed. Anyone who had any dealings with Cuba in those days, including the newsmen who visited the Sierra Maestra, could see it.

But almost no one in Latin America, let alone in the United States, was prepared to take Castro seriously in the political sense. While those who were sufficiently interested in Cuban affairs were beginning to admit the possibility of a rebel victory, the consensus was that once Batista had fallen, more experienced men than Castro would take over the island's helm. And the failure of the general strike in Havana in April, 1958, intended as a major showdown between the revolutionaries and Batista, made Castro's limited stock decline even more. As always, democracies were complacent about revolutions.

New Clouds Gather

In the spring of 1958, the Latin American democracies were becoming outwardly consolidated, despite periodic but not particularly significant right-wing and military conspiracies in Argentina, Colombia, and Venezuela. It was generally felt that the danger to the democratic regimes, if any, could come only from the right and the military.

But under the surface new forces were gaining momentum and new clouds were gathering. The Cuban revolution, still largely confined to the mountains, was a distant rumble that few, if any, observers related to the over-all Latin American picture. Yet, what was occurring in Latin America threatened to affect the form, if not the actual posture, of the new democracies and the standing of the United States in the Hemisphere.

New relationships, internal and international, were in the making, though it was not yet clear, even to those who were engaged in developing them, what their nature would be. In the crucible, numerous ingredients, never interrelated before, were beginning to be blended. They included the mounting social and economic pressures that the palliatives could no longer satisfy, the question of relations with the United States, and the problems of nationalism.

Internally, the weight of the new populations and the scourge of inflation were making the situation of the urban masses intolerable; it was becoming increasingly clear that far-ranging solutions would have to be found soon. Strikes and food riots were almost daily occurrences from Argentina to Mexico. People were plainly becoming impatient with their lot.

Because of its many past sins of omission and commission, the United States was a handy scapegoat for the whole gamut of difficulties in those troubled days. No conversation with political leaders, students, or intellectuals was possible for an American anywhere in Latin America without his being subjected to a whole litany of complaints covering past United States support for dictators, its insufficient economic aid, its economic policies in restricting imports of certain metals, its lack of attention and appreciation for Latin America, its business practices, and its foreign policies. Some of the complaints were well taken, others were wholly or partly imaginary. But the important thing was that unhappiness and disenchantment with the United States and its leadership were spreading across the Hemisphere. It was not clear just how the Latin Americans proposed to modify the relationship with the United States, but it was unquestionable that they did want a change.

Nationalism, that other effervescent but ill-defined element in the crucible, was closely related to both the internal and the international problem as a largely psychological manifestation of the multifarious pressures facing the Latin American republics. Though it was not a new phenomenon, it was now acquiring a new dimension, becoming linked to the whole fundamental question of where the Hemisphere was going and looming as a key component of the entire revolutionary psychology. It was also being intensely encouraged by the Communists and by extreme left- and right-wing groups, each for its special individual reasons. But instead of understanding and accepting this nationalism as a surging historical tide, the United States chose in the beginning to be hostile to it— and to be bewildered by it—thus leaving this whole fertile field to its enemies.

Along with nationalism, or as a part of it, there also soared the desire for political "independence," ending the traditional and disturbing sense of "being taken for granted" by the United States. As a reaction to old slights, this sentiment existed at both extremes of the political rainbow, edging steadily toward the middle.

Subdued for decades, except for occasional isolated eruptions, this nationalism made up of so many ingredients always had a latent power and was never altogether absent from the relations between the United States and Latin America. The "antigringoism" and assorted resentments against the "Colossus of the North," curiously mixed with admiration for the Yankees and a strong desire to imitate their ways, had been associated for a hundred years with Hemispheric history.

Politically, the resentments had their first roots in the interventions by United States Marines in the Caribbean, Mexico, and Central America early in the century and running well into the 1920's. Although President Roosevelt ended the era of interventions in 1934, when he abrogated the Platt Amendment to the Cuban constitution, which had allowed the United States to step into domestic situations, and committed this country to the policy of nonintervention, suspicions about American motives lingered in Latin America. These feelings returned forcefully after the Guatemalan incident of 1954.

Economically, Latin American nationalism took the shape of the Mexican and Bolivian expropriations of foreign oil properties, largely United States-owned, in 1938. Vargas experimented with nationalism on and off throughout his career, and it was under his influence that the Brazilian oil-monopoly law setting up Petrobrás was passed in 1953. In Argentina, Perón relied heavily on the nationalism theme, expropriating the British railways and later an American telephone company and several power plants. Interestingly, the tone of political speeches and newspaper articles in the Cuban press in the early 1930's and again in 1940 was almost identical with the outbursts against the Yankee "economic imperialism" reiterated in the Castro days.

The overshadowing economic presence of the United States in Latin America through its investments of nearly $8 billion and its massive trade was a fact of life that made resentments and manifestations of nationalism inevitable.

In the 1950's, under the pressure of new conditions, this nationalism continued to develop. Politicians throughout the Hemisphere clamored for laws expelling or curtailing foreign investors or, at least, limiting severely the remittances of their profits. There was almost unanimous agreement that public utilities should be transferred to national control, and presently, some United States companies began to come over to this viewpoint. Negotiating for compensations for plants seized by the Perón regime in Argentina, a major New York power company agreed to reinvest the indemnity payments in other industrial fields and applied similar policies in Mexico and Colombia.

Though Peru and Colombia revised their legislation to allow the entry of foreign companies into oil exploration, Brazil and Chile remained adamantly opposed to them. Perón was prevented in his last days by his own oil unions from granting concessions to a United States company. But President Frondizi did it later as part of a complicated scheme involving foreign companies and the state monopoly. This brought him the undying hostility of the Peronistas and left-wing groups, manifested indirectly in the 1962 congressional elections, which led to his ouster by the military. Bolivia's revolutionary regime, in a desperate bid to earn urgently needed dollars, allowed foreign oil companies to work alongside the state monopoly. But in Venezuela, after the ouster of Pérez Jiménez, the ruling junta decreased the percentage of the foreign companies' profits from oil, and rumors started about the formation of a national petroleum company.

A major diplomatic effort by the United States was required in 1957 to obtain an agreement authorizing the use of Brazil's Fernando de Noronha Island, off the Northeast coast, as the site of a tracking station for the South Atlantic missile-test range. Earlier, Brazil denounced an agreement with the United States for joint prospecting for uranium and canceled an arrangement for bartering thorium-bearing monazite sands for wheat. Interminable hearings went on in the Brazilian Congress on "sell out" atomic pacts with the United States, on the behavior of the American oil companies distributing petroleum products, and on the alleged harm caused Brazil by the agreements that supplied her on loan hundreds of millions of dollars of surplus wheat. The Federal Congress rang with indignant speeches by the members of the fast-growing Parliamentarian Nationalistic Bloc. Campaigns were afoot to lead Brazil into diplomatic and economic relations with the Soviet Union.

While a great many of the nationalistic attacks on the United States were unjustified and malicious, nationalism nonetheless constituted a major historical process. But United States policy-makers of the Republican era tended to dismiss it with undisguised irritation as a pernicious movement influenced by Communist minorities or fellow travelers. Though the Communists were undeniably taking advantage of the nationalistic spirit, Washington was inclined to confuse cause and effect.

The Republican philosophy, frequently expressed in official statements, was that private foreign investments were the magic key to the development of Latin America. Consequently, any questioning of this fiat was viewed with alarm and suspicion. When Latin American economists argued that a region so dramatically underdeveloped and plagued by natural obstacles and rising populations could never achieve a meaningful breakthrough with the methods that worked in the United States in the nineteenth century, they were greeted with derision and patronizing implications that all Latin America really wanted was plenty of money to squander. In short, the official United States attitude was that Latin Americans should be like North Americans and that they should apply North American methods to develop the region, instead of searching for solutions of their own that might be better suited to the Hemisphere's peculiar needs and problems.

When the United Nations Economic Commission for Latin America (known as CEPAL from the initials of its name in Spanish, Comisión Económica para América Latina) came up with studies calling for integrated economic planning in each country and in the Hemisphere as a whole, the United States Government gave it a cold shoulder, and high officials in Washington spoke openly of CEPAL as a "hotbed of socialism."

The Latin Americans' insistence on pushing economic and social development along Latin American patterns was a sophisticated form of nationalism, eschewing radical political ultranationalism in favor of pragmatic nationalism. When the pleas of Latin American economists and government officials for a re-examination by the United States of the aid patterns continued to fall on deaf ears, many of them shifted to political nationalism in some of its more extreme forms.

And the disappointments were frequent. At the conferences of American Economic and Finance Ministers in 1955 and 1957, United States Secretaries of the Treasury made perfunctory appearances, mostly to say "No" to Latin American proposals. Among other ideas, a suggestion for an Inter-American Bank was turned down. In 1956, as if to assuage hurt feelings, General

Eisenhower flew to Panama for a meeting of the Hemisphere's Presidents. He mingled with democrats and dictators, and platitudes were exchanged for two days. The result, a top-level committee of Presidential advisers, was hardly worth the trouble for what it produced in terms of serious inter-American understanding or cooperation. But the fault appeared to lie on both sides: Nobody seemed particularly interested.

In Brazil, much headway had been made toward comprehensive planning of aid and development through the studies of the Joint Brazil–United States Commission in the late 1940's. Outstanding Brazilian and American economists worked together on this plan, the most articulate one ever evolved in Brazil, and relations between the two countries rose to an unusually high pitch of confidence. But the Eisenhower Administration, upon taking office in 1953, let the entire program lapse because its own economic philosophies rejected the thesis of over-all planning.

The demise of the Commission dealt Brazilian faith in the United States one of the most severe blows of the postwar years. Subsequently, many of the young economists, sociologists, and planners who had been associated with the Commission, or had favored its work, found a political haven for their resentments in the Brazilian Institute of Superior Studies (Instituto Superior de Estudos Brasileiros, or ISEB), a highly influential grouping of intellectuals and leftists preaching ultranationalism. The Joint Commission incident was a typical example of a denial of alternatives to young, impatient, and visionary Latin American thinkers and of the United States propensity for alienating or undercutting the moderate elements. It was, in a way, a synthesis of the fundamental political and psychological problems facing the United States in Latin America in those days of rapidly changing conditions.

It was under those circumstances that Vice-President Nixon stepped into the hornets' nest on his South American trip in May, 1958. It proved to be the turning point in the whole relationship.

The Nixon Calvary

The Nixon tour was designed to accomplish several specific missions fitting into the broad concept of stressing the good will of the United States toward Latin America and its new democracies. The unpleasant past involving the flirtations with dictators had to be erased, and in general, it was beginning to dawn on Washington that its relations with Latin America were not all they should be.

Mr. Nixon's itinerary was arranged to meet all these objectives. His first stop was to be Buenos Aires, for the inauguration on May 1 of President Frondizi, marking Argentina's return to democratic rule after the ouster of Perón and the transitional period. Initially, the Vice-President had planned to go only to Buenos Aires because he had attended the inauguration of Brazil's President Kubitschek in 1956, and it seemed proper to give Argentina the same treatment as its big neighbor. Presently, however, it was decided to expand the Buenos Aires visit into a continental tour. Montevideo, the capital of Uruguay, was then made the first port of call. From Argentina, Mr. Nixon was to go inexplicably to Asunción, Paraguay, where General Stroessner, the local dictator, had just re-elected himself in an uncontested race. But the official justification for this piece of political levity was that it would be an affront to Paraguay to skip its capital and that, anyway, Mr. Nixon's presence there might stimulate democracy.

The next stop was to be La Paz, Bolivia, where the United States was keeping the social revolution alive. Then came Lima, Peru, where the Prado government had replaced General Odría, the dictator to whom the Eisenhower Administration had earlier awarded a medal. Quito, Ecuador, was selected as the following stop because the United States did not want to give an impression of partiality in the bitter border feud between the Peruvians and the Ecuadorians. Finally, Mr. Nixon was to stop at Bogotá, Colombia, and Caracas, Venezuela, where dictators for whom Washington had displayed its usual sympathies had been recently thrown out.

Thus, the only two South American countries excluded from Mr. Nixon's two-week tour were Brazil and Chile. The Brazilians were not upset because the Vice-President had visited them two years earlier, but the Chileans were furious. Actually, it was an oversight of the kind that continually damaged the United States in Latin America. Chile's President Ibáñez, an irascible old cavalry general, reacted by legalizing the Communist Party.

It was anticipated that the tour would be pleasant and profitable politically, despite the tight and exhausting schedule. Mr. Nixon, therefore, took along his wife and a large contingent of high-ranking officials. He was followed by an aircraft chartered by the press.

Before the departure from Washington, Mr. Nixon was advised by the intelligence agencies that he could conceivably run into some very minor displays of displeasure over his presence in South America but that nothing serious was to be expected. An advance party of the Secret Service had preceded him in all the capitals he was to visit, and no one gathered any impression that the Vice-President might run into dangerous situations. Only two months earlier, a high State Department official concerned with Hemisphere affairs had assured a Senate committee that relations between the United States and Latin America were perfectly good.

Mr. Nixon received a very slight foretaste of these relations when he landed in Montevideo. Nothing particularly significant occurred there, except for the disturbing note of some university students booing him, and the Vice-Presidential entourage was pleased with the beginning of the tour. In Buenos Aires, the climate was still reasonably favorable. The Argentines, mainly interested in their President's inauguration and the events that accompanied it, greeted Mr. Nixon with considerable warmth that may have been a response to the large-scale financial aid that the provisional government had been receiving in the past year. But at the University of Buenos Aires, in a debate with the students, Mr. Nixon ran into polite hostility. Many of the questions were, actually, charges that the United States had engineered the overthrow of the Arbenz regime in Guatemala almost four years earlier. The Vice-President adroitly fielded the questions, denying that the United States had actually intervened there and stressing the dangers of a Communist government in the Hemisphere. This, however, was as far as the hostility to Mr. Nixon went in Argentina.

Arriving in Asunción, the Vice-President was met at the airport by an eager General Stroessner, the only South American President to do so, and he was quickly exposed to the dictatorial climate of Paraguay. While he drove through the city, students waved United States flags and chanted "Liberty, Liberty"—using the occasion to express their sentiments about their dictatorship. Police plain-clothes men weeded the noisemakers out of the crowd and led them away to jail. One arrest took place in Mr. Nixon's sight and another resulted in an incident between an American press photographer, who had snapped a picture of an arrest, and a Paraguayan policeman. Later in the day, Stroessner told American newsmen who accompanied Mr. Nixon that the students shouting for liberty were Communists, "because I say so." The visit was concluded with the Vice-President's speech before the Paraguayan Congress, in which he spoke fervently of freedom and democracy, but the forceful allusions seemed to be lost on the legislators hand-picked by General Stroessner.

The next day, in La Paz, Mr. Nixon received a pleasant welcome, though anti-American leaflets circulated in the crowd lining the route from the airport. But the debates with students at the university and with labor leaders at a union headquarters revealed the same suspicions of the United States, its motives, and its attachment to democracy as were evinced in the Buenos Aires university roundtable. The Bolivians were encouraged to speak out frankly, and they did so as the Vice-President occasionally winced.

Then, on Wednesday, May 7, the Nixon party arrived in Lima, Peru, and what had been a dignified tour became a calvary road. From the moment Mr. Nixon set foot in Lima, it was clear that trouble was brewing. The students at San Marcos University had decided they did not want to receive the Vice-President and that they would display violent hostility if he insisted on making an appearance. They gathered in front of the hotel where the Nixon party was staying, booing and shaking their fists.

Their grievances at that moment against Mr. Nixon and the United States were not particularly clear. The posters they carried protested United States tariffs on Peruvian zinc and lead, but this was not really a national issue despite considerable agitation in the press. Other posters described the United States as a protector of dictators, chided it for the Guatemalan affair, and demanded independence for Puerto Rico. It looked as if the San Marcos students had searched hard for issues to support their decision to dislike the United States and its Vice-President. The Communist Party, for which any cause was good so long as it was aimed against the United States, was clearly manipulating many of the levers of the gathering demonstration. Printed leaflets bearing the name of the Peruvian Communist Party, Lima Committee, urged the crowds to keep Mr. Nixon out of the university and show him what Peruvians were supposed to be thinking of him.

The evening was spent in urgent strategy conferences as to whether the Vice-President should attempt the sortie to San Marcos University scheduled for next morning. The Peruvian authorities indicated they could assure Mr. Nixon's safety, but they wished dearly that he would not go before the students, and they said as much. But United States Ambassador Theodore C. Achilles urged the Vice-President to go ahead, correctly arguing that American prestige demanded that Mr. Nixon not be cowed by intimidation from Communists or rowdies. Mr. Nixon agreed with the Ambassador.

On Thursday, May 8, the Vice-President headed for the showdown. First, he marched across the plaza from his hotel to place a floral wreath at the monument of San Martín. As soon as he turned his back, the wreath was torn to bits and the United States flag attached to it was desecrated. It was one of the first times the Stars and Stripes was publicly dishonored in Latin America, but Americans soon became accustomed to the sight of their flag being burned or shredded.

From the monument, Mr. Nixon, accompanied by Ambassador Achilles and the interpreter, drove in a convertible the two city blocks to the entrance to San Marcos University. There, a compact mass of shouting students and adults stood in the street blockading the gate. The Vice-President and Ambassador Achilles, who calmly sucked on his pipe as if he were at a garden party, dismounted from the convertible and took a few steps toward the students. The youths moved forward, and from the crowd, there rose cries of "Fuera Nixon!" ("Out, Nixon!") and "Aquí no le queremos!" ("We Don't Want You Here!"). Mr. Nixon, not short on physical courage and visibly furious, buttonholed the first student before him. "Are you afraid of debating with me?" he shouted. His American military interpreter repeated the question in Spanish. For the next few minutes, Mr. Nixon, Ambassador Achilles, and the interpreter were engulfed by the student mob, everybody shouting at the same time and pushing in all directions.

Concluding that nothing useful could be accomplished, Mr. Nixon retreated to his car. Stones and rocks flew as the motorcade departed. A flying missile chipped the tooth of a Secret Service agent. The first deed of violence was done, but the Vice-President was not giving up so easily. He ordered the cars to drive to the Catholic University, where a visit had also been tentatively scheduled and where the atmosphere was expected to be more amenable to debate. Standing on the rostrum at the head of a classroom, the Vice-President spent thirty minutes answering questions from the students. The youths were not especially friendly but not openly hostile, either.

All that was left of the morning's schedule was the return to the hotel. Finding a large crowd massed in the plaza, Mr. Nixon alighted from the car and proceeded to walk toward the building. Instantly, he was set upon by screaming, fist-shaking Peruvians. As policemen and Secret Service agents opened the way for him, the Vice-President walked a gantlet of shouted hatred. Just as he neared the hotel entrance, several youths, their faces distorted with savagery, spat at him. A jet of saliva hit Mr. Nixon in the face. At this point, the Nixon journey in South America became the spit-and-stone trip, and a new dimension in the treatment of visiting foreign dignitaries came into being, one that was to be imitated far and wide.

From Lima, the Vice-President flew to Quito, Ecuador, and a reception that was relatively pleasant, largely because of the contrast provided by the events in Lima the day before. But, just to be on the safe side, a planned university debate was canceled. Kicking off the ball at a soccer game became the most spectacular moment of the Quito visit. But it was also in Quito that the Nixon party met the New York Philharmonic Orchestra and its conductors, Dimitri Mitropoulos and Leonard Bernstein. The orchestra was on a South American tour of its own, but it was moving counterclockwise to the Vice-President's itinerary. Representing American culture and music, the Philharmonic had already played in Caracas, Venezuela, among other capitals, and scored an unprecedented triumph. But as Mr. Nixon and the orchestra met at the American Embassy to exchange impressions, press reports were beginning to arrive from Caracas that students there were planning a Lima-type reception for him.

In Bogotá, Colombia, where Americans are usually liked, Mr. Nixon again found a pleasant reception—and tight security. A truckful of demonstrators parked in front of his hotel, shouting imprecations, but pro-American Colombians and the police chased them away. In the evening, a band of urchins staged a tiny anti-Nixon demonstration. Spirits were rising in the Vice-Presidential party despite insistent press reports from Caracas that bad trouble lay ahead. But State Department officials minimized these stories, and the only special precaution that was ordered on the eve of the departure for Caracas was to have Mr. Nixon use a closed limousine there instead of a convertible. It was a precaution that probably saved his life.

It was Tuesday, May 13, when the Air Force plane carrying the Vice-President landed at Maiquetía Airport, which lies on the shore of the Caribbean, about twenty-five miles from Caracas. Mr. Nixon was arriving in a restless and nervous country. The Pérez Jiménez dictatorship had been overthrown not quite four months earlier, and Venezuela was going through an immensely difficult adjustment in every field. The government junta was facing rightist conspiracies, there was a dire financial problem resulting from the debts left by the dictatorship and the flight of nervous foreign capital, and unemployment in Caracas was dangerously high. There was considerable leftist agitation among the poor in the *ranchos* and among the university students. There was also a growing feeling that the revolution that ousted Pérez Jiménez had not even begun to solve Venezuela's problems. But the bulk of the bitterness was directed against the recent dictatorship, and since the United States had supported it until the end, it was easy for the agitators to turn this whole complex of frustration against the Americans. Mr. Nixon thus loomed as a first-class target, and careful preparation went into making his stay in Caracas unforgettable.

The day before his arrival, the leftist-dominated Caracas city council had voted not to receive him. But a reception committee of a thousand or more persons went to Maiquetía to meet the Nixon plane, and they were the first to let him know what kind of feeling was running in the capital. Carrying posters declaring, "Fuera Nixon!" and "Down with the Yankees!," they shouted insults as the Vice-President walked from the aircraft to meet the waiting Venezuelan dignitaries. And on his way to his car, he again ran the hateful gantlet of the spitting men and women.

The drive up the mountain speedway toward Caracas was uneventful. But when the motorcade reached the workers' suburb of Catia, the hostility was again on display. Knots of sullen people watched the passage of the cars. Some shouted insults, others shook their fists. Moving up Avenida Sucre and approaching the downtown section of Caracas, the motorcade ran into a traffic jam that the police outriders could not break. Obviously, no thought had been given beforehand to clearing the avenue for the Nixon party.

As the drivers honked their horns impatiently, a mob suddenly surged from around the corner of an intersection and bore down on the paralyzed motorcade. A truck had been deliberately stopped in the path of the Nixon party to make the limousines a sitting-duck target for the attack. As the Venezuelan motorcycle policemen looked on helplessly, about five hundred people—mostly students and workers from the nearby housing projects—surrounded the motorcade. Swinging with rocks, bats, and lengths of pipe, they engulfed the car in which Mr. Nixon sat with the Venezuelan Foreign Minister and two Secret Service agents and the car carrying Mrs. Nixon, the Minister's wife, and a United States Air Force aide. Rotten eggs covered the black automobiles with their greenish-yellow putrescence. The bulletproof windows of the cars were shattered.

Then the attackers began tugging at the locked doors of the Vice-President's limousine so that they could drag him out. The Secret Service agents drew their guns. Flying glass broke the spectacles of the Foreign Minister. For a few seconds, the lives of the Vice-President and his party hung in the balance. If the enraged mob could have dragged him out, he would certainly have been beaten to death. Then, miraculously, the driver of the limousine saw an opening ahead, gunned the engine, and pulled out of the mob and the traffic jam at breakneck speed.

The original plan called for Mr. Nixon to stop at the National Pantheon to lay a wreath on the grave of Bolívar. But now the idea was hurriedly dropped, and instead, the motorcade rushed to the American Embassy residence atop a hill overlooking Caracas. It was just as well that Mr. Nixon canceled the visit to the Pantheon. An even bigger crowd had gathered there, ready to set upon the Vice-President if he escaped the Avenida Sucre ambush. A few hours earlier, an Army platoon with drawn bayonets had to rescue the Embassy's military attaché, who had gone ahead with the wreath.

No sooner did Mr. Nixon reach the refuge of the Embassy residence than Washington was advised of the situation. President Eisenhower immediately ordered Marines and Army paratroopers in Caribbean bases to stand ready for a landing in Venezuela if it was necessary to rescue the Vice-President. Although the official announcement said that the troops were held in readiness in case the Venezuelan Government requested aid in maintaining public order, the fact was that the plan called for the paratroopers and the Marines to secure Maiquetía Airport by sea and air in case the Venezuelans lost control of the situation. Helicopters from Navy ships steaming toward Venezuela at top speed would then be sent out to Maiquetía and on to the Embassy residence in Caracas to bring out Mr. Nixon and his party and transfer them to the vessels. If Mr. Nixon were in any danger at the Embassy, the paratroopers and Marines would be ordered to take the city. The troops could also be available to assist the evacuation of the 40,000 American residents of Venezuela if the mob violence turned against them.

But none of these measures had to be put into effect. After its first moment of horrified surprise, the Venezuelan Government called out its security forces and the Army surrounded the Embassy with a protective ring. Admiral Larrazábal, the junta President, called on Mr. Nixon and expressed his dismay, and the Vice-President showed himself to be singularly understanding of the forces that had set off the riots under Communist provocation. The rest of the official program in Caracas was canceled, and after a desultory lunch given by the junta the next day, Mr. Nixon drove back to Maiquetía through deserted streets guarded by heavily armed soldiers stationed every few paces. The South American trip was over, and relations between the United States and the rest of the Hemisphere would never be quite the same again.

Back to Oblivion

Mr. Nixon was greeted in Washington like a returning hero but the impact of his *via crucis* experience had hit the United States like a megaton bomb. Congress and public opinion demanded to know how it could have happened. Why did the State Department and the intelligence agencies not know that this sort of sentiment against the United States existed in Latin America, Senators, Congressmen, and editorial writers inquired. Urgent top-level meetings were held in the Administration to assess the situation. After ignoring Latin America for years, Washington rushed to the other extreme of breast-beating and wondering where we had gone wrong. Alarmed by his hard-earned discoveries in South America, Mr. Nixon proclaimed that the new United States policy in the Hemisphere should be of cordial embrace for the democrats, cold handshakes for the dictators, and greater economic aid to the Latin American republics. He promised to write a report with specific recommendations.

After the first excitement died down, Washington turned to other matters, and for all practical purposes, Latin America slid back into official oblivion. Secretary Dulles, who was never greatly impressed by Mr. Nixon's foreign-policy ruminations, continued to be bored by Latin America and his ennui kept all these brave ideas about cold handshakes for dictators from being implemented. In fact, he and the Department went on regarding the Batista dictatorship rather warmly, and later in the year he figuratively gave it an embrace by attending a reception at the Cuban Embassy in Washington on the eve of the elections in which one Andrés Rivero Agüero was selected as the figurehead for the regime. This was at the time when Castro's columns were fanning out of the hills, preparing to administer the *coup de grâce* to the dictatorship that was foundering in its own corruption and weakness.

But if the United States did not seem to know, or care, how to draw profitable lessons from its Vice-President's adventure, the Brazilians saw in it a golden opportunity for setting Hemisphere relationships on a new basis.

Within weeks of the Caracas affray, Brazil's President Juscelino Kubitschek sent President Eisenhower a long letter setting out proposals for an "Operation Pan American" designed to save Hemispheric solidarity through cooperative economic and political action. Dr. Kubitschek's main point was that the old concepts of Pan-Americanism had to be given a modern meaning if the system was to survive. He called for "a policy of ardent fraternity and indestructible continental unity" under which the American nations would jointly mobilize their efforts and resources to overcome economic and social underdevelopment.

The Brazilian President and his advisers who drafted the proposal saw beyond the anti-American display in Caracas the shadow of deeper economic and social problems besetting the continent. Obsessed as the Kubitschek government was with economic development, it readily sensed the gathering forces of the Latin American social revolution in all their aspects. The ferment was visible in Brazil, and it was obvious that it was setting in everywhere in the Hemisphere. The crux of Kubitschek's thinking was that unless Washington joined quickly with the democratic Latin American governments in a grandiose and imaginative program of development, the impatient region might shift toward revolutionary solutions and the United States would lose its standing and influence in the Hemisphere. Fidel Castro was still six months away from victory in Cuba, but it took no particular prescience on Dr. Kubitschek's part to see what was in store for Latin America—regardless of Cuban rebels—if something were not done rapidly.

Thus, in the middle of 1958, when there still seemed to be

enough time, Brazil handed the United States a potential instrument for building a democratic movement of revolutionary scope that could swing all the Latin American relationships to its side and make the region's future bright and secure. And it was well that the initiative had come from Brazil: Any action by Washington in the immediate wake of the Caracas affair would have smacked of the obvious and insincere. Dr. Kubitschek's "Operation Pan American" contained all the political, psychological, and economic concepts required to make it a success. Handled imaginatively, it could have become anything the United States wanted it to be, for the idea met with great receptivity.

But General Eisenhower knew little about Latin America, and Mr. Dulles' interest in the potentialities of imaginative policies there was limited, to say the least. Mr. Nixon had vanished from the Latin American scene as quickly as he had entered it.

In short, the Administration took a look at the Kubitschek proposal and concluded that it was just another scheme for prying loose large United States credits. No thought, apparently, was given to its political implications and possibilities when both the Cold War and the social revolutions were nearing the Hemisphere's shores in full force. President Eisenhower signed a cordial letter to Dr. Kubitschek and Assistant Secretary of State for Inter-American Affairs, Roy R. Rubottom, Jr., flew down to Rio de Janeiro to deliver it.

The missive was couched in conventional banalities, but startlingly, it included a reminder of the Caracas Declaration of 1954 enjoining all American governments to fight Communism. This was the document obtained from the Conference of Foreign Ministers in connection with the Guatemalan episode, and it had no visible relationship to Dr. Kubitschek's ideas for social and economic development. When Mr. Rubottom came to Rio, he also made it known that the United States wished to be polite to Brazil, but that it did not intend to be bamboozled into a Latin American Marshall Plan.

This is how the United States missed one of the great historic opportunities for Hemispheric leadership, declining to do willingly, and with all the credit accruing to it, that which it was to do three years later under the gun of a Communist revolution. It still refused to recognize that strong winds of social revolution were blowing and that unless democracy moved fast, it could forfeit the faith in it and be left behind in Latin America.

Actually, the idea of "Operation Pan American" did not die outright. President Kubitschek stubbornly kept it alive, and no Brazilian statement on any international subject failed to refer to it. The Communists, who had no serious quarrels with the Kubitschek regime, paid the proposal the compliment of attacking it violently. Out of regard for Brazil and because anti-American sentiment in the Hemisphere was noticeably mounting, the United States played cautiously with the proposal, but it was always careful not to become committed to anything.

In August, a month after Mr. Rubottom's visit, Secretary Dulles went down to Brazil to talk about "Operation Pan American" and other topics. He planted a magnolia tree in Brasília and authorized a "consolation prize" loan of $10 million to finance prefabricated steel structures for government buildings in the new capital. He also told Brazilians that it was a mistake to have a state oil monopoly and announced that Washington would not lend any money for it. The visit ended with a "Declaration of Brasília," the usual sort of document, which denounced "atheistic" Communism but proposed no measures to fight it in the way that would do the most good.

Brazilian pressure resulted, however, in an "informal" conference of American Foreign Ministers dedicated to the idea of "Operation Pan American." It met in Washington in September as the "Committee of the 21" and recommended that a special committee prepare the organization of an Inter-American Development Bank, an idea that the United States had rejected in 1955 and 1957. Its acceptance in 1958 was the only tangible concession to the new realities of Latin America that were discovered as a result of Mr. Nixon's experience in Caracas. There was also agreement on drafting general proposals for Hemisphere development to be submitted to the next session of the Committee of the 21 the following spring, but Washington emerged safely uncommitted to any programs.

The United States thus was learning slowly and reluctantly how to cope with a dangerous though still controllable brushfire. Then came the explosion.

4. The Explosion

___

The Shock Waves

THE EXPLOSION whose successive shock waves staggered Latin America was the victory of Fidel Castro's revolution on January 1, 1959. The collapse and disappearance of the Batista dictatorship fulfilled the political revolution—which was all that had been expected from the rebels—but without stopping to catch a breath, Castro plunged into a social revolution of a violence and thoroughness never seen before in Latin America. In fact, it was the most rapid, radical, and complete revolution to occur in the world since the Communists had taken over China, ten years earlier.

As Castro is fond of repeating, "We made a big revolution, not a small one." Launching far-ranging reforms in the first year of his rule—the slashing of urban rents by 50 per cent, then the cut in utility rates, the tax reform, and finally the sweeping land reform—Castro and his companions merged the concepts of political and social revolutions, unlike the democratic revolutionaries of South America, who halted at the traditional political line. This was the first and most fundamental step in their undertaking.

The second step was for Castro to turn away—imperceptibly and gradually in the beginning, then openly and irrevocably—from the idea of a democratic social revolution. It was generally assumed in Cuba and in Latin America that Castro would fit what had become his social revolution into democratic molds, as democracy was then understood in the Hemisphere. This had, indeed, appeared to be his program while he was still in the Sierra, talking of democratic government and the restoration of the 1940 constitution. Accustomed to the tradition that victorious democratic revolutionaries promptly order elections, Latin America waited for Castro to issue the call. Initially, he spoke vaguely of elections in eighteen months, but even before six months of his revolution had elapsed, Castro made it clear that he had no intention of holding elections. By late 1959, he implied that all the talk about elections was downright counterrevolutionary.

Castro's point was that elections and old-style representative democracy would hamper his revolution and divert the nation's attention from the revolutionary fervor he was striving to keep alive indefinitely. Although there was no question during that first year that he could have been elected to the Presidency by an overwhelming majority, or almost unanimously, and that a Congress enthusiastically responsive to his ideas would likewise be chosen, Castro had disturbing visions of his revolution bogging down in the free debate and practices of a democratic society. The democratic framework, with its checks and balances, would also deprive him someday of the supreme power that he now held as the revolution's "Maximum Leader." He also feared that Congress and the political parties would be infiltrated by "counterrevolutionaries" and economic interests opposed to his reforms, and thereby would tie his hands in carrying out the revolution that he already intended to be more radical each day. As a justification, he reminded Cubans of the venal practices of what had passed for representative democracy in the old days—and on this point he was on solid ground, even though logic might have suggested that the solution lay in cleaning up democracy, instead of in discarding it.

Therefore, Castro conceived the alternate device of "pure democracy." Addressing crowds at Havana's Plaza José Martí or elsewhere—while television carried his rhetoric to every corner of Cuba—he put forth the notion that the audience's applause represented approval of the policies of the revolutionary government and was, in fact, a better popular referendum than old-fashioned elections. He would ask the excited crowds whether they approved of executions of the Batistianos or of land reform, and when they roared that they did, Castro beamingly announced that the nation had just endorsed his policies. It was a very effective system in the midst of all this revolutionary ardor—and the huge crowds were more responsive than any traditional political party could be expected to be. Castro described it as the democracy of the market place, "purer than Greek democracy because there are no slaves among us."

As a natural consequence of this practice of direct contact with the jubilant but unsophisticated and politically obedient masses,

Castro then moved to silence all forms of free expression and criticism. Gradually, through devious and imaginative means, the newspapers and the television and radio stations were placed in the hands of the regime, and their owners, editors, or commentators fled abroad while the "workers" took over. The revolutionary government thus did not have to resort to censorship, an unpopular method reminiscent of the old dictatorships. Arrests and persecutions disposed of persons who might have been fully in favor of the revolution's goals but disapproved of Castro's means. The military secret police, the G-2, became one of the chief tools of the revolution. President Manuel Urrutia Lleó was unceremoniously fired over television because he spoke out against Communism. Matters thus became greatly oversimplified in Castro's Cuba: One was either for the revolution as Castro was conducting it, or one was against it. And to be against it was to be a "counterrevolutionary," the worst villain in the new Cuban demonology. Thus, hope died that the Cuban revolution might prove to be a democratic social revolution.

At this point, Castro ran into the inescapable problem of providing his revolution with an ideological content. The *"Humanismo"* of the early days no longer served its purpose, and "pure democracy" was nothing but a political gimmick. After getting rid of the moderates in the government late in 1959, Castro proceeded in the next year or so to fill the ideological vacuum of his revolution with "socialism" and "Marxism," before finally calling it by its proper names—Marxism-Leninism and Communism. Having rejected representative democracy and the United States, Castro had no choice but to turn to Communism and the Soviet Union, because in this polarized modern world there is no other alternative for a revolution. A revolutionary middle position is a myth.

But aside from this search, and eventual discovery, of an ideology for his movement, Castro was practicing social revolution in a sweeping and uncompromising manner. Until the use of the techniques of dictatorship and the advent of Communism split Cuba down the middle, this was the way the vast majority of Cubans seemed to want it. And this was the way in which Latin America saw the Cuban phenomenon. It was a revolution that no longer tolerated the delays, temporizing, or palliatives with which Latin American democratic and authoritarian leaders, with the approval of the United States, sought to pacify their own restless populations.

Cuban peasants were apparently receiving land, the city workers seemed to be getting low-cost housing, free education was available to everybody, racial discrimination had vanished, and this little island in the Caribbean sun was gaining full sovereignty and self-respect. It was a great social revolution, inspiring to the Latin Americans, and, many thought, worthy of imitation. That colossal deceit and a Communist dictatorship might have been hiding behind the brave and exciting façade of the Cuban experiment was a reality Latin America was not prepared to face for a long time—at least until another alternative was going to be offered to it.

The Mystique of Revolution

The Cuban events perforce had an extraordinary impact in Latin America in those early days, not only because they represented such an appealing social revolution but also because of their unusual, romantic, and picturesque features. There was a touch of the glorious, inebriating fiesta about everything the victorious rebels did, whether it was Castro and his aides strutting proudly around Havana with their telescopic-sight rifles slung over their shoulders, or Castro lecturing his nation on television about the glories of a revolution, or Castro handing a peasant family acres of land confiscated from some escaped Batistiano official. Newspaper stories, photographs, and newsreels disseminated the growing Fidelista legend and mystique across the Hemisphere, beards became the fashion among the younger set, and editorial writers far removed from Havana let their pens and typewriters run away with them in sublime comparisons between Havana and the Bastille and between the Cuban revolution and the French revolution.

Consciously or not, Castro was also convinced of the historical parallel. His activities in the first six or seven months of his rule underscored his wish to see the Cuban revolution break out of the narrow confines of his island and spread into the Caribbean, if not into all of Latin America. Tiny invasion forces of Cuban *guerrilleros* fanned out into the region like miniature Napoleonic armies carrying the revolutionary gospel to all the peoples.

Since Latin America still thought of the Castro revolution in the dual terms of an antidictatorial campaign as well as of social justice, sympathies were largely with the bearded invaders, particularly when they accompanied or led exiles from dictatorships in attacks on such strongholds of tyranny as the Dominican Republic of Generalissimo Trujillo or the Haiti of President Duvalier. This was still the antidictatorial phase in Latin America, and while the responsible governments were slightly alarmed over the way in which the Cubans were taking matters into their own hands, public opinion displayed considerable tolerance for these picaresque undertakings, and even encouraged them.

Hindsight, of course, suggests that Castro was perhaps less concerned with the fate of fellow Latin Americans suffering under dictatorship than with the need to assure himself of friendly revolutionary regimes in the Caribbean and Central American arc surrounding Cuba. It was the concept of the *cordon sanitaire* in reverse, the idea the French revolution first practiced for its own protection, that the Soviet revolution repeated in 1920 with Trotsky leading the all-out attack on Poland in retaliation for its penetration of the Ukraine, and that the Chinese Communists used in their capture of Tibet and their expansionist activities along the Indian border and in the countries of what was formerly Indochina.

Castro's second objective in practicing these geopolitics of revolution was aggressive rather than defensive: The dynamics of the revolution required that its influence be extended as far as possible into Latin America as a condition of its own survival in immediate as well as historical terms. Such ideological conquest, Castro obviously reasoned, would undermine the Hemispheric position of the United States, which he regarded from the first moment as his foremost—and natural—enemy.

If the Castro-engineered attacks on the Dominican Republic, Haiti, or Nicaragua could in those days be explained through his alleged sympathies for the nations under dictatorships, the assault on Panama in April, 1959, offered no such justification and, in a way, showed his hand perhaps too soon in the game. Whatever can be said of the quality of Panamanian democracy and social justice in 1959, it was not a dictatorship, and the Cuban "liberators" had a singular mission there. The facts were both tawdry and ridiculous: the Cubans had outfitted some shrimp boats to carry about 100 invaders, led by César Vega, a Cuban Army major, to help a disgruntled Panamanian politician, "Tito" Arias, to overthrow the government and presumably to set up a regime, astride the Panama Canal, that would owe a debt of gratitude to

Havana. The ridiculous touch was provided by the participation in this affair of ballerina Margot Fonteyn, Arias' wife, and the whole unhappy experience became known as the "Aquatic Ballet."

The invaders got absolutely nowhere. The Panamanian National Guard promptly broke up the invasion force, much of which capsized in the water, and imprisoned its members. Contrary to Arias' and Castro's expectations, the population did not rise to help oust the government, and the invasion ended in ridicule. Caught red-handed, Castro did the only thing left to him: He disavowed the entire adventure, insisting that it was staged without his knowledge and against his orders. When Panama sent back his invaders, Castro went through the motions of putting them in jail, which was unfair to both the hapless warriors and to Arias and his emissaries in Havana, who had held long and hopeful conferences with the top Cuban leadership before the shrimp boats took off on their mission. As food for added meditation, it may also be mentioned in passing that several United States businessmen were involved in the Panama operation.

A considerably more serious undertaking was sponsored by Castro in June of 1959, two months after the Panama fiasco. This was the attempted invasion of Trujillo's fief in the Dominican Republic. Here, not only was Castro eager to establish an allied regime in a country that was ripe for a political and social revolution, but he also seriously feared Trujillo and his armed forces, which, in those days, were incomparably more powerful than Cuba's ragtag and ill-equipped Rebel Army. In fact, Castro anticipated a Dominican attack on his island for reasons that exceeded the mutual hatred between him and the old Generalissimo and had their roots in the fact that the Caribbean was not big enough for both of them. Despite a subsequent truce when the Cubans and the Dominicans became concerned with their own problems, the basic hostility persisted. After Trujillo's assassination, in 1961, and the eradication of the remnants of his regime, the latent Cuban-Dominican conflict became a contest between a Communist dictatorship with its own expansionist ambitions and an infant democratic regime striving for stability.

But in 1959, the outward target was the Trujillo oppression. Recruiting a number of legitimate Dominican opponents of Trujillo, Castro on June 14 sent out a Venezuelan C-46 aircraft filled with Dominican exiles and a few Cubans, who were to land at the Constanza air strip in the Dominican mountains in a daring air commando raid designed to set up a guerrilla operation. Simultaneously, two assault launches carrying other Dominican contingents sought to land in Maimón Bay, on the north coast of the Dominican Republic.

Captain Enrique Jiménez Moya, a Dominican, and Major Delio Ochoa Gómez, a Cuban, were in command of the operation and both flew in aboard the C-46. The invasion was a military failure, but as it developed later, it planted the seeds of the rebellion against Trujillo, leading to the emergence of an active underground in the Dominican Republic and the assassination of the old tyrant two years later.

At Maimón Bay, Dominican aircraft had no trouble sinking the launches with their rockets. Most of the rebels drowned or were killed on the beach. The few survivors were caught and dealt with summarily. In Constanza, Trujillo enjoyed the added advantage that one of the officers who flew in aboard the rebel plane was a Dominican agent, an Air Force jet pilot who had earlier staged a prearranged spectacular escape from the Dominican Republic to join and infiltrate the rebel movement. It is another story that the pilot-agent subsequently vanished in Trujillo's hands. The invaders lasted only a few days as an organized force, and within two weeks the Dominican troops and loyal peasants flushed out all the unsuccessful *guerrilleros*. Captain Jiménez was killed and Major Ochoa was captured. Later, in one of those weird vignettes of the Trujillo dictatorship, Ochoa briefly reappeared to recant on television, then disappeared forever.

In this instance, Castro did not deny his involvement in the affair, and he mused to foreign visitors that he almost felt like personally leading another guerrilla force to the Dominican Republic to show Trujillo how those things should be done. But he never again tried to sponsor a direct attack on the Dominican Republic, perhaps realizing that the example he gave in Cuba of destroying the regular army after his victory—and of executing hundreds of Batistiano officers and soldiers for good or indifferent reasons—discouraged even the potentially anti-Trujillo officers from turning against the regime. During late spring and summer of 1959, Castro allowed small undertakings in Nicaragua and Haiti, but presently he abandoned the method of direct action, which was beginning to damage his position, and turned to Hemispheric political activity and then to subversion. By 1963, this method reached unprecedented sophistication, by Latin American standards.

Actually, Castro's personal inter-American action began even before he sent out his *guerrilleros* into the field. Three months after his victory, he flew to Caracas—where Vice-President Nixon had been stoned less than a year earlier—for a hero's welcome that began when he broadcast a speech to Venezuelans from aboard his aircraft flying over the city. Caracas, the ideal breeding ground for social revolutions, received the Cuban Premier regally, but President Betancourt—the shrewd veteran revolutionary—managed to be out of town for the occasion. Though even this early he had spotted Castro as a future danger to Latin America, he was aware of Castro's immense popularity among Venezuelan students and urban *rancho* dwellers, and he was not anxious for a confrontation. Castro, whose stay in Caracas included a strange bathroom conference with Gustavo Machado, the General Secretary of the Venezuelan Communist Party, immediately sensed Betancourt's hostility. He told a companion that he did not think that Betancourt could be counted upon for a joint action "against the Americans."

In April, just before the Panama invasion, Castro came to Washington at the invitation of the American Society of Newspaper Editors. There, he was on his best colorful behavior, and his immense charm was turned on with full force to the extent of impressing Vice-President Nixon, Secretary of State Christian Herter, and assorted Congressmen and journalists. At this stage, the United States, utterly perplexed by the Castro phenomenon, was far from understanding him, his social revolution, his political gravitation toward Marxism, or his methods and techniques. It was sufficient that he had spoken against dictatorship and indicated his dislike of Communism. And, to the general surprise, he did not even want money, unlike most Latin American leaders.

From Washington, Castro flew to Buenos Aires to represent Cuba personally at the meeting of the "Committee of the 21," the group set up to study President Kubitschek's proposals for "Operation Pan American." Most of the members were half-hearted, and the United States remained extremely lukewarm about the idea, even though the Cuban revolution had taken place in the interval between the Washington and the Buenos Aires conferences. There was still no imagination on the United States side, and the delegation still concentrated on avoiding any commitment toward Latin America rather than on working one out. If there was any clash of ideas in Buenos Aires, it was a personal one between Assistant Secretary of State for Economic Affairs Thomas C. Mann and Brazil's Augusto Frederico Schmidt, a wealthy industrialist and poet who was Kubitschek's *éminence grise* and the real author of "Operation Pan American."

Then, Castro, his olive-green rebel uniform open at the throat and his eyes flashing, descended upon the conference as the personification of the Latin American revolution. Cutting through the caution and the technicalities of the meeting, he proposed that the United States give Latin America the fantastic sum of $30 billion over ten years for her economic development. The figure was picked out of thin air, but Castro was addressing himself to Latin American public opinion above the heads of the gathered delegates, and the effect was exactly what he had calculated. The American delegation, the prisoner of its own conservatism, pooh-poohed the proposal, suggesting that the Cuban rebel was an eccentric, if not worse. The upshot was that Castro ran off with the headlines of the conference. Castro's departure made the rest of the conference an anticlimax. The irony of the situation was that two years later, under another Administration, the United States was to come forward with an offer of $20 billion in Western aid over ten years. Thus, while Castro was allowed to steal the thunder in Buenos Aires, the United States still preferred to bring up the rear of history rather than to be in its van.

The trip to Buenos Aires was Castro's last Latin American foray, though he stopped in Uruguay for a little revolutionary agitation after the Argentine Government prevented him from holding mass rallies in Buenos Aires. From then on, the missionary work in Latin America was done through his overt and covert emissaries, sometimes successfully, sometimes disastrously.

In August, 1959, Caribbean tensions, specifically the tension between Castro and Trujillo, led to the conference of American Foreign Ministers in Santiago, Chile. Castro's Foreign Minister, Raúl Roa—a nervous intellectual who veered from violent anti-Communism during the Budapest rebellion in 1956 to violent pro-Communism in subsequent years—was followed there by Castro's brother Raúl, accompanied by a planeload of armed rebel soldiers whose dispatch there can be explained only as revolutionary exuberance. With Roa's concurrence, the conference signed the Declaration of Santiago, enhancing representative democracy, for which Castro had no use, and reaffirming the principle of nonintervention, which Cuba accepted only when it could be applied to her defense. Raúl Castro's visit angered the Chileans, though it permitted him to make some useful contacts with the Chilean left.

Early in 1960, Castro further clarified his views about democracy in Latin America by issuing attacks, couched in gutter language, on Betancourt, Lleras Camargo, and other democratic Hemispheric leaders. As his quarrel with the United States intensified, he deputized President Osvaldo Dorticós Torrado to make a Latin American tour during which he spouted accusations against Washington for organizing "daily" air raids against Cuba, and blandly sought to convince Latin Americans that Cuba enjoyed the fullest freedom of the press and religion. It was during Dorticós' trip, on which the touring President helped to popularize the slogan *"Cuba sí, Yankee no!,"* that the last independent Cuban newspaper was taken over.

Simultaneously, Castro embarked on his policy of infiltration and subversion in Latin America. Cuban diplomats were caught time after time helping local revolutionary movements with money, advice, and propaganda. Tons of Cuban propaganda materials poured into Latin America—much of it innocent-looking publications vaunting land reform—and some of it even appeared among the relief shipments for the victims of the Chilean earthquake of May, 1960.

Cuba began to extend its political activities to Latin American students in July, 1960, when Castro celebrated the seventh anniversary of his movement's attack on the Moncada Barracks in Santiago. A Latin American Youth Congress was held in Havana, and the hundreds of young people brought there largely at Castro's expense were subjected to intense indoctrination, which ranged from revolutionary discussions to hiking and preguerrilla training in the Sierra Maestra. It was probably one of Castro's best propaganda investments: The students went home as potential revolutionary cadres and enthusiastic propagators of the Fidelista faith. The vast majority of those brought to Havana already had leftist sympathies, but the visit to Cuba served as a catalyst for their ideas. For the first time, they had a channel and an outlet for their frustrations and anxieties, and the sense of revolutionary euphoria and togetherness was highly contagious. With political life as narrowly based as it is in Latin America, the importance of students cannot be exaggerated. Castro, himself once a student leader, knew it, and he took the youths with utmost seriousness.

Not only are students the loud "activists" of movements of social and political protest today, but within a short period, they graduate to leadership, playing significant roles in government, professions, and political parties, and they often enter parliaments. Cuba was thus trying to invest in tomorrow's leadership generation.

Two more of Castro's investments were the purchase and operation of powerful short-wave radio transmitters beamed at Latin America and the establishment of his Prensa Latina news agency. As a rule, short-wave radio propaganda has limited impact in Latin America, unless it is rebroadcast locally by standard-band stations, and outside of the pro-Cuban fanatics, few South Americans confined to short-wave reception do listen to the Havana broadcasts. But Castro's medium-wave stations, with their booming signal, later blanketed the Caribbean from Mexico to Venezuela and the Dominican Republic, enhancing the Cuban influence.

Prensa Latina was designed to distribute Latin American and world-wide news written in Havana, but since the bulk of the Latin American press is in the hands of moderates or conservatives, the agency never gained more than a few minor outlets and, in time, was reduced to an instrument for gathering political intelligence.

Over the years, as Castro openly pushed for Latin American revolutions and insistently described Cuba as the first "Free Territory of the Americas," he amassed a large coterie of left-wing Hemispheric leaders—or prospective leaders—who either lived in Havana or commuted back and forth, always available to advocate Fidelismo and revolution or to attack the United States at various congresses and manifestations throughout the region.

The group as a whole was not greatly impressive, but each of its members had some followers at home, and as a tiny Hemispheric Comintern of sorts, it had considerable value for Castro. From Mexico, there was former President Lázaro Cárdenas who had volunteered to go and defend Cuba during the Bay of Pigs invasion but was stopped by his own government. Instead, he helped operate a pro-Communist Latin American congress in Mexico. Another Mexican member of the coterie was Vicente Lombardo Toledano, the head of the pro-Communist but not very influential Confederation of Latin American Workers (Confederación de Trabajadores de América Latina, or CTAL). Then there was Chilean Senator Salvador Allende, who was almost elected President of his country in 1958, and Guatemala's Jacobo Arbenz, who was thrown out of the Presidency in 1954 and gravitated to Havana by way of Prague. The Brazilian member of the group was Francisco Julião, the head of the Northeastern Peasant Leagues. From Ecuador came Manuel Araujo Hidalgo, the diminutive Marxist with a Lenin-like beard who briefly served as Minister of Interior under President Velasco Ibarra. Hilda Guevara, Major Guevara's ex-wife, came from Peru, representing the Fidelista wing of APRA. From Venezuela came Fabricio Ojeda, the young newspaper reporter who had directed the Patriotic Junta against the Pérez Jiménez dictatorship and later was elected to Congress. In time, Havana became his second home and Ojeda acquired a military uniform and a Cuban officer's rank. In 1962, he returned to Venezuela as a backlands *guerrillero* and was promptly captured and sent to prison. A onetime Peronista leader, Juan William Cooke, represented Argentina.

In addition to these relatively well-known names, there was a steady stream of lesser lights among Latin American journalists, student and labor leaders, and congressmen, all of whom served the useful function of liaison agents, propagandists, and revolutionary helpers. By 1962, this informal organization of Latin American Fidelistas had become an important asset to Castro in his unflagging effort to spread his revolution to the rest of the Hemisphere. It represented the hard core of ready and indoctrinated leadership in the event that another revolutionary movement should succeed somewhere else in the Hemisphere.

The Collision Course

That the Cuban revolution had to become militantly anti-United States was implicit from the very start. This trend was organically necessary, and it stemmed from the ideological convictions of its leadership. It could not find its historical fulfillment as a major act of Hemispheric defiance without pitting itself against the United States, which the Cuban revolutionaries regarded as the symbol of a social order that they rejected. It was required by the revolution's dynamics at home and by its dynamics of foreign expansion. As dynamics are a law of physics and of motion, so they are also a law of revolution, which, by definition, is a phenomenon of powerful forward movement. Obeying these immutable laws of history and physics—of what might be termed historical physics—the Cuban revolution, in its determination to change the face of the island and then of Latin America, inevitably had to collide with the United States. And, in fact, Castro deliberately embarked on this collision course to force an epochal showdown. His effort to spread a Cuban-type revolution to the rest of the Hemisphere was a challenge and a defiance to the United States that he knew Washington could not ignore.

As was noted earlier, a great social revolution is compounded of multifarious ingredients. Social justice, of course, is the principal one, but the other elements are attached to it organically in the manner of atoms revolving around their core. If the chain is broken in one place, the entire molecular structure must disintegrate, because the unifying magnetic pull has been destroyed. Thus the concept of social justice in Cuba under the revolutionary pressure became related to intense nationalism, which, in turn, was channeled against the United States. The next step in this revolutionary logic was to seek to expand the Cuban anti-American nationalism into Latin American anti-Yankee nationalism. It provided a second common denominator between Cuba and Latin America, in addition to the fundamental urge to see social justice established. The suggested conclusion was that these two common denominators implied a sense of Latin American solidarity with Cuba against the United States, which Havana deftly sought to present as the entire Hemisphere's historical enemy.

By the time Castro openly espoused Communism late in 1961, the majority of moderate Latin American governments had rejected Castro's overtures for an anti-Yankee front. Subsequently, they joined in proclaiming at the Punta del Este Conference of Foreign Ministers in January, 1962, that Cuba's Marxism-Leninism was incompatible with the Hemisphere's idea of representative democracy. But important segments of the Latin American population—led by some students and leftist intellectuals, ambitious politicians, and professional agitators—were not ready to reject the notion of Hemispheric solidarity with Cuba. Nor were the governments of Brazil and Mexico.

The Cuban appeal to Latin American nationalism, sometimes dormant but never extinguished, found considerable response. While in Cuba the Castro regime represented the United States as the wrongdoer, blaming it for the island's history of corrupt dictatorial politics and for her deep economic and social distortions, the line in Latin America was to portray the United States as the chief obstacle in the path of social justice and political emancipation and sovereignty. Again, the slogan preached by Cubans was that in order to achieve social justice and true independence, Latin America must break away—as Cuba had—from United States political influence and "economic domination," getting rid of the "trusts and the monopolies."

The Cuban propaganda—and, to some extent, the Cuban mirage distorted as it was by the distance—thus held out the attractive prospect that in following Castro's example, all Latin America could acquire a new identity and a new sense of destiny. The showy ribbon adorning this package of social revolution proffered by Cuba was aggressive anti-Americanism.

The first United States reaction to this attitude was something of bewilderment, in which concern about the future was mixed with the unfounded hope that somehow the United States could come to reasonable terms with this perplexing revolutionary phenomenon.

The initial policy toward the Cuban revolution was one that the Eisenhower Administration described as "patience and tolerance," and it was based on the premise, sound as far as it went, that any precipitate hostility against Cuba could be interpreted in Latin America as representing an attack on social revolution. At that point, Washington had acquired a vague mystical respect for the notion of social revolution, but it used it as a catchall cliché, without really understanding it. The proof of this was in the fact that the "patience and tolerance" policy was essentially hollow and negative.

Though it did win the approval of Latin American moderates— and this did count in the long run—the Eisenhower policy was basically a defensive holding operation lacking the complement of positive and imaginative actions that, in a manner of speaking, would have won the United States some influence in the social revolution. Instead, U.S. officials were content to point gleefully to the numerous and glaring shortcomings of Castro's helter-skelter revolution and to emphasize self-righteously how Washington suffered with Job-like patience the Cuban provocations and injustices. But these were revolutionary times in Cuba—and in Latin America—and cries of offended and indignant righteousness were not an acceptable substitute for the craving of millions of moderates and liberals to see the United States assume a posture of political and social-revolutionary leadership. When Washington failed to do so, it again left the field to Castro.

This was the first instance of the West's failure to comprehend fully the phenomenon of an onrushing social revolution, although such an understanding did emerge to a limited degree two years later—or two years too late—when President Kennedy launched his Alliance for Progress. Since in the first year of the revolution, Cuba herself was far from ready for socialism, let alone Marxism-Leninism, it is fascinating to speculate how matters would have developed if the United States had strengthened the hand of the moderates in the Castro government by outdistancing Castro as a champion of social revolution—a pursuit in which it is now involved in the face of severe handicaps.

The second instance of the West's—and the United States'—failure to comprehend the complexity and the ideological momentum of a social revolution was its almost pathetic refusal to recognize that Castro was dynamically and historically bound to radicalize his anti-Americanism more and more, and to move toward Communism to fill the political vacuum he had created. To do so, he capitalized on every American error, watching, with the diabolical pleasure of a cat poised before a mouse hole, as the United States responded just as he had planned to his deliberate provocations. In fact, each nervous United States reaction, from the cutting of the Cuban sugar quota in 1960 to the Bay of Pigs invasion in 1961, made it easier for Castro to push his revolution a step closer to the ultimate unveiling of his Marxist-Leninist ideology. It was a superb cat-and-mouse game, a projection of mountain-guerrilla tactics into the field of foreign policy, and the United States had no chance of winning so long as it persisted in defensive policies, failing to challenge Castro with more than words on the terrain where he was the most vulnerable—that of a true democratic social revolution.

Both the Eisenhower Administration and liberal public opinion in the United States bogged down, instead, in speculations as to the nature of Castro and his revolution. Some compared him to Kerensky and others to Colonel Nasser. Some spoke of him as a Nenni Socialist and others saw in him a budding Tito. Yet the truth was that Castro was like none of them, and the American exercise in comparisons obscured the correct analysis. For Castro was a radical revolutionary equipped with extraordinary dialectical talents, undergoing a rapid process of political and ideological evolution that could lead him in only one direction. Only one side in the Cold War offered him help and encouragement in his efforts to revolutionize Cuba and Latin America, and since that side also offered an ideology, Castro inevitably espoused it.

According to the clichés popular during those days of the Castro transformation, his revolution was like a melon—green outside and red inside—or like an iceberg with the visible half being the impressive social revolution and the submerged half being the pro-Communist trend. It should be added that powerful forces were at work to propel Castro in the Communists' direction: There was constant persuasion by some of his closest wartime companions, who never had any doubts about *their* ideology.

Yet the infinite American capacity for self-criticism and breast-beating caused influential liberals in the United States to concentrate on the nation's own past guilt in her dealings with Cuba at the expense of an objective analysis of the trends of social revolutions. It was true, of course, that the United States political stewardship of Cuba over the half-century of independence, beginning with the Platt Amendment and culminating with the excessive influence of the American Embassy in Havana, had caused deep resentments. It was equally true that the United States had in effect held the strings of the Cuban economy through the complicated system of sugar-quota allocations, tariffs, and private investments. But much as Castro used this past history as ammunition against the United States, what mattered after January 1, 1959, was the present and the future. The important task was to recognize the gathering political dangers in Cuba and to develop in the United States the kind of leadership for a democratic social revolution that could wrest the initiative away from Castro. Such a policy was continually but unsuccessfully urged on the Eisenhower Administration by farsighted segments of liberal public opinion in the United States, but these spokesmen of reason weakened their own case by minimizing and overlooking the degree of Communist inroads in Cuba, even as late as the middle of 1960, when it was perfectly clear to those on the spot that Castro had already crossed the Rubicon. There was still a tendency to look for the silver lining in what was rapidly becoming a dictatorial police state instead of the promised social revolution and to play up the apparent benefits of the land-reform and the housing and educational programs, while largely ignoring the disappearance of the free press and free institutions and the mounting terror of the Castro secret police. But democracy learns its lessons the hard way.

Inevitably, the showdown came between Eisenhower's America and Castro's Cuba because the revolutionary Premier was finally ready for it. He had the internal situation well in hand, and his economic and political arrangements with the Soviet bloc guaranteed him protection against any United States reprisals. Soviet oil and Soviet credits were available to him, and a sugar market awaited him in the Soviet bloc. Premier Khrushchev was about to announce that Soviet rocket-artillerymen were capable of striking at the United States if any harm came to Cuba, and Soviet weapons had already begun to fill the island's arsenals.

With the "patience and tolerance" of the Eisenhower Administration and of Congress rapidly changing into anger, Castro precipitated a crisis late in June, 1960, by ordering two United States and one British-owned refineries to process Soviet oil, which he said was being purchased much more cheaply than petroleum from "imperialist" sources. While Cuba's right to import whatever oil she pleased was not at issue, the Havana regime coupled its order with the ultimatum that disobedience by the refineries would lead to their immediate seizure and to the forfeiture of more than $60 million due the companies for past oil imports.

Under the circumstances, the companies refused to carry out Castro's orders, and forthwith, militia units occupied the refineries. The first major move in the showdown had been made, and the two countries had reached the road of no return in their relations. While the United States had earlier tried patiently to negotiate compensations for American-owned land, utilities, and other companies already seized by Cuba—and found itself criticized by Castro for doing so—the seizure of the refineries was taken to be an openly hostile act, as Havana had intended.

In Washington, not surprisingly, Congress immediately granted the Eisenhower Administration authority to cut the Cuban sugar quota. Castro, whose regime had long complained that the quota was a form of economic slavery, yelped that Cuba had been made the victim of economic aggression. Castro countered at once by seizing all the American property remaining in Cuba, while the Soviet Union announced that she would buy every ounce of Cuban sugar that could no longer be sold on the United States bonus market. Castro thanked Khrushchev profusely for this gesture, although the difference between the American premium price and the barter price offered by Moscow represented a loss to Cuba of more than 2 cents per pound—or 40 per cent. Subsequently, in June, 1963, when the world price shot up to 13 cents, the Soviet Union raised its payments on Cuban sugar from 4 cents to 6.

From the time the Cuban sugar quota was cut, a physical clash between the United States and Cuba, directly or indirectly, was unavoidable. As it began to run out of its patience and tolerance toward Castro, the Eisenhower Administration, in the late spring, 1960, set up training camps in Guatemala for a rebel Cuban force to be used in a contingency of one sort or another. Soon, it was tacitly accepted on both sides that an invasion was inevitable sooner or later, and that it was only a question of time before it came.

In August, 1960, the United States tried and failed to win from the Conference of Foreign Ministers at San José, Costa Rica, a direct condemnation of Cuba for accepting Soviet military protection. The sympathies for what Latin America considered to be the Cuban social revolution still ran very high in most of the republics, and the ministers recoiled before the rash step of citing Cuba as being guilty of anything. They approved, instead, a watered-down resolution proclaiming that no American republic should accept Sino-Soviet protection, but the Cuban delegation took the view that it was an insult addressed to the revolution, and it walked out of the conference shouting *"Cuba sí, Yankee no!"* Castro declared, aptly, that he could not visualize the Organization of American States moving militarily to defend Cuba from an American attack. After the economic round, the diplomatic round thus ended with Castro clearly leading on points.

The climax came early in 1961. In January, just two weeks before President Kennedy's inauguration, Cuba advised Washington that it had to cut its diplomatic mission in Havana down to twelve persons. President Eisenhower saw in this another provocation and ordered the rupture of diplomatic relations with Cuba. Castro, who did not want Americans with diplomatic immunities running loose around the island and helping his enemies, had expected precisely this reaction. In addition, he could now claim that he was the victim of diplomatic aggression.

Taking office on January 20, 1961, President Kennedy discovered that he had inherited a Cuban rebel invasion force in Guatemala almost ready to jump off. The Central Intelligence Agency, which had organized the rebel army, assured him that the operation had excellent chances of success and that Cubans were certain to rise against Castro as soon as the rebels landed.

The Joint Chiefs of Staff testified to the military soundness of the enterprise. The CIA had also warned the President that Cuban Air Force cadets were about to return from training in Czechoslovakia and that it was essential to launch the invasion before Castro's recently acquired Soviet MIG jet fighters became operational.

Impatience and anger overrode reason and political sophistication as President Kennedy presently gave the CIA the green light. On April 17, the 1,500-man force landed at the Bay of Pigs in southern Cuba, only to be destroyed in seventy-two hours by Castro's well-armed militiamen. The Cuban population did not rise in rebellion partly because the CIA refused to take the anti-Castro underground into its confidence and partly because the secret police moved with lightning speed to round up tens of thousands of the regime's enemies. The operation wound up as a bitter military and intelligence fiasco for the United States and generated considerable political capital in Latin America for Castro. To be a victim of an act of United States military aggression, however indirect, was precisely what he had wanted, and he extracted from it useful political mileage at home and abroad. His enemy had again walked into a trap.

But before and since, Castro has been careful to stay away from the United States naval base at Guantánamo, on Cuba's eastern coast. He realized that a military attack on Guantánamo could not succeed in the face of United States power and that, instead, it would invite the American Marines to defend the base all the way to Havana. Further, the likelihood of Soviet armed support for him in such an adventure was exceedingly slim. So in the curious state into which United States-Cuban relations finally settled, Castro was content to leave Guantánamo in American hands, drawing millions of precious dollars annually from the wages paid the Cuban workers at the base. On a miniature scale, it is somewhat similar to Communist China's allowing Britain to continue holding Hong Kong right on her coast.

The Bay of Pigs incident was the event that led Castro to shed whatever caution or hesitation preventing him from fully espousing Communism as his own political allegiance and as the ideology for his revolution. But the preceding two years had seen Castro personally exercise great care to avoid a final public commitment, even as he let his companions and the regime as a whole move gradually but steadily toward the establishment of a state dedicated to the pursuit of Communism.

This process had become particularly accentuated after November, 1959, when the group of revolutionary moderates—the "26th of July" group of professionals and intellectuals—was removed from the government and other posts of influence. But for reasons of his own political evolution and out of his precise and instinctive sense of timing, Castro for a long time did not feel that the psychological moment had arrived to tie Cuba officially to Marxism-Leninism or Communism. It was possible, indeed desirable, to continue advancing at full speed with the revolution's structural reforms, but an ideological shift of such magnitude required considerable indoctrination at home and special preparation in Latin America.

After Castro and his regime had insisted for almost a year that they were "Humanists" and not Communists, it was necessary to proceed with utmost care to avoid damaging Castro's personal image as the great "Maximum Leader" and the over-all image of the social revolution. Additional persuasion and indoctrination were required in Cuba to wean a great many otherwise loyal revolutionaries from their traditional suspicion of Communism. In Latin America, care was necessary to prevent important non-Communist backers of the Cuban revolution from turning away from it in shock and surprise. This, incidentally, was also the view of the Soviet Union, which occasionally was disturbed by Castro's radicalism and his breathless pace of reform and was apprehensive that the Latin American apple cart might be upset by his exuberant excesses.

By the time the rebel invaders hit the Bay of Pigs beaches in April, 1961, and short-circuited the situation, Cuba's process of preparation for Marxism-Leninism and Communism was already well advanced, both internally and internationally. Though Castro and most of his colleagues still went through the carefully staged fiction of avoiding in public—but no longer denying—identification of themselves and the revolution with Marxism or even socialism, the erection of the ideological edifice was nearly complete. Only a few more touches were needed before the scaffolding could be removed and the tenants invited to inspect the new premises.

The manner in which this edifice was patiently and gradually constructed shows why what had occurred in Cuba after 1959 cannot be described as a Communist takeover. Unlike in the

Eastern European countries, where Communism had been implanted at the war's end by native Communist cadres moving under the shield of advancing Soviet troops—or even in Czechoslovakia, where a sudden coup in 1948 put a Communist regime in power —the advent of Communism in Cuba was a step-by-step scientific process conducted under controlled conditions, with the participation, conscious or not, of the entire body politic of the nation. Yet, as subsequent events demonstrated, it was an undertaking in which the chief architect was not quite certain of what he was doing and often allowed his foremen to draft the blueprints as well as direct the laying of the bricks.

The unfolding of this process is important not only in terms of the Cuban story but even more so today as an object lesson in how a legitimate social revolution, initially supported by an overwhelming majority of the nation, can be led into a totalitarian channel by a small minority of the leadership, if a political and ideological vacuum is permitted to exist. Since, demonstrably, a revolution requires an ideology because it cannot survive in political emptiness, an understanding of this phenomenon in the West and the United States is essential because of the possibility of new social revolutions in Latin America. To put it crudely, the West has to come forward with its democratic ideology even before an actual revolution erupts if a repetition of the Cuban situation is to be prevented.

In Cuba, the ideological and political vacuum was deliberately created by Castro himself immediately after his victory, when he banned elections and prevented the functioning of the traditional political parties. Though his 26th of July Movement was an ideal framework for a revolutionary political party of his own, Castro refused to use it in that way, arguing that he could not practice himself what he refused to others. It would have been a commendably consistent position if Castro had not made a significant exception for the Communist Party, which in Cuba went under the name of the Socialist Popular Party (Partido Socialista Popular, or PSP).

The decision to let the PSP function and publish its newspaper *Hoy* was part of the agreement Castro worked out with the Communist Party in the early autumn of 1958, when Carlos Rafael Rodríguez, one of the Party's top leaders, visited him in the Sierra Maestra. Until then, the Communist Party, which had once worked closely with Batista—Rodríguez served as a

Batista minister in the 1940's—had withheld its support for Castro's revolution. The 1953 attack on Moncada had given Castro the reputation of a putschist among the Communists, whose dogma denied that power could be captured by a small band of ideologically unprepared revolutionaries operating in a political vacuum. Castro's landing in Cuba late in 1956 and his guerrilla operation, supported in the cities by the 26th of July Movement underground, still fell short of convincing the Communists that they should commit themselves to a man who not only was not politically reliable but was as yet by no means a sure winner.

It was the Party's view that the whole Castro operation was a bourgeois undertaking and even the presence in the Sierra of a number of officers who seemed to be Communists did not recommend the revolution to the Communists, for these officers were not local organization men. When the 26th of July Movement staged a general strike in Havana in April, 1958, in support of Castro, the Communists pointedly refused to cooperate with it. Since they had not been invited to help plan it from the beginning, they felt it was poorly organized and they did not wish to be associated with a failure at a time when nobody was sure how the revolution would come out. Their opposition to the strike accounted in part for its collapse, and for a while relations between the Communists and the Castro rebels were strained.

But by late summer 1958, the Castro operation began to look increasingly formidable and the Batista regime increasingly shaky. The Party then decided that it could not afford to be left out of what could develop into a victorious revolution, and Dr. Rodríguez was dispatched to the Sierra Maestra to observe Castro at close quarters and arrive at an understanding with him. Though Castro was still angry over the Party's lack of cooperation in the Havana strike, he proved to be tractable and, Dr. Rodríguez thought, ideogically promising—if his colossal ego could accept the Communist discipline.

After several weeks in the Sierra, Rodríguez worked out a deal with Castro, who turned out to be as shrewd a political bargainer as he was a military leader. Rodríguez asked guarantees that the Party's structure would not be touched—the Communists wanted to be sure they would not have to go underground again just when a major revolution was triumphing—and Castro was prepared to agree to this, provided that the PSP's organizing facilities and experience would be at his command. It may not have been clear at that point who had put what over on whom, but as events were to prove to Castro three years later, the purchase of a Communist apparatus can be an expensive transaction.

The apparatus went to work at once in the face of what appeared to be Castro's tolerant insouciance. The first target of Communist infiltration was the Rebel Army, whose ranks were swelled in the closing weeks of the revolution with Party volunteers. The "nonorganization" Communist officers from the Sierra, controlled mostly by Raúl Castro and "Che" Guevara, took over G-2, the Army's intelligence service. The protests of anti-Communist revolutionary officers were ignored or they were invited to resign. At the same time, a defensive mentality developed in the revolutionary ranks about Communism. Castro explained, as if with embarrassment, that he allowed the PSP to function because he did not want to divide the united front of the revolution, and the Communists, too, were for the revolution.

In July, Castro carried out his ouster of President Urrutia for having spoken out against Communism and named Dorticós Torrado, a Cabinet minister very close to the old-line Communists, as a replacement. It was, presumably, a telltale sign of the direction Castro's mind was taking, but he and most of his companions still denied any special affinity for Communism and insisted that what seemed to be their protection of Communism was simply an effort to prevent a fissure in the ranks of the revolution. Most people still believed it because they wanted to believe it, and aside from these disquieting signs and occasional excesses, the social revolution was going well and commanded the support of almost the entire population.

The land reform was already on the books, the first *fincas* were being seized and apparently prepared for division and distribution to peasants. The urban workers had more money than ever before because rents had been cut by half and utility rates decreased. A tax reform had been written and people were paying their taxes honestly, perhaps for the first time in Cuba's history. Graft and corruption no longer existed, also for the first time. The Ministry of Public Works was energetically repairing roads and bridges and building new ones. New schools and housing projects were being erected in the neglected rural areas. The hot and dusty cities were beautified with tree-shaded public squares, and youngsters received sports fields. The once-private beaches, the preserves of the rich, were opened to the people and equipped with beach facilities, a pet project of the Premier's. The peasants and the workers were treated with attention, care, and tenderness by the government and they could not fail to respond enthusiastically to such a departure from past practices.

So it was of no importance if the PSP was allowed to exist and publish its newspaper that almost no one read, and if a few Communists did work in the revolutionary government.

In his speech of December 1–2, 1961, when he announced his Marxism-Leninism, Castro provided a series of interesting insights into his political thinking processes, and a partial explanation for his pro-Communist leanings in the early days.

"Revolutions are not born in the minds of men," he said. "Men can interpret a law of history, a given moment in the development of history, make a correct interpretation, and give impetus to the revolutionary movement."

Although it is not clear—and it is still lost in the labyrinth of Castro's rhetoric—at what point he interpreted these laws of history in favor of Communism and impelled his "revolutionary movement" in that direction, he did say he had been a Marxist when he graduated from college and when he fought in the Sierra. But, of course, being a Marxist does not necessarily mean being a Communist—particularly among left-leaning Latin American youths. Perhaps the most accurate interpretation of his political evolution is that when he came down from the Sierra to find himself in control of Cuba, he was a partly indoctrinated Marxist with vast radical inclinations that his friends had little trouble in stimulating toward the ultimate extremism.

In perspective, then, it must have seemed natural from Castro's point of view for him to tolerate—and even appreciate—the activities of the Communists, convinced like so many men before him that he would be able to use the Communists for his own purposes. But it was a matter of tactics for him during the Sierra period and the opening months of that first year of his rule to appear at first as a leader interested only in the overthrow of Batista and then as a head of government concerned primarily with a good and even liberal social revolution.

Actually, the revolutionary laws of the Sierra and his post-Moncada speech of 1953 made it clear that he pursued the goals of a social revolution, yet few Cubans or foreigners paid much attention to this. However, in his December, 1961, speech, Castro obliquely explained his Sierra political tactics. He was describing how carefully his incipient revolution had to be presented to the nation so that support for the 26th of July Movement would not be scared off by fears of radicalism.

> In the first place, we should not be taken into account; in the second place, many people thought we were romantics who were going to die there; in the third place, they thought we were a crowd of ambitious people; in the fourth place . . . they thought that the group of revolutionary people was a group of leaders of conservative ideas or nonradical ideas. . . . It is beyond dispute that if we, when we started the effort, had been known as people of very radical ideas, it is indisputable that all the social classes—the social class which today is waging war on us—would have done so from that time. . . .

But by November, 1959, Castro no longer seemed to care how radical he was. As Jean-Paul Sartre remarked correctly in his book about the Cuban revolution, every time the "Maximum Leader" felt himself being attacked, he countered by taking another step toward radicalism. But since, consciously or unconsciously, he provoked most of these attacks, this was something of a deliberate chain reaction that carried him further and further and faster and faster toward Jacobinism.

Two events occurred late in 1959 that produced the phenomenon described by Sartre. One was a leaflet-dropping air raid on Havana by Pedro Luis Díaz Lanz, once chief of Castro's Air Force and now his archenemy. The other was the attempt by Major Huber Matos, a veteran of the Sierra campaign and then commander of the Camagüey Province garrison, to resign from the Army in protest against Communist infiltration. There was not much that Castro could do about the Díaz Lanz raid except to be indignant. But Matos was within easy reach, whereupon Castro had him arrested, charged with treason and subsequently sentenced to twenty years in prison.

Castro's political reaction to these two episodes was to reshuffle his Cabinet, ousting virtually all of his companions from the 26th of July Movement underground who were moderates. Major Guevara became President of the National Bank and thereby the chief of the Cuban economy, in addition to his function as the organizer of the Revolutionary Militia, which he had conceived to take the place of the politically less reliable Rebel Army. Other extremists and Communist sympathizers entered the Cabinet simultaneously. A major step had been taken toward the radicalization of the social revolution.

During the same period, Castro moved to win control over Cuba's organized labor. Although the Confederation of Cuban Workers (Confederación de Trabajadores de Cuba, or CTC) was fully in support of the revolution, a rank-and-file movement developed, especially among the urban unions, to prevent the Communists from winning a foothold in the organization. At a CTC Congress late in 1959, separate 26th of July and Communist slates' emerged in the elections for the Confederation's officers. When it became clear that the Communist slate would be crushed by the 26th of July candidates, Castro erupted into the meeting hall to make an impassioned plea for a "unity slate," browbeating the delegates into accepting it by shouting that rejection of unity was counterrevolutionary treason. The "unity slate" was, of course, heavily loaded with Communists, and presently the CTC began purging all the anti-Communist officials on trumped-up charges that they were Batistianos.

That labor Congress was the last time that the 26th of July Movement attempted any political action as a non-Communist revolutionary group. The Communist apparatus, with its organizational talent, provided new provincial and municipal heads for the Movement, and what had once been the hope of the democratic revolution became an empty shell. The regime preferred to look for regimented support in new revolutionary groups that it indoctrinated directly: the Militias, the paramilitary Association of Rebel Youth (now the Association of Communist Youth), the children's Juvenile Patrols directed by the Revolutionary Police, the Federation of Women, and a multitude of other groups that kept springing up as soon as someone in the regime thought of another group of the population to regiment.

In February, 1960, Soviet First Deputy Premier Anastas I. Mikoyan came to Havana to open a Soviet exposition and to sign a trade pact with Cuba providing for the purchase of a million tons of sugar annually and a $100-million credit line for industrial equipment. Thus, the first link with the Communist world was forged, to be followed by the establishment of diplomatic relations with the Soviet Union and Communist China. Castro was thus coordinating his internal moves toward the extreme left with a foreign policy and trade shift toward the East. Ideology and Cold War politics marched together.

Meanwhile, the socialization of the economy was advancing rapidly. Land and ranches were nationalized faster than records could be kept, inexperienced new managers were found, and plans for the operation of agriculture were evolved. The regime was proud of the pace of the social revolution, unaware that its magnificent chaos was undermining the economy and with it the whole social revolution. Industrial establishments were seized without much advance planning, and productivity began to plummet, but the revolution wanted to do more and more, faster and faster. The exodus of the middle class from Cuba acquired the proportions of a flood, and in time, the island lost most of her experienced managerial class. Left to their own devices, the revolutionaries ran the country into rapidly growing confusion. By mid-1962, looking back at what the revolution had done, Major Guevara wrote frankly that "terrible errors" had been committed. The degree to which the Cuban economy had been shattered made his words an understatement.

In the political field, Castro proclaimed that to be anti-Communist was to be counterrevolutionary, and his minions wasted no time putting this edict into effect by flushing out all the known and suspected anti-Communists. At Havana University, armed leaders of the Federation of University Students carried out their own purge. Anti-Communist TV and radio commentators and newspaper writers were removed from their jobs by various forms of pressure. Subsequently, the TV and radio stations were seized by the regime. The newspaper workers' unions forced the publication of *"coletillas"*—"corrections"—at the foot of every article they found objectionable. Later, economic pressure in some cases and outright seizure in others put the end to the free press.

Marxist jargon began to creep into Castro's pronouncements and into the propaganda of the regime. "Imperialism" and "colonialism" were chastised along with the United States and the democratic governments of Latin America, while no praise was sufficient for the Soviet Union. The U-2 incident and the collapse of the Paris summit meeting between Eisenhower and Khrushchev in May, 1960, were presented to the Cuban public in the words of the official Moscow line. Soviet-bloc technicians began to flock into Havana and the provinces. Cuba was moving fast toward the extreme left at home and abroad.

There remained the problem of how the Catholic population of Cuba would accept the conversion to Communism. The Archbishop of Santiago, who after Moncada interceded for Castro's life, was already on record with a warning in a pastoral letter that the Communist enemy was "within the gates." Priests throughout the island were speaking out against Communism, though still praising the regime and the social revolution. But Castro solved the problem rather simply, confounding those who had blindly believed that the Cubans' Catholic faith would be an unbreachable barrier to Communist penetration. In the first place, he played heavily on the theme that the revolution respected the religion and opposed only "counterrevolutionary" priests. That the bulk of Cuban clergy was made up of Spanish priests, often truly reactionary, helped him considerably in this line of persuasion. Besides, the real hold of the Church on Cubans was never strong despite the great nominal devotion to the Virgin of Charity, Cuba's patron saint. In the second place, Castro used the image of the social revolution as a manifestation of the aspirations for Cuba's future.

Through tireless repetition, he established his credo that those who opposed the revolution and the benefits it was bringing the people were using anti-Communism as a cover for their counterrevolutionary activities. It was simple but it was effective, particularly with the *guajiros* of the sugar plantations and the mountain villages to whom Communism as a concept had no meaning at all. It was indoctrination at its uncomplicated best, and when the time came for the official espousal of Communism, the unsophisticated peasant masses were ready for it. More drastic means of persuasion, however, had to be used later with the Havana workers, who knew Communism when they saw it.

But in general, it was a useful demonstration of what can happen to a social revolution for those who believe that Latin America's Catholicism is an effective bar to Communism.

The erection of the ideological edifice was quickened still further in Cuba after the cutting of the sugar quota by the United States. Castro already had a virtual, though not actual, military alliance with the Soviet bloc; Communist weapons had begun to flow into Cuba, and Khrushchev had made his promise about using rockets to protect Cuba from the United States and buying up all the Cuban sugar.

A significant though largely unnoticed event occurred in Havana a few days after the cutting of the sugar quota. Castro had called a mass rally to address the crowds from the terrace of the Presidential Palace to protest the United States action, and among Cabinet members and other revolutionary luminaries gathered around the rostrum, there were two key leaders of the Communist party. Nattily attired and wreathed in smiles, Carlos Rafael Rodríguez and Juan Marinello, the President of the PSP, sat in chairs reserved for the top leadership of the revolution. It was the first public appearance of high Communist leaders with the cream of the Fidelistas, and it clearly was not accidental. Amusingly, their well-tailored suits contrasted sharply with the revolutionaries' khaki uniforms, with their open-throated sport shirts. The PSP had made the grade officially and pointedly, in high sartorial style.

A few weeks later, Dr. Rodríguez directed the takeover of Havana University and its loss of autonomy. In his capacity of Professor of Economics, he led a student movement designed to force out "reactionary" and anti-Communist professors from the faculty. There was little resistance, and within days, the University became another appendage of the regime.

From then on, the process of Communization moved in a routine pattern. Cuban leaders in droves visited the Communist capitals of Europe and Asia. Diplomatic and "cultural" relations were established with such implausible countries, from the Latin American viewpoint, as Outer Mongolia, North Korea, and North Vietnam. In September, 1960, Castro attended the session of the United Nations General Assembly in New York, proudly consorting with Khrushchev, Poland's Wladyslaw Gomulka, and other Communist chiefs of government, and insulting American officials in his formal address.

At home, Communist indoctrination was carried out openly in schools, factories, and land cooperatives. But Castro still refrained from calling a spade a spade as far as he and his revolution were concerned.

Then the Bay of Pigs invasion enabled him to make the first open admission. During the week of the invasion, the Cuban radio devoted long programs to marking the anniversary of Lenin's birth and narrating the history of the Soviet Union's victory over the "reactionary" forces attacking her after the 1917 revolution. Radio announcers suddenly began to talk about "our glorious socialist revolution," and finally, at the May Day celebration, which also marked the victory over the invaders, Castro rose to proclaim that Cuba would henceforth be a socialist state.

From Socialism to Communism

To call Cuba a socialist state was the preliminary step on her path toward Marxism-Leninism and the ultimate identification of her social revolution with Communism. The use of this terminology was still a matter of Castro's tactics, but it set off a world-wide discussion whether Cuban socialism meant Communism, or what. Experts on Communism pointed out learnedly that outside of the Soviet Union, only Czechoslovakia rated the denomination of Socialist Republic, while all the other Soviet satellites and even China were merely Popular Republics or People's Republics. Others chose to think that Castro was turning toward a European form of socialism, and jubilantly repeated that he was not a Communist after all.

But the evident truth was that in the wake of the rebel invasion, Castro had made his final decision to lead Cuba to Communism. Powerful internal and international reasons propelled him toward this objective.

While Sartre's theory that every new attack pushed Castro in the direction of further radicalism is correct within the general context of the postinvasion situation, the Premier's reactions at this stage were deliberate political acts and not fits of pique. In a sense, the Bay of Pigs was a narrow escape, in which Castro's luck and good internal organization, combined with his foes' glaring errors, saved the day for him. But, unable to predict President Kennedy's thoughts and the future mood in the United States, Castro had to assume that the danger of external attack had not necessarily ceased with the rout of the exiles' little army.

Though his own military establishment was adequate to cope with the kind of limited operation staged by the rebels, it obviously could not withstand alone a new assault that, for all he knew, might have the backing of the entire armed might of the United States. From this premise, it followed logically that Cuba quickly had to become associated with a major world power system in order to be assured of protection in any conceivable future event. It, therefore, loomed urgent to Castro to obtain a full-fledged military alliance with the Soviet Union that would operate automatically in the moment of need.

Prior to the rebel invasion, Cuba enjoyed ample military cooperation with the Soviet bloc, receiving considerable quantities of armaments and technical advice, but the relationship was markedly short of iron-clad guarantees, and it certainly was not an alliance in the full sense of the term. To be sure, Premier Khrushchev had fired off a long letter full of ominous warnings to President Kennedy while the attack was still in progress—presumably to discourage the United States from stepping into the fray—but at no point could Castro be sure of how Moscow would actually react in the event of a full-scale American operation.

As happens in relations between individuals, Castro's political strategy toward his Soviet friend was to commit and compromise him as much as possible in order to make it extremely difficult for Moscow to turn its back on Cuba—should such a rejection ever suit its larger objectives. To set his revolution squarely within the ranks of the Communist family of revolutions—to use Theodore Draper's apt phrase—Castro felt it necessary to identify it completely with the Communist ideological system, even if he aimed at a tropical variant of Marxism-Leninism. The rationale of this move, which really amounted to an application for membership in the Warsaw Pact, was presumably that if the Soviet Union should ever choose to let a fellow Communist state, and an ardent new convert at that, be devoured by the "imperialists," then her posture in the eyes of the revolutionary world would be seriously undermined. The subsequent agreement for the installation of Soviet nuclear missiles in Cuba, and Castro's tortuous policies after their withdrawal late in 1962, were a logical extension of this basic approach to relations with the Soviets.

Since Castro's overwhelming interest lies in the success of his revolution and its eventual extension to Latin America, it stands to reason that he is not above exercising subtle forms of blackmail against the Soviet Union. His new dedication to Marxism-Leninism does not necessarily contradict such practices, and it is also evident, particularly since the missile crisis, that the objectives of Moscow and Havana are not always the same. While Castro obviously sees the problem of Cuba as the overriding consideration in all his policies, the Soviet Union, on the other hand, must see Cuba in the global context of its relations with the United States and of the Cold War everywhere in the world. Khrushchev's decision to pull out the missiles under United States pressure in October, 1962, made this point with complete clarity.

Because deep differences in approach must inevitably persist in Cuban-Soviet relations, Castro does not consider himself the head of a Soviet satellite state, and it is erroneous for the West to dismiss Cuba as just another Soviet satellite. Just as profound fissures and conflicts exist within the Western alliance, they are also present in the extremely complicated relationships between Cuba and the Soviet Union and between Peking and Moscow, even if on a different level. But the aftermath of the missile crisis brought the Soviet, Chinese, and Cuban situations into a common focus.

In her own way, even before the missile affair, Cuba posed a difficult and delicate policy problem for the Soviet Union in what is essentially a marriage of political convenience. The story circulated at the time of the arrival of the Soviet Ambassador in Havana in 1960 that Castro told him that while Moscow unquestionably knew a great deal about the world in general, he could teach the Russians just as much about Cuba and Latin America. Although this may be apocryphal, it does reflect Castro's judgment of the situation, and as later developments showed, Castro applied some of his most subtle maneuvers to the political intercourse with the Soviets.

Always operating on several parallel levels, Castro combined his international policies with what he saw as the internal requirements of the Cuban revolution to shape his island in the Communist mold. In addition to using Communism as an instrument for establishing what he hoped would be an unbreakable bond with the Soviet bloc in order to serve Cuba's military and economic purposes, he also needed the ideology to fill the political void that was presenting more and more of a domestic problem. As has been repeatedly stressed here, Castro was always convinced that a revolution cannot prosper in an ideological vacuum, and it was becoming increasingly urgent to create a form of political cohesion to maintain his new society and to glue it together. The revolutionary fervor of 1959 was beginning to wear thin in the face of the mounting problems and hardships of the transition, and furthermore, a revolution, like every political phenomenon, is affected by the law of diminishing returns. In other words, a nation can be kept only so long in a state of revolutionary pageantry and agitation before a new and durable substitute has to be devised to keep alive the allegiance to the revolution. From Castro's viewpoint, considering his natural leaning toward Marxism and his lack of real alternatives, Communism, based on powerful indoctrination, was the only possible answer. And if he had any doubts on this score, there were enough Marxist believers in his entourage to help him make up his mind.

For all these reasons, then, the Bay of Pigs invasion supplied the ideal framework for the switch that he had already been preparing to make for some time. From what had until then been no more than a betrothal, the Cuban relationship with Communism turned into a marriage of convenience. The new strength that Castro extracted from his victory at the Bay of Pigs provided the political springboard for making the plunge.

In his victory speech and then in the May Day oration, Castro defiantly spoke of how his little island had dared to implant a socialist revolution "under the very nose" of the United States. If there were any doubts as to what this socialism meant to him, Castro supplemented his discussion of the doctrine with dire predictions of the approaching disintegration of "imperialism," in phrases borrowed from the Moscow lexicon. Carried away by his rhetoric, he proclaimed that the defeat at the Bay of Pigs was the beginning of the end of this imperialism. And to make Castro's intentions crystal-clear, listeners to Havana Radio were treated to the interminable programs celebrating the anniversary of Lenin's birth and the Soviet Union's victory over her "reactionary" attackers. In fact, before the invasion, Cuban propaganda acquired its definitive tone when the assistant editor of *Hoy,* the Communist newspaper, became the director of the daily official radio program, "Venceremos" ("We Shall Win").

But even Castro could not turn Cuba overnight into a Communist state by issuing a decree, and a period of formal transition was prescribed. The task of carrying out this transition was delegated to the leadership of the PSP—the Communist Party—and the seed of what was to become Castro's first deep disenchantment of his revolution was thus planted.

The plan, worked out in May and June and announced by Castro on July 26, called for the creation of the Integrated Revolutionary Organizations (Organizaciones Revolucionarias Integradas, or ORI) as the first step toward setting up the unified proletarian revolutionary party to be known as the United Party of the Cuban Socialist Revolution (Partido Unido de la Revolución Socialista Cubana, or PURSC). The idea was to bring all the existing revolutionary organizations under one roof in order to prepare the cadres of the new party and develop a grass-roots political structure based on a system of cells and "democratic centralism," modeled on the structure of the Soviet Communist Party. To set the pace for the process of unification, Castro announced the fusion of the PSP with his 26th of July Movement and with the virtually defunct Revolutionary Student Directorate. Actually, the fusion was a farce because both the 26th of July Movement and the Directorate were empty political shells and, for all practical purposes, the ORI was just a new label for the old Communist Party, which was now being given an official status as the chief political organ of the revolution. But only much later did Castro realize the real extent of this farce and of the damage it had inflicted on him and his revolution. Meanwhile, he was delighted to accept nomination as the General Secretary of the future proletarian party, the PURSC.

But from that moment, Cuba was wholly under the control of the old-line Communists fully loyal to Moscow—the efficient organizers—and they wasted no time in making their influence felt. In the political field, the Communist leadership handed over the ORI to Aníbal Escalante, the old party's Organizational Secretary. Escalante immediately proceeded to turn Cuba into the tightest possible little island for the benefit of traditional Communism rather than of the idealistic social revolution of which Castro still talked incessantly. On becoming the ORI's Organizational Secretary, Escalante established the first national directorate, which was a replica, on the party level, of the Cuban Government. Provincial and municipal ORI directorates were then set up, and the local secretaries of the old Communist Party were automatically designated as their heads. Veteran Communist officials took over the "nuclei"—the cells—of the ORI in farms, factories, and government offices. Within a few months, the ORI emerged as Cuba's shadow government, holding all the power, and on a day-to-day basis, Escalante actually wielded more influence than Castro.

In the nominal governmental structure, important changes were made to conform with the new situation. The military secret police—the dreaded G-2—was elevated to the status of the Ministry of the Interior, on the Soviet MVD pattern, incorporating all the other police organizations and assuming control of the Committees for the Defense of the Revolution, the vast network of neighborhood and work-center informers. Major Ramiro Valdés, one of Castro's Communist companions from the Sierra Maestra, was raised from chief of G-2 to Minister of the Interior.

The party thinking also spread to the planning and the operations of the Cuban economy. Hundreds of farm cooperatives officially became People's Farms, or collectives. Communist leaders took over the formulation of the economic-development plans on the theory that their alleged experience qualified them and that it was imperative for them to do so in the light of the urgent need to remedy chaotic conditions created by the young Fidelista amateurs. Little by little, the Fidelistas were removed from posts of influence. When a "self-criticism" congress was called in Havana in August, 1961, to discuss the severe food shortage, it was Carlos Rafael Rodríguez who delivered the keynote speech, while "Che" Guevara—theretofore the leading economic spokesman for the revolution—took a back seat. But Castro still appeared pleased with the way his Communist friends were managing the situation, and in a speech to cheering supporters, he declared that "if this is Communism, this is what we want."

And, in fact, he was having Communism, but of a wild variety, and the waste and arrogance of the ORI operators—old and new Communists alike—made the Soviet technicians in Havana shudder. Castro and his companions kept telling each other, and the nation, that mistakes were inevitable in trying to set Cuba on the path of socialism. They promised to correct them, and doubtless they meant it, but in practice, the regime kept finding itself deeper and deeper in errors and confusion. The national resources—and much of the Soviet-bloc aid—were going down the drain, and seen through an accountant's cold eye, the revolution had less and less to show for its efforts.

While the official propaganda emphasized the immensely ambitious task of wiping out illiteracy in Cuba during 1961, one of the main and certainly commendable goals of the revolution, the national economy was in a tail spin. Deprived of the traditional food imports from the United States, the island could not be expected to become self-sufficient overnight even under the best of circumstances. But under the stewardship of the omnipotent ORI, the circumstances were the worst imaginable. The big cooperatives and collectives were producing sluggishly and usually at a loss. The small farmers produced just enough for their own necessities either because they were afraid of having their land seized and nationalized, as often was the case, or because the government set the prices and forced them to sell all their marketable produce to the National Institute of Agrarian Reform. The irony of this situation was that thousands of these farmers were supposed to be the beneficiaries of the social revolution, for they had received their land from the agrarian reform.

A good part of the 1961 coffee crop, important to Oriente Province, was lost because there were no workers to pick it; the peasants had lost interest in the harvest. This happened again in 1962, and in February, 1963, coffee rationing had to be ordered in Cuba. The regime's allegation, repeated the following year during the sugar-harvest crisis, was that the *guajiros* were making so much money in other activities that they could not be bothered picking the coffee beans. But if this was the case, then a high percentage of the Cuban work force had simply vanished, because industry was also greatly undermanned. In mid-1961, contradicting its own allegations about the abundance of satisfactory employment, the regime unveiled a nationwide campaign against absenteeism, almost desperately pleading with the nation to work instead of sabotaging the revolution by staying away from its jobs. The revolutionary slogan that "Revolution Means Work" was simply ignored by thousands of Cubans who found that it no longer paid to work because not enough could be bought with their money, and because they were forced to contribute more than 15 per cent of their salaries to various revolutionary causes.

It developed later, when Castro himself became sufficiently alarmed over the conduct of the revolution by his Communist specialists in good management to intervene personally, that much of the fault for the growing crisis lay with the ORI. Here was an example of how a political bureaucracy, greedy for power for power's sake, was derailing a social revolution that, despite its immense drawbacks and its steadily stiffening dictatorial features, had not so long ago loomed as the great hope and promise for the nation. Castro's subsequent explanation that he did not realize what was happening is difficult to accept. The fact that he allowed himself to be blinded by his faith in the Communists and the ORI— and that he isolated himself from his own revolution—in itself constitutes an indictment of him as a revolutionary leader.

In a broader sense, the Cuban events of 1961 were a grim warning of how a rapacious and predatory ideology can be manipulated by professional political bureaucrats to devour a social revolution. It was a warning as well to the starry-eyed Latin American radicals who saw in the Cuban revolution only a radiant inspiration and were willing to accept the Communist presence in it as a not too disturbing fact of life. But perhaps the greatest lesson of the ORI episode in Cuba was that when a social revolution allows the creation of a political and ideological vacuum, it invites predatory Communism to come to fill it.

Communism Cuban-Style

But when the autumn of 1961 rolled around, Castro, still in the throes of his new conversion, was perfectly satisfied to let the professional Communist apparatus go on running the country for him. In his mind, the old Communists were still the great organizers, and their presumed experience in such fields as planning and economics was expected to clear up the amateurish confusion from which Cuba continued to suffer toward the end of the third year of the revolution.

Consequently, in November, it was Carlos Rafael Rodríguez who took in hand the task of drafting the economic-development program for 1962, and the four-year plan that was to follow it. Economy Minister Regino Botí, a figurehead left over from the earlier revolutionary days, was assigned to work with Rodríguez on the master blueprint, but his influence was negligible. Major Guevara, once the boss of the economy, was relegated to the presentation of the industrial plan in his now restricted capacity of Minister of Industries. In a speech hailing the vague goals of the new plan—a typical Communist document making no reference to current production and making its projections in terms of meaningless percentages—Castro himself made a point of stressing that Rodríguez was the brain behind the new program. If you have any questions, he told his listeners, "ask Comrade Carlos Rafael."

A little earlier, in October, the new Cuba demonstrated her complete ideological allegiance to the Soviet Union. A delegation from the ORI, headed by Blas Roca, the General Secretary of the old Communist Party, traveled to Moscow to participate in the debates of the Twenty-second Congress of the Communist Party of the Soviet Union. The ORI delegation was the only group outside of official foreign Communist parties attending the Congress, but the Cuban leaders felt so much a part of the family that they actively supported Premier Khrushchev in his dispute with Communist China over Albania. Almost literally, the Cubans knew on which side their bread was buttered—at least at that time.

It is not known whether, or to what extent, the question of

formalizing Castro's adherence to Communism was discussed during the Moscow visit of the ORI leaders; there are many available accounts, all of them contradictory. But on the night of December 1, Castro rose in Havana to announce that he was a Marxist-Leninist and would remain one "until the last day of my life." He said that the ORI would soon complete its preparatory task and Cuba would be ready to launch her official Marxist-Leninist party, the PURSC. He explained at length that, in its new maturity, the Cuban revolution could no longer look to one "Maximum Leader" for guidance and that the country now would be directed by a "collective leadership."

The declaration had an electrifying effect in Cuba as well as in Latin America and the United States. The last remaining shreds of the cherished myth that the Cuban revolution was an independent movement had been destroyed by the Premier. But, contrary to some expectations, Castro's confession did not cause him quite as much political harm as it might have earlier. It was a calculated risk, internally and internationally, and in a way it paid off.

In Cuba, the highly indoctrinated masses, particularly the youth, received the announcement gleefully. Those who were already opposed to the revolution, perhaps one-half of the population, turned even more bitterly against it. Their ranks were swelled by a limited number of fence-sitters, but Castro always preferred to be rid of the nonreliables. In Latin America, a similar phenomenon of polarization occurred, and significantly, the extreme leftist groups began talking openly for the first time of Marxist-Leninist revolutions. In the opinion of Cuban Communist leaders, this was a necessary and important test to discover to what extent the leftist militants in Latin America were willing to be identified clearly with Marxism-Leninism, or Communism. The returns were not discouraging to the Cubans. A great many lesser revolutionary lights in Latin America—like Brazil's Francisco Julião—rushed to proclaim their own Marxism-Leninism, and there were no indications that the segments of the masses who all along had a penchant for revolutionary solutions were repelled by Cuba's new Communist label. To a large degree, it was the old story, so successfully played out in Cuba, that the concept of Communism is largely meaningless to hungry and frustrated people and not particularly disturbing to the intellectuals.

Much of the non-Communist left in Latin America reacted with remarkable coolness to Castro's confession. As we have already seen, the United States had to live through a diplomatic nightmare at the Foreign Ministers' Conference at Punta del Este in January, 1962, before it obtained Cuba's exclusion from the Organization of American States on the grounds of her avowed Marxism-Leninism. Brazil and Mexico favored some kind of co-existence with Cuba's Communist regime, and several other governments were fearful of the internal reactions if they supported the move.

But perhaps the most interesting immediate reaction came from the Soviet Union. It took the form of utter silence. Instead of greeting Castro at once as a desirable new convert, the Soviet press and radio waited three days before even reporting. When they finally did, it was through brief and underplayed TASS dispatches from Havana. But because even in the Communist world there is a sense of *noblesse oblige, Pravda* after a while came forth with an editorial welcoming the new member of the family.

Later in December, Blas Roca and President Dorticós went to Moscow and Peking to negotiate the renewal of trade agreements. In a sense, then, Castro got his way with the Soviet Union, even though Moscow may have appeared to be the reluctant dragon. There has been unending controversy over the Soviet attitude toward having Castro force himself upon the Communist family of nations, and there has been some reasonably founded suspicion that Moscow, for its own larger tactical reasons, might have preferred to keep the ebullient Cuban at arm's length. But Castro, a specialist in facing friend and foe with *faits accomplis,* had won a kind of political alliance, with many of its implications, and had led to its logical conclusion the internal political process initiated six months earlier with the creation of the ORI.

Yet Moscow had not granted Castro all he had expected. The Premier had told a visiting Chilean Congressman that Cuba now was ready to join the Warsaw Pact, but no invitation ever came from the Soviets.

Though Castro may have been pleased with the over-all effects of his ideological coup, even despite his exclusion from the Warsaw Pact, it soon began to develop that at home he was being hoist with his own petard. To use another metaphor, the ORI, which he had ordered built, suddenly started following its own ends, like Frankenstein's monster. The signs of this state of affairs began multiplying in big and small ways. On lower levels, the ORI-directed Communist bureaucracy had assumed control of all activities in

Cuba, and Castro's original revolutionary companions were frozen out. On higher levels, the Communist leaders moved in to occupy key positions of power. Lázaro Peña, the veteran labor specialist and member of the Central Committee of the old Communist Party, took over direction of the Labor Confederation. In January, 1962, Juan Marinello, formerly the President of the Party, was named the "Magnificent Rector" of Havana University. In February, Carlos Rafael Rodríguez became the President of the Agrarian Reform Institute, thus emerging as the nominal as well as the actual boss of the Cuban economy.

Months before these appointments were made, it had become clear to observers both inside and outside of Cuba that the old-line Communist apparatus had completely taken over the country and its revolution. Castro's own importance and influence were diluted in the context of the Communist-controlled "collective leadership," and the former "Maximum Leader" gradually began to seem a mere figurehead or mouthpiece. His Fidelista friends were reduced to impotence. Whispered tales designed to discredit him and his old *"compañeros"* were circulated by the ORI organizers. The apparatus began to question the soundness of the two experiences of which Castro was proudest: the 1953 Moncada attack and the Sierra Maestra guerrilla campaign. It was becoming apparent that, in a Communist system, it was no longer enough to be a latter-day Communist and that an old-line Communist leadership could be as exclusive a club as the worst "imperialist ruling circle."

But it was not until mid-February that it began to dawn on Castro that matters had gotten out of his hands. In the preceding months, he had publicly derided all the reports made by United States observers that Fidelismo and Fidel had been elbowed out of the way by the Communists, somewhat in the self-righteous manner of the husband who not only is the last man in town to discover that his wife has taken a lover, but who cannot conceive that such a thing could happen to him.

Marital infidelity or political treason, however, cannot remain hidden forever from the most innocent husband or politician, and Castro was no exception to this age-old rule. In February, as more and more indignant reports from hapless Fidelistas reached him, Castro undertook his own investigation of what was being done to his revolution. He virtually disappeared from public view and even refrained from speechmaking. When he was seen in Havana, it was in the company of his old Sierra *comandantes,* most of whom had been out of circulation for well over a year. Reports started filtering out of Cuba of Castro's angry outbursts against the Russians and the local Communists. He was now in a slow boil and began gathering his old friends for a counterattack, particularly after discovering early in March that a large group of disenchanted Rebel Army officers had begun to plot a coup against the regime. Though he had been willing, even eager, to share his revolution with the Communists—and to embrace their ideology—Castro was not the man to accept a subordinate role in the revolution, or to give it away altogether.

To compound his problems, the new political difficulties had coincided with the worst economic crisis in the revolution's history. On March 7, 1962, drastic food rationing had to be instituted throughout Cuba. The sugar harvest, Cuba's lifeline, lay ungathered in the fields because the *guajiros* simply would not cut it, although the plantings had been much smaller than the year before. Desperate appeals by the regime to bring in the harvest before the advent of the rains, in late May, did not move the Cuban peasants, who proved that they could be just as maddeningly, stubbornly uncooperative as the kulaks of Russia had been.

In fact, what Castro had on his hands was a Cuban version of the kulaks' passive resistance. Though the propaganda organs trotted out the previous year's story of so much new employment that there was no manpower left for harvesting the sugar cane, the regime's newspapers at the same time bitterly complained that, for the *guajiros,* the weekend began on Thursday night and that, in practice, they worked only four days a week. Not only were the peasants refusing to cut cane for the regime, but a great many of them were setting the crackling dry canefields on fire, in that sullen and furtive way peasants have of sabotaging governments they dislike.

The alternate methods worked out by the frantic regime were of little avail. Army troops and militias, students and city workers organized in "volunteer brigades," could not solve the problem because they were inexperienced in the tough job of cutting cane and because many of these "volunteers" were reluctant to do the job at all. The labor force was shifted from one province to another in what amounted to little migrations, but still the cane stood in the green fields in silent defiance of the revolutionary regime. By the end of May, official statistics showed that 30 per cent of the crop was lost; if Cuba had planted the big crop of the preceding year, the loss would have exceeded 50 per cent.

As Castro remarked later, it is easy to socialize industry, but with agriculture, where each individual is a separate problem, it is a different story. He was discovering, belatedly, what every Communist regime since 1917 has learned the hard way: that the rulers can surround factories with soldiers and policemen and make the men work, but there are not enough armed guards under the sun to make each farmer plant the seed and harvest the crop. Much as he confidently repeated after Khrushchev that Communism was the "wave of the future," Castro was finding out that the system could not feed its own people in the present.

Economic hardships, combined with political resentments—both largely created by the ORI—began to erode seriously Cuba's faith in the revolution, and popular support for the regime began to dwindle very noticeably, even among the fanatical masses. Time was running out for Castro if he was to save his concept of the . revolution and his own ascendancy over the regime. The man who had betrayed his own revolution for Communism was in turn being betrayed by the Communists to whom he had handed so much power.

March, 1962, turned out to be the critical month, and it seemed as if the soothsayers had warned Castro to beware of the ides and of political annihilation at the hands of the Communist Brutuses. But one more event occurred before Castro jumped into the fray with a gusto reminiscent of his guerrilla days. This was the formal unveiling on March 8 of the permanent twenty-five-member National Directorate of the ORI, described as the island's collective leadership. The list included ten old-line Communists, among whom were all the top leaders of the Party, virtually its entire Central Committee. Aníbal Escalante, the overseer of the ORI, was high on the list. Experts on Cuban affairs assumed that the final deed had been done and that the ultimate control of the revolution by the Communist apparatus had been achieved.

Then, almost overnight, the storm broke. On March 13, Castro went to Havana University to attend a function in tribute to the memory of José Antonio Echevarría, a student leader who was killed in an attack on Batista's Palace. A Communist official, reading Echevarría's political testament, deliberately omitted the dead hero's invocation of God. Castro, who had countenanced an almost complete eradication of organized Church activity in Cuba, blew up. He said that the omission was dishonest and inexcusable and that it demonstrated the "sectarian" spirit of many ORI officials. But because in the same speech he went on to urge young Cubans to join the Communist Youth organization, this first attack on "sectarianism"—a term that came to occupy a leading place in the Fidelista demonology—went generally unnoticed.

The fact that the next day in *Hoy,* the Party newspaper, Blas Roca endorsed Castro's attack on sectarianism also contributed to lessening the impression that a serious split was developing between the Fidelistas and their Communist allies. The truth, however, was that the apparatus was in no position to pick a public quarrel with the Premier.

But on March 16, only three days after the university incident, the rest of the old Castro team went to bat. Major Guevara, removed by the Communists the previous autumn from his old post of boss of the economy, took the microphone at a "self-criticism" session at his Ministry of Industry to lash out viciously and mercilessly at the new planners of revolutionary economics.

"We made an absurd plan," he said, "disconnected from reality, with totally disorganized supplies. . . . We have entered the fourth year of the revolution with more problems than we had on the first day, so we cannot give ourselves the luxury of losing the revolutionary spirit."

The plan he mentioned was the one that Carlos Rafael Rodríguez had drafted the previous November. Denouncing it in such violent terms, Guevara clearly was in reality denouncing the old-line Communist leadership. Despite his long-standing Communist leanings, or allegiance, Guevara was primarily a Fidelista revolutionary, and he left no doubt as to where he stood.

The Fidelistas were now on the offensive, and twenty-four hours after Guevara's harangue, Castro was back at the speaking stand with another attack. Not yet mentioning names, he charged that "some people" in the ORI were sabotaging the revolution in the belief that "to be a member of the ORI means to give orders and impose or create a state within the state."

"They have destroyed authority and created problems of all types because they cannot distinguish between the functions of an administrative apparatus and the functions of the political apparatus. There are people who have a talent for hiring and firing and . . . who are capable of doing the revolution tremendous harm. They must be eliminated," he said.

In reconstructing this breath-taking chronology, it appears that the climax in the showdown between Castro and the Communist apparatus came between March 16 and 22. Acting swiftly, Castro moved not only to smash the ORI organization but also to protect his rear guard by deploying his trusted followers in key positions. Célia Sánchez, his personal secretary, was named Minister of the Presidency, as if to keep an eye on President Dorticós, whose allegiances were not too clear. Fauré Chomón, a leader of the Student Directorate of the Escambray Front and later Ambassador to Moscow, was handed the vital Communications Ministry. Raúl Curbelo, another Sierra veteran, became chief of the MIG-equipped Air Force. Raúl Castro, long ago designated Castro's successor, was formally appointed Vice-Premier, a newly created post. Then, on March 22, the Havana newspapers published the membership list of the ORI Secretariat. Castro led the list as the First Secretary, followed by Raúl and Guevara. The old Sierra trinity was back in charge of the revolution.

But the assertion of Castro's power did not—and could not—mean a drastic break with the Communists. The crisis proved that although Castro had again emerged on top of the pyramid, he still needed the Communists and they needed him. The situation was reminiscent of the old Cossack tale of the peasant who shouted to his friends that he had captured a bear, but when they urged him to bring the animal over, he replied, "I can't because he's holding me, too."

Political realism dictated that the Communists could not openly oppose Castro because of the risk of having the Fidelista masses turn on them. The masses' allegiance was primarily to Castro personally, and only secondarily to Marxism-Leninism. Castro, on the other hand, after a full year of praise for Marxism-Leninism, could not denounce Communism and all the Communists without discrediting himself and smashing the whole political structure of the revolution. Because of his international problems, he could not afford to damage his hard-won alliance with the Soviet bloc and leave himself unprotected against the United States. It was, then, a forced relationship from which neither party could fully extricate itself. A compromise was worked out, providing for the continued presence of the old Communists in the high councils of the government but with the clear understanding that the Fidelistas, or the "new" Communists, would control the political apparatus.

Accordingly, Escalante was singled out as the foremost scape-goat. He was fired from his ORI post and forced to flee to Czechoslovakia. On March 24, *Hoy* published an editorial in which, without batting an eye, it called Castro "the most responsible Marxist-Leninist in Cuba and the best of the Communists." The Communists, great masters of the tactical retreat, knew how to back down when faced with superior force.

On March 26, Castro delivered his famous five-hour speech narrating in painstaking detail the entire sordid story of the ORI and Escalante and announcing that the revolution would flush out all the other culprits. For the sake of appearances, he urged unity between "old" and "new" Communists and reaffirmed his Marxist-Leninist faith. But the furious tone of his speech left no doubt that he held the Communist apparatus responsible for the "criminal chaos" in Cuba and the attempts to undermine him and his wartime companions. He told how Escalante had placed the country in a "yoke" and how his organization—there were 500 Escalantes in Cuba, Castro said—had created a state within a state, paralyzing all administrative activities and imposing sectarianism, favoritism, and nepotism, with special privileges reserved for the "old" militants.

He recounted angrily that 100 of his wartime commanders had been deprived of positions of responsibility because they allegedly lacked political sophistication. Speaking of the Communists who had been critical of his companions-at-arms, Castro savagely accused them of having hidden under the "beds" when the revolution against Batista was being fought in the Sierra. No matter how often he kept returning to the theme of unity, his description of the vast scope of the ORI operation made it clear to his audience that not just Aníbal Escalante but the whole Communist apparatus had been behind it. And it was, indeed, hard to understand how one man could have carried out such an undertaking singlehandedly, without the blessings of his fellow Communists.

Having no other choice, the Communists rushed to endorse Castro's speech and straight-facedly pitched in with their own accusations against Escalante and "sectarians." The Premier then proceeded to carry out his own purge and revised all the basic economic policies in an attempt to save the country from impending disaster.

But although the local Communist apparatus took the Castro

offensive in stride, the Soviet Union required three full weeks to swallow both the insult and the injury. Not only had Castro dismantled the Moscow-backed organization through which the Kremlin presumably had expected to control Cuba in the orthodox way, but he committed the additional ideological sin of discontinuing the usual praise for the Soviet Union—a courtesy customarily rendered by satellites or aspiring satellites.

Moscow, however, was hardly in a position to punish Castro. The centrifugal movement of power from the great nations into the hands of their allies was afflicting the Soviet Union just as it had earlier affected the United States. Defiance of the leaders by the smaller states—violently in the case of Albania, or more subtly as in Cuba's case—was the fashion of the day. The split between the Soviets and the Chinese Communists was widening rapidly. Each of the great powers stood ready to scavenge benefits from the rebellions against the other. For broad political reasons, Moscow could not afford an open quarrel with Castro without endangering its position as the source of the "wave of the future," and Moscow finally gave its endorsement to Castro's proclamation of independence. On April 11, *Pravda* published an editorial joining in the attacks on the hapless Escalante and on sectarianism, and pronounced Castro a fine Marxist-Leninist.

But the Premier pressed his advantage, and presently he confronted Moscow with a new economic shopping list, including substantial requests for food, which, relatively, was as scarce in the Soviet bloc as in Cuba. Until then, the Soviet bloc had resisted the demands for major shipments of foodstuffs, but the new situation created by the ORI crisis, and its political implications, now made Castro's pressure irresistible. Through gentle blackmail, Castro had impressed on Moscow the notion that it could be immensely embarrassing for the Soviet Union to let the Cuban economy collapse, especially after the revolution had asserted both its independence and its continued affection for Marxism-Leninism. Thus, on May 31, the Cuban regime was able to announce that during the balance of 1962, the Soviet bloc would supply it with 600,000 tons of food.

But even the apparently successful denouement of the ORI crisis and the additional Soviet aid did not change the fact that Castro's social revolution had fallen upon dangerously hard times. It had taken another Castro speech, a careful address delivered in Matanzas on May 10, to show just how dangerously close the

Cuban revolution had come to a total breakdown economically and politically.

"We were falling into errors and deviations that were much more grave than we knew ourselves when we decided to begin to rectify them," he said. "One of the contributing factors was that a loss of faith by the people in the revolutionary leaders was taking place. . . . It was not only Comrade Fidel but it was also a series of comrades who were losing authority in the eyes of the people."

Castro went on to say that if Escalante had succeeded in his endeavors and no crisis had arisen to halt him, then it would have meant "a sort of a defeat like that of the Paris Commune, with a general collapse that would have meant for the revolutionaries the triumph of a counterrevolution."

He stressed that the ORI policies were largely responsible for the production crisis, and he acknowledged that the people had begun to realize something was wrong in the country even before the leaders had become aware of it.

In addition to these denunciations and warnings, Castro began switching in May to a new economic policy and to a careful relaxation of the revolutionary controls. He had concluded that the revolution had overreached itself and that it could founder before his eyes unless quick corrective measures were taken.

Blaming the excesses on the ORI, he spoke indignantly of people being arrested without reason by overzealous secret policemen and of unjustly confiscated farms. Some officials, he said, did not know the difference between a sugar mill and a small farm. Castro announced that these farms would be returned to their owners, and Carlos Rafael Rodríguez chimed in with the statement that the fate of the revolution was tied to the fate of the 160,000-odd smaller farmers of Cuba. They both promised that henceforth the farmers would be free to sell their produce on the open market without fear of imprisonment or confiscation.

This seemed to be a major reversal in Cuba's economic policies, clearly designed to persuade the stubborn *guajiros* to start producing food. But the new policy was short-lived. By August, the regime moved toward full-scale collectivization and later to the nationalization of retail commerce.

Castro also gave a new emphasis to the political content of the revolution, aware as ever before that no revolution can function in a vacuum. Hardly had he recovered from the ORI crisis when he began reorganizing the political foundations of his revolution and preaching his own brand of Marxist indoctrination. He insisted in the Matanzas speech that the political apparatus must be even superior to the public administration and that, having weathered *"l'affaire* Escalante," Cubans must now seek to create a "perfect" Marxist-Leninist party that could stand as a "worthy example to all the peoples of Latin America."

In calling again for Latin American revolutions on the Cuban model, Castro was returning to the ideological offensive and spreading his revolutionary gospel, now purified by the Escalante experience. Righteously asking Cubans "who said that Marxism means not to have a soul and not to have sentiments," Castro was skillfully presenting himself not as the dupe of the ORI Communists, but as the savior of the revolution and of the Cuban concept of Marxism-Leninism. He was again demonstrating his great gift for making a near disaster appear a noble victory, and through the extraordinary chemistry of his revolutionary appeal, Castro appeared to be retaining his psychological hold over his Latin American sympathizers.

The Missile Crisis

But from an international as well as internal viewpoint, Castro must have concluded that his relationship with the Soviet Union needed further cementing and that, in fact, their destinies must become virtually intertwined. Having survived the Escalante experience, Castro evidently realized that he could again become the victim of Moscow's machinations in a continuing contest for control of Cuba and her revolution. Though it obviously suited the Soviets to have a Communist-type state ensconced within the Western Hemisphere, it suited them much less to have Castro acting as an independent operator—with his own views on internal and international policies—at the financial, political, and military expense of Moscow. The Escalante affair and its handling by Castro had been a great revelation for Moscow, too.

Aware of the new Soviet attitude toward him, Castro moved in the direction of a policy that would assure him of iron-clad guarantees of military, economic, and other support from Moscow. This was a continuation of his earlier efforts to force the Soviets into a full-fledged alliance—including participation in the Warsaw Pact—so that no shift in political thinking in the Kremlin could ever bring a curtailment of support, no matter how independent Castro chose to be.

It was in this manner, then, that the Bay of Pigs and the Escalante affair spawned the great missile crisis of 1962. These two events in Cuban revolutionary history may at first glance seem unrelated, but Castro succeeded in establishing a relationship between them in terms of his own political needs.

The Escalante episode, as we have seen, convinced Castro of the urgency of tying the Soviets to Cuba's future—instead of the reverse link that exists in other satellite relationships. The Bay of Pigs, or the memories of the Bay of Pigs, became the instrument for his policy in seeking such a tie.

The precise history of how the missile crisis developed is still shrouded in mystery. We do not yet know just what the Cubans said to the Soviets and what the Soviets said to the Cubans during the crucial period running roughly from May to July, 1962. But enough clues are available to permit a sketchy reconstruction of this extraordinary occurrence.

About the time that Castro extracted the additional trade protocol from the Soviets in May, 1962, he also began to warn Moscow that a new invasion of Cuba was being prepared in the United States. It is not known exactly how the Soviets reacted initially to these warnings, but Castro had in his favor the precedent of the Bay of Pigs and the general knowledge that the fundamental Cuban policy of the Kennedy Administration remained one of somehow getting rid of the revolutionary regime.

The Soviets were, therefore, faced with the possibility that Castro might again be under an invasion threat and that he might not simply be crying wolf. If it was true that a new attack on Cuba was being prepared, then it followed that the attack would be based on United States military power, for nobody would think it possible that President Kennedy would allow a repetition of the rebel fiasco at the Bay of Pigs. Cuba's own military strength, considerable as it was, would not be sufficient to withstand an American invasion. Equivalent Soviet support was, therefore, required if Cuba was not to be overrun by the Yankee invaders.

This, apparently, was the argument first presented by the Cubans to Moscow through diplomatic channels and then reinforced during Major Raúl Castro's visit to Premier Khrushchev in July. The unsolved mystery in this situation is, of course, why the Soviets believed, or chose to believe, the Castro brothers' assertion that an invasion was imminent. As far as any well-informed person in Washington could tell, nothing was further from President Kennedy's mind in those spring months. While the desire to see the bearded Premier vanish was as great as ever, the Administration was interested in exploiting, if possible, the Communist-Fidelista quarrel that came to light in the Escalante incident. The rather naïve thinking in Washington was that since Castro had shown himself to be independent of Moscow and Communism during the Escalante affair, some kind of understanding might in time be worked out with him if his differences with Moscow could be pushed to the point of an outright split. The old-line Communists were still seen by the Administration as the chief villains in the situation, and the last thing Washington wished to do under the circumstances was to undermine Castro. This thinking emphasized again that the United States was still unable fully to understand the revolutionary dynamics of Cuba and the Florentine turn of mind of her "Maximum Leader."

To be sure, the Soviets made discreet inquiries in Washington to learn whether an invasion was being indeed prepared. Questions were asked of United States Government officials and of Washington newspaper correspondents, but by late spring, the tone of these inquiries revealed that the Russians had already convinced themselves that an invasion was coming and all they were seeking was confirmation of an a priori idea.

Whether it was Castro's idea that Soviet nuclear missiles should be stationed in Cuba, or whether this was Moscow's condition for all-out support, is a matter still open to speculation. Castro has been quoted as claiming that it was Khrushchev who insisted on the rockets in Cuba, and subsequently, Communist China accused the Kremlin of "adventurism" for having done it. Then there was the strange, almost incoherent Soviet note to the U.S. early in October tying together Cuba and the Berlin crisis, as if to suggest that through some event, the U.S. would have to capitulate on both. Evidently, the Soviet decision to install rockets on the island fitted into the Kremlin's broader policy ideas, and here, unquestionably, Premier Khrushchev was attempting to use the Cuban situation for his own Cold War purposes. Once Khrushchev made up his mind, Soviet military supplies began flowing into Cuba at a rapidly increasing rate.

Information that came to light in 1963 suggests that Khrushchev decided that the alleged invasion threat provided him with an extraordinary opportunity to gamble on establishing a sudden and dramatic tactical advantage over the United States in the nuclear power race. There are good reasons to suppose that the Cuban missile episode was his final and desperate gambit to win nuclear superiority and blackmail Washington with it. The failure of his attempt marked the end of the openly aggressive phase of Soviet postwar policies. The next phase began immediately thereafter and led to the open Chinese-Soviet split, to new attempts at co-existence with the West, and to the August, 1963, limited test-ban treaty. The Cuban crisis, therefore, will appear in retrospect as a hinge of fate upon which turned the Moscow-Peking division and the start of the coexistence period. The clandestine movement of missile-laden Soviet ships to the little Caribbean island was, then, one of those events fated to change the course of history.

When this traffic was discovered by United States intelligence, as it was bound to be, the Soviet Union and Cuba engaged in a curious maneuver designed to prove to the world that the new build-up was defensive and justified by the belligerent American posture. This became a self-perpetuating cycle: Because the United States Government expressed concern over the build-up and because Congressmen began clamoring again for action against Cuba, Havana and Moscow could take the position that American "warmongering" made the new military assistance to Castro necessary. It was a repetition of Castro's now perfected technique of inviting that which he professed to dread.

Then, because the United States increased its air and naval patrols around Cuba, Havana and Moscow pointed to this activity as irrefutable proof that Washington had aggressive designs against the Cubans. Havana daily published charges that Cuban air and sea space was being violated by the Americans. It was a cunningly contrived game in which only the Cubans and Soviets seemed to know what they were doing.

The subsequent events in the crisis are well known. In mid-October the United States discovered the presence of Soviet nuclear missiles and jet bombers in Cuba, the United States–Soviet nuclear confrontation was set in motion, and it was ultimately settled through direct Kennedy-Khrushchev negotiations.

But from Castro's viewpoint, the missile affair seemed to boomerang badly and initially did him immense political damage. The withdrawal of the missiles and bombers over his violent protest emphasized once more that Soviet and Cuban interests were not always identical and that the Kremlin was prepared to sacrifice its Caribbean associate in some measure if it suited its larger world interests. The whole fantasy of the alleged American invasion threat had been intended to establish an unbreakable bond of common interest between Moscow and Havana, but suddenly it threatened to break down over the harsh imperatives of the world situation.

And yet, Castro's own extraordinary political instinct, combined with the very real fact that neither could afford to let go of the other, in the end led to a Soviet-Cuban stabilization that resulted in the reaching of their original goal: the tacit acceptance by the Kennedy Administration of the physical inviolability of Cuba. With the collapse of the broader nuclear maneuver, at least this much was gained.

As the situation developed, the period between October and the end of 1962 was given over to a reformulation of the Soviet-Cuban relations, beginning with a long visit to Havana by Anastas I. Mikoyan, a First Deputy Premier, who had laid the cornerstone of the alliance two and a half years earlier, and ending in painful economic negotiations in Moscow in December. At that stage, the only known Soviet concession to Havana was the permission to release for direct sales on the world market about 1 million tons of sugar from the quota earmarked for the Soviet bloc. This allowed Castro to earn some hard currency to build up his reserves.

Though relations between the Soviets and Cuba would never be precisely the same again, both sides had a stake in maintaining a considerable degree of cooperation. Castro could not afford to break openly with Moscow—he literally had no other place to go—and the Soviet Union could not afford to let Cuba collapse, particularly after Communist China voiced loud charges that the withdrawal of the missiles had been a "Munich" and a betrayal. Thus, as in that old Cossack anecdote, the bear and the peasant went on holding each other in a desperate embrace. In February, 1963, this relationship produced the further Soviet agreement to grant Cuba several hundred million dollars in additional import credits. This was the prelude to Castro's triumphant Soviet visit two months later.

At home, the frictions between the old-line Communists and the Fidelistas erupted again and in a much more serious manner than at the time of the Escalante incident. Castro this time was determined to assert his complete control over the country. The power of his personality and his political apparatus broke down the resistance of the orthodox Communists. In the strange way in which the emphasis keeps changing in Cuban affairs, the old Communists suddenly began to look to Washington like "good guys," relatively speaking, while the Fidelistas acquired the reputation of being the "bad guys."

Here, the new theory was that the old-line Communists, presumably representing the Moscow views on world affairs—including "peaceful coexistence"—could be more amenable, while the Fidelistas appeared to be hugging the "Chinese line," which urged immediate revolutions throughout Latin America. But, again, this thinking showed Washington's confusion over what was really happening in Cuba.

What was really happening was that Castro had to regain balance, while the basic problem of his relationship with Moscow was not quite solved. In his classical Florentine style, he launched a new line of maneuver. It was still the line of subtle blackmail of the Soviets—this time designed to force them to continue supporting him economically and to maintain their conventional military establishment on the island while recognizing his status as the real "Maximum Leader" in Havana—but now the tool in Castro's hands was the Soviet-Chinese split. However, the outside observer had to keep in mind what fundamental interests were involved, and it was important, in making judgments, not to mistake political maneuvering for a real split.

In two speeches in January, 1963, Castro announced that Cuba was equidistant in the Moscow-Peking ideological dispute, which meant, in effect, that he seemed to move far toward espousing the Chinese line. Only a year earlier, by contrast, the ORI delegation in Moscow had firmly supported Premier Khrushchev against the Chinese and the Albanians. In the same speeches, Castro returned to a violent advocacy of immediate revolutions in Latin America—again taking the Chinese ideological line against the gradualist Soviet approach. Simultaneously, United States intelligence services reported that Cuban propaganda, financial, and infiltration efforts in Latin American countries had risen sharply since the October crisis.

As 1963 opened, Castro appeared determined to play his final revolutionary card in Latin America, aware that the missile crisis and a general reshuffling of Hemispheric political attitudes had made his direct appeal in the region decline to its lowest level in four years. As a United States diplomat remarked at the time, Castro's heart was in Peking, his stomach was in Moscow, and his battlefield was in Latin America.

Late in April, 1963, as the Soviet-Chinese ideological confrontation approached, Castro flew to the Soviet Union to be received there as no foreigner had ever been received before. He reviewed the May Day parade at Khrushchev's side atop the Lenin Mausoleum, and the two men spent the next five weeks together in interminable discussions. By the end of May, the deal was finally concluded. A lengthy joint communiqué repeatedly underlined Cuba's devotion to "peaceful coexistence"—the political concession Castro granted Khrushchev—while the Soviet Union committed itself to go on supporting Cuba to the hilt. Soviet troops —some 13,000 men—remained on the island, Castro was given recognition as the indisputable high priest of revolutionary Communism in Latin America, and the price for his sugar was increased.

Almost a year after the missile crisis had been first conceived, it seemed to have finally paid off for Castro. The United States was effectively at bay, Castro acted as if he were a full partner with Khrushchev in the political councils of Communism, and he was assured of an uninterrupted flow of Soviet material aid.

Yet, the inexorable course of world events again conspired to change the Havana-Moscow relationship, even before the ink could dry on the joint communiqué. The May agreement with Khrushchev may have created the impression that Cuba and the Soviet Union had found a lasting basis for a mutually profitable relationship, but the consummation of the Chinese-Soviet split in July, and the subsequent signing of the nuclear-test-ban treaty between Moscow and the Anglo-Saxon powers, threatened to shatter this basis.

This Soviet-American *rapprochement,* followed by the promise of new agreements, suddenly shifted all the world relationships, leaving Castro in a dramatically exposed position. With the bitter experience of the October, 1962, Soviet pull-back on the missiles, Castro now began to have acute fears that another deal with him as the pawn might be concluded between Moscow and Washington. Simultaneously, as a by-product of its feud with China, the Soviets began denouncing the line of violent revolutions, so dear to Castro's heart.

Predictably, Castro's reaction was of the usual Florentine variety—here involving blackmail. First, he delayed adhering to the test-ban treaty; Cuba had not signed up to the end of September, though more than ninety other nations had done so. Among the Communist bloc, Cuba's apparent opposition to the treaty was shared by China and Albania—the two anti-Soviet hard-liners—and North Vietnam and North Korea, still trying to remain on the fence in the Moscow-Peking rivalry. Pointedly, Castro told diplomats at a Brazilian Embassy reception early in September that nobody, "but nobody," dictated Cuba's foreign policy, and that he could not say whether or when she would join the pact.

As it turned out, she never did, and as the first anniversary of the treaty's signature came in August, 1964, Havana along with China and *her* followers remained in the ranks of Communist opponents of the test ban.

Economically, Cuba's position had become so difficult that in mid-1963, the regime had to order a fundamental policy change in its approach to revolutionary economics. Whereas the battle cry of the Castro revolution in 1959 had been to end Cuba's dependence on sugar and to seek diversification and industrialization, by 1963 this policy was declared to have been erroneous.

Having destroyed their sugar economy—the 1963 crop was 3.8 million tons as compared to 7.0 million tons in 1957—the Cubans, again acting under Soviet pressure, decided that, after all, sugar was again to be the mainstay of their economy. Castro took to the radio to promise that by 1970, Cuba would produce 10.0 million tons of sugar and, in effect, control the world market.

But the 1964 harvest, estimated at even less than the previous year's 3.8 million tons, made it doubtful that the goal set by Castro would be fulfilled on schedule. Further, the high world sugar prices that had prevailed in 1963 dropped alarmingly by mid-1964, destroying Castro's hopes for a long-lasting bonanza. The 1963 prices had made it possible for Cuba to accumulate a promising reserve of foreign exchange and to turn to Western Europe for purchases of buses and locomotives—briefly threatening to break the United States blockade—but late in 1964, Cuban trade prospects again seemed bleak.

As the sixth year of the Cuban revolution neared completion late in 1964, its stresses, weaknesses, and contradictions remained unresolved. But, at the same time, there was little or nothing to indicate that these pressures would result in a change in Cuba in the foreseeable future.

5.   The Reaction

The Cuban Impact

THE CUBAN REVOLUTION in its peculiar form or in any of its possible violent variations may never find imitators in Latin America. With the present perspective of nearly six years on the Castro phenomenon and its repercussions in the Hemisphere, it may be possible to argue that it is by no means certain the great Latin American revolution will join the Communist families of revolution. Although flat predictions are ruled out by the very nature of Latin American politics, it does appear that a new dimension of revolution—intellectual rather than violent—may be evolving in the region.

But whatever course is ultimately taken by the Latin American revolution, the pivotal importance and influence of the Cuban revolution in Hemispheric history can never be erased. In launching his revolution, Fidel Castro released an uncontrollable genie from its bottle, and five years later, the genie still hovered over the Hemisphere.

To be sure, the potential for a great revolution has existed for decades throughout Latin America. That in Cuba it became clothed in the Communist ideology was perhaps an accident of history and an outgrowth of the Cold War. But fundamentally, the revolution was a logical historical development—quite aside from the ideology that subsequently captured it.

The Western response to the revolution that thus exploded in the Caribbean was the American-sponsored Alliance for Progress, which the Kennedy Administration inaugurated in March, 1961—two years and two months after Castro's rise to power—to foster a peaceful and evolutionary process in Latin America. It was suddenly discovered that a "revolution of rising expectations" had come to this vast region, and in the pragmatic ways of the Anglo-

Saxon West, Washington proposed as an alternative "evolution instead of revolution."

That two years and two months elapsed between the Cuban explosion and the West's political and philosophical response was clear proof that the opulent and affluent nations had lost the habit of revolutionary thought and action. Though the United States from the outset proclaimed its own revolutionary heritage, the slowness and caution of its response to this new revolutionary challenge showed again that it had not yet come to terms with the revolutionary present.

Unquestionably, however, the Cuban revolution has performed a major historical function, not only because it awakened new aspirations and anxieties among Latin Americans but also because it did, belatedly, produce the Western response of the Alliance for Progress.

As far as Latin America was concerned, the advent and the march of the Cuban revolution affected the region in an extraordinary variety of ways. Its effects have ranged over the years from the hopeful and starry-eyed reaction of 1959 to today's uncomfortable but resigned acceptance of Castro's climactic and defiant identification with Marxism-Leninism. Not even the stationing of thousands of Soviet troops on the island and the installation of Soviet nuclear missiles there could bring a full-fledged rejection of the Cuban revolution by Latin America, and five governments continued to maintain diplomatic relations with Havana during and after the missile crisis of October, 1962.

Though all the governments agreed, with more or less reluctance, that Cuba's Marxism-Leninism was incompatible with the Hemispheric principles of democracy, five of them opposed Cuba's exclusion from the Organization of American States at the January, 1962, conference of American Foreign Ministers at Punta del Este. All of them joined in endorsing the United States actions that led to the removal of the Soviet missiles from the island, but the five governments—Bolivia, Brazil, Chile, Mexico, and Uruguay—recoiled from any further pressure on Havana once the offensive weapons were dismantled and evacuated. Brazil remained an outspoken advocate of coexistence with Cuba, while Mexico continued to serve as the bridge for communications between the revolutionary island and the rest of the Hemisphere.

By early 1964, it became increasingly unlikely that the pressures by the United States, despite Cuba's growing difficulties and inner contradictions, could bring the collapse of the Castro regime in the foreseeable future. Regardless of its ultimate fate, however, the Cuban revolution as an accomplished fact has altered forever all the internal and external relationships in the Hemisphere and modified all the balances of forces. The genie was out of the bottle, the political and psychological clock could not be set back, and the existence of a major historical process could not be ignored.

To assess the relationship of the Cuban situation to the larger picture of the Latin American social revolution—always remembering that Castro unleashed certain forces but did not invent them—it is necessary to examine the political reactions the Cuban phenomenon evoked in the United States and the Hemisphere. These reactions must be considered first in terms of their individual national components—nationalism, foreign policy, and the state of democracy in each country—and then in the context of subsequent occurrences, such as the Alliance for Progress and the shrinking of United States power in Latin America.

The American Response

The first phase of United States and Latin American reaction to the Cuban revolution is comprised in the twenty months between Castro's victory in January, 1959, and the signing of the Act of Bogotá by the Hemisphere's Finance and Economy Ministers in September, 1960. The advocacy of this act by the United States —after the Eisenhower Administration had reached the point of no return in its bitter quarrel with the Castro regime—marked the end of its hollow policy of "patience and tolerance" toward Cuba and the belated beginning of its understanding of Latin America's immense potential for social revolution. The Act of Bogotá laid the foundation for the concept of self-help by Latin America to be matched by United States aid, implemented through the new Inter-American Development Bank. It thus became the forerunner of the Alliance for Progress, and for the first time, there was recognition of the need for social improvement alongside economic growth.

The "patience and tolerance" policy made considerable if limited sense in the early days of the Cuban revolution, for Washington realized that it would be unpolitic to hit hard at Cuba at a time when the image of Castro reforms was firing Latin

America's imagination. Despite the growing and deliberate Cuban provocations, the United States displayed remarkable and commendable self-restraint in dealing with Castro and his revolution. The underlying policy thinking in Washington was that in demonstrating monumental tolerance for the revolutionary excesses, the United States would acquire an unassailable moral stature in the eyes of Latin Americans, who would then turn away in disgust from Castro and side with the Yankees in the cause of anti-Jacobin reason.

But the trouble with this policy was that it contained built-in limitations: the underestimating of Castro as an adversary and the American inability to perceive at that time the depth of revolutionary sentiment uncorked by the Cubans. It was a policy fatally flawed by an astounding lack of imagination, by facile simplicity, and by that extraordinary talent for being patronizing that United States bureaucracy—and even United States public opinion—has perfected almost to the status of a suicidal art.

"Patience and tolerance" was a good idea as far as it went, but it was an essentially negative enterprise, having no real objective beyond the implausible hope, nurtured by wishful thinking, that Castro and his revolution would vanish in thin air. While the Cubans hurled at the United States the great challenge of the Latin American social revolution and set the Hemisphere tingling with excitement and anticipation, Washington insouciantly, or naïvely, chose to ignore this defiance.

It is, of course, easy to render hindsight judgments, but in terms of the alertness of American policy to historical developments, it may be valid to inquire why it was eighteen or twenty months before the Act of Bogotá was set in motion and why the United States waited more than two years before proclaiming the Alliance for Progress. Both policies were almost casual improvisations. The idea of the Act of Bogotá emerged from an Eisenhower announcement at a Newport, Rhode Island, golf course late in July, 1960, and it became a reality six weeks later; the Alliance was invented aboard a Kennedy campaign bus in Texas about December of the same year, and it was fashioned into a major prop of United States foreign policy less than two months after the new President took office. Since the United States is blessed with such a gift for spectacular improvisation—and with vast funds available to back it up—is it not bewildering that this country waited so long to unveil its counteroffensive against Castro on the plane of social revolution?

Again, there was no lack of encouragement to the United States in these opening months of the Cuban revolution to try and steal Castro's thunder by responding to his challenge with a democratic social revolution—something that in the end Washington decided to attempt, belatedly and awkwardly. There was the indefatigable President Kubitschek of Brazil, single-mindedly pushing his "Operation Pan American" in the face of continuing incomprehension in Washington of what was behind the Cuban revolution and what its repercussions were likely to be. There were the appeals from Latin America's great liberal leaders, like Colombia's President Lleras Camargo and Venezuela's President Betancourt, urging some sort of grandiose and imaginative United States approach to the new realities of the Hemisphere. And there was finally—and ironically—Fidel Castro appearing in his olive-green fatigues at the Buenos Aires conference of the "Committee of 21" in May, 1959, proposing half-seriously that the United States earmark $30 billion for Latin America's development in the next ten years. Two years later, the United States earmarked $20 billion for it.

But in 1959, the immobilism of the Washington bureaucracy and its lack of historical and political imagination were still supreme. The principal reaction emanating from the Department of State was that it would be just too crude for the United States to embark on something like "Operation Pan American" only to placate the new Latin American appetites aroused by an unsophisticated Caribbean revolution. Officials talked derisively of Latin American hopes for a Marshall Plan, pointing out that the problem was that the Brazilians and all the others were simply hoping to get something for themselves out of the Cuban revolution.

The Eisenhower Administration and principally its foreign-policy architect, Secretary of State Dulles, were fascinated with the power plays in Europe and the Near and Far East, concentrating on the Cold War in the great traditional world arenas and relegating Latin America to the bottom of their list of concerns. Less than four years later, Washington pleaded with its allies to recognize that Cuba was squarely in the midst of the Cold War.

But as the summer of 1959 came and the freshly proclaimed Cuban land-reform law was fast becoming the talk of Latin

America, the United States became embroiled in an unnecessary dispute with Brazil over financial stabilization policies and her relations with the very orthodox International Monetary Fund. This dispute is worth mentioning because the situation at its root was a fundamental issue that the Alliance for Progress has to face today just as it had to be faced by the Eisenhower Administration in the preceding years. It remains to be seen whether the Johnson Administration will have any greater success with this problem.

For a number of years, the United States had made it a condition of financial assistance to countries with balance-of-payments problems that the assistance programs be tied to the International Monetary Fund's policies of currency stabilization. The reasoning behind this was that dollar aid from the United States or the Fund would not produce lasting effects unless the recipient country committed itself to certain stabilization measures—such as combating inflation and related steps in the field of credit control, governmental expenditures, import restrictions, currency printing, and administrative and fiscal orderliness. In the case of many European countries—France and Turkey, for example—and in most of Latin America, United States financial-assistance programs were conditioned upon the signing of stabilization agreements between the Fund and the recipient governments. In theory, it was a highly sound policy, particularly in Latin America, where fiscal irresponsibility often reached poetic heights inasmuch as the local governments found it easier to clamor for United States aid than to adopt politically dangerous and unpopular anti-inflation measures. Both Washington and the Fund took the rational view that balance-of-payments loans under such circumstances were money down the drain, creating no new sources of economic wealth in the Latin American countries and only adding to their already staggering external debts. But the drawback of this policy was that, implemented by bureaucrats and dogmatic economists, it was too inflexible in its execution, failing to take into consideration the political realities in each country.

In the particular case of Brazil, the problem of inflation and of external and internal deficits was not only monumental in scope but also immensely disheartening from the viewpoint of those in Washington who sincerely hoped to help the country out of its financial and economic morass. With the vastly ambitious economic-development program of the Kubitschek Administration and the uncontrollable dynamism of the Brazilian society, infla-

tion had become both a source of nourishment and a scourge
striking directly at the country's foundations. Where money could
not be found to finance the great adventure of national development, it was borrowed from anybody who made it available at
any rate of interest, or it was simply printed in dizzying cascades
of orange-colored 1,000-cruzeiro bills. The peculiar political
make-up of Kubitschek's government, and his personal dislike
of policies tending to antagonize any group in the population,
led Brazil to continuous violations of its stabilization agreements
with the Monetary Fund. But by June, 1959, Brazil was again
in dire financial straits and it again appealed to the Fund and to
the United States for relief.

The Fund replied by insisting that a new stabilization agreement
be signed. Washington then announced that it would not lend
Brazil one cent unless Dr. Kubitschek made his peace with the
international monetary authorities. To act differently, the United
States stressed, would be to undermine all the other financial
programs throughout the world. The attempt to try to force Brazil
to behave responsibly was a logical consequence of a basically
sound general policy. But the inflexible manner in which it was
handled succeeded only in stirring up a nest of political hornets
—with Dr. Kubitschek doing a great deal of the stirring himself
and demonstrating how readily an otherwise moderate and responsible Latin American leader will, when in a fit of pique,
embark on a wild flight of demagoguery.

Annoyed by the steadfast position of the Fund and of the United
States and possibly frustrated by the cool reception continually
given his "Operation Pan American," Dr. Kubitschek took to the
microphone to denounce the "slavery" of the Fund and to charge
that it and the United States were seeking to force Brazil into
social convulsions. Such convulsions, he insisted, would inevitably
result from the anti-inflation measures proposed by the Fund. He
then invited Luiz Carlos Prestes, the General Secretary of the
Brazilian Communist Party, to join him in a round of speechmaking in the gardens of the Presidential Palace. The two spent
some time in ringing denunciations of their enemies in the Fund
and in Washington, as American officials in Rio de Janeiro gasped
in disbelief.

In the actions of both sides, Brazilian and American, the Fund
dispute provided a classic lesson on how two friendly governments
should not behave. Dr. Kubitschek gained nothing by his petulance,

except in adding a head of steam to the rising Brazilian ultra-nationalism that the Communists were avidly encouraging. The United States lost a chance to carry out some imaginative and skillful diplomacy. As it was, the incident—played out under the shadow of the Cuban revolution—helped to harden the image of the United States in Brazil as an inflexible banker doing its heartless business as usual among the gathering clouds of the social revolution. Politically speaking, it was too much to expect from the oversensitive Brazilian public opinion that the economically sound motives of United States policy at that moment should be fully and seriously appreciated.

A similar but less spectacular dispute arose at the same time between Peru on one hand and the Fund and the United States on the other. Elsewhere in Latin America, the approach of the United States to the urgent problems of development remained as conservative as ever, with continuing emphasis on stabilization programs and on encouragement of private foreign capital. Imagination played no role at all in policy, though a social revolution was rumbling menacingly within the confines of the Hemisphere.

All of 1959 and the first half of 1960—the first eighteen months of the Cuban revolution—were thus spent by the United States in a motionless contemplation of the rising social revolution. Washington still hoped, or appeared to hope, that its policy of "patience and tolerance" would solve the problems created in the Hemisphere by the Cuban revolution, although the stubborn absence of an imaginative follow-up for this rigid attitude made it quite unlikely even to the most casual observer of the passing scene.

When it finally became clear that Castro and his revolution would not go away and that the contagion of the social revolution was spreading in Latin America instead of being erased by Washington's conservative righteousness, the Eisenhower Administration switched to a new Cuban policy—but still refused to fit it into a larger Hemispheric approach. The central preoccupation was that Castro was violently anti-United States and probably pro-Communist, and therefore, the policy became focused on destroying him physically rather than undercutting him politically.

By March, 1960, General Eisenhower authorized the training of anti-Castro rebels in Guatemala and Florida for what was to be the following year's invasion. Washington had become reconciled to the notion that force in one form or another would have to be used to put an end to the Cuban experiment. In July, economic sanctions of great magnitude were applied to Castro with the cutting of the Cuban sugar quota in the premium-bearing United States market. The step was taken as the direct result of unceasing Cuban provocations that culminated a few days earlier in the seizure of American-owned oil refineries and other properties. With the training of a military force in Guatemala and the cutting of the sugar quota, the United States finally dropped its sterile "patience and tolerance" policy and embarked openly on the course of seeking the destruction of the Castro regime as a danger to itself and to the Hemisphere.

Only then was a thoughtful effort made to relate the Cuban problem to the question of the Latin American social revolution. As Washington officials worked on the preparations for a Foreign Ministers' conference that they hoped would condemn Castro, simultaneous plans were made for a social-development fund for Latin America and a new economic policy in the Hemisphere.

The news that the United States would become actively engaged in assisting social progress in Latin America was announced by General Eisenhower in Newport a few weeks after the Cuban sugar quota was cut. Whatever may be said of this coincidence and of the disturbing lateness of the decision, it was a major breakthrough in United States policy toward the Hemisphere and the starting point for what was to emerge later as the Alliance for Progress.

In its own way, the new approach was quite revolutionary as United States policies went. Until then, Washington had taken the traditional position that official aid to Latin America should consist only of balance-of-payment loans or Export-Import Bank loans for specific industrial and related projects. The underlying philosophy had been that foreign private capital should be the mainspring of Latin American economic development and that official loans should complement it only in special areas to which private investments were not attracted. Thus, American money had been made available for carefully engineered power projects or steel mills—such as Brazil's Volta Redonda—as well as for harbor improvement, railroad modernization, occasional roads, and a host of other infrastructure undertakings.

The so-called social aspect of development—land distribution, housing, schools, and hospitals—should, in Washington's view, be carried out by the countries themselves. Since these projects were not profit-generating, private capital had no interest in them. As a matter of policy, the United States had not financed them from official funds. And since the inflation-ridden underdeveloped countries of Latin America, with their immense budget deficits and vast civil-service payrolls, could spare no funds for these social projects, they had been undertaken only in spotty areas and on a totally inadequate scale. The furiously growing populations added to the magnitude of the social problem and fanned the revolutionary winds that nobody seemed disposed to try and control. That Latin America's traditional inability to harness its own resources for development had long been responsible for the mounting pressures, did not change the urgent realities of the moment.

The extent of the human and social neglect in Latin America was so vast—the heritage of centuries—that to secure means for remedying it on its own, each Latin American country would have to embark upon a fantastic program of money-printing and inflation that would probably wreck it instead of accomplishing the objective. The inevitable solution, therefore, appeared to be United States aid on a selective basis—at least until some stability was attained and Latin America learned how to use its own capital resources.

The first step in persuading the United States of the need for assuming responsibilities in the realm of social development in Latin America—as both a deterrent to revolutions and as a means of strengthening the social structures—came from Peru's Pedro Beltrán, then Prime Minister. Drawing on his long-standing personal friendships in Washington, on his successful stabilization policies, and on his powers of persuasion, Beltrán convinced the Eisenhower Administration in July, 1960, to agree to a loan of nearly $60 million for land reform, low-cost housing, and the building of "penetration" roads in the jungle and in the Andes.

The disbursement of the funds was to depend, however, on the passage by the Peruvian Congress of enabling legislation for land reform and an agrarian institute and for the creation of a system of savings and loan associations for cheap housing. This, in effect, was the germ of the idea of self-help that through the Act of Bogotá and the Alliance for Progress was to become the foundation of the whole cooperative development program. That in the subsequent two years the Peruvian Congress failed to approve the land-reform legislation, and thus prevented the disbursement of the

United States loans, is a tragic second act in the drama of American aid to Latin America and a problem that today is plaguing the Alliance for Progress almost everywhere in the Hemisphere.

The Act of Bogotá, calling for the creation of a social-progress fund and setting forth the self-help obligations of the Latin Americans, was thus an outgrowth of Señor Beltrán's earlier campaign of persuasion. But by the time Eisenhower announced the program and committed the United States to an initial investment of a half-billion dollars, the concept of social development already had also won the strong support of Under Secretary of State Douglas Dillon and Assistant Secretary for Inter-American Affairs Thomas C. Mann.

Dillon and Mann went to Bogotá in early September, a few weeks after the conference of American Foreign Ministers at San José, Costa Rica, had grievously disappointed the United States by refusing even to name Cuba in a vague resolution deploring the acceptance of Sino-Soviet military aid by an American state. No political *quid pro quo* thinking, however, had been involved on the part of the United States in unveiling the social-fund ideas in Bogotá.

At the economic conference, Dillon and Mann ran into the unexpected opposition of the big Latin American governments, notably Brazil and Argentina, to the new social-development notion as well as to the suggestions that the Hemisphere countries embark on land, taxation, and other reforms as the condition for United States aid.

The argument of these countries was that since they had already reached a relatively high degree of development, their needs were not for land reform, housing, or other social-purpose aid but for massive infusions of United States public capital to finance economic growth—and preferably with no strings attached. If great new sources of wealth and production were created, they contended, then the social problem would take care of itself through high employment and the consequent rise in living standards. While the special-fund concept might be all right for such backward countries as Haiti, Ecuador, or Bolivia, they argued, the big countries required fundamentally huge sums of economic-development money.

The United States response was that economic growth on such a scale would, of necessity, be a long-range undertaking and that it would be difficult if not impossible for any country to build almost overnight an industrial society based upon an uneducated, undernourished, ill-housed, and unhealthy population. The point made by the Americans and opposed by many Latinos in a surprising reversal of traditional attitudes was that man and not dams and machines must be the cornerstone of a nation's progress. United States delegates were sufficiently tactful not to stress that Brazil, and to a lesser extent Argentina, suffered from awesome human and social problems.

An understanding was finally reached on the basis that the creation of the social fund would not exclude subsequent economic-development projects.

Inevitably, the Bogotá conference hall felt the shadow of the Cuban revolution—given body by the harangues of the Cuban delegation—and after the participants went home, the comments about this new $500 million United States social fund were often accompanied by the sarcastic aside, "Gracias, Fidel!" Yet, late as it was, the United States had made its first headlong plunge into the unfathomably deep ocean of the Latin American social revolution. And as time went by and new policies emerged, the United States became more and more inextricably tied to this overwhelming historical movement.

The Emotions

The differing United States and Latin American attitudes and views on the questions of rapid economic and social development were only one aspect of the total reaction to the Cuban revolution. Deeper and incomparably more important were the political, psychological, and emotional repercussions because they colored the basic national behavior in the face of the Cuban phenomenon and in relation to the United States and to the Cold War. In fact, the prime historical function of the Cuban revolution was to serve as a catalyst in releasing pent-up sentiments of nationalism and general protest against all the old ways.

Before the Cuban revolution, the internal upheavals in the Latin American republics were judged and evaluated on their own, at most, in terms of what now seemed to be such relatively simple Hemispheric patterns as the transition in the 1950's from military dictatorships to a tenuous form of representative democracy.

The 1958 Venezuelan revolution that ousted Pérez Jiménez was the last of these eruptions that could be considered as essentially a domestic event, not really connected with the great movements sweeping the world. Castro's rebellion against Batista was believed to be likewise a local Cuban situation until it suddenly and dramatically became clear that the bearded chieftain from the Sierra Maestra had launched a major social revolution aimed at his own country and at the rest of Latin America and that he proposed to link it to one of the two great ideologies struggling for control of the world.

After the emergence of the Cuban revolution, therefore, every political development of some significance in Latin America was immediately—but not always accurately—related to the exploding social revolution, a concept that rapidly became a household word and the new cliché of the dawning decade of the 1960's.

Attitudes toward the whole problem of Latin America's future, the Alliance for Progress, and the United States thus became politically motivated because, inevitably, social revolutions in potential or in actual development must have a political content. The fatal weakness of the United States policy in Latin America in response to the Cuban revolution—even long after the Alliance for Progress was launched—was that it blindly insisted on ignoring this political syndrome and stubbornly sought to deal with the seething Hemisphere on a purely technical level of massive economic and social development. Even as late as 1964, it was not fully understood in Washington that the success—even the acceptance—of the Alliance for Progress as a workable cooperative scheme hinged to an immense extent on its political impact on the Latin Americans.

Indeed, Latin American reactions to the Cuban revolution, to the Alliance, to the United States, and to the Cold War were intrinsically inseparable. The reluctance by some of the big and small Latin American nations to go along with collective action against Cuba—even after Castro's public espousal of Marxism-Leninism and the disclosure of the Soviet military and nuclear presence on the island—was related to their views on how the Alliance should or should not be conducted. The new phenomenon of the erosion of United States political power in Latin America, so evident after the Cuban revolution in countries like Brazil, was similarly a part of these immensely complex and still undefined attitudes. And so was the readiness of Brazil—and, to a lesser extent, several of the other republics—to engage in active relationships with the Communist bloc and to move toward a form of "independent" foreign policy frankly bordering on neutralism.

Many of the Latin American attitudes in response to the Cuban revolution may be explained through the curious parallel between the Hemisphere situation after 1959 and wartime events in China. The Chinese Communist movement gained a considerable degree of acceptance among Chinese liberals beginning in 1942 and 1943, primarily as a reaction against the corruption and the high-handedness of the Kuomintang during the war against Japan, and the Fidelista revolution won great sympathies in Latin America for roughly similar reasons.

While much of that sympathy was subsequently forfeited after Cuba turned to Communism—particularly among the liberals of the more mature Latin American generation—a vast residue of good will toward the Cuban revolution did remain. In part, it was a sense of identification with the over-all revolutionary concept that appealed to Latin American youth in a manner transcending all reservations about the Communist or totalitarian character of the Cuban experiment. In part, it was the belief that what Castro did in Cuba represented the opening of a new era of emancipation from traditional and exaggerated United States influence—and this desire for real or imagined emancipation is one of the funda-mental cravings now sweeping Latin America. And, finally, the continuing sympathy for Cuba—her Communism notwithstanding—finds its roots in the growing disenchantment of Latin American youth with the system of life and government that is known as Western representative democracy. Among the many elusive and often contradictory feelings now rising in the Hemisphere is an un-definable malaise that can only be described as a "weariness of the West."

Having mentioned the Chinese parallel in explaining some of the Latin American reactions to the Cuban revolution, one must also note the very considerable influence exercised by Communist China in the Hemisphere even before Castro's appearance on the scene and before the repercussions of the Sino-Soviet ideological split. Although no Latin American government—except, of course, Castro's Cuba—maintains official relations with the Peking regime, the impact of China on Hemisphere thinking is actually much greater than that of the Soviet Union and of her satellites. While the Soviet Union and her East European partners have active embassies in Argentina, Brazil, Mexico, and Uruguay (as well as in Cuba), and enjoy increasing trade and cultural ties with Latin America, Communist China holds much deeper interest and appeal for the Hemisphere's younger politicians and intellectuals. Though some of this appeal may be traced to the fact that China's antipodal exoticism in itself is intriguing to Latin Americans, Chinese influence ranges well beyond the realm of curiosity and novelty. Indeed, it may have highly significant implications for the political future of the Hemisphere.

The first—and more general—point of contact between Latin America and China is that the Hemisphere experiences a considerable feeling of identification between its current problems and aspirations and those of the Chinese Communists. Both Latin America and China are essentially agrarian societies, traditionally suffering from land-distribution and land-tenure problems. Both have been faced with the immense, if not impossible, task of trying to feed and clothe their huge populations. Both desire— for emotional as well as economic reasons—a rapid process of industrialization in order to free themselves from their backward status. Both are human societies equipped with extraordinary latent or actual dynamism.

Significantly, the Peking regime's Communist ideology and its oppressive system do not seem greatly to disturb the Latin Americans, who are so impressed by what they think they see as the accomplishments of the Chinese revolution in land reform, in industrialization, and in emancipation from Western influences. The attraction, therefore, is to the revolutionary image. Considerations of ideology and of the political and personal liberties of the Chinese are subordinated to the central interest in Peking's real or alleged achievements. The net result is that scores of Latin American leaders, who vociferously defend freedom and democracy at home, unprotestingly accept the fact of Communism in China just as they now do in Cuba.

This reaction emerges with considerable clarity from reports by outstanding Latin Americans who have visited Communist China in the last five or six years. Dozens of books, articles, and speeches almost uniformly praising China—or at least showing a grudging admiration for it—have been written by Latin American Congressmen, intellectuals, artists, and labor- and student-union members on their return from guided tours of the Chinese mainland. In issuing their invitations, the Chinese have been imaginative enough to concentrate on known non-Communists and on respected liberals of slightly leftist leanings, presumably on the sound theory that praise from Party-liners would not evoke much credibility and

would do little to influence local public opinion in favor of relations with Peking, peasant revolutions, and anti-Western doctrines.
Latin American Communists who travel to China are not expected
to write books when they go home; other tasks are expected of
them.

It is interesting to note that João Goulart, then Brazil's Vice-
President, was in Peking heaping praise on the Chinese regime when
he was propelled to the Presidency by Jânio Quadros' resignation in
August, 1961. Hélio Almeida, a noted Brazilian engineer, toured
China in 1962 as a non-Communist guest, and on his return was
named by Goulart to be Minister of Public Works. He later returned to private life as Goulart kept reshuffling his Cabinets.

In the context of Latin American revolutionary sentiment, the
travelers to China not surprisingly show a rather limited interest
in the Soviet Union, which they usually cross on their way to and
from Peking. For all those who are not faithful Moscow-line Communists, the Soviet Union, in contrast to Red China, is already a
country of *status quo* and does not offer the revolutionary excitement that the Latin Americans feel to be emanating from Peking.

This Latin American attitude toward China and the Soviet Union
is already reflected within the local Communist parties and other
extremist revolutionary groups. Although all the Latin American
parties, including Cuba's, lined up with Premier Khrushchev in his
controversy over Albania with the Chinese at the Twenty-second
Congress of the Soviet Communist Party in February, 1962, a
strong "Chinese" current could nevertheless be detected at that
time among them. In 1963, the big Brazilian and Venezuelan
parties were visibly split over doctrine, and Castro was advertising
himself as an example of unity for the "socialist family."

Essentially, the difference between the Moscow and Peking
revolutionary doctrines that concerns Latin America is that the
Russians still advocate the gradual takeover through "national
fronts" and, whenever possible, in cooperation with the "progressive
bourgeoisie," while the Chinese and the Cubans frankly prefer outright rebellion.

Ideologically, this difference has its roots in the basic interpretation of Marxism-Leninism. The Chinese believe in the inevitability
of violent revolutions—as they believe in the inevitability of the
war against "imperialism"—and the Russians think that the same
objective can be achieved by the inevitable, if peaceful, collapse of
"capitalistic" regimes.

Following the open Chinese-Soviet split in the summer of 1963, it became clear that Moscow actually feared violent Latin American revolutions because they could complicate its delicate relationship with the United States and because such upheavals could lead to the establishment of pro-Chinese—and, therefore, anti-Soviet—regimes in the Hemisphere. As part of this mounting contest with Peking for Communist allegiances in the underdeveloped countries, the Kremlin issued urgent warnings that premature rebellions could "compromise" premanently the cause of the "movements of national liberation" everywhere.

In Latin American terms, the Cuban revolution comes much closer to the Chinese recipe. It was started in classic fashion as a guerrilla operation—carried out with the aid of Mao Tse-tung's manual on guerrilla warfare—and later expanded into a peasant-based social revolution on the Chinese model. Indeed, there is much kinship between Castro's Sierra Maestra and Mao's Yenan caves or Ho Chi Minh's Vietnamese jungle hideouts. The middle-class background of Castro and his companions does not affect this parentage of the Cuban revolution; modern peasant revolutions are seldom, if ever, led by peasants.

It is logical, then, that from the very beginning of his rule in Cuba, Castro has been urging violent revolutions in Latin America and promising that the Andes would be turned into a new and vast Sierra Maestra. But even more interesting than Castro's rhetoric, the Cuban guerrilla manual written by "Che" Guevara specifically proposes peasant-based agrarian revolutions in "our America." Copies of his manual and of Mao's old guerrilla handbook regularly turn up throughout Latin America at the headquarters of extreme leftist factions, at schools and universities. French-language translations of Guevara's *La Guerra de Guerrillas* have been discovered at, among other places, the University of Dakar in Senegal.

There is recent evidence that the Soviet Union is cool toward the prospect of the violent revolutionary cycle for Latin America that the Chinese advocate from afar and the Cubans help to encourage on the spot. Partly out of concern that premature violent revolutions may lead to United States interventions and inevitably involve the Soviet Union in a major world crisis that may not be at the time or place of its choosing—and Premier Khrushchev's commitment in 1962 to support and defend Cuba with nuclear missiles may have been made more grudgingly than it is generally realized—Moscow is believed to be much more interested in a slower process of establishment of socialist and anti-American regimes in Latin America through gradual political means.

A second reason for favoring the more conservative approach is that Moscow is not any more prepared than is the United States to cope with major chaos in Latin America. The four years of cooperation with Castro's Cuba has been a highly expensive and immensely frustrating experience for the Soviet Union, which found itself in the position of having to support at all costs a Communist enterprise in Latin America, however much it may be appalled by the methods being employed by the local revolutionaries.

Castro's continuing inability to make a going concern of his frantically disorganized island, despite new crash programs of Communist-bloc aid that now include emergency food shipments along with thousands of technicians, does not speak too well for Communism. Moscow, therefore, may be understandably reluctant to become involved in repetitions of the Cuban affair throughout the width and length of the Hemisphere.

It is not an accident that since the 1961 rebel invasion attempt and the 1962 nuclear-missile affair—both of which could have easily pushed Premier Khrushchev into unwelcome conflicts with the United States—Soviet diplomats have been quietly but per·sistently passing the word in Washington and elsewhere that nothing would please Moscow more than a coexistence agreement between the United States and Cuba. They have been careful to stress that such an agreement should include the resumption of normal trade between the two countries, presumably in the hope that the Soviet Union would no longer have to purchase annually millions of tons of Cuban sugar and siphon off to the Castro regime food that is desperately needed in the Communist bloc, as well as provide a mounting flow of import credits. After the Castro-Khrushchev agreement of May, 1963, the Soviets resumed their quiet campaign for "normalization" of U.S.–Cuban relations.

Under the circumstances, then, the current Soviet interest in such key countries as Brazil and Chile, where leftist leanings toward neutralism are growing perceptibly, may in the long run be incomparably more profitable than its involvement in Cuba. In the present stage of the Cold War, Moscow can benefit much more from reasonably orderly neutralism and ultranationalism in a country like Brazil than from a wild revolutionary explosion in, say, Bolivia or Ecuador.

In the curious and often contradictory manner in which the impact of the Cuban revolution has affected Latin America, the echoes from Havana have stimulated in the more mature Hemisphere nations a movement toward neutralist, nationalistic, and doctrinaire leftist sentiments instead of encouraging serious revolutionary violence. Thus, Brazil moved steadily toward a Nehru-Nasser form of neutralism in international affairs, while developing at home a strong tendency toward extreme nationalism and doctrinaire leftism. In Chile, leftist and nationalistic feeling had been running so strong that many observers were surprised at the resounding defeat the extreme left suffered in the 1964 elections. In Argentina, neutralist and nationalistic tendencies were temporarily and superficially arrested by the March, 1962, military *coup d'état* that ousted President Frondizi, but they subsequently returned to the fore through the growth of neo-Peronismo. In Peru, the military junta that overthrew the government of President Prado in July, 1962, and canceled the results of the general elections of the preceding month, busied itself making overtures to Communist-led labor unions, while proclaiming its anti-Communism.

Significantly, the Soviet military build-up in Cuba in the late summer of 1962 threatened to encourage further the neutralist sentiment as the image of the United States as the traditional "protector state" began to look tarnished. The resolute action of the Kennedy Administration in the ensuing missile crisis reversed this particular trend, but in countries like Brazil the tendency toward neutralism returned later in a still more sophisticated form.

Much as the Cuban revolution may have contributed to the release of all these new forces and sentiments, they have been alive or in gestation for a long time. It was perhaps inevitable that they should have finally erupted to the surface. They are part of Latin America's historical process, and henceforth they are bound to affect all Hemispheric reactions and attitudes. Upon them will hinge the fate of the Alliance for Progress and of the whole relationship between Latin America and the United States.

The Brazilian Phenomenon

Setting aside Cuba as a special case in which the Castro explosion triggered all forms of extremism, an overwhelmingly important phenomenon in Latin America's process of historical change is the political and psychological evolution of Brazil that began in earnest about a decade ago and is now approaching a still unpredictable denouement.

Even accepting the premise that the Cuban experiment served as the rocket to propel Brazil along her course of ultranationalism, leftism, and quasi neutralism—at least until the April, 1964, revolution—all the ingredients for the emergence of the new Brazilian national personality were present long before Castro came to power. It is probable that Brazil's act of self-assertion would have taken place in any event, and that it was merely a historical accident that the Cuban revolution occurred to accelerate and short-circuit a process that was already close to fruition.

In the perspective of Latin America's present and future, Brazil's ultimate course—it could be a form of military Nasserism as easily as a swing back to leftist radicalism—is certain to overshadow the Cuban revolution. Cuba's contribution to the Hemisphere's social and political revolution may even now be a thing of the past, an already fulfilled historical function, while the center of gravity may move to the South American mainland—notably to Brazil.

Because of its size, population, potential and actual resources, tradition, and influence, Brazil's actions profoundly affect the rest of Latin America. Had Goulart managed a definitive shift to the left, it would certainly have set off leftist trends elsewhere. Conversely, Brazil's firm cooperation with the Alliance for Progress, to which the government of President Castelo Branco is now committed, may well give this program an important boost.

In terms of U.S. foreign policy, Cuba and its alliance with Communism could be regarded as a local aberration that might be isolated and controlled in the end. But a determined move by Brazil toward full-fledged neutralism—if not its outright entry into the Communist orbit—could have shattered the U.S. position in the Hemisphere and turned the traditional safe back yard into a zone of danger and hostility.

Even before Goulart was swept from power, Washington had sought desperately to work out a *modus vivendi* with Brazil, hoping to stabilize its economy and halt the drift toward chaos and extremism. The 1964 revolution averted the immediate danger, but Brazil remains one of the keys to Latin America's stability. If the Castelo Branco government undertakes the needed reforms resolutely and without the demagoguery of the Goulart years, the whole Latin American situation will look brighter. But the Brazilian crisis has not yet run its full course, and new anxieties and pressures have been added to the existing ones. Late in 1964, despite the new regime's progress against inflation, the coalition of the political forces that had ousted Goulart had come apart, and the lines among contesting groups became sharply etched.

To sum up Brazil's new attitude toward itself and toward the world, suffice it to say that "the giant has awakened" after a slumber that lasted since the Brazilians won their freedom from Portugal in 1821. Despite periodic commotions and upheavals punctuating Brazilian history—the end of the Empire and the advent of the Republic in 1889, the emancipation of slaves, and the Vargas social revolution bridging the 1930's and the 1940's—Brazil has lived for a century and a half very much at the margin of the world and even of Latin America. Its domestic life was largely characterized by somnolence, its growth was painfully slow, its degree of under-development was staggering in view of the amazing natural resources, and, as far as Brazilians and foreigners were concerned, it was fated to remain forever "the land of the future" of Stefan Zweig's 1940 book.

As is the case with other traditionally backward nations, weighed down by the burden of a hostile nature and climate and by a sense of national inadequacy in the face of the present and the future, Brazil developed over the years an acute colonial inferiority complex. Brazilians were quick to deride themselves and their country in bitter little jokes, evidently intended to beat the foreigner to the punch before he launched on the usual litany of complaints about Brazil. The recurring theme was that nothing that was Brazilian could be any good, and that if you wanted anything decent—goods or people—you had to import it from abroad.

That through writers like Machado de Assis, Euclides da Cunha, and others Brazil had produced an outstanding if little-known literature, that it had borne a number of great statesmen like Ruy Barbosa and Rio Branco, and that it had spawned famous artists and musicians were matters to be minimized rather than to be vaunted. It was typical that the Brazilians never seriously pressed the claim—still open to debate—that their engineer Santos-Dumont preceded the Wright brothers as the first man to fly an airplane.

Afflicted with a suffocating provincialism, even in the years after World War II, Brazil's impact on the outside world predictably did not surpass the Brazilians' own self-estimation. The country was thus famous for its abundance of coffee, for the carnival, samba and

Carmen Miranda (who was actually born in Portugal), for the Sugar Loaf and Christ Redemptor of Corcovado, for its occasional revolutions (rather infrequent by Latin American standards), and for the fact that Brazil was a place to get rich easily and quickly. To official Washington, Brazil was famous for its great balance-of-payments deficits, which appeared irreversible, since every cent the country earned was spent on frequently unnecessary imports.

But the Brazilian awakening, or the breakthrough, had to come sooner or later. A nation of Brazil's size and with its breathlessly growing populations had only the alternatives of coming of age or of decomposing gradually. Having finally awakened, Brazil—and Latin America—had the immediate problem of getting through its hectic period of young adulthood. There was the danger that the young giant might trip and fall in the take-off.

The slow process of the giant's real awakening began with Brazil's participation in the war. Having sent an Army division and a fighter squadron to Italy to fight the Axis powers, it abruptly and dramatically entered into contact with the outside world. The expeditionary force won a major battle at Monte Castello, and forthwith a new sense of patriotism and pride was evident in Brazil. The returning soldiers were greeted as heroes, and hardly a few months went by before their influence, at first indirect, began to be felt all through the country. Under growing public pressure, the generals agreed that a country that sent troops abroad to fight foreign dictatorships could not tolerate a dictatorship at home. In late 1945, in a tank-led but bloodless *coup d'état,* Getúlio Vargas was ousted from office after fifteen years in power.

The first psychological step toward ending Brazil's colonial attitude toward itself was thus taken. From that moment on, the great ferment began. Free elections were held in 1946 and the new Congress busied itself writing a democratic constitution. Political democracy, then the cynosure of the young nations, was practiced furiously and incessantly, though it was sometimes hard to tell where the exercise of rational democracy ended and the hectic game of graft-ridden politics for its own sake began. The long-dormant ambitions for national development and industrialization surged to the forefront of Brazilian attentions. Almost everybody who could command an inch of newspaper space or a few minutes of public exposure sounded and acted like a professional economist, propounding grandiose if often fantastic solutions for the country's future.

Yet, there seemed to be lacking an effective channel for putting all that energy and dynamism to proper use. The glittering schemes were not quite thought out and conflicts were beginning to appear. Extreme nationalism quickly entered the scene to add its contribution to the country's great debates, centering on the emotion-laden slogan of "Petroleum Is Ours," which rapidly became the surest way of winning votes and evading basic issues.

The election of Getúlio Vargas to a Presidential term five years after his ouster as a dictator—one of those astounding Brazilian paradoxes—ended in tragedy when he shot himself in 1954, rather than allow the military to throw him out once more because of his misrule, which had almost sunk Brazil in a "sea of mud."

Then, weathering crisis after crisis, Juscelino Kubitschek took office as elected President in 1956, and Brazil's true breakthrough suddenly came. Pledged to "Fifty Years of Progress in Five Years," Dr. Kubitschek fell considerably short of accomplishing his impossible goal, but he did succeed in producing an amazing psychological change among his fellow citizens.

Vibrating with boundless enthusiasm for what he turned into a mystique of *"desenvolvimentismo"*—"economic development"—the new President plunged into the task of remaking Brazil with a total and almost admirable lack of understanding of the mechanisms of economics and finance. His cavalier disregard of the country's financial capabilities and of consequent inflationary dangers led him to push such extraordinary projects as the building of the new national capital in Brasília and the crisscrossing of the vast and largely uninhabited territory with a wide network of highways slashing open the jungles and the savannas.

Perhaps a man more versed in economics and less endowed with imagination would not have even attempted to carry out the program that Dr. Kubitschek drew up for himself. But Brazil needed a visionary, and there was no stopping Dr. Kubitschek and his dreams. So, for five years, Brazil lived through an amazing and exciting era of contagious enthusiasm that propelled the nation from its erstwhile inferiority complex directly to a new sense of manifest destiny.

With the building of Brasília as the great symbol of growth and with everything else that the tireless Dr. Kubitschek did to attract attention to his country, Brazil landed firmly on the world map. Stimulated by the Kubitschek vision of the future, foreign capital poured into Brazil at a dizzying rate. Whereas in pre-Kubitschek days, Brazil imported the bulk of what it produced, in these five years it assembled Latin America's largest and most spectacular industry. By the end of Dr. Kubitschek's tenure, the brand-new automotive plants were exporting buses, cars, and Jeeps to a number of Latin American countries and even to the United States. The suburbs of São Paulo turned into the "Brazilian Detroit," the new highways carried Brazilian-made trucks, driving on Brazilian-manufactured tires and burning Brazilian fuel. To own a Brazilian-built car suddenly became a source of pride for upper-class Brazilians.

The giant that had slept for so long was suddenly awake and flexing his muscles in all directions. The vast country was swept by a feeling of excitement, of being on the go, of things happening all over and all the time. And President Kubitschek, the exalted missionary of his development creed, was everywhere, inaugurating new projects, promising new projects, and talking about new projects. Making a second home of his Presidential turboprop aircraft, he lived in the air, flying from one corner of Brazil to another in a tireless crusade to awaken his country. It was not unusual for Dr. Kubitschek to breakfast with politicians in Rio de Janeiro, fly up to Brasília for lunch to inspect the progress of the new capital, and turn up in a Northeastern city for a dinner speech. In a country depending as greatly as Brazil does on air transportation and radio, the Presidential sorties played an important role in bringing a sense of national unity and purpose to the population living in widely separated areas of the Brazilian land mass.

And it seemed that Brazil was growing under one's very eyes. The São Paulo industrial complex broke out of the confines of the city to spread all over the state. Monumental excavations were in progress in the state of Minas Gerais for power and irrigation projects. Rio de Janeiro, no longer the capital but still Brazil's key city, was bursting at the seams. To cope with its expansion, it began to cut down its hills and to fill in Guanabara Bay to provide more lebensraum. In the remote Territory of Amapá, tough young Brazilian engineers were supervising one of the world's largest manganese industries, complete with its own towns, ports, and railroad. Through the virgin jungles of the state of Pará and the Territory of Acre, surveyors planned new highways, and tree cutters and bulldozers crowded in their footsteps.

The newly found Brazilian sense of pride and destiny was gratified in other fields as well. Brazilian architecture and its daring inventions soared to world fame. São Paulo became the scene of one of the world's most important modern art competitions. Brazilian airlines flew jet transports to the Near and Far East and the United States. The Brazilian soccer team twice in a row won the coveted world championship, and wild joy swept the country. A Brazilian tennis player became Wimbledon's women's champion. Brazilian motion pictures twice captured the gold medal at the film festival in Cannes. Miss Brazil, in 1963, was named Miss Universe. The music of the "bossa nova" swept the world. To enhance its prestige, Brazil spent $30 million to buy itself a second-hand aircraft carrier, which became promptly known as "our floating debt." Argentina immediately imitated this example.

But this intoxicating national flight into progress and prominence was accompanied by massive distortions and weaknesses that imperiled the future of the whole enterprise.

Prosperity and progress proved a blessing for the relatively developed areas of Rio, São Paulo, and Minas Gerais, but the huge Northeastern region with its 20 million inhabitants remained a wasteland of droughts, misery, disease, and virtual feudalism. The rising discontent, channeled through the Marxist-oriented Peasant Leagues, encouraged feelings of rebellion. The excess rural populations migrated in mounting waves to the big cities, creating social problems and prerevolutionary tensions. The runaway inflation, due partly to Dr. Kubitschek's magic-wand operations, was sapping the nation's energies and resources.

Despite its formidable leap forward in national development—underlined by the incredible 7 per cent annual increase in the gross national product between 1959 and 1961—and its amazing psychological breakthrough, Brazil lived in a deepening crisis. The Kubitschek solutions were no longer satisfactory, new pressures were emerging daily and the country was ready for a new phase.

The "Independent" Policy

This new phase was inaugurated early in 1961 with the rise to the Presidency of Jânio Quadros, a bizarre and unpredictable personality, full of contradictions, complexes, and his own brand of mystique and sense of mission. Quadros was elected by the greatest plurality in Brazilian history in what was described at the time as the "White Revolution" of the ballots, supposedly marking the end of the Vargas tradition and all the ills associated with it. If

Dr. Kubitschek, personally an heir of the Vargas machine, had represented the great period of transition, Quadros was to mark the advent of the new age. His electoral slogan was: "Don't Despair, Jânio Is Coming."

But when Jânio did come, all the earlier predictions proved hopelessly confused. Though he had defeated a Communist- and nationalist-backed candidate largely because of the support of the rising Brazilian middle class, Quadros instantly switched to a policy of intense nationalism and courtship of the Communist and neutralist worlds. Though he never bothered to explain his policies, his aides made it known that this two-pronged approach was designed to win the backing of the powerful Brazilian leftist movement for his unpopular but vital plans to fight inflation and put the country's financial house in order. If this rationalization had ever been valid, it very soon became a goal in itself and a widely supported foundation for national policies toward the world.

This new policy, launched by Quadros during his seven months in office and continued after his abrupt resignation by President João Goulart, who succeeded him, took the shape of an "independent" attitude in world affairs. Its immediate effect was to make Brazil, once a close ally, edge away perceptibly from the United States.

In a larger sense, the Brazilian policy shift was part of the continuing phenomenon of the erosion of United States power in Latin America and in the world. In Brazilian terms, it represented a desire, first expressed by Quadros, to turn the country into a major world power. Psychologically, it was a logical consequence of the great breakthrough of the previous five years in which the Brazilians' own sense of their world importance and of their manifest destiny grew so spectacularly. Radical nationalism was a natural adjunct of this attitude. That the nation increasingly supported the new policy, once it got over the initial shock, was the proof that Quadros was correctly interpreting the sentiments of Brazilians, rather than merely seeking to improvise them.

Clearly, the Cuban revolution—a powerful assertion of Latin American nationalism, aside from its other aspects—played an important role in leading Quadros to espouse his new policy. He had visited Castro in Havana in April, 1960, when he was a candidate, and earlier he had met with Khrushchev in Moscow, presumably to determine what kind of relationship useful to Brazil could be developed with the Soviet bloc. The pressure in Brazil that called for trading with the Communist world and establishing political relations with it had been mounting over the years, and evidently Quadros was receptive to these entreaties. The rationale was that Brazil should be guided by her own interest in deciding with whom to maintain relations.

But it is more likely that Quadros' decision on how to turn Brazil into a world power, or at least to give her a loud and respected voice in international affairs, was reached pragmatically. Despite his unpredictable personality, Quadros is a pragmatic and practical politician who had no trouble in shifting from earlier opposition to Jacobinist nationalism—including the national oil monopoly, which is its most sacred symbol—to an intense advocacy of it.

In formulating his "independent" foreign policy, he had obviously reached the conclusion that Brazil's rise to world stature could best be achieved through a middle-of-the-road position, free of Cold War commitments to either side. His first thought, often expressed by others long before his election, was that Brazil should not place herself in a position of vulnerability if the Cold War should ever become a hot one. There was growing sentiment in Brazil for the country to concentrate on her economic development instead of becoming involved in and threatened by the East-West conflict. If Brazil could benefit economically from the East-West rivalry, so much the better, Quadros thought.

In another dimension, responding to the pressures of nationalism, Quadros believed that as a nation of 75 million inhabitants rich in immense untapped resources, Brazil had reached a point in her political development where she could and should practice her own foreign policy, without turning to Washington for inspiration, as she had done throughout her history.

Quadros thus proceeded along the avenue of closer relations with the Soviet bloc and Cuba because he felt that this line would be politically useful to Brazil in the intricacies of world affairs. He simultaneously indulged in a good deal of gratuitous baiting of the United States, presumably on the theory that it would be helpful to keep Washington off balance. When Adolf A. Berle, an emissary of President Kennedy, arrived in Brasília in March, 1961, with a good-will offer of a $100-million loan to help out the incoming Brazilian Administration in its first months, Quadros coldly notified him that he would advise Washington when he was ready to request a much broader aid program.

Within months of his inauguration, Quadros ordered the establishment of diplomatic relations with the Soviet Union and all the European satellites with whom Brazil had not previously had ties—including Albania—and dispatched a mission to seek expanded trade with the Communist bloc. He went out of his way to recognize the Soviet annexation of the Baltic states, announced that Brazil would support the debate in the United Nations on the admission of Communist China, and invited Yugoslavia's Marshal Tito to visit him.

His active support of the Castro regime in Cuba, including awarding Brazil's highest decoration to "Che" Guevara for no discernible reason, appeared to be motivated by his determination to convince the United States that he held the key to any inter-American action on Cuba. Quadros, in effect, intended to be the judge of whether the Havana government should or should not be tolerated by the Hemispheric system.

In sum, Quadros—with his political and intellectual sympathies gravitating toward men like Tito, Nehru, and Nasser—seemed to believe that his foreign-policy acrobatics would give Brazil the best of both worlds. Under the circumstances, it is easy to see how the march of affairs under Quadros incited the interest and the expectations of the Soviet Union in her world-wide efforts to separate the United States from its traditional friends and allies. Significantly, Quadros was one of the few world leaders in the nonaligned group to receive a lengthy personal letter from Khrushchev outlining the Soviet position on Berlin. It was an honor that no other Latin American ruler, not even Premier Castro, was accorded by Moscow.

But if Brazilians seemed to approve of the Quadros quasi neutralism, they did not equate it even remotely—then or later—with the possibility of implanting a Castro-type regime in their own country. During the August, 1961, crisis resulting from Quadros' resignation, Castro's appeals to Brazilians to form guerrilla bands to put the then Vice-President Goulart in power in face of military opposition brought considerable derision. A pro-Goulart newspaper in Rio expressed the prevailing sentiment when it remarked in an editorial that "this crisis is ours, absolutely ours."

The new political course taken by Brazil in the wake of the anti-Goulart revolution put a halt to the disorderly foreign-policy experimentations of Quadros' Presidency and the more deliberate neutralist and pro-leftist policies of Goulart's tenure in office. The new Castelo Branco government broke diplomatic relations with

Cuba and aligned itself again to a marked degree with the United States, but the Brazilian penchant toward neutralism had sunk some roots in the previous three years, and it may once more come to the fore, even if in a more discreet form.

Men identified with neutralism and nationalism had been placed in key posts in the Foreign Ministry, and the bulk of the career diplomats have accepted the new line. The establishment of diplomatic relations with the Soviet Union was carried out by Goulart. The Brazilian delegation to the Geneva Disarmament Conference joined the nonaligned group, along with India and Mexico, and played a key role in formulating the neutralist proposals on a nuclear-test-ban agreement. A Brazilian delegate attended the 1961 neutralist conference in Belgrade as an observer. A Brazilian delegation went to Cairo in 1962 to participate in the conference on the economic development of the new nations, a markedly neutralist conclave. At the ministerial conference of Punta del Este in January, 1962, Brazil actively opposed the exclusion of Cuba from the inter-American system, and instead advocated coexistence with her. In the summer, the Brazilian and Polish Foreign Ministers exchanged visits and warm expressions of friendship. A pro-Communist Congressman, who once had been awarded the Stalin Peace Prize, was named Ambassador to the United Nations office at Geneva.

When President Goulart visited Washington in April, 1962, he made it perfectly clear to President Kennedy and to a joint session of Congress that much as Brazil wished to be friendly with the United States, she intended to maintain her nonaligned foreign policy. Significantly, however, the Goulart regime did not think of denouncing the military-assistance pact with the United States, and American military missions continued to train Brazilian troops— including courses in antiguerrilla and antisubversive techniques.

But a few months after Goulart's visit, when the Soviet Union announced the dispatch of military "technicians" to aid Castro, Brazil formally reaffirmed her policy of "hands off" Cuba, which, in effect, meant the full acceptance of a Communist military alliance within the Hemisphere.

Another curious aspect of the new Brazilian attitude was that while it seemed to favor a high degree of neutralism, it did not imply any official hostility toward the United States, despite growing criticism in many quarters of Washington's policies. This point was brought out in detail in a comprehensive survey of Brazilian public opinion carried out in September, 1961, by the Institute for International Social Research, of Princeton.

The survey found that President Kennedy and General Eisenhower rated as high as Quadros and Kubitschek in the opinion of the urban public, 34 per cent of whom also declared that the United States is a sincere friend of Brazil. But 43 per cent of those asked professed not to have an opinion. A total of 41 per cent believed that relations between the United States and Brazil were good; 60 per cent of the legislators gave the same opinion.

But, significantly, 37 per cent of the legislators felt that Brazil should cooperate with "all the countries wishing to cooperate" with her, and only 11 per cent favored restricting cooperation to the "free world."

The legislators favored military balance between the East and the West by 55 per cent. In response to the question whether Brazil should be "as neutral as possible" in the "Cold War," 63 per cent of the legislators voted Yes. The prevailing opinion among legislators and the urban public also held that Brazil should side neither with the United States nor with the Soviet Union.

The Institute's survey showed that persons favoring closer relations with the Soviet Union are found in the larger cities, in the higher income groups, and especially among university graduates. A strong penchant toward ultranationalism was also found in Congress and among the urban public. A close relationship was discovered between neutralist and nationalistic sentiments.

Brazilian policy gestures during the Quadros-Goulart period and the additional evidence of public-opinion sampling suggested the degree to which Brazil had chosen at that time to proceed along its own path in foreign policy—and thereby carve out an independent position in relation to the United States. Unquestionably, the profound switch in Brazilian attitudes prior to the 1964 revolution was one of the most important and far-reaching developments in Latin America since the war. Its long-range significance and implications loomed as greater than those of the Cuban revolution.

Foreign policies in particular during the Goulart period created growing difficulties in United States–Brazilian relations, not because Washington was necessarily opposed to an "independent" foreign posture, but because this posture was accompanied by frank hostility. After Goulart's visit to Washington in 1962 failed to lead to an improved understanding, each step by one side led to resentment and suspicion on the part of the other.

Brazilians—of both right and left—resented U.S. insistence that internal financial orderliness must precede the disbursement of aid, while Washington felt that continued assistance to Goulart's fiscally irresponsible regime would be money down the drain. In the latter part of 1963, all aid to the Federal government was stopped, and the only American funds flowing into Brazil went to specific state development projects, private industry, and long-term infrastructure works in the Northeast. The exception was the continuation of loans of surplus farm commodities under Public Law 480.

The restrictions gradually being placed on foreign capital and the pressures by Goulart's supporters for the expropriation of United States utilities and other property without compensation were irritating both Congress and the government in Washington. Congress expressed its sentiment toward Brazil in 1962, when the so-called Hickenlooper Amendment—providing for the cessation of all assistance if steps were not taken to settle expropriation disputes—was tacked onto the foreign-aid legislation. Early in 1963, the Goulart regime did settle the cases involving properties of the International Telephone and Telegraph Company just in time to prevent application of the amendment. But a political battle raged over Goulart's earlier commitment to buy out the plants of the American and Foreign Power Company.

A complete breakdown in economic and political cooperation between the United States and Brazil became a real threat early in 1964, when Goulart had surrounded himself almost entirely with far-leftist and anti-United States advisers. These men, many of whom also earned substantial profits from their positions, demanded expropriation of U.S. property and the declaration of a moratorium on Brazil's vast external debt. Brazil, they said, had to "go it alone," perhaps with aid from the Communist bloc, rather than allow itself to be "bled white by American imperialism."

However, realists, even in nationalistic quarters, were fully conscious that, aside from geopolitical facts of life and Brazil's own Western tradition, the country's dependence on trade with the United States was so immense that a self-imposed isolation, motivated by politics and petulance, could not fail to bring economic ruin and the end of all the dreams of economic and social development. The Communist bloc, particularly in the light of its failure to put even little Cuba on a sound basis, could never match the $1.5 billion in annual commercial exchanges between the United States and Brazil—to say nothing of the Alliance for Progress. The Russians themselves were aware of this, and both the Soviet Embassy in Rio and the Soviet-controlled faction of the Brazilian Communist Party quietly warned Goulart against a break with the United States.

Early in 1963, a major effort to find a common ground for sound cooperation—it was, in fact, the final effort before the United States abandoned hope of dealing with Goulart—was undertaken in Washington when the Kennedy Administration agreed to provide Brazil with nearly $400 million in credits during that year, in exchange for a pledge that the Goulart regime would carry out its new anti-inflation and stabilization program.

Brazil urgently needed the credits to improve its disastrous balance-of-payments situation and to make possible the continuation of development projects under the Alliance for Progress. The agreement rested on the belief that Goulart himself was a moderate and, as such, needed U.S. support to bolster him against the assaults by extremists, whose stock was rising sharply in direct ratio to the country's economic and social deterioration. The question of Brazilian foreign policy, including its position on nonintervention in Cuba, was left completely out of the financial talks on the theory that it would only exacerbate the explosive internal situation in Brazil at a time when stability was so essential.

The New Relationship

But despite all the good will on the part of President Kennedy and of the Brazilian negotiators in Washington, no lasting new relationship seemed possible so long as Goulart remained in power. The 1964 revolution and the Johnson Administration's speed in promising cooperation to the new regime may provide a basis for such a relationship in the future.

The key to a mutually profitable relationship between Brazil and the United States lies in political stability in the great South American republic. A sound government, fully in control of the domestic situation, including its finances and inflationary forces, and a Congress prepared to embark on fundamental social reforms (such as land reform) without demagoguery, can enjoy a satisfactory and advantageous relationship with the United States.

United States aid for Brazil's rational development—with full respect for her "independent" policy ideas—can be provided when Brazilian leadership, in and out of government, begins facing up to the nation's basic problems. The Goulart regime talked about these problems, but neither it nor the Congress did much about them. The 1964 coup may yet bring about such responsible attitudes—the Castelo Branco government is committed to them—but time alone can tell if such a breakthrough is possible.

Although in both countries much stress is being laid on the obligations of the United States in assuring a sound relationship, it must be recognized that despite Washington's desire to help, it cannot—and must not—live the Brazilians' political life for them. Nor can the United States force Brazil to embark now upon the desperately needed democratic social reforms and stabilization measures, any more than it could when Goulart was in power.

While the solution of the long-range Brazilian problem lies in economic and social betterment—in an end to the long-entrenched and rapidly deepening economic structural distortions and in an improvement in the socially decisive patterns of revenue distribution—immediate political stability is a crucial prerequisite for achieving this goal. It is demonstrably impossible to launch complex and often unpopular reforms in the midst of political crises in which civilian and military groups jockey for position and power—and no better example of this truism is needed than the Brazilian crisis that erupted in mid-1961 and continued even after a plebiscite in January, 1963, restored full Presidential powers to Goulart.

The Brazilian case provides, in fact, probably the most convincing answer to the argument as to whether political stability is a precondition for rational economic and social improvement or whether there can be no political stability until the economic and social problems are licked. In this chicken-or-egg controversy, the pragmatic Anglo-Saxon view, widely supported by United States policy-makers and editorial writers, holds that if the structural problems are solved, then political instability will vanish by itself. This theory, accepting as its main premise the diagnosis that Latin America's problem is essentially economic (and, therefore, social, as well), has become the fallacious philosophical basis of the Alliance for Progress. Because the Alliance's framers rejected the complex and contradictory reality of the profound political and ideological ferment in the hemisphere, they have founded its edifice on quicksand, with the result that its labor of construction often became paralyzed. If any major lessons were suggested by the first few years of the Alliance, as seen against the backdrop of the Hemisphere's political developments, it is that political stability must march hand in hand with economic and social programs and new investments of funds.

In Brazil's case, all the planning for basic reforms and all efforts at healing the ailing economy were brought to a virtual standstill by the constitutional crisis resulting from Quadros' resignation in August, 1961, and the subsequent political infighting that brought the country to the brink of civil war. The inherent dynamism of the Brazilian society, which, despite all the adverse pressures, maintained the national economic product at high levels, could not prevent the menacing drift of the nation into chaos and confusion.

In the sixteen months—from September, 1961, to December, 1962—of President Goulart's rule under the parliamentary system imposed as a compromise between his supporters and opponents, the principal achievement of the Brazilian Congress was to set the date (January, 1963) for the plebiscite to determine whether the Presidential system should be restored. During that entire period, land-reform legislation could not be reported out of a Congress whose attentions were divided between the political crisis and its own vested economic interests. Although tax reforms were written, they were never properly implemented.

The struggle between Goulart, who demanded full Presidential powers, and his congressional foes, who long opposed them, rapidly deteriorated into a polarization between the left, supporting him, and the center and the right, fighting his efforts.

Brazil's foreign policy was in tune with the domestic political pressures. As we have seen, the general principle of an "independent" policy was largely acceptable to the nation, but the impression also grew that Goulart in his latter phase—in 1962—increasingly used foreign policy to bolster his domestic position. Again, Cuba was the great case in point; Brazil stubbornly refused to see any special dangers in the Soviet military build-up. When the missile crisis came, in October, 1962, the Goulart regime did support the United States, however, in ringing Cuba with a naval blockade.

While the Goulart regime thus navigated between domestic nationalism and neutralism abroad, the situation at home in late 1962 was nearing an economic breakdown, and it was difficult to say who, if anybody, actually governed the country. The successive parliamentary governments barely went through the motions of attempting to control inflation and maintaining vigilance over Brazil's balance of international payments. Each recrudescence of the crisis pushed the government into printing more paper money. Inflation and the cost of living rose accordingly—and alarmingly— to the point where the index of living costs showed a 52 per cent increase for 1962. The government could not control the speculators who withdrew food staples from the market, and bloody food riots around Rio de Janeiro resulted. Throughout the republic, armed squatters occupied land—a do-it-yourself land reform—and tensions mounted from the desolate Northeast to the wealthy South, and from the jungle frontiers of the West to the over-crowded coastal cities in the East.

The January, 1963, plebiscite that restored the Presidential system offered a promise that a respite would be granted Brazil from 'its political crisis, which would make it possible for that vast nation to concentrate on its vital problems of reform and development. But in a historical sense, the events following Jânio Quadros' resignation—apparently intended as a protest against the perpetual politicking that was destroying his domestic policies—showed clearly that in awakening, the Brazilian giant had stumbled into a political and psychological swamp that almost brought him to his knees.

Quadros' supremely irresponsible act—or perhaps it was only a frustrated grandstand play—had interrupted Brazil's march toward the greatness that seemed to lie within reach. It rocked the country to its very foundations, shattering its national fabric and much of its newly won self-confidence. It demonstrated again that without a minimum of political—and democratic—stability, a nation is ill-prepared to begin solving its fundamental problems and benefiting from the Alliance for Progress.

The period following the 1963 plebiscite seemed to offer briefly the hope that the Brazilian pendulum was swinging toward the center. President Goulart launched an apparently promising stabilization program, began to move away from extreme leftist influences, and sent his Finance Minister to Washington to negotiate the $400-million agreement.

But in mid-year, Goulart switched policies again, fired the Finance Minister, and moved toward an increasingly rapid radicalization. With the Goulart policies drying up the flow of new foreign investments essential for Brazil's continued economic development, the financial situation deteriorated at a steady pace. The cruzeiro further lost value, inflation continued to mount, and industrial production dropped alarmingly.

Government-inspired strikes added to the unrest, and in October, 1963, Goulart made an inept attempt to declare a state of siege, close Congress, and set up a "trade-union dictatorship." Even the orthodox Communist Party opposed this maneuver, but undaunted,

Goulart went on preparing a new coup, hoping for the support of noncommissioned officers and young line officers.

By early 1964, a series of conspiracies against Goulart began throughout Brazil. Initially, they involved a number of state governors and civilian politicians; later, they attracted groups of younger and older officers, especially in the Army. But the key troop commanders resisted revolution, in line with the Brazilian military tradition of staying out of politics. In the end, it was Goulart himself who forced action upon the same generals who had first opposed a military coup, and thereby brought about his own ouster.

In March, he staged a mass rally in Rio to announce a partial land reform that circumvented the constitution. Goulart also disclosed other measures for economic control designed to vest in the government complete power over the nation's affairs. The response was the eruption of a national civilian movement "pro-democracy," and the switch of additional military to the growing conspiracy.

Later that month, Goulart committed his most grievous error when he refused to punish a group of mutineers in the Navy and the Marine Corps. It was in the Marines that Goulart seemed to have his principal military support, including the Corps commandant, but this act of defiance was the last straw for the older generals, who now feared a complete breakdown of discipline. Simultaneously, word circulated that Goulart had prepared to proclaim a leftist radical state in Brazil on May 1, closing down Congress and setting up a "popular" dictatorship.

On March 31, the first Army rebellion broke out in the central state of Minas Gerais, and the state's governor declared himself in revolt. Goulart ordered loyal troops to march on Minas, but within a day the powerful São Paulo garrison joined the revolution, and for all practical purposes, the revolution had triumphed. Goulart fled to Uruguay after a futile day in the new capital of Brasília, when none of his military, labor, or student supporters lifted a finger to defend him.

The Speaker of the Chamber of Deputies was immediately named Provisional President, in accordance with constitutional provisions, and within three weeks, Marshal Humberto Castelo Branco, who had been Chief of Staff of the Army, was elected to serve out Goulart's unexpired term, which was to have ended in 1966.

The Brazilian constitution was, to be sure, stretched almost to the breaking point in order to give a semblance of legality to this change-over, but a vast body of the nation believed that it was by the deposing of Goulart that democracy may have been saved in

Brazil. But whether this was the case is a political and philosophical argument that is certain to go on for years to come.

The Vicious Circle

The thesis that internal political stability is absolutely essential for rational development in Latin America and avoidance of the pitfalls of violence and revolution applies to the rest of the Hemisphere as it does to Brazil. But such stability is unattainable in the long run unless the economic and social structures are rapidly shored up and the living standards raised, thereby making the climate inhospitable to revolutionary agitation.

What faces Latin America and the United States, then, is a race against time in breaking the vicious circle, in resolving which must come first: stability or development. The inevitable conclusion is that they must be made to grow together.

By mid-1964, more than three years after the Alliance for Progress was proposed by President Kennedy, the instability of Latin America had increased sharply, though there was also some ground for optimism here and there. The instability did not stem, of course, from failures of the Alliance as a program—it was just beginning to get off the ground—but from the fact that the political and psychological fever, accompanied by a continued weakness of the economies, was acting faster than the tranquilizer and body-builder that the Alliance was seeking to apply.

Brazil, after drifting from crisis to crisis, finally underwent a revolution that ousted Goulart and left the future uncertain. The constitutional governments of Argentina and Peru were overthrown by the military in 1962 because the generals disapproved of results of elections—a civil war in Argentina was, in fact, narrowly averted in September of that year—and the return to democratic rule in 1963 was accomplished through considerably enervated institutions. Peru's new President, Fernando Belaúnde Terry, seemed to have the situation in hand a year after his inauguration, but Argentina's President Illia was skating on thin ice.

Late in 1963, Venezuela weathered a major pro-Communist conspiracy that was aided by Cuba, but the terrorists began regrouping in 1964 after Raúl Leoni, the new President, took office. Guatemala and Ecuador lost their constitutional governments to military coups in the first part of 1963. In 1964, there was no evidence that democracy would be restored in either country in the foreseeable future.

The Dominican Republic, liberated in 1961 from three decades of the Trujillo dictatorship, reverted to military rule in September, 1963, after a brief fling at democracy. President Juan Bosch, an attractive social reformer but an inept politician and administrator, was overthrown by a military *coup d'état* after seven months in office. With his fall, the United States' dreams of a democratic showcase in the Dominican Republic vanished. The military-backed civilian "triumvirate" changed members three times in less than a year—none of the original members remained in office by July, 1964—and stagnation and corruption returned to that Caribbean republic.

The democratic government in Honduras was ousted by the Army two weeks after Bosch's fall, and a military dictatorship turned its back on the Alliance-inspired reforms. Haiti, the Dominican Republic's neighbor on the unhappy island of Hispaniola, vegetated under the cruel and murderous dictatorship of François Duvalier, a sorcerer-like tyrant obsessed with the Haitian African heritage and its history of bloodshed. In mid-1964, Duvalier proclaimed himself President for life.

Chile prepared for the 1964 Presidential elections in a state of increasing polarization between the rightist and leftist extremists, and the overwhelming victory of Christian Democrat Eduardo Frei Montalva surprised even veteran observers. In Bolivia, racked by critical problems raised but not solved by the 1952 revolution, President Víctor Paz Estenssoro was inaugurated for a third term amid a rising tide of strikes and political conspiracies. Early in November, a military junta sent Paz Estenssoro into exile, and instability loomed ahead. Paraguay, accustomed to successive dictatorships, went through another extension of the rule by President Stroessner, who for the second time won rigged elections.

Colombia elected a new President in 1962, under the National Front system of alternating governments of rival parties, but the fourteen-year-old backlands violence showed no sign of abating, and political ferment was spreading to the cities. In 1963, a dangerous political crisis threatened the coalition regime.

British Guiana, impatiently awaiting independence under a Marxist Prime Minister, saw its capital wrecked by arson and rioting in 1961, as political and racial feelings exploded into violence and threatened to do so again. The local government was drawing increasingly closer to Cuba and the Soviet bloc, and in mid-1963, a general strike against Marxist Prime Minister Cheddi

Jagan led to racial strife between East Indians and Negroes, bringing in British troops and delaying independence indefinitely.

Mexico, Uruguay, and Costa Rica were the only islands of relative stability in the storm-beaten Latin American ocean, but even in Mexico, the tranquillity was illusory, and subsurface forces were gathering strength.

The great Latin American crisis was, therefore, an essentially political phenomenon, drawing powerful nourishment from economic problems and mounting social protest. Under the stimulus of the Cuban upheaval, it was a full-fledged political-social revolution in the making, advancing under the shield of instability and agitation.

One of its most disturbing aspects was that democratic institutions and the notion of representative democracy seemed unable to provide a stabilizing influence on the tension-gripped Latin American stage. In fact, the very concept of representative democracy had faced a critical challenge since the outset of the 1960's.

While the decade of the 1950's had witnessed a great surge toward the restoration of democratic institutions after the postwar dictatorial cycle, many of the people who had fought then for political democracy were now becoming disillusioned and doubtful about its merits and its workability. This attitude of doubt and disillusion provided the military and their civilian supporters in Argentina and Peru with the rationalization for the *coups d'état* that dismissed the constitutional governments in 1962. What may well be the last chance for democracy in these two countries came, however, in mid-1963, with the holding of elections and the inaugurations of the new Presidents.

Elsewhere, the younger people were skeptical of the feasibility of democracy in their underdeveloped countries. There was a growing tendency to equate the representative democracy preached by the United States with the capitalistic system and "Yankee imperialism," a line that the Communists and their allies were actively encouraging.

In her drive for change and self-assertion, Latin America was beginning to grope for new forms of political expression, though nobody could tell just where this quest would lead and precisely what was desired. Events in Argentina and Peru demonstrated that democracy and all its implications—including the results of elections—could not be fully accepted by powerful groups in those countries. The apparently successful 1963 elections in these two countries, conducted under military supervision, did not significantly alter this fact.

In the postrevolutionary decades, Mexico had solidified her one-party system—a peculiar form of democracy that operates even more efficiently than the Democratic primaries in the United States South to preserve political power for a dynastic ruling faction. The Brazilian revolution of 1964 led to the establishment of a hybrid regime, which purged Congress and sharply limited its powers. Under military pressure, President Castelo Branco had to accept the decision of Congress that his term should be extended.

The Colombian bipartisan system, an emergency measure approved in a popular plebiscite, has successfully entered its second stage, but it is not a structural democracy and it was becoming increasingly doubtful whether it would function for the full sixteen years for which it was planned. The National Front formula was approved in a plebiscite in 1957, providing for the Liberal and Conservative parties to alternate in power every four years until 1973. Alberto Lleras Camargo served the 1957–61 term for the Liberals, being succeeded by Guillermo Leon Valencia, a Conservative.

A Relative Democracy

As we have seen, the modern political history of the individual Latin American republics has always adhered to the nominal concept of representative democracy, though the actual practice has left much to be desired.

As a regional entity, Latin America has likewise made the principles of representative democracy the cornerstone of its political life. Thus, Paragraph (d) of Article Five of the Charter of the Organization of American States, signed at Bogotá in April, 1948, proclaims that "the solidarity of the American States and the high aims which are sought through it *require* the political organization of those States on the basis of the effective exercise of representative democracy."

The OAS Charter, which contained this inspiring paragraph, was solemnly signed by all the twenty-one members of the inter-American system. Yet the irony—or the paradox—is that at the time the Foreign Ministers drafted their exhortation, democracy in Latin America was in shocking straits. The institution of representative democracy, which had never been noted in Latin American history for its vitality or seriousness of purpose, despite impassioned oratory and constitutional provisions in its favor, was undergoing one of its worst cycles of regression since the turn of the century, just as the ministerial conference was convening in Bogotá.

Argentina was under the Perón dictatorship, for the 1946 elections that had brought him to power quickly led to authoritarian, mob-supported rule instead of a reign of democracy. Prior to Perón, the Argentines had alternated since 1930 between dictatorships and pseudo-democratic governments controlled by traditional oligarchies. The Dominican Republic and Nicaragua neared the end of the second decade of oppression under the respective dictatorships of the Trujillo and Somoza families. Paraguay was in its customary state of dictatorship. Bolivia was under a strongly authoritarian, Army-backed regime. Cuba had an ostensibly democratic government, but widespread corruption and politicking made representative democracy there something less than a responsible undertaking. Haiti had a *de facto* dictatorship. Panama was ruled by one of the families that took turns running the country in a game of musical chairs that made a travesty of democracy. And Colombia, the host country to the OAS conference, was entering a period of civil war that was to continue for the next fifteen years. In fact, this internal strife, which was to cost upward of 300,000 lives, exploded during the inter-American conference itself, following the murder of a leader of the opposition Liberal Party at a time when the ruling Conservatives were increasingly turning to violent repression against their political enemies.

Subsequent events showed even more tellingly how little the Latin American governments and the region's political and military leaders respected the Charter's requirements for the "effective exercise of representative democracy."

Before the year 1948 had ended, Peru and Venezuela had joined the camp of military dictatorships with the overthrow of their elected constitutional governments. In March, 1952, Fulgencio Batista mounted another dictatorial coup in Cuba, ousting the elected government of President Carlos Prío Socarrás. It is inconceivable that in returning to the old pattern of personal rule, Batista realized that he had sown the seed for the Castro rebellion and the ensuing explosion of the Latin American social revolution. But, as the record continues to show, history hinges upon the most improbable events performed by the most unexpected personages.

In Argentina, Perón was re-elected in 1951 in another travesty of democratic processes, after his opponents were imprisoned and prevented from campaigning. But significantly, the element of "social justice" injected into his dictatorship made it in a way the forerunner of the modern social revolution in Latin America, presaging the emergence of the still unsolved fundamental conflict between political freedom—or democracy—and the attempts to free the Latin Americans economically and socially.

This new turn of history was soon reflected in the situations in Bolivia and Guatemala. The 1952 Bolivian social revolution, which exploded over an ostensibly political issue—as the Cuban revolution was to do seven years later—took the shape, perhaps inevitable at that time and place, of authoritarian rule bordering on dictatorship. Víctor Paz Estenssoro, a revolutionary social leader, seized power through a bloody coup after the traditional rulers of Bolivia—the conservative classes and the military— sought to deprive him of the Presidency to which he had been elected. Launching his social revolution with the support of the tin miners and peasants, Paz Estenssoro had little choice but to gravitate toward harsh rule to prevent reaction against his social and economic experimentation.

In Guatemala, where the social ferment was as explosive as in Bolivia, a leftist quasi dictatorship of President Jacobo Arbenz Guzman was the delayed product of the earlier overthrow of the Ubico dictatorship. Unlike the Bolivians, however, Arbenz turned toward Communism for assistance in pushing forward his chaotic social revolution, which, classically, began with the distribution of land to the peasants.

By 1954, when the United States, concerned over the growing Communist control of the little Central American republic, organized anti-Arbenz forces to overthrow his regime, a major historical trend was already developing in the Hemisphere. Under this trend, the threat to the democratic institutions, historically confined to right-wing or military dictatorships, was now appearing from the extreme left of the political spectrum, offering as its justification the need for social justice. In the Mexican revolution of 1910, the political problem had not arisen in this context, and furthermore, the world was not split in those days by the East-West conflict and there was no Communist bloc poised to exploit the widening fissures in the Western system. But as Dr. Milton S.

Eisenhower remarked in his book on Latin America, in the postwar years only the pro-Communists seemed to be concerned with social justice.

In 1954, therefore, the West, notably the United States, was completely unprepared for this new historical phase. Representative democracy, sadly neglected and much too often sacrificed to rightist dictatorships under the benevolent eye of the United States, was not being strengthened to face the new challenge from the left. Secretary of State Dulles went to Caracas, Venezuela, where the tough military dictatorship of General Pérez Jiménez was in power, to seek inter-American support for anti-Communist action on Guatemala. But it seemingly had not crossed Dulles' mind that to be successful, the long-range battle with Communism in Latin America would have to be fought on the issues of liberal democracy and social progress. As it was, then, the Caracas Declaration against Communism, extracted by Dulles from the Hemisphere ministers, loomed as a sterile and negative instrument. Only tiny Costa Rica, a practicing democracy, made the *beau geste* of staying away from the ministerial conference on the reasonable grounds that Caracas, as the capital of the Pérez Jiménez dictatorship, was an odd place indeed to launch the defense of democracy against Communism— or any other challenger.

Even though Peronismo in Argentina and the subsequent Bolivian and Guatemalan revolutions made it abundantly clear that history now required that representative democracy be tailored to the realities of social protest and justice—in fact, that these two concepts should be wedded to produce a modern Latin American democracy—the West and the traditional ruling groups of the Hemisphere went on displaying a thoroughgoing blindness to the new imperatives.

Between 1955 and 1958, the formalistic concept of representative democracy surged forward in Latin America through the revolutions that overthrew Perón, Rojas Pinilla, and Pérez Jiménez, and through the political pressures that forced the holding of free elections in Peru to replace dictator Odría.

Significantly, in each case, these democratic revolutions were led by the students and supported by the intellectual, professional, labor, and even conservative economic communities, and, ultimately, by the military. But in no case were they followed by concerted efforts at democratic—and peaceful—social revolutions, though the writing on the wall was plain enough. Democracy in its deep sense, therefore, remained a purely political concept super-imposed upon the seething Latin American societies, with diminish-ing relationship to the daily realities. The outstanding exceptions were Costa Rica and Venezuela, since February, 1959, under the regime of President Betancourt, whose efforts at social reform were also hamstrung by a myriad of obstacles.

Inevitably a major question had to be faced: How could democ-racy prosper in the new age—after failing so utterly in the earlier age—unless an intimate and working relationship were established between its political and social justice aspects. But, as we have seen, even the advent of the Castro revolution in January, 1959, did little to bring this problem into focus in Latin America and in the United States.

Trying hard to atone for its past practice of happy coexistence with the rightist dictatorships, Washington was content in the clos-ing years of the Republican era to accept passively the emergence of political democracy in the region. Latin Americans who now enjoyed political freedom were satisfied to do so at home, but there was still little disposition to view representative democracy as a Hemisphere-wide obligation. There was widespread public sym-pathy for the early attempts by Castro's *barbudos* to try to over-throw the dictatorships in the Dominican Republic, Nicaragua, and Haiti, but the Cuban methods of seeking this goal were objection-able to the law-abiding governments. While these governments rightly determined to oppose this kind of forcible democratization coming from another country, they did not provide a responsible alternative to the Castro techniques. Nor did they seem to realize that behind the Cuban revolution, there were powerful forces of social explosion gathering, ready to find a propitious climate every-where else in Latin America.

Thus, when the so-called Caribbean tensions (mostly the mutual threats of Castro and Trujillo to do away with each other) reached a point of real danger, the inter-American system responded by calling the Foreign Ministers' Conference at Santiago, Chile, in August, 1959.

The resulting decisions again sounded inspiring, but again, they did little to equip the inter-American system to deal with the new state of affairs. The Declaration of Santiago, drafted mainly by the Brazilian delegation, succeeded in tying together—for the record—the concepts of democracy and human improvement, but its prac-tical effects in both fields remained elusive. Yet, the ideas set forth in the Declaration should have immediately become the cornerstone for United States and Latin American policies, for it was then already eight months after the advent of the Cuban revolution. The Preamble to the Declaration said:

> The faith of the peoples of America in the effective exercise of representative democracy is the best vehicle for the promotion of their social and political progress, while well-planned and intensive development of the economies of the American countries and improvement in the standard of living of their peoples represent the best and firmest foundation on which the practical exercise and the stabilization of their institutions can be established.

The Preamble went on to state that "the existence of anti-democratic regimes constitutes a violation of the principle on which the Organization of American States is founded, and a danger to united and peaceful relationships in the hemisphere." The operative section of the Santiago Declaration spoke of a contribution "to the eradication of forms of dictatorship, despotism, or tyranny," and it stressed that "perpetuation in power, or the exercise of power without a fixed term and with the manifest intent of perpetuation, is incompatible with the effective exercise of democracy."

A separate resolution issued in Santiago ordered the OAS Council to prepare a "draft convention on the effective exercise of representative democracy, and the establishment of the procedure and measures applicable thereto."

These were, indeed, sonorous words and praiseworthy aims. But again, the seriousness with which they were taken was illustrated by the identity of some of the Foreign Ministers signing the Declaration and the accompanying resolutions. The list included Raúl Roa García of Cuba, which was quickly turning into a leftist dictatorship; Louis Mars of Haiti, where President François Duvalier was building one of the Hemisphere's toughest tyrannies; Porfirio Herrera Báez of the Dominican Republic, where Trujillo was in the twenty-ninth year of dictatorial rule; Alejandro Montiel Argüello of Nicaragua, where the Somoza family continued to control the country; and Raúl Sapena Pastor of Paraguay, where President Stroessner had developed a masterful technique for self-perpetuation in power through elections in which he was the only candidate.

All these gentlemen straight-facedly signed the exhortations in favor of representative democracy, and their colleagues watched it just as straight-facedly. There could have been no serious expectation that their governments would ever voluntarily enforce these democratic precepts, and the inter-American system was not prepared, legally or politically, to encourage their observance. Legally, the principle of nonintervention—at one time a vital principle of protection for the Latin American republics, but now a paralyzing influence on all Hemisphere actions—presented a formidable obstacle against any effort, even in terms of political persuasion, favoring democracy in the countries victimized by the local dictatorships.

Politically, Latin America stood ready to condemn dictatorships —and the United States for once having supported them—but she had a deep-seated aversion to doing anything practical to enhance the democratic cause on a Hemispheric level. Though in 1946, Uruguay suggested a method for discouraging dictatorial coups by making it a rule that the American states would not accord diplomatic recognition to new regimes without a two-thirds decision of the entire body, the majority of the republics turned it down. However, the United States did support the idea.

For a wide variety of reasons—one of them being a broad sense of mutual protection—Latin America is something of a political club in which no member can really do any wrong. There have been very few occasions indeed when one of the governments has defended the rule of democracy when it was violated by a fellow clubman. In this respect, Latin America has been historically much more guilty of double standards in dealing with dictatorships than was ever the case with the United States. If the principle of nonintervention could be invoked to prevent any forcible action, it was the sense of clubmanship that led many of the democratic governments to maintain cordial relations with some of the worst dictatorships in the region. Even after the overthrow of the Argentine, Colombian, and Venezuelan dictatorships, most of the republics sent high-ranking delegations to the inauguration of Paraguay's Stroessner after he re-elected himself in 1958 for a new term. Brazil dispatched two Cabinet ministers for the ceremony, and Venezuela, freed from her own dictatorship barely a month earlier, also sent a special deputation. What Dr. Milton Eisenhower and Vice-President Nixon had recommended as a United States policy of a "cool handshake for the dictators" was not accepted by the Latin Americans for their own use.

By mid-1960, it was amply clear that the Hemispheric battle lines were being drawn along ideological lines. Cuba under Castro had given up all pretense of being engaged in a liberal or democratic social revolution, her alliances with the Communist bloc were rapidly taking shape in the political, economic, and military fields, and Premier Khrushchev had already uttered his first threat that Soviet "rocket artillerymen" would strike at the United States to defend the Cuban experiment.

To counter the mounting Communist threat identified with the new aspects of the Cuban revolution, the Hemisphere urgently needed a revitalization of her democratic structure so that her own masses could be persuaded that the wave of the future lay not in revolutionary totalitarianism but in democratic evolution or gradualism. But with a few exceptions, the Latin American governments preferred a "do-nothing" attitude in relation not only to Cuba but, even more importantly, to their responsibilities for Hemispheric democracy. As the Cuban regime gathered its forces for an ideological offensive in Latin America, the Hemisphere, caught between a misinterpretation of the principle of nonintervention and a sense of clubmanship, supinely crossed its collective arms.

The Dominican Case and Other Tests

A classic example of this attitude came in August, 1960, when the Foreign Ministers of the Americas met again, this time in San José, Costa Rica, to deal with the problems of Cuba and the Dominican Republic—two presumably unrelated matters. In the first instance, the question was how the Hemisphere should react to Cuba's acceptance of the Soviet offer of military protection and to its growing interest in promoting its brand of revolution throughout Latin America. In the second instance, the ministers were to decide on how to cope with the dangers posed by the Trujillo dictatorship after its participation in a clever but miraculously ineffective plot to murder Venezuela's President Betancourt earlier that year.

The theory that circulated in the conference corridors was that if the ministers took strong punitive action against Trujillo, a rightist dictatorship, then they would acquire political and moral authority for voting some measures against Cuba. But the theorem was not properly posed, and it illustrated the Latin American governments' continuing lack of understanding of the great problems they faced. A condemnation of Trujillo should not have been intended to pave the way for a condemnation of Cuba—as an impartial "plague on both your houses" gesture against a rightist and a leftist dictatorship—but rather as a deliberate move in favor of Hemispheric democracy. The ministers failed to recognize that Communist and revolutionary sorties emanating from Cuba could not be successfully controlled if the Hemispheric community continued tolerating such aberrations as the Trujillo rule over the Dominican Republic. If the Latin American masses were to take democracy seriously, then the inter-American system should have acted with equal seriousness in its defense when the issue arose.

As it happened, the Latin Americans showed their traditional reluctance in dealing conclusively with Trujillo, even though there was ample proof that he had attempted no lesser offense than to assassinate the President of a "sister republic." Again, it was the United States that advocated, in vain, a harsh but intelligent course of action, aimed not only at the punishment of the Dominicans for the murder plot, but also at the very heart of the Dominican problem.

Secretary of State Christian A. Herter, representing the much-maligned Eisenhower Administration, proposed that diplomatic and economic sanctions be imposed on the Dominican Republic and maintained until the Trujillo regime allowed free elections and a general democratization of the country. This would have been a novel but possibly effective way of trying to enforce a return to democracy in a dictatorial country, but the Latin Americans balked at the idea. Their view was that Herter's formula would constitute a form of intervention in Dominican affairs, and a continuation of the murder-punctuated Trujillo dictatorship thus seemed to be preferable to a violation of the hallowed but hollow principle of nonintervention.

In the end, the ministers voted to break diplomatic relations with the Trujillo regime and to order economic sanctions until some vague and undetermined time when it ceased to be a danger to Hemispheric peace. A great opportunity to encourage democracy was thereby lost out of timidity. When, in January, 1961, the OAS Sanctions Committee met to prepare the procedures for the application of the economic sanctions, several of the big Latin American powers, notably Brazil, abstained from voting.

The Dominican story is worth examining further as an example of how the inter-American system acted subsequently in what might have been a great demonstration of its determination—so solemnly proclaimed in Bogotá and Santiago—to encourage the effective practice of representative democracy.

On May 30, 1961, history came to the aid of the inter-American system and the Dominicans: Trujillo was assassinated by a group of civilian and military plotters, whom the Kennedy Administration, which knew of their plans, had not discouraged from acting. The Dominican government remained in the hands of President Joaquín Balaguer, who had for some time served as Trujillo's hand-picked chief executive, and of the late dictator's son General Rafael L. Trujillo, Jr. The entire Trujillo structure remained intact, and there were strong indications that Balaguer and the young Trujillo intended to keep the system going, though in a slightly modified form, despite their promises to democratize the country.

The United States immediately took the view that the future of the Dominican Republic was a Hemispheric responsibility, particularly since the inter-American system had become involved in Dominican affairs through the application of sanctions against the Trujillo regime nine months earlier. Washington's appraisal, idealistic as well as realistic, was that unless the Dominican Republic was effectively and promptly placed on the road to democracy, a political vacuum would rapidly develop and invite a Cuban-type revolution. A major ideological contest—and a race against time that is still going on—was involved in the Dominican issue, and the Kennedy Administration believed strongly that a maximum of inter-American surveillance was required to ensure the transition to democracy in a country that was just emerging from thirty-one years of dictatorship.

The Latin American response was careful, timid, and unreceptive. Diplomatically, the overriding consideration of most of the governments was to prevent any OAS action that could smack of intervention. In most capitals, even enlightened public opinion somehow failed to relate the Dominican crisis to the larger problem of the developing ideological battle over the destiny of the Hemisphere. The respective governments, which should have known better, did little if anything to educate their public opinion.

In short, the United States had to use all its prestige and influence to bring even a modicum of inter-American action to bear upon the Dominican situation. It took unrelenting State Department pressure before a subcommittee of the OAS Sanctions Committee was authorized to make several trips to the Dominican Republic during the fateful summer and fall of 1961 and, by its presence, curb some of the excesses of the Balaguer-Trujillo rule. In justice, it must be recorded that several individual Latin American members of the committee had done all they could to make the OAS operational in the Dominican Republic.

But it was the United States, through an intricate double diplomacy, that carried the burden of negotiating with the Balaguer regime to guarantee a transition to democracy and of persuading the nascent democratic forces in the Dominican Republic to avoid upsetting the political apple cart, which might have brought about a new military coup. When, in November, 1961, the two brothers of the late dictator—the "wicked uncles"—attempted such a coup on their own, the United States moved alone to block it. Rather than risk becoming bogged down in a juridical debate in the OAS Council while the "wicked uncles" would presumably be grabbing power, the United States dispatched a Navy task force that anchored menacingly at the edge of the territorial waters, in front of the capital, ready to land Marines if a coup materialized. The presence of the Navy saved the day for Dominican democracy, but the Latin American governments refrained from either applause or criticism—though Brazil issued a bizarrely worded statement indicating its displeasure.

Having inaugurated an effective, unilateral system to protect—though not to enforce—democracy in the Dominican Republic, the Kennedy Administration had to repeat the Navy stratagem in January, 1962. This time, it was designed to discourage a young Air Force general named Pedro Rodríguez Echevarría, who hoisted himself to power after the November incident and liked the idea of being top dog. Here, however, the Navy did not even have to show the flag to put down the Echevarría coup; the knowledge that the ships were lurking nearby was enough.

To be sure, the United States did not relish the notion of calling out the Navy to look after democracy in a Latin American republic when the inter-American system was not prepared to do what it had proclaimed twice as its supreme goal. Such unilateral actions, commendable as they may be, gave ammunition to anti-American elements in the Hemisphere who charged that the United States was again practicing intervention and that its behavior in the Dominican Republic was the forerunner of a new invasion of Cuba. Castro's propaganda machine, which had discovered at one point that Trujillo was a good nationalist sacrificed by the "Yankee imperialists," was busy hurling accusations at the United States interfering with Dominican "freedoms" and seeking to impose its control. It is useful to note that Havana, as well as the extreme left-wing movements in the Dominican Republic, in its attacks zeroed in on the United States-supported "Council of State," the transitional democratic regime in the country. These groups clearly sought to undermine all efforts to lead the Dominicans to elections and rational social and economic reforms under the Alliance for Progress. The Communists were wasting no time in placing the battle for the Dominican Republic on a political and ideological level.

This political and ideological problem in terms of representative democracy again faced the United States and Latin America in March, 1962, when the Argentine military ousted the elected government of President Frondizi, blaming him for the important Peronista victories in congressional and gubernatorial elections. Here the democratic process, plagued by the underlying political problem of Latin America, had come full circle. A dictatorship had been overthrown nearly seven years earlier, but the restored political democracy had disregarded the need for both strengthening its ideology and adequately handling the mounting social problems. That more than 2 million Argentines were then ready to vote for Perón's slogans seven years after his departure demonstrated that the nation's basic ills had not been tackled and that the faith in democratic procedures had not been inculcated in an important segment of the population. Two ironic facts in the situation were that the Peronistas had used elections—a technique of representative democracy—to register their protest, and that the bulk of public opinion reacted with complete apathy to the end of constitutional rule in Argentina.

Since the Charter of the Alliance for Progress did specifically relate the practice of democracy to the cooperative inter-American development programs—and the political aspect was really a Latin American idea that was spelled out in the Santiago Declaration and later in the 1961 Alliance articles—the Argentine coup placed the Kennedy Administration in the first of many dilemmas concerning the democratic problem of Latin America. Washington's initial inclination was to withhold diplomatic recognition and financial aid indefinitely. But the military-backed regime in Buenos Aires rationalized its existence in terms of a rather far-fetched interpretation of the constitution, and the Latin American reaction was far from helpful to the United States in trying to make a stand on the Argentine case. Only Venezuela stood firm in her refusal to recognize the Buenos Aires regime. Reluctantly, Washington restored relations with Argentina a month later, and within two months, it resumed financial aid.

The Argentine coup became a dangerous example to all those among Latin America's military and conservative classes who felt justified in staging *coups d'état* whenever the results of an election displeased them. This group was joined by those who feared and resented the social reforms proposed under the Alliance for Progress, and who preferred a return to military dictatorships rather than to see their governments in the hands of left-of-center groups —even if non-Communist or anti-Communist. The need for countering Communist or Fidelista penetration was offered as a justification for strong-arm regimes, in total disregard of the historical truism that Communism and its subversion thrive the best under dictatorships. It was forgotten that Castro and his social revolution, which ultimately turned toward Communism, would not have occurred in all probability if Cuba had not been ruled by the Batista dictatorship.

The second urgent test for the cause of representative democracy in Latin America—and for the Alliance for Progress—came in Peru four months after the Argentine coup. The apparent victory in the Presidential elections of Víctor Raúl Haya de la Torre, a leftist but anti-Communist leader of the APRA Party (whom Castro had been denouncing for two years in the vilest terms), led to a coup by the Peruvian military, largely because they hated Haya de la Torre and his party for a series of revolts, nearly thirty years earlier, in which a number of the military had been killed.

In this instance, President Kennedy reacted with unprecedented violence, charging that the military junta had defied the principles of the Alliance in overthrowing the outgoing government of President Manuel Prado and preventing the inauguration of an elected President and Congress. Diplomatic relations were immediately suspended and all military and economic aid was cut off, except for minor humanitarian programs.

But, here again, the United States was a voice in the wilderness. Most of the Peruvian public accepted the junta, and a majority of the Latin American governments refused to echo the indignation voiced by Washington. The Communists, who feared that Haya de la Torre's government would damage their revolutionary cause, rejoiced in the collapse of democratic institutions in Peru and gave their backing to the military junta. The junta responded in kind, flirting with them, then finally cracking down early in 1963.

An attempt by a group of Latin American governments—notably Venezuela and the Dominican Republic, who had their own reasons for fearing military coups—to convoke a conference of Hemisphere Foreign Ministers on the threat of military takeovers was voted down by a majority in the OAS Council. Though both the OAS Charter and the Santiago Declaration seemed to provide a sound basis for such a debate in favor of representative democracy, the majority agreed with the Lima junta that to do so would be a violation of the principle of nonintervention. A watered-down attempt by the United States to establish at least the principle that a ministerial conference should be called was likewise defeated a few weeks later.

Latin American clubmanship had again prevailed. Washington sheepishly resumed diplomatic relations with Peru and restored economic and military aid under a greatly weakened political concept of the Alliance. The dispirited Administration also succumbed to pressure from Lima and recalled Ambassador James Loeb, who had supported the policy of sanctions against the junta that President Kennedy had so determinedly tried to apply.

What the Argentine and the Peruvian military coups intended to do in regard to the basic political and social problems of the two countries was not clear. They had weakened the political front of the Alliance countries in the contest with Communism and Castro-type revolutionary pressures, enabling the enemies of democracy to argue again that the democratic system was not workable. The futility of trying to solve problems of political instability through military coups that eliminated large numbers from political life was demonstrated in Argentina in September, 1962. In a brief but bloody engagement, a faction of the Army vanquished the advocates of dictatorship and briefly restored the rights of the Peronista electorate. All that Argentina had gained from the six-month period of strict military rule was a dramatic deterioration of her economy under the impact of the crisis and a strengthening of the leftist revolutionary elements.

As a political entity, the inter-American system merely watched these events with passivity, preoccupied as ever with the sanctity of the principle of nonintervention. And it may be added that not a word of the "Draft Convention on the Effective Exercise of Representative Democracy," ordered by the Santiago Conference in 1959, has ever been written, despite the solemnity with which the resolution was signed.

As we have noted, new elections were ultimately held in Peru in June and in Argentina in July, 1963, in a cliff-hanging atmosphere. Fernando Belaúnde Terry, a left-of-center architect, was the winner in Peru, and Arturo Illia, a middle-of-the-road physician, was elected in Argentina, where a part of the Peronista electorate finally tired of obeying the exiled dictator. But the great question remained whether Belaúnde and Illia would know how to inject a social sense in the painfully re-emerging democracy in their countries or whether they would again court disaster.

The Loss of Faith

This entire record of the performance of representative democracy in Latin America seems to lead to the conclusion that after a century and a half of political independence, the Hemisphere remains uncertain as to whether the democratic system—desirable as it is in theory—is indeed practicable in this unsettled, crisis-ridden, and revolution-prone region. Small wonder, then, that Latin America's faith in representative democracy and in the political aspects of the Alliance for Progress seems to be waning, particularly among the younger people and the intellectuals.

That the validity of the democratic system has come under critical questioning in Latin America is without doubt one of the most important and disturbing developments to occur in the Hemisphere in the wake of the Castro revolution. It emphasizes the ideological erosion of the Western position in Latin America under the impact of the new Jacobin revolutionary forces that proclaim the concept of representative democracy to be a myth and a fraud. This ideological problem is, then, the real heart of the contest between the democratic elements in Latin America and the revolutionary influence of the Castro phenomenon.

The continuing popular attraction toward the radical and ultra-nationalistic left—which rejects the democratic gradualism of the Alliance and portrays the United States as the Hemisphere's chief enemy—is a manifestation of this rising doubt over democracy. While the United States has based the philosophy of the Alliance for Progress entirely on the premise that economic and social progress *is* compatible with democratic freedoms and the human dignity they imply, the Castro retort is that representative democracy, as it has traditionally been practiced in the American republics, has been a sham and a failure, leading to dictatorship, oppression, and corruption. Going even further, Castro has charged that the concept of Western democracy is used by the United States, in conjunction with the Alliance for Progress, as a cover-up for a streamlined version of "imperialism" and aggressive capitalism.

There is, to be sure, an enormous body of historical evidence to support Dr. Castro's evaluation of so-called democratic practices in the Americas over the last century and a half. The events of the last few years—especially the Argentine and Peruvian situations of 1962, undermining, as they did, the Alliance philosophy —would appear to confirm his assertions. But where the Johnson Administration and the democratic liberal groups in Latin America would like to see a rebirth and an improvement of democratic practices, Castro recommends outright abolition of traditional representative democracy as being totally unsuited to the new needs of Latin America.

Castro's earlier views favoring a liberal and democratic solution for Cuba's problems, along with far-reaching measures of social and economic betterment, were subsequently ground into dust by Cuba's impetuously developing history. Castro's new theory, and one that is gaining intellectual disciples throughout Latin America, is that the only "true democracy" is his brand of "people's democracy." This, he says, is intended to do away with social and economic privileges, destroy the old order without the hesitations implicit in democratic gradualism, and assume justice and equality for all.

This point, underscoring Castro's revolutionary impatience with the slow and often dubious procedures of the old-fashioned democracies in seeking social reform, was one of the first conclusions he reached after capturing power, and long before he turned his revolution over to Communism. Presenting it as his "political revolutionary philosophy," Castro argued in speech after speech that this "true democracy" drew nourishment from the support shouted by his followers in public squares. Consequently, he said, old-fashioned elections were no longer necessary. And, indeed, the starry-eyed Fidelistas chanted that "We've already elected Fidel," and Castro talked endlessly and emptily of a democracy purer than that of the ancient Greek market place.

All this, of course, was superb demagoguery, and in time, it became a rationalization for his emerging dictatorship and a bridge for his switch to Socialism and Communism. Also, Castro had to build a powerful secret-police apparatus, shored up by an army of civilian informers organized in the "Committees for the Defense of the Revolution," to assure that his "true democracy" went on functioning as smoothly as possible. In the end, Castro's regime finally became a repetition of other Latin American dictatorships that leaned on the secret police and oppression to perpetuate itself.

Yet the Castro dictatorship—before and after its identification with the Communist ideology—was a dictatorship with a difference. Even before accepting Marxism-Leninism as its political foundation, and replacing the "Greek democracy" of the earlier days with the "democratic centralism" copied from the Soviet Communist Party, the Castro regime had broken away from the mold of the Hemispheric political traditions and rhetorics. Unlike all the other dictatorships, Castro had the courage, or the bravado, to come out openly against the notion of representative democracy and advocate a completely new system.

His predecessors in Latin America used to—and still do—go to incredible pains to pay lip service to democracy and to dress up their cavalier management of their states in democratic legalisms. Thus Trujillo rewrote the Dominican constitution repeatedly to fit, retroactively, into his policies and practices. Venezuela's Pérez Jiménez, Colombia's Rojas Pinilla, Paraguay's Stroessner, and Haiti's Duvalier went doggedly through the motions of one-candidate elections or plebiscites. For the word "democracy" has been sanctified in Latin America along with "God" and "family," it has been enthroned in inter-American jurisprudence—often over the signatures of tyrants—and it has become the most overworked cliché in the speeches of demagogues of the left and of the right. As a sage Latin American once observed, "We are constant sinners against democracy, but we are not heretics against the religion of democracy."

Castro, however, has contributed a new factor to the Latin American political scene by disavowing the practice, concept, and rhetorics of representative democracy—and thereby becoming the great heretic. He has thus hurled the most telling challenge to the democratic forces of the Hemisphere and narrowed the issues in the great contest to the fundamental question of whether democracy can survive in the changing Latin America.

Regardless of the ultimate fate of the Castro regime, the seed of doubt he has cast on the validity of democracy as a system suitable for Latin America will persist for years. There are millions of young Latin Americans, who, while rejecting Communism, are no longer certain about the desirability of representative democracy as they have understood it from history books or contemporary observation. The passive acceptance by the Argentine and Peruvian masses of the destruction of democratic institutions in their countries has underscored the loss of faith in the democratic concept. The soul-searching and the uncertainties about the political road Latin America must take in the midst of her social revolution are heard elsewhere in the region, from crisis-torn Brazil to the precariously developing democracy of the Dominican Republic, and from the long-oppressed Haiti to the mountains of Bolivia, still trying to make sense from her decade-long revolution. The apparent return of constitutional rule to Peru and Argentina at best places them on democratic probation.

In terms of pure politics and ideology, Western democracy has allowed a dangerous vacuum to develop. It is a vacuum that Castro's infectious revolutionary pressures have helped to widen and that he hopes to fill with his "wave of the future." But in a social revolution, politics and ideology are tied to the economic and social realities of the new age through a cause-and-effect relationship. The doubts concerning the democratic system are linked to the ability of representative democracy to function in a social revolution.

This is the cardinal point that Castro has raised and that has not yet received a satisfactory answer. The question is whether a democratic government—responsive to a Congress, a free press, and the interplay of political and economic forces—can carry out the imaginative but complex and often unpalatable programs of social and economic development.

During the first three years of the Alliance for Progress, the experience has not been overly encouraging. The continuous failure of most of the democratic, semidemocratic, or allegedly democratic Latin American governments to practice the reforms to which they are pledged under the Alliance Charter, and which common sense requires, has been one of the principal reasons for the erosion of faith in democracy and for the propagation of revolutionary ideas. Small concessions, like the approval of new tax laws, have not really lessened the ossification of the Latin American societies.

A vicious circle has been created as the processes of democracy do not seem adequate to force the implementation of reforms upon which the very future of this democracy depends. One cannot deny the shortcomings of the United States leadership in failing to break this vicious circle. But ultimately, the fate of Latin America lies in the hands of Latin Americans, and the United States obviously cannot and should not try to live their lives for them, nor can it carry out their social revolution for them. Like the "effective exercise of representative democracy," this is, in the final analysis, the responsibility of each Latin American republic and of the inter-American system as a whole.

While, evidently, a regime's desire to implant far-reaching reforms is not a justification for establishing a rightist or a leftist dictatorship, the great question that arises is how the "revolution of rising expectations" is to be conducted in the face of the powerful pressures and vested interests that, by definition, operate freely in a democratic society. Premier Castro's belief that the social reforms of his revolution could never be carried out in the midst of an electoral campaign, or under a representative political democracy of the type Cuba has known in the past, cannot, of course, excuse his refusal to hold elections and his ultimately implanting a Communist dictatorship. But it is a thought-provoking argument, one that has captured the attention of millions of increasingly impatient Latin Americans. After years of national debate, Brazil has not been able to move ahead with any form of land reform, and this is true everywhere except for Venezuela, and to a small extent for Colombia and the Dominican Republic. Whether the new government and Congress in Peru and Argentina will be able to make a breakthrough in social reform is the great question overshadowing the fact of their election.

The Castro argument, when examined with the benefit of hindsight, suggests, however, that if the revolutionary regime had to contend with a free Congress, a free press, and a free public opinion, it might have found it extremely difficult, if not impossible, to convert itself into the Marxist-Leninist apparatus it is today. Yet, this flaw in the Cuban argument—and the Cubans nowadays regard it not as a weakness but as a strength and as a vital part of the revolutionary dialectics—does not greatly impress the young people of Latin America as they search for new directions and new definitions. Millions of them are ready to accept Castro's defiant cry that "If this is Communism, then we are Communists." Though most of these young people do not wish to see the advent of Communism in their countries, they are increasingly willing to go along with any short cut to a successful social revolution.

The next step in this process is the acceptance of the oversimplified Castro doctrine that the state must have complete power in order to put the needed social and economic reforms into effect. Thus the notion is accepted that a bit of what seems like dictatorial rule may not be such a bad thing, after all, though it is easily forgotten that there is no such thing as a "bit of dictatorship" and that power corrupts, and absolute power corrupts absolutely.

What these attitudes add up to is nothing less than an abdication of the democratic principle. But because the sacrifice of one ideology to a social revolution inevitably creates a vacuum that in turn is filled by another ideology (this is an immutable law of politics), the trend to rationalize or to compromise with democracy is the most important and dangerous by-product of the Cuban revolution operating against the background of Latin America's traditional negligence toward its democratic institutions.

Upon the ability of the Alliance for Progress to arrest this trend depends the entire future of the Hemisphere in the decade of the 1960's. Either the Alliance, as a broad political concept shared by all the Hemispheric countries, can evolve a new form of democracy adapted to the social revolution, or it is bound to fail. Its first three years of existence, as a reaction to the problems not produced but brought into the open by the Cuban revolution, does not warrant very optimistic conclusions.

Yet, because the Latin American revolution is not a black-and-white phenomenon but a live, surging, and receding situation, hope is daily blended with discouragement.

On the positive side—though what seems positive at this writing may quickly cease to be so—there have been elections of moderate candidates in Peru and Argentina in 1963, and in Panama in 1964. There has been the sudden emergence of the Christian Democrats in Chile as the strongest single democratic party there, and the success of Rómulo Betancourt in serving out his Presidential term in Venezuela in 1964. Senator Frei's overwhelming victory in the Chilean elections over his Marxist opponent constituted perhaps the brightest political event on the Hemisphere scoreboard, not only because the pro-Communist candidate was defeated but even more important, because Frei is deeply committed to democratic reforms. All these, and other, moves toward political stability are a boon for the Alliance for Progress, but the life-or-death struggle for Latin American democracy in its new revolutionary context and amidst the leftist and rightist pressures will not be settled so easily or quickly.

6. The Alliance

The Alliance Is Born

THE ALLIANCE FOR PROGRESS was officially born as a policy idea and a broad cooperative concept on March 13, 1961, when President Kennedy gathered the Latin American Ambassadors to the White House to invite their governments and people to join with the United States in "a vast effort, unparalleled in magnitude and nobility of purpose, to satisfy the basic needs of the American people for homes, work and land, health and schools."

This effort, he said, would be a new "Alliance for Progress" between the United States and Latin America, aimed at raising the Hemisphere's living standards and strengthening democracy in the Americas. The plan unveiled by the President implied that the United States would commit itself to massive aid to Latin America, while the republics themselves initiated broad self-help measures. The third element implicit in this equation of the Alliance was that the sum of the first two would bring stability and eventually prosperity to Latin America, thus bolstering her democratic structure in the midst of the revolutionary age.

In relating the economic and political aspects of Latin American development, the new Administration's thinking represented, at least in principle, an immense step forward in the United States approach to the Hemisphere. In the past, Washington had advocated Latin America's rational economic improvement just as vaguely and incomprehensively as it encouraged its political development. It had passively hoped for economic stability revolving around the practice of free enterprise and Export-Import Bank lending, and for a maximal anti-Communist position that was expected to grow even in the absence of the truly healthy roots of a positive exercise of democracy. Washington's relations with the dictators underscored this casual attitude.

The Kennedy Alliance concept stemmed, to be sure, from the challenge to the United States posed by Castro's defiance and, in a larger way, by the whole revolutionary ferment of Latin America. The obvious idea that a major effort was needed in the Hemisphere was not, of course, a Kennedy innovation. Brazil's Juscelino Kubitschek had been advocating it since 1958 through his "Operation Pan American" proposals, and the Eisenhower Administration had made a sound beginning in that direction through the Act of Bogotá of September, 1960. The chief architects of the Act— Douglas Dillon, then Under Secretary of State, and Thomas C. Mann, Assistant Secretary of State for Inter-American Affairs— had made an important contribution to the emerging new American thinking when they had related the concept of social development to that of economic growth and launched the principle of self-help in Latin America.

But the introduction of the political approach to the situation was due mainly to the young Kennedy Administration, a very politically minded group. The recognition of the need for bringing the United States into the revolutionary situations, for shoring up the democratic structures in Latin America, and for meeting the special requirements of the Hemisphere in central planning and financing emerged during the 1960 campaign. This awareness had its origins in Kennedy's personal appreciation of the shortcomings in our relationships with Latin America even before he became a Presidential candidate.

Senator Kennedy wrote in 1960, in his *Strategy of Peace,* that "just as we must recall our own revolutionary past in order to understand the spirit and the significance of the anticolonial uprisings in Asia and Africa, we should now reread the life of Simón Bolívar . . . in order to comprehend the new contagion for liberty and reform now spreading south of our borders."

Quite perceptively, he noted that "Fidel Castro is part of the legacy of Bolívar" and that he "also is part of the frustration of that earlier revolution which won its war against Spain but left largely untouched the indigenous feudal order." All this was written after Castro had already embarked on an anti-American line but before he had openly espoused Communism, and Senator Kennedy, like most Americans, was at a loss to understand the revolutionary leader.

But, then as later, Kennedy showed his preoccupation with the larger problem of Latin America. "Cuba is not an isolated case," he said. "We can still show our concern for liberty and our opposition to the status quo in our relations with the other Latin American dictators who now, or in the future, try to suppress their people's aspirations. And we can take the long-delayed positive measures that are required to enable the revolutionary wave sweeping Latin America to move through relatively peaceful channels and to be harnessed to the great constructive tasks at hand."

Almost two years earlier, in a speech delivered in San Juan, Puerto Rico, in December, 1958, Senator Kennedy urged a new political approach to Latin America, remarking that "in the final analysis, I think this question of attitudes will prove to be more important in improving or worsening relations between the United States and Latin America than dollars, tariffs, and treaties of friendship."

In a statement that is as applicable in 1964 as it was in 1958, he added that "unless we in the United States re-examine our attitude toward Latin America, there is little value in re-examining our policies and programs."

He recognized the mounting Latin American complaint against Washington's demands that all economic development be based on private investments, saying that "they resent our insisting upon a larger role for their private enterprise, which cannot cope with many of their problems, or a larger role for our private investors. . . ."

This was the philosophical foundation of Kennedy's thinking on Latin America as it emerged in the plans for the Alliance for Progress, less than two months after he took office. In subsequent months and years, he frequently said that the Alliance was one of the most important foreign-policy undertakings of his Administration.

President Kennedy's launching of the Alliance policy in early 1961 coincided with a series of developments in Latin America that promised to mark new milestones in the Hemisphere's history.

In Brazil, Jânio Quadros had been sworn in as President eleven days after President Kennedy's own inauguration, and there was optimism that the new Administrations, taking office almost simultaneously in two of the Western Hemisphere's biggest and most important countries, could together set in motion a new era in inter-American relationships. In the Dominican Republic, a key point in the seething Caribbean, anti-Trujillo conspiracies were mounting under Washington's benevolent eye, and the days of the old dictator seemed to be numbered.

And there was the problem of Cuba that, in its own way, was also rushing toward a decisive crisis. Though the Castro regime had entertained high hopes that, as a liberal, President Kennedy would accept its increasingly radical revolutionary status and come to terms with it, the new Administration was, on the contrary, prepared to destroy it physically in order to start its Latin American policy with a clean slate—and without the problem of a pro-Communist state in the Hemisphere.

Having inherited from the Eisenhower Administration the rebel army secretly trained in Guatemalan and United States camps, President Kennedy decided to go ahead with the attack on Cuba even while he was unveiling the plans for the Alliance for Progress. There may have been, as many people have observed, a moral contradiction in these two steps, but Kennedy was convinced that in authorizing the Cuban invasion, he was acting in the cause of freedom.

A White Paper on Cuba issued by the State Department on the eve of the Bay of Pigs assault charged Castro with the betrayal of his own social revolution and reaffirmed the United States' dedication to the principles of social justice, progress, and democracy to which the Cuban revolutionaries had once been pledged.

But, as also became evident later with the Alliance, a deep gulf existed between the ideas and pronouncements of the President and the field activities of his subordinates. In the case of the invasion, the Central Intelligence Agency tied itself to right-wing elements among the Cuban exiles in Miami, who had no sympathy for social justice of the Castro or even of the Kennedy variety, and it proceeded to banish from the operation all the left-of-center democratic Cuban groups—actually in defiance of the White House policies. It is now a matter of history that the failure of the Bay of Pigs enterprise, from which the Cuban underground was almost entirely eliminated, was due largely to these tactics.

But the phenomenon of the void between the President's policy ideas—and inspiration—and their execution by the bureaucratic establishment, beginning with the Cuban invasion, persisted and worsened as time went by, affecting the Alliance for Progress perhaps more than any other single major foreign program of the Administration. In analyzing the progress of the Alliance in its first three years, it is clear that much of the inspiration President

Kennedy provided for the new Latin American foreign policy was destroyed by the professional bureaucracy's defective imagination and follow-up. This was true particularly in the vital job of linking the large concept of material development with the political and psychological realities of the Hemisphere.

The Cuban invasion, coming five weeks after the announcement of the Alliance, obviously did little to enhance the standing of the United States in Latin America. Predictably, charges were made— and they were echoed even by friends of the United States—that the Alliance for Progress was nothing more than a shield for renewed efforts to overthrow Castro and liquidate his revolution. On another level, the Alliance was described as simply a grudging United States gesture to counteract the impact of the Cuban revolution.

Both charges were unfair and at best vastly oversimplified, but the Bay of Pigs venture unquestionably did put the United States and the newborn Alliance in an unsavory light, after it had been greeted with immense enthusiasm throughout Latin America. The difficulty was that Cuba could not be separated from the larger question of the Hemisphere's future, and hard as the Administration tried to isolate Castro's island and concentrate on the essential tasks in Latin America, the relationship between the two issues could not be broken.

In a larger sense, this relationship was, of course, a political and historical reality, inasmuch as the Alliance was conceived as an answer to the Jacobin turn of the Cuban revolution. Its central idea, overshadowing everything else, was that if the United States and Latin America could really cooperate in development and reform programs, the fundamental point could be made that progress is not only desirable but also possible in free, democratic societies, and that the neglected masses of the Hemisphere need not seek solutions in the extremisms of violent revolutions. All this carried the implication that the democratic social revolution, which President Kennedy so warmly promoted, would have an ideological content. But ideologically meaningful social revolutions must possess their own dynamics, just as Communist revolutions do, and this is where the Alliance started off on the wrong foot—and appeared to continue on it.

In the meantime, before Cuba again cast its pall over the Hemisphere, Latin America's first reactions to President Kennedy's inauguration and to his March speech on the Alliance were en-

thusiastic. The expectations raised by the advent of a Democratic
Administration in Washington were so high that an anticlimax
seemed unavoidable. President Kennedy was described in emo-
tional editorials and speeches as a spiritual heir of Franklin D.
Roosevelt, whose legend still lives throughout Latin America. The
Kennedy election presaged a new and a better era of Good
Neighbor policies, Latin American writers declared in their news-
papers.

In short, the reassessment of United States–Latin American relationships promised by Kennedy could not have been carried out
under better circumstances and in a more favorable climate. United
States image and prestige, steadily plummeting in recent years,
had suddenly risen to a new high. Even Fidel Castro ordered a
demobilization of his militias for the day of President Kennedy's
inauguration.

Three factors rendered the Kennedy Administration particularly
appealing in those days to Latin American youth and intellectuals,
helping to spread pro-United States sympathies in some of the
Hemisphere's most influential quarters.

First, there was the attraction of the aura of political liberalism
surrounding the new President and his team. Vastly disturbed
by the McCarthy period in the United States and the eight-year
Republican era, whose conservatism—and political negativism,
expressed in policies that, being single-mindedly anti-Communist,
offered nothing new and positive to the anxious Hemisphere youth
—went far to tarnish the American image, Latin Americans wel-
comed the different political climate heralded by Kennedy's election. Their belief was that a liberal Administration in the United
States would play a major role in strengthening democratic influences in Latin America and bringing about the social reforms
that theretofore were resisted by the entrenched "oligarchs."

Second, Latin Americans were impressed by what they viewed as
the economic liberalism of the new Administration in the sense
that it recognized the peculiarities of the Hemispheric development problems, even though what the Hemisphere sought was the
opposite of classical economic liberalism. The new trend meant,
primarily, that the United States would now accept the concept
of central economic planning—which had been rejected by the
Republican Administration as a highly suspect undertaking smack-
ing of socialism—and would abandon its insistence on assigning the
chief role in development to private capital. Likewise, the Latin

Americans were pleased that the new Washington Administration seemed to believe in the principle of highly accelerated development. The politicians, economists, and intellectuals were intimately familiar with the thinking of the Harvard and MIT groups, and Walt W. Rostow's theory of economic "take-off" became a sacred precept for Brazilians, still enamored of their *"desenvolvimentismo."*

Third, Latin Americans respected an American government that included more noted intellectuals than generals and bankers. When Arthur M. Schlesinger, Jr., the Harvard historian who became a special Presidential adviser, arrived in Brazil on the first Latin American mission of the Kennedy Administration, one of the top Brazilian negotiators opened the session with a discussion of his books. The feeling in Latin America was that "now we can talk with the Americans," who, for the first time, would understand the Hemisphere problems. The Latin tradition of respect for intellectuals—an attitude in some ways peculiar to underdeveloped societies—served to enhance the prestige of the United States.

In sum, all the political and emotional ingredients were present for the United States to assume the long-neglected positive leadership in Latin America at the time of the rising social revolution. The Alliance for Progress seemed to offer the perfect vehicle for this leadership.

But this leadership began to falter even before it hit its stride. Many controllable and uncontrollable factors combined to create this state of affairs. Most important, the concept of the Alliance somehow failed to electrify Latin America, contrary to what optimists in Washington had hoped and notwithstanding the early Latin American enthusiasm for the new Administration. Despite the noble and inspiring words of President Kennedy, the Alliance quickly proved to be virtually empty of the desperately needed political and psychological content. It was unable to project a mystique that would captivate the attention and imagination of Latin Americans—as the Castro revolution had done in Cuba and in the rest of the Hemisphere. As a result, the Alliance gradually lost its freshness and its force as an ideological weapon in the contest with the Jacobinism emanating from Havana and supported by the organizational talents of the Communists.

Instead, it became a somewhat pedantic program of financing for economic and social projects, punctuated by a self-conscious in-

sistence on domestic reforms in Latin America and largely ineffective sallies into the field of public relations.

What seemed to have happened was that having invented the
Alliance, the United States did not quite know what to do with it.
But, in 1964, with the establishment of the multinational CIAP
setup, there was new hope that it might regain its original impetus
and begin to exude a mystique of its own. As Mr. Kennedy had said
in 1958, what counted was "this question of attitude" rather than
all the billions of dollars of the Alliance.

Other factors, of course, aside from the continued inability of
the United States to exercise acceptable leadership, contributed to
the slowing down of the Alliance.

For one thing, the honeymoon with Latin America that followed President Kennedy's inauguration ended perhaps sooner
than was anticipated, largely because the expectations that had
been built up in these first months could not have been fulfilled by
any reasonable, or even mystical, standards. The Bay of Pigs
incident inevitably contributed to this cooling-off process.

For another thing, a democratic social revolution turned out to
be a much more complex process than anyone had imagined.
Foot-dragging by the Latin American governments—bedeviled by
their own immediate internal problems—combined with the powerful resistance to change by the traditional economic interests in
the individual republics to help block the Alliance. The never-
ending game of Latin American politics prevented any of the
major breakthroughs that had been expected in the first years of
the Alliance.

However, as the third year of the program came to a close, a
truly agonizing reappraisal of the Alliance, its functions, and its
potential was undertaken by the Hemisphere's Finance Ministers at
the São Paulo Conference, resulting in the creation of CIAP as the
steering committee and the possibility that the whole enterprise
may finally begin functioning as a real alliance. And it may
now have a chance to work among the Latin American masses.

The Objectives

Historically, the next milestone in the life of the Alliance after
President Kennedy's initial speech was the conference of the
Hemisphere's Finance Ministers at Punta del Este, Uruguay, in
August, 1961, to draft and sign the Charter of this new under-
taking.

In it, the Latin American governments and the United States set vastly ambitious goals, summarized in the opening phrase of the Charter's Preamble: "We, the American Republics, hereby proclaim our decision to unite in a common effort to bring our people accelerated economic progress and broader social justice within the framework of personal dignity and political liberty."

The articles of the Charter, spelling out the specific objectives to be achieved under the Alliance, stated that to raise Latin America during this "decade of progress" to levels where self-sustaining development is possible, "the rate of economic growth in any country should be not less than 2.5 per cent per capita per year." They also provided for "a more equitable distribution of national income"; for "programs of comprehensive agrarian reform"; for accelerating "the process of rational industrialization"; for eliminating adult illiteracy and assuring all children in Latin America by 1970 of at least six years of primary education"; for increasing "life expectancy at birth by a minimum of five years"; for reducing housing shortages; for maintaining stable price levels and avoiding inflation or deflation; and for joint programs designed to prevent the ruinous fluctuations in the prices of the Hemisphere's basic export products.

These goals of the Alliance constituted, in effect, a catalogue of the Hemisphere's fundamental ills, along with a promise of attempting to cure them through well-integrated economic and social programs. The underlying theorem of the Alliance was that social improvement—through better distribution of income and better housing, health, and education—will inevitably lead to greater economic activity and thus to higher living standards and greater general welfare. The broad image, in short, was of a rising spiral of economic improvement and social improvement, each aiding the other.

To set this spiral in motion, the Charter offered two principal stimulants. One was to be the preparation and execution of national development programs in each Latin American republic, based on the Bogotá principle of self-help and on the maximum use of domestic material and human resources. The other stimulant was to be, in the words of the Charter, "sufficient external financial assistance," which was loosely defined as adding up to at least $20 billion over the ten years of the Alliance, or $2 billion annually, in fresh development funds. The bulk of these external resources was to come from public-sector financing—thus extinguishing the earlier myth that private investment alone could build a new Latin America—and the United States committed itself to supply at least $1 billion a year.

What the Alliance equation—or the Alliance *quid pro quo*—meant, then, in practice, was that if Latin America actually began to help herself while maintaining her democratic political structure, the United States and the international financial community would match her efforts with a massive infusion of loans and grants. In speaking to Latin America, the Punta del Este Charter employed the old adage that if you help yourself, then God, or somebody, will help you.

Inspiring and commendable as the Alliance goals and principles looked on paper in Punta del Este, they were immediately faced with formidable obstacles stemming from the very nature of the Latin American structure and from the attitudes of men both in the southern lands and in the United States.

That these obstacles did arise, and that the Alliance had perhaps set its aims too high in terms of the Latin American realities, should not, of course, be a cause for criticism. The usual assumption is that the higher one aims, the higher one will reach. But what did happen at Punta del Este was, as a perspicacious Latin American statesman observed, that the United States failed to realize the incredible difficulties lying ahead of the Alliance, while the Latin Americans, realizing them fully because they knew themselves and their problems, signed the commitments for self-help and reform without much intention of seriously living up to them.

The ink on the Charter signatures had hardly dried when a few fundamental, and disturbing, facts and problems became apparent. Seen with the hindsight of the Alliance's first three years, these problems were inevitable, yet, at the time, they produced anguish, impatience, and harsh criticism in the United States.

Obviously, it was incredibly optimistic to expect the 2.5 per cent rate of per capita economic growth in any Latin American country in the first, second, or even third or fourth year of the Alliance. With the sky-high rate of population increase, simple arithmetic would have made it clear that this aspect of the Alliance's goals could not be attained in the overwhelming majority of cases.

About ten Latin American republics could report a 3 per cent annual rise in the gross national product in recent years, while the population rate growth ran somewhere between 2.5 and 3.1 per cent. In these instances the annual per capita income growth was 1 per cent. Argentina, Bolivia, and Haiti actually suffered a steady decline in per capita income—a 2 per cent annual loss in the case of Haiti—as their stagnant and declining economies lagged far behind the increase in population. When the Alliance was born, therefore, a good part of Latin America was progressively losing ground, with their economies and their populations' living standards unable to stand still.

A few of the countries had independently maintained a per capita annual increase close to or even above the Alliance's goals in the late 1950's and early 1960's. Guatemala's income growth hovered around the 2.5 per cent level, and Brazil, riding the crest of the tremendous wave of foreign capital investment during the Kubitschek period (1956–61), was able to show a 7 per cent gross national product growth and a 3 per cent rise in per capita income. But even these achievements were in a sense illusory and susceptible of reversal. In the case of Brazil, the apparent per capita increase figure was produced by an actuarial sleight of hand, because the new income was concentrated mainly in the south-center industrial triangle and did not extend to the majority of the population. The runaway inflation of the early 1960's—the result of the headlong rush into unplanned development and of irresponsible financial policies—began to curb the growth in the gross national product, and the consequent cheapening of the currency made the impressive rise in the per capita income meaningless in terms of actual costs and purchasing power. In 1962, the Brazilian increase in per capita income fell to less than 1 per cent.

Taking all the Latin American realities into consideration—and they ranged from the soaring birth rate and inflation to the decline in export prices of commodities and the flight of capital—it was naïve to talk in Punta del Este of raising the per capita income by at least 2.5 per cent annually, even under the best of circumstances. And, as it presently developed, these circumstances were far from favorable, let alone the best.

As soon as economic planning was begun, it became evident that many, if not most, of the Latin American republics simply lacked experienced planners and economists to draw up the necessary long-range development blueprints. By the end of 1962, almost a year and a half after Punta del Este, only five countries had submitted national development plans for study and financial implementation by the Alliance mechanism. Of these five, Bolivia,

Chile, and Colombia presented slightly revamped versions of studies that had been prepared earlier for the World Bank. The other two, Mexico and Venezuela, came up with fresh blueprints late in 1962. Brazil drafted an anti-inflation and investment program based on earlier similar efforts, but it seemed to be intended more for domestic use and consumption than for review by the Alliance's panel of "Nine Wise Men."

The other republics entered 1963 with serious gaps in their own knowledge of their resources and development needs, and thus far unable to come up with comprehensive national plans. A major structural problem of the Alliance was that, in a sense, it was a headless enterprise, deprived of an executive agency. In highly critical reports to the OAS, Colombia's ex-President Alberto Lleras Camargo and Brazil's ex-President Juscelino Kubitschek proposed in June, 1963, the creation of such an executive body, to be known as the Inter-American Development Committee.

Illustrating the serious obstacle presented by the absence of professional planning is the fact that the United States, which committed well over $1.5 billion in loans and grants to the Hemisphere between March, 1961, and December, 1962, could disburse only two-thirds of this total because there were simply not enough fully studied and engineered projects to be financed. About one-half of the disbursed funds were Export-Import Bank loans, many approved in pre-Alliance days and covering everything from balance-of-payments ritualism to private-enterprise projects. Some of the money disbursed in that period was in the form of emergency grants and loans that the United States had promised at Punta del Este to make available within six months to aid its partners' limping economies.

If over-all measures of self-help—and rational economic planning certainly fitted into this concept—were stymied by the lack of technical competence, the Latin American countries likewise were singularly unenthusiastic about putting into practice the reforms to which they had committed themselves in theory in signing the Punta del Este Charter.

To be sure—and in all fairness to the Latin American governments, this must be stressed—such complex undertakings as agrarian or taxation reforms require a great deal of thought, study, and preparation. When the Alliance was launched, only Mexico and Bolivia had had an actual experience of land reform, and their accomplishments—going back fifty years in the first case, and eight years in the latter—were somewhat short of sensational or orderly. Guatemala had had a brief and hectic experience in the field. Venezuela, which had had none, launched a land-reform program two years before the Alliance's advent, and slow and error-punctuated as it was, it had at least the advantage of showing some tangible results. Colombia passed land-reform legislation late in 1961, but a year later, its achievements were hardly noticeable, and the Conservative government that took office in August, 1962, seemed to have little stomach for pushing it ahead. Honduras legislated a reform program, but it died with the 1963 military coup.

Elsewhere in Latin America, agrarian reform remained a slogan and a bone of contention among the local politicians and between the country's government and an impatient Washington. First, of course, it was necessary to define what reform meant as a general proposition and what it meant to each Latin American country and to its different regions. But these definitions were not formulated clearly at the outset of the Punta del Este commitment, and in the eyes of the United States Congress and of United States public opinion, this signified that Latin America was merely dragging its feet on reform.

However, to alter the system of land tenure, as the Charter puts it elegantly, it is not enough to approve legislation dividing up vast tracts of land owned by the "oligarchs" and giving it to the peasants. Except to radicals, land reform does not mean, either, expropriating, nationalizing, or collectivizing the land—as was done in Cuba—but instead, it means creating a new class of landowners who can realistically and efficiently till their new properties. The Alliance Charter has made it clear that the *minifundio* (the dwarf holding) is economically and socially just as harmful as the *latifundio* (the giant holding). The temptation among those inexperienced in land reform is simply to divide the landlord's property like a cake and give each available family a slice, regardless of whether it can cultivate the holding economically. When a nation's agriculture suddenly switches from the *latifundio* to the *minifundio* pattern—primarily to satisfy political urges—an economic catastrophe can easily result.

It is essential, therefore, for each Latin American republic to organize what Venezuela's President Betancourt has called an "integrated" land reform. The first step, obviously, is to survey what type of land and how much is in the hands of the federal and state governments so that the reform program can be at least initiated without pushing a country into the immense and inflationary enterprise of paying compensations to private owners. In the opinion of land-reform experts, a giant step toward settling rural families on their own properties can be taken simply by the rational use of government lands that often lie idle. Until now, however, little if any attention has been given to this obvious move. The political spotlight has been primarily on expropriating private land, a procedure that, at least initially, is frequently unnecessary.

Once the surveys are completed, and modern agrarian technology makes this a relatively easy task, economic studies are required to determine how—and in what amounts—land should be divided among the peasant families. Obviously, different criteria should apply to areas where vegetable truck gardening seems indicated than to those where, say, climatic and economic conditions favor crops like coffee or sugar, or cattle-raising. Thus a family of five can prosper on five acres of good land if they concentrate on vegetables, but it does not make any sense for one family to try to grow sugar cane on a plot of similar size. In such cases, when economical production demands efforts on a large scale, cooperatives of the type existing in northern Europe or northwestern United States may be preferable.

The next steps in an "integrated" approach to agrarian reform include construction of at least minimally adequate housing, electrification when possible, and provision of technical advice and of seeds and implements. Land infrastructure investments are required for building access roads from farms to markets because, clearly, agrarian reform will be valueless if the peasant is unable to take his produce where it can be sold. The guiding aim here is, naturally, to take the Latin American peasant out of his situation at the margin of the money economy and to integrate him into modern society. When he has ceased merely eking out enough food to survive with his family—being neither a producer nor a consumer in the economic sense—he can become instead a positive factor in the national agricultural supply, which in most countries lags further and further behind the population increases. Once he becomes a producer of goods and a consumer of goods, his living standards will rise and with them the national economic activity.

Accompanying all these steps, there must be a supply of housing and production credits and other forms of settlement assistance so that the peasant family can become properly fixed on the soil.

Schools and medical and hospital services would complement this "integrated" land reform.

In the cases where not enough public land is available, or when this land has already been distributed, the governments may move toward the next step, which is actively discouraging absentee landlords who maintain large and unproductive estates. This can be accomplished through severe and punitive taxation, which will lead the landlord to sell his properties at reasonable prices either to the government or to his own farm hands or tenant farmers. This system, incidentally, is now in practice in the Brazilian states of São Paulo and Rio Grande do Sul.

Clearly, this is an ideal blueprint that will take years to turn into reality. Immense funds are required to set it in motion—in Brazil, for example, it is calculated that it takes $1,500 to settle one family on new land—and vast technical expertise is required. Yet, no country today possesses the reserve of money needed to launch land reform on an impressive scale, and even with an annual disbursement of $1 billion under the Alliance programs, the United States alone cannot even begin to foot the bill for this job.

The shortage of professional agronomists, without whom a land reform can become a nightmare instead of a brave success, is another brake on this undertaking. The Inter-American Institute of Agricultural Sciences reported in 1962 that there were only 16,000 trained agronomists in Latin America, while to serve minimal requirements, even without a major land-reform program, 43,000 were needed. There are only 60 agricultural schools in the region, graduating about 2,000 agronomists annually. At this rate, the Institute said, it would take thirteen years just to cover the present gap. In an effort to provide some emergency training, the Organization of American States has set up, through the Institute, a special school at Turrialba, in Costa Rica, where thus far 8,000 farm specialists have been given intensive short courses. With the Alliance support, the Turrialba school has also graduated 1,135 agronomists in the last two years.

But these fundamental difficulties do not justify delaying efforts toward "integrated" land reforms. Unfortunately, though, the record shows that most of the governments have not taken even the initial steps in that direction. Bogged down in domestic politics, paralyzed by their parliaments, and held back by the local vested interests, they have preferred to stand still, as if awaiting a miracle that will solve the awesome economic and social problems of Latin American land tenure.

That no start has been made constitutes the greatest fundamental failure of the Alliance thus far. It emphasizes that the Alliance has not been able to awaken the revolutionary mystique that could act as an irresistible stimulant to the governments and the political parties to put the reforms into action. As a leading Latin American statesman who is deeply involved in the Alliances remarked recently, "Nobody except the Communists is really against the Alliance, but nobody is prepared to go out and fight for it and nobody will put his hand in the fire for it."

Since the reform concepts of the Alliance have struck no spark in most of Latin America, it is small wonder that the social and political unrest in the Hemisphere is growing instead of diminishing, contrary to what the signers of the Punta del Este Charter thought at the time.

Having heard promises of land reform for years but not seeing any practical results, land-hungry peasants all over the Hemisphere have been taking matters into their own hands. Francisco Julião's Peasant Leagues had been talking of armed revolt until the 1964 anti-Goulart revolution broke their strength, at least temporarily. The new Brazilian Government immediately promulgated an agrarian-reform bill, but it may take years before it is translated into reality. Indian peasants in the Peruvian highlands have been invading landlords' *haciendas* and clashing with troops and police, though the long-delayed passage of a moderate land-reform law by Congress in 1964 promises to slow down these invasions. Obviously, Communists have been exploiting all this restlessness, but the answer to the problem lies not in repression but in rapid structural changes.

Writing of his own country, Brazil's former Economics Minister Celso Furtado has warned that unless a land reform is begun, the danger of "Marxist-Leninist" revolution based, China-like, on the peasant masses has to be reckoned with.

But if the governments and the political leaders of Latin America continue to balk at reforms that are so obviously needed for their own survival and for the survival of the democratic system, their slowness and irresponsibility are matched by those of the economic leadership groups. In most of the republics, the fear of tax reforms, along with the fear of political unrest, has set off in recent years an immense flight of capital. It is admittedly impossible to estimate precisely how many millions of dollars annually are fleeing Latin America, but this exodus by the early 1960's is already one of the most massive movements of capital in postwar years.

First to go was much of the "hot" speculative money, which does not really belong anywhere but had alighted in Latin America in the late 1950's to take advantage of what then appeared to be prospects for quick and easy profits. Some of it had come from the United States and Canada, some from Europe, some from as far away as Indochina and North Africa, as French capitalists moved their resources away from these danger areas.

The "hot" money was followed by short-term investment capital, which had lost interest in Latin America and became attracted again by United States and European stock markets and the prosperity of Europe. Its departure coincided with a marked retrenchment of serious investment capital—especially in the United States —which slowed down and even discontinued some of its new operations in Latin America, fearing the inroads of inflation and the threats of nationalization by governments that found it easier to take over foreign firms than to develop national resources. Nobody can estimate how much the nationalization of several United States public utilities in 1962 by politically minded State Governors cost Brazil in terms of potential capital that refused to invest there.

But perhaps most painful for Latin America was the continuing flight of its native capital, which preferred to find new havens in Miami real estate, the New York stock market, Swiss banks or Nassau dummy corporations, rather than face the danger of taxation or political unrest. The capital fled through the purchase of dollars on free or black markets, incidentally adding to inflation, and through a myriad of banking stratagems. Big corporations and landowners exported their pesos and cruzeiros and bolívars, and much of the middle class did likewise with their savings, to protect them from taxes and inflation. What the total figures are nobody knows, but the estimates of Latin American capital invested abroad range from $5 billion to $25 billion—or more than the external financing under the Alliance is to bring over a decade. At the end of 1961, Department of Commerce statistics showed that $4 billion in Latin American funds were held in the United States alone and that $316 million of this had gone during that year.

The blow was damaging because the formation of national investment capital through savings had all along been one of the key elements in the shoring up and developing of the economies. The Alliance had placed a special stress on the mobilization of national financial resources so that local private enterprise could fruitfully cooperate with the public-sector investments from the United States.

This, then, was how, in the first three years of the Alliance for Progress, the almost overwhelming problems of trying to alter a social and economic structure frozen for generations had come into collision with the noble goals of Punta del Este.

The Response

Again, one must return to the political problem of the Alliance as the hinge upon which its ultimate success or failure will rest. Looking back over the program's march in its first years, the observer cannot fail to find ample evidence that the Alliance, as a political and democratic revolutionary concept, has not seeped down to the mass levels of the population and has not set off the kind of generalized support that would be reflected in pressures on the governing classes to move ahead with the needed reforms.

Lincoln Gordon, currently United States Ambassador to Brazil and one of the founding fathers of the Alliance, remarked in a recent speech that the program suffers from its inability to spawn the kind of mystique that Franklin Roosevelt's "New Deal" evoked in the United States thirty years ago. And, unquestionably, if the Alliance is to succeed, it must be to Latin Americans the same kind of a democratic social revolution that the "New Deal" was to North Americans.

Likewise, the Alliance has evoked no marked response from the political leadership in the Hemisphere—with the exception of the top governing levels in such countries as Venezuela, Colombia (under the Lleras Camargo regime), and Costa Rica, which have traditionally been sympathetic to the notion of democratic social revolution. Most of the democratic political parties in Latin America have remained cool to the cooperative notion of the Alliance, partly because of disbelief in its future and partly because both the United States and the Latin American governments have made no real effort to relate the domestic problems and anxieties in each country to the over-all idea of a revolutionary partnership under the Alliance for Progress.

During a 1962 visit to Washington, Senators Eduardo Frei and

Radomiro Tomich of Chile's Christian Democratic Party told this writer that if any effort had been made by the Alliance director to interest them in the program, they would have gladly used their and their party's considerable influence to spread the Alliance's gospel on the grass-roots level back home. It is impossible to work in a political vacuum, they remarked, yet the leadership of the Alliance has made no concerted effort to attract the political forces of the Hemisphere to what was intended as a joint enterprise.

Dr. José A. Mora, the Secretary General of the OAS, has proposed privately that the Alliance seek to acquire a political arm by creating some sort of an active interparliamentary Hemispheric group, somewhat like Strasbourg's European Assembly, which provided political support for the notion of the European Community more than ten years ago. Though Dr. Mora's suggestion was heard in high places in Washington, it was never acted upon.

In intellectual, labor, and student circles in Latin America, the Alliance has caused no visible stir, and yet these are the groups that are vital in any effort to animate the revolutionary concept President Kennedy had in mind when he launched the program. The primary reason for this apathy is that the Alliance leadership in Washington has made very little attempt to communicate a sense of excitement and participation to these restless groups; in addition, the local governments have done even less to convince them that the Alliance is as much their own undertaking as it is Washington's.

Anti-Alliance propaganda, relentlessly pushed by the Communists and other extreme leftist factions in Latin America, has had its effect among the Hemisphere's youth. The intellectuals, traditionally inclined toward the left, have often been openly hostile to the Alliance, seeing in it nothing more than a clever scheme for the United States to perpetuate its political and economic influence in Latin America.

In a reasonably sophisticated country like Brazil, Leonel Brizzola, who campaigned on a virulently anti-Alliance platform, was elected to Congress from the city of Rio de Janeiro in October, 1962, by the greatest plurality ever accorded a Federal Deputy. Brizzola, who served at the time as Governor of Rio Grande do Sul, hammered his point home by expelling the Peace Corps volunteers from his state. It is hard to find more telling evidence of how poorly the Alliance is faring politically. But there are other examples.

Juan Bosch, elected in December, 1962, to the Presidency of the Dominican Republic, arrived in Washington in January, 1963, and told the Administration that although the Alliance had operated in his country for a full year after the fall of the Trujillo dictatorship, it remained an unknown quantity politically, despite its loans and grants. Neither Bosch nor his opponent, Viriato A. Fiallo, had dared to bring the Alliance into their electoral campaigns. This point is extremely important because from the day Trujillo was assassinated, in May, 1961, the United States had proclaimed that a great opportunity now loomed to make the Dominican Republic a showcase of the Alliance—and indeed the opportunity existed.

But as events showed, it was a short-lived opportunity. On September 25, 1963—seven months after he took office—Bosch was overthrown by a military *coup d'état*. The generals announced at once that a "rightist state" would be set up, thus dealing the Alliance one of the worst blows of its young life. Ten days later, the Honduran constitutional regime fell, and with it, the Alliance reform programs.

What can be concluded, then, is that the Alliance's principal failing is that it has not become an Alliance in a real sense nor the catalyst of a democratic social revolution. Operating in a virtual political vacuum, it is battered by the cross winds of the opposition from the extreme left, which fears its democratic "social reformism," and from the right and the business interests of the center, which, for their own reasons, fear these reforms.

Thus, the Chilean newspapers that speak for the economic interests of the right had no hesitation in accusing the United States of "betraying" its old friends in Latin America through a "courtship" of the left and through its insistence that the Alessandri government rapidly institute land and tax reforms as a condition for Alliance aid. It is notable that such an attitude should have arisen in a country where the left is a powerful political force and threatened to capture Chile's Presidency in the 1964 elections.

In Brazil, business and industrial interests, including United States corporations operating there, were able to raise millions of dollars to try to influence the voters in the 1962 congressional elections away from the left. But the same men, with a few exceptions, had no interest in constituting themselves into a political force in favor of democratic reform. With the harsh winds of nationalism and extreme leftism blowing over Brazil in recent years, the affluent classes allied themselves with the middle class and the military in bringing about President Goulart's overthrow in April, 1964. But no sooner did the new regime take power than the so-called conservative classes immediately began sabotaging its efforts to combat inflation and push through the needed economic and social reforms.

That the Alliance desperately needs a political content has been demonstrated by the Latin American response, right down to the grass roots, to the personality of President Kennedy and to the gospel he preached on his visits to the Hemisphere. His trips to Venezuela and Colombia in 1961, to Mexico in 1962, and to Costa Rica in 1963 showed that the United States, as personified by the President and his political ideas, still exercises a powerful magnetism on the Latin Americans and that his Alliance pronouncements echo their own wishes.

But naturally, the mystique of the Alliance cannot be left to depend entirely on flying Presidential visits to Latin America, frequent as they may be, and in the ideological field, there has been a destructive lack of follow-up. It may be said that no bureaucracy, and particularly no Anglo-Saxon bureaucracy, can light the fires of revolution and of a sense of participation in a great adventure. Yet, an effort by the United States to communicate to the political forces of Latin America such a sense of participation could finally evoke this mystique, with all its extraordinary implications for the march of the Alliance and the Hemisphere's future.

It should be recorded here that Teodoro Moscoso, who was the Alliance's immensely devoted United States Coordinator until 1964, was fully alive to the need to inject a political and ideological content into the program he directed for nearly three years. But overall foreign policy and psychological-warfare strategies were not formulated by Moscoso and his Alliance operation, and the political aspects of the Alliance were continually lost in the huge transmission belt of the Administration's far-flung activities. After President Kennedy's death and the emergence of the new policy team for Latin America under Assistant Secretary of State for Inter-American Affairs Thomas C. Mann, recalled by President Johnson from his post as Ambassador to Mexico, the political aspects of the Alliance continued to be neglected for a long time. However, Carlos Sanz de Santamaría, the Colombian Chairman of the program's new steering committee, is dedicated to the political idea, and the Alliance may gain new life through his efforts.

Yet, political inspiration is the very heart of the Alliance, and without it, the whole brave program may wither away like a plant deprived of the sun's rays. This point is being stressed increasingly by the key Latin American statesmen involved in the Alliance, but thus far it has been falling on deaf ears in Washington. The underlying theme of this approach is that the Alliance is not an economic abstraction, but a living program, designed for human beings, and as such, it must rely on human reactions and human support. And since articulate human beings are politically motivated, the program must have a political content. Chile's Felipe Herrera, the President of the Inter-American Development Bank, sought to make this clear in a speech in Washington in June, 1962:

> In practice, the Alliance has placed particular emphasis on the economic aspects, even though any process of economic and social development is, in the last analysis, *a political undertaking* in which the creative forces of society are mobilized. . . . In my opinion, postponed consideration of the political problems inherent in the Alliance is one of its chief limitations and may impair its chances of success.

Like Dr. Mora of the OAS, Sr. Herrera turned to the example of Western Europe, pointing out that "adequate functioning of the Alliance at the political level also includes the need to create machinery for cooperation which will make it possible to coordinate national and inter-American policies at the highest possible level." He recalled that the Treaty of Rome, which laid the foundation of the European Common Market, set up the Council of Ministers, and the 142-member Parliamentary Assembly elected by the individual parliaments, to supply the political direction to the European brand of the modern revolution.

Until early 1964, the Alliance was completely devoid of such instruments of political inspiration and follow-up. However, the creation of CIAP and the belief of Dr. Sanz de Santamaría, Chairman of CIAP, that his committee should be the "political engine" of the program are promising. Yet, a broader, ministerial-level organ like the European Council of Ministers still seems to be required.

The nine-man panel of economists, a sort of presidium of the Alliance that operates without a legal existence, is empowered to pass only on the validity of national development plans, and even these judgments are not binding. Occasionally, however, these

"Nine Wise Men" succeed in smuggling out a political idea, as was the case in July, 1962, with Raúl Saez Saez of Chile. In an unusually outspoken address, in Santiago, Saez had this to say:

> To me the Alliance for Progress is an unknown topic because it has not yet reached the people of the Hemisphere. The people are unaware of the provisions of the Alliance for Progress, they do not know of their responsibilities in the Alliance for Progress, they have not been informed of its benefits, not those referring to such a vague thing as the economic growth of nations, but those which can be immediately felt and understood by man. . . . The Alliance for Progress program should be a Latin American program, and this is the main reason why I think that the countries of Latin America are unaware of what the Alliance for Progress really is. . . .

Blaming the United States and Latin America equally for the failure to make the Alliance a living and effective undertaking, Saez said that "to my mind, the United States has not succeeded in creating public opinion favorable to massive aid to Latin America; neither has it been able to create a favorable political climate for aid to our countries. . . ."

But, he went on, another "basic defect" is a "lack of force in the representation of Latin American political thought, if such thought can be said to exist." Worst of all, he said, "national opinion has not been won over to the idea of the Alliance for Progress, and this is a phenomenon in practically all Latin America."

Because this Latin American "national opinion" indeed has not been won over to the Alliance, and the Hemisphere governments have been so slow in making it their own program, enormous complications arose for the United States in its relationships with the region between 1961 and 1964.

The Political Gap

Perhaps the key lesson of the three years of the Alliance's life is that the program cannot succeed as a major historical movement unless it becomes a Latin American as well as a United States undertaking. This truism—which really means that the Alliance must be a real alliance—dawned on the more perceptive officials in the Kennedy Administration fairly late in this first period, along with the disquieting realization that until now the Alliance had been far from an alliance in fact and that Latin Americans had by no means espoused it as their own program.

Again, it took a Latin American statesman who has a deep personal commitment to the Alliance concept to diagnose its ailment. Colombia's former President, Lleras Camargo, put it thus: "The program is fascinating, and the surprising thing is that it fails to fascinate. It is attractive, and it is astounding that it does not attract as it should those who are going to be its immediate beneficiaries."

Lleras' comment, and its sense of bewilderment, also served to synthesize the United States judgment: that the Alliance, in its initial two years, had proved incapable of winning enthusiastic support from one end of the Hemisphere to another, and thus was incapable of solving the great and awesome problems in the New World.

Enthusiastic support for the Alliance did come from Washington, both in the idealistic speeches by President Kennedy and in the more tangible earmarking of substantial funds for Latin America's social and economic development along paths never tried before by the United States alone or in cooperation with the region. Concessions to Latin American thinking—and to the new revolutionary thinking—that were written into the Alliance concept by the Kennedy Administration were in themselves a revolution in the North American approach to the whole notion of development. The idea of centralized and comprehensive planning had been accepted and championed by Washington since early 1961, after having been consigned to opprobrium during the Republican years. Land reform, a subject no United States government would ever before have touched in propounding changes in the Hemisphere, became the battle cry of the Kennedy advocates of the Alliance. Tax reforms and fiscal responsibility became watchwords for the officials dealing with the new program.

Wasn't the Alliance and all its shiny new ideals precisely what the Latin Americans had been talking about for a decade or more? Wasn't Kennedy's reaffirmation of support for representative democracy, and its rebuff of rightist as well as leftist dictators, the answer to the prayers of a generation of Latin American liberals?

If logic determined the reactions and responses of national and political groups, the Alliance should, by all rights, have been greeted in Latin America with an explosion of enthusiasm and devotion, dwarfing the impact of the Cuban revolution and hurling into oblivion the frustrations of bygone years.

Yet logic seldom applies to politics or to emotional responses, and the reaction to the Alliance in Latin America was ambivalent, not to say schizophrenic. While there was initially an emotional response to the Kennedy program, it withered away almost completely in the two years that followed. Difficult as it is to assess precisely the reasons why people do or do not fall in love with other people or ideas, some suggestions can be advanced in an effort to explain the resistance in Latin America to the Alliance.

It may be argued that the Alliance came too late. The Latin Americans were asking for it in 1947, when the Marshall Plan was launched, and after the first glow of satisfaction with the Alliance, Hemispheric public opinion sensed that, in the form in which it was offered, it no longer suited the needs of the region. And contrary to the Washington view, Latin America's needs are as much psychological as material. Perhaps the Latin Americans thought that, as it was being administered from the banks of the Potomac, the Alliance smacked too much of the familiar patronizing Yankee undertaking. Such an assessment, incidentally, would not be too far off the mark because even despite the October, 1962, Alliance conference in Mexico City—which United States officials described with the unfelicitous term "confrontation" when they meant "cooperation"—the fact remained that Washington was not prepared to yield any part of its complete control over the basic policies and planning of the program.

If Latin Americans had trouble in projecting themselves wholeheartedly into the Alliance spirit because of what Marxists would call "the contradictions" of colonial or feudal societies—or what can be described less dramatically as the disorientation of changing societies—they were not encouraged by the United States attitude in keeping the brain, the heart, and the purse of the new program safely tucked away in Washington.

Notwithstanding the grandiloquent assurances that the Alliance was a joint enterprise, it remained three years after its inception a largely one-sided effort, principally because Washington wanted it to be so. All the decisions were made in Washington by AID (Agency for International Development) officials, by the State Department's specialists in Latin America, or frequently, by the White House in free-lance sallies into the situation. The overwhelming majority of these decisions were in the field of financing and project-approval—sometimes for sound economic reasons and sometimes for less sound reasons of political expediency—because the character of the Alliance as managed from Washington left no room for other kinds of decisions.

The Latin Americans were expected to act responsibly in executing the specific projects Washington set for them for their own good (the reforms and the stability measures), but they were not given any tangible sense of sharing authority when it came to the formulation of Alliance concepts. The Latin American governments were fairly reduced to bilateral relations with the United States in the context of the Alliance, which meant agreeing or disagreeing with what Washington proposed—or bargaining over it—and to the risk of having aid cut or reduced if they disregarded too blatantly the pafernal advice from headquarters. A variant on this situation was Washington's willingness to abandon its political and philosophical criteria when a military or dictatorial regime asserted its right to thumb its nose at the Alliance's democratic principles and to threaten to look for help "elsewhere" if the Americans persisted in their unreasonable demands for elections and democracy.

What was then lacking in the whole relationship was not just a snug togetherness, whose value might well have been exaggerated, but rather a structural system of joint operations that could have made the Alliance into an alliance. Conceived as a multilateral undertaking, the Alliance was bogging down in old-fashioned bilateralism on all levels that some Latin American governments were actually and selfishly finding convenient.

A New Structure

Unlike the European Community or the Common Market, the Alliance has lacked during its first three years a multilateral executive body on any level, be it political or economic. On the economic level, this was remedied with the creation of CIAP, but there still is no permanent ministerial council to look after the political aspects of the program and no equivalent of the Strasbourg Assembly.

The Organization of American States and its Economic and Social Council were, in theory, to perform the executive role in the Alliance. The annual conference of Hemisphere Finance Ministers (designated officially as an Economic and Social Council meeting on the ministerial level) was to review each year's progress, or lack thereof. But in practice, the Council, sitting in Washington, had little if any influence on Alliance policy-making.

The ministers met in Mexico late in 1962 for the first review

THE ALLIANCE · 259

conference after Punta del Este, and their conclusion after this
"confrontation" was that the first year of the Alliance was characterized by all the difficulties of a new enterprise but that the next
year would show better results. Economic-development procedures
were clarified at this "confrontation," at which the United States
sought to have Latin Americans push each other into accomplishments. But somehow it seemed to a great many people on both
sides of the Hemisphere that these results fell somewhat short of
the earlier great expectations of a formidable democratic social
revolution.

The only concession the Mexico conference made to the political
problem of the Alliance was an agreement to invite former Presidents Lleras Camargo and Kubitschek to find out why the program
was not making much headway. Again, the ministers—who were
shocked in Punta del Este when Cuba's "Che" Guevara introduced
the political features of the Hemisphere's situations into the Alliance Charter debates—failed to face up to the most grave short-
coming of their program. Likewise, the United States made no effort
to bolster its own undertaking in the field in which it lagged the
worst. To be sure, Secretary of the Treasury Dillon was concerned
with the Cuban missile crisis that was simultaneously brewing, and
his subordinates had no visible interest in stepping into the tricky
area of political debate. The United States policy that prevailed at
that time was that, in a sense, this country had done its part by
inventing the Alliance and making the money available, and it was
now up to the Latin Americans to do something about it. This may
have been true as far as it went, but leadership in a venture of this
type cannot be so easily abdicated.

The notion of asking Lleras Camargo and Kubitschek to recommend remedies for the Alliance had something tragic and absurd about it. It was tragic that after nearly two years of Alliance
efforts, the entire future of the grandiose program had to be tied
to the imaginations of two men—hopefully labeled "superangels"
—and it was at the same time absurd that the idea should have occurred to the conference in the first place. It was as if a council of
learned physicians at the bedside of a desperately ill patient had
decided to confess its own incompetence by summoning two out-of-
town specialists not just for a consultation but to take over the whole
treatment.

Dr. Kubitschek, who had long felt that the Alliance should have
been organized along the lines of his own "Operation Pan Amer-

ican," arrived in Washington with a staff of advisers, prepared to reshuffle the entire inter-American structure. Dr. Lleras, who is a political realist and knows his fellow Latin Americans well, remarked sagely upon his arrival that the OAS could reorganize itself as much as it wanted and name as many new committees as it desired, but that this would not make much difference to the Alliance so long as there was no spirit favoring it in the Hemisphere. In the end, however, their reports settled on recommending precisely the creation of a new committee. This committee was to operate as the long-needed executive agency, but it took President Kennedy's personal intervention in overruling the State Department to make it possible for the United States to accept it.

In a move typical of the prevailing approach to the Alliance, the United States Government gave the OAS the sum of $1.6 million to "publicize" the Alliance in 1963, and to make it "multilateral." A few professional public-relations specialists fanned out across Latin America to form citizens' committees for the Alliance. Though the budget for "publicizing" the Alliance was considerably less than what a self-respecting cigarette company spends a year on advertising in the United States, Madison Avenue soft-sell techniques were borrowed; pro-Alliance comic books were produced, along with more esoteric projects that could hardly elicit a mass veering toward the democratic social revolution.

Considering how the Alliance was faring in 1962, it was not surprising that President Kennedy, who theretofore had missed no opportunity to vaunt the program's promise and future, remained silent in August, when the anniversary of the Punta del Este Charter rolled around. He also remained silent when the Ministers met in Mexico in October, but at that point, of course, his concern was with the confrontation with the Soviets over the missiles in Cuba. The second anniversary, in March, 1963, of his Alliance speech also went unnoticed.

It is easy, of course, to blame the United States for the Alliance's failure to gain momentum. Many Latin Americans and many thoughtful North Americans do, in fact, charge this up to its bureaucracy and its lack of imagination. It has been said, not unjustly, that the United States, with its immense resources and with its not inconsiderable talents, could have presented the Alliance in a more fascinating and attractive light—particularly when a liberal Administration was in office in Washington. It has also been said that the great fault lies in the inability of a mature and affluent society like ours fully to comprehend revolutions and to become attuned to them. But this has become the great historical problem of the West in the premillennium decades and a part of what can be called, in a paraphrase of Toynbee, the Western malaise.

But every problem has its obverse side, and the Alliance is no exception. It would be fatuous to blame the United States for all the failings of a program and to forget that Latin America, too, has immense responsibilities to which she has not quite lived up.

Because the reaction to the Alliance has become polarized to a considerable extent on both sides of the Hemisphere, there is a mounting tendency in the United States to shift the bulk of the blame to the Latin Americans. This school of thought is especially prevalent in Congress and is beginning to gain converts in the Administration, including the officials closely connected with the Alliance. In recent congressional appropriations, the Alliance has been seriously threatened.

In this camp, the view—and it is one of hurt and bewilderment —is that the United States went to extraordinary lengths to produce the kind of development program that Latin America had always seemed to desire. But instead of embracing it with wild enthusiasm and committing themselves to the democratic social revolution "by the book," the Latin Americans were lukewarm, uncooperative, irresponsible, or sometimes hostile. In its resentment, Washington spreads the blame among the extreme leftists, who indeed conspire against the program, the "oligarchs," who have been deliberately dragging their feet and thereby sabotaging all the reform efforts, and the politicians, who simply oscillate between the two poles and seem unable or unwilling to assume Alliance leadership at home.

This reading of the Latin American attitudes has led to impatience in Congress—which had already cut $75 million from the Alliance appropriations in 1962—and within the Administration. Beginning late in 1962, there has been more and more agitation among Washington officials for a redefinition and reappraisal of the Alliance, perhaps confining its efforts to the five or six countries that have responded positively to the program, and cutting off the others to drift on the seas of their own incompetence and lassitude. But petulance is presumably not the best foreign policy at times of crisis—and what has been happening to the Alliance is definitely a crisis even if it is not sharply etched in day-to-day terms—and perhaps what may be in order at this juncture is a reappraisal of the entire policy.

If such a serious fresh look at the Alliance were indeed taken, two points would probably emerge as the basis for a reconsideration. One is the pressing need to inject a political content into the Alliance, giving it a life it has not yet had, and adjusting this approach to the deep and extensive psychological changes that have been taking place in the Hemisphere, not only since the Castro revolution but also since the riposte of the Kennedy program.

The other point is the equally pressing need for turning the Alliance into a real partnership in which the Latin Americans could participate in the broadest possible scope, sharing both responsibility and authority with the United States.

That both these requirements are essential to the future success of the Alliance is evident from its failings to date. Since human nature tends to create vicious circles in human affairs, the Alliance's initial shortcomings—in the fields of both political inspiration and organizational partnership—have led to the deep disenchantment with the program. Because nothing succeeds like success, and because, conversely, nothing brings more failures than a failure, the Alliance has begun to acquire the reputation of a somewhat aborted undertaking. Yet, to a large extent, this verdict is a psychological rather than a factual judgment and one that could conceivably be remedied by a fresh approach to the whole question.

A Reappraisal

Numerous suggestions and recommendations on how to achieve a breakthrough in the Alliance have been offered from both within and without the program. In reviewing them here, it may be useful to look first at its structure, since greater Latin American participation may also help to sharpen the program's political content and attraction. These organizational aspects of the Alliance are wholly intertwined with the political problems.

As it is now set up, the Alliance lacks organs of political direction. It may, therefore, be necessary to entrust the OAS, through the conference of Foreign Ministers, with an Alliance role. While the function of the Hemisphere's Finance Ministers, operating through the Inter-American Economic and Social Council, would remain one of supervising broad economic, financial, and development planning, the Foreign Ministers could act as a permanent organ of political stewardship for the Alliance, on the pattern of the NATO Council.

This is crucial if the United States and Latin America are to implement their recognition that the Alliance must have an attractive political content if it is to awaken from its present lethargy. Since the OAS Council constituted itself into a ministerial-level "organ of consultation" to face the Cuban missile crisis in October, 1962, and still retains this status, there should be nothing to preclude it from operating on this level for the purposes of the Alliance as well. In its own way, after all, the Alliance represents as much of a crisis as the Cuban affair. Therefore, the political and psychological coordination of the Alliance should be in the hands of the highest organ of the inter-American system, instead of being relegated to a few OAS functionaries who have the vague task of "publicizing" the program.

Under this scheme, the ministerial conference, working directly or through the OAS Council, would be empowered to deal on the *political* level with member governments to bring about the fulfillment of Alliance commitments and to review political activities pertaining to the program. Inevitably, this would lead the inter-American system to face up to basic problems that it has thus far refused to consider because of the traditional principle of non-intervention. This principle, justifiable in another age, demands contemporary reinterpretation and redefinition. Otherwise, the regional system will remain burdened forever by antiquated and hollow precepts that can have only the effect of paralyzing any efforts to march forward with Latin America's great revolution. If Western Europe has been capable of sacrificing a substantial degree of national sovereignty—and the 1963 French "rebellion" does not fundamentally alter this—as much can surely be expected of Latin America if she truly aspires to an orderly and progressive future.

To succeed, the Alliance cannot—and of course should not—avoid a relationship to political life. But the direction of this common political life should be turned over to the inter-American community, as a part of the Alliance concept, and not rest exclusively in United States hands.

Specifically, there are continually decisions to be made on the extent to which United States financing of the Alliance should hinge upon a country's performance of Punta del Este commitments —in both the material and the political spheres. Until now, for reasons of expediency and practicality, the United States has decided unilaterally whether the failure of a given Latin American republic to move ahead with tax, land, and fiscal reforms was cause for discontinuing or slowing down Alliance disbursements. And it is pertinent to note in this connection that United States attitudes do color those of the international agencies, such as the International Monetary Fund, the World Bank, the Inter-American Development Bank, and the European groups, and even those of private New York bankers.

Although the problems of "bail out" aid or project investments are matters of bilateral negotiations between Washington and the affected country—Brazil and Chile were cases in point in 1962—the final decision inevitably rests with the United States Government. As Washington has to reappraise its attitude toward its Alliance partners—now that the glowing hopes of Punta del Este have been replaced by the harsh awareness of what is and what is not feasible—its position, paternalistic perforce, has led to frictions and recriminations, even if much of this unhappy dialogue has been kept beneath the surface. When local national pride clashes with the "I-hate-to-do-it-but-it-is-for-your-own-good" attitude of Washington, the unavoidable result is the weakening of the broad Alliance concept. It brings the exacerbation of anti-American feelings, their quick and gleeful exploitation by extreme leftist forces, and the transfer of the whole problem into the field of political negativism. The difficult relations between the United States and Brazil—largely due to the long-lasting political crisis during which the Goulart regime was both unwilling and unable to undertake even minimal "self-help" measures prior to the January, 1963, plebiscite—became dangerously colored by such political bitterness.

It has been suggested, therefore, that such negotiations in highly sensitive situations be conducted multilaterally by a standing committee of the Foreign Ministers, rather than unilaterally by the United States. Of course, the United States cannot be automatically bound by the decisions of such a committee, although it would be represented on it, as it is now represented in CIAP. U.S. views would inevitably influence the group's consensus, and the outstanding political advantage of such an arrangement would be to counter the impression that the Alliance is a unilateral undertaking and to spare the United States the politically awkward role of conducting negotiations singlehanded. CIAP, as it is now constituted, can fulfill this role at least up to a point—and much will depend on the extent to which its chairman can assert his powers—but the committee's frame of reference has considerable political limitations.

Political Responsibility

An even more difficult task awaits the inter-American system in the context of relating the Alliance to Hemispheric political life. That task is to encourage the exercise of representative democracy in the region.

As has been mentioned, the notion that the Hemisphere must be governed by the principles of representative democracy is embodied both in the OAS Charter and in the Alliance Charter of Punta del Este. As has also been mentioned, this notion has been cavalierly disregarded in practice by a vast number of the republics, not only after the OAS Charter was signed in 1948, but also after the Alliance Charter was signed in 1961. Since the latter date, military coups ousted elected governments in Argentina and Peru, both countries with reasonable political sophistication by Latin American standards. Elected but completely ineffective regimes in Guatemala and Ecuador were ousted in 1963, with the latter experiencing its second political upheaval in two years when the military deposed President Carlos Julio Arosemena, an alcoholic whom they put in office in 1961. Early in 1963, the strong-man regimes of Nicaragua and Paraguay were confirmed for another period in power through carefully staged travesties of free elections. In Haiti, a dictatorial regime that is medieval in its cruelty, but highly modern in its corruption and its use of organized terror, has remained in power in defiance of all Hemispheric trends and pressures, including a war threat by the Dominican Republic and near intervention by the United States. The constitutional governments of the Dominican Republic, Honduras, Brazil, and Bolivia were subsequently overthrown for a variety of reasons.

The ancient arguments held either that Latin America is not yet prepared for a modern exercise of democracy—the classic assertion of the dictators—or that the republics need an indefinite period of time, free from external interference, to "learn democracy." But at this time of revolutions, these excuses can no longer apply, for the Alliance's entire existence hinges upon the Hemisphere's ability to make democracy a workable enterprise. It is not the naïve hope of starry-eyed democrats, but the stark reality of events that makes the success of democracy in Latin America so crucial at this juncture. Though it may be argued that Arosemena's alcoholism made him unacceptable as President of Ecuador, it can also be asked why his removal had to be accomplished through a military coup rather than through a parliamentary act of impeachment.

The realities of the Hemispheric situation point up the fact that Latin America faces two basic alternatives for her future: one is material progress within freedom and democracy, and the other is an attempt to solve economic inadequacies and social injustices through totalitarian experiments.

If the democratic way fails because Hemispheric society is not capable of making it work, then a disenchanted young generation of Latin Americans, even now attracted by radical and revolutionary solutions, will have no choice but to seek solutions in left-wing Jacobinism, or Communism on Cuban or similar patterns. If this new generation is forced to decide between military dictatorships of the right, even if they are seasoned with nationalism, and a leftist experiment of the Cuban type, it may well be that a form of Castroism or Nasserism will appear preferable.

If the Hemisphere—and the Alliance—tolerates the maintenance or the proliferation of dictatorships or quasi dictatorships, it will be extremely hard to argue against the validity of the Castro thesis that "justice" can be achieved in Latin America only through the regimentation imposed by a revolutionary regime.

This thesis has been emerging in Guatemala, Ecuador, the Dominican Republic, Honduras, and Brazil since the recent military coups in these countries. Although their military or military-backed regimes violently reject Communism (growing Communist influence was, in fact, one of the excuses the armed forces invoked for their assumption of power), they, too, now tend to the notion that social reforms can be accomplished only under authoritarian regimes free of democratic politics. In most cases, this argument is used to justify continuation of nondemocratic rule, but the sad truth is, of course, that both the ousted legal governments and their militarist successors have done little to push basic reforms.

That military thinking is beginning to take this turn is one of the major new phenomena occurring in Latin America in recent times. The new military generations, unlike their predecessors of ten or twenty years ago, are full of a social-reformist zeal that, although commendable, also threatens to demand the sacrifice of democratic institutions. This spirit, suggesting the advent of a Latin American "Nasserism," is present in other countries—notably Brazil—and it blends easily with hard nationalism. Indeed, the fact that present-day Latin American generals and field-grade officers are increasingly recruited from the ranks of the socially conscious middle classes—rather than from the aristocracy, as in the past—is quickly turning the military establishments into powerful progressive forces. But if this new sense of social participation and leadership is to result in an abdication of democracy, then, in the end, the Alliance will offer a political program very little different from the leftist authoritarianism of Castro. It will be a question only of degree and of political coloration.

The obvious difference will, presumably, lie in the Alliance dollars, as opposed to Soviet-bloc rubles, and in anti-Communism as opposed to Cuban pro-Communism. But the politically conscious Latin American masses—led by the politicians and the intellectuals, who mold public opinion and reactions—are not likely to support such a sterile version of the Alliance for long.

The disenchantment with the Alliance, with United States leadership, and with the very concept of Western democracy is already clearly visible in the region. The search for new solutions peculiar to Latin America or its individual components has inevitably begun, and judging from the trend this quest is taking, it can be foretold that these new answers will not fit into the Washington concept of the Alliance—which is the unglamorous and antiseptic approach to economic development as a goal in itself—or into the classic definition of democracy. Further, unless democratic rule and a modicum of faith in democracy prevail in Latin America, it will be increasingly difficult, if not impossible, to harness the Hemisphere's articulate leadership, as well as the masses, to the orderly, patient, and self-sacrificing procedures of economic development championed by Washington. The Nasser-type experiments are not likely to provide the answer.

Still another argument for concerted fostering of democracy—and it is indeed extraordinary that justifications for democracy have to be adduced in this day and age—is that even enlightened military dictatorships, no matter what the excuse for their presence, will surely breed radicalism, not to say Communism.

In the light of all these considerations, it should be evident that the restoration of faith in democracy as a road to the future is the most urgent task of the Alliance for Progress. But this restoration cannot and should not be undertaken by the United States alone. There is a limit to the capabilities and responsibilities of this country in helping Latin America to find a reasonable destiny, and clearly, this responsibility must, in the final analysis, lie within the Hemisphere.

Since the end of the Eisenhower period, attempts to aid and regulate the fortunes of democracy in Latin America have foundered in failure and embarrassment, and they have evoked only resentment against the United States. Gradually, they have been replaced by policies of self-conscious expediency as the once-shining political principles of the Alliance have become more and more uncertain. Therefore, it should be up to the inter-American system to act as the guardian of Latin American democracy, overcoming the obsoletely inflexible and moth-eaten doctrines of nonintervention. It would seem to follow, in terms of intellectual and political honesty, that if the inter-American system were able to act in January, 1962, to exclude Cuba from the OAS on the grounds that her Marxist-Leninist regime is incompatible with the Hemispheric principles of democracy, it should also be able to cope equally forcefully with right-wing dictatorial deviations from democratic doctrines.

It did, in fact, deal in this way with the Trujillo regime in the Dominican Republic (in 1960 and 1961), and there can be little question that the Hemispheric isolation imposed on the Caribbean dictator played a large role in encouraging the conspiracy that led to his assassination. But in the Dominican case, it took an extreme offense by Trujillo—rigging a murder plot against Venezuela's President Betancourt—to rouse the OAS into action. It seems inconceivable that a crime against another country's President would be required before the inter-American system would become concerned with freedom and democracy in the Hemisphere.

It is not suggested, of course, that the inter-American system engage in physical intervention against old or new dictatorships. Clearly, the OAS cannot involve itself in overthrowing the governments of member states, objectionable as they may be.

Much as many of the republics may have sympathized with President Juan Bosch of the Dominican Republic in his attempt in April and May, 1963, to provoke military action to oust the Duvalier dictatorship in neighboring Haiti, they could not go along with him in this endeavor. The United States, which still fears that Communism may in the long run result from the Duvalier rule, played a decisive role in holding back the Bosch maneuver, though the Kennedy Administration itself went to incredible and confused lengths to engineer the fall of the Haitian regime. Hoping for a provocation—and doing all it could to bring such a provocation about—the United States dramatically evacuated the dependents of its official personnel from Haiti, stationed an aircraft-carrier task force at Port-au-Prince's doorstep, and briefly suspended diplomatic relations with the Duvalier government. But in the end, both the United States and the Dominican Republic had to bow to the reality of Duvalier's hold on his own country.

The irony of the Haitian-Dominican controversy was that Bosch was ousted by his own military a few months later, while Duvalier continued in power. In fact, Bosch's crusade against his neighbor was seized on by the Dominican generals as one of the excuses for the coup.

But the Haitian incident did provide an interesting insight into what the OAS might someday decide to do about the dictatorial problem in the Hemisphere. An OAS committee, charged with conciliating in the Dominican-Haitian conflict, came up with a report that, in effect, linked the Duvalier regime's violations of human rights in Haiti with the threat to American peace and security. This concept was not original in itself—a precedent for such a conclusion can be found in the Inter-American Peace Commission study in 1950 of a dispute between Cuba and the Dominican Republic and, to a lesser extent, in the resolutions of the 1959 Conference of Foreign Ministers—but it was stated in 1963 with unprecedented forcefulness.

The OAS Council did not act on the committee report on Haiti, but the document stands as a highly significant new precedent that may, in time, lead to a breakthrough in the inter-American system's handling of dictatorships. The thought behind this linking of domestic oppression with international peace lies in the notion that dictatorial practices lead to the creation of exile movements abroad that, in turn, may cause an exacerbation of relations between the governments protecting the refugees and the tyrant regime. However, the real, if unexpressed, idea was that tolerance of dictatorships encourages their emergence elsewhere.

If, on the other hand, the system formally proclaimed its disapproval of a dictatorship—or declared it incompatible with the principles of representative democracy, as was done with Cuba —then powerful moral and political pressures would arise around the usurping government that might quicken its downfall. If the OAS should choose to act on a finding that connects violations of human rights with danger to peace and security, then sanctions under the Rio Pact would be possible, further increasing the pressure on the dictatorship. Aside from the immediate moral and philosophical problems involved, a resolute inter-American stand on protecting democracy would unquestionably strengthen its position in the eyes of those who doubt the validity of democratic institutions and would promote the contention that the Castro revolution in Cuba indeed violates the American ideology.

Since Punta del Este, unilateral United States interventions in favor of democracy have been, as already noted, highly unsuccessful. With rare exceptions, they have created almost as much resentment as the earlier interventions in favor of the dictatorships or the tolerance of their existence.

When the military ousted the Frondizi government in Argentina, the United States went through a soul-searching in order to decide whether to establish diplomatic relations with the new regime and whether to continue economic aid under the Alliance. The point was made in Washington that the military coup had violated the basic principles of the Alliance and that another agonizing reappraisal of the situation was required. But looking at the rest of the Hemisphere, the Kennedy Administration soon realized that only a few governments, notably the Venezuelan, were prepared to support the United States in any moves toward isolating Argentina. Furthermore, the Argentines argued successfully that the coup was legal because their constitution provides for the deposition of the President of the republic and that constitutional continuity was not affected because José María Guido, the President of the Senate and the next man in line to become chief executive, was named to the top job. The pretense that Guido was an effective and independent democratic leader was readily accepted, along with the generals' contention that to let the Peronistas occupy seats in Congress and take over a few governorships would lead to a return of Peronismo and totalitarianism in Argentina.

Diplomatic relations were continued, and in June, 1962, Washington announced new credits for Argentina. The Administration's sense of timing, often curious, here proved to be disastrous. The extension of financial aid to the military-backed regime in Argentina was the final argument for the Peruvian military, who were then considering a coup of their own in connection with their country's Presidential elections the same month.

The coup was carried out a month later, after the elections, with the excuse that the results threatened a breakdown in public order. This time the Kennedy Administration reacted with missionary zeal upon the transgression against the Alliance's democratic principles. The President delivered an unprecedented public denunciation of the coup, and followed it up by suspending diplomatic relations and cutting off all military and economic aid.

But hardly a week went by before the Administration found itself considerably embarrassed. The majority of Latin American governments refused to treat the Peruvian incident as a serious breach of the Alliance principles, or of anything else. Much of Peruvian public opinion, including those who once were loud in the defense of democracy, failed to muster indignation about the junta's takeover. A general strike called by APRA, the leftist but anti-Communist party that almost won the elections, never got off the ground. Outstanding Peruvians immediately charged the Kennedy Administration with unjustified interference. United States business interests in Peru pressed the White House to restore diplomatic relations and resume aid in order to avoid damage to their investments.

Isolated in its well-meant venture of defending Latin American democracy, the United States Government had no choice but to back down sheepishly. Relations were restored, along with economic and military aid. As a scapegoat was needed, Ambassador James Loeb, who had carried out the initial Presidential policies, was recalled.

When a group of Latin American governments sought subsequently to call a meeting of Hemisphere Foreign Ministers to debate the problems of *coups d'état* (their fear was that the Argentine and Peruvian examples would be followed elsewhere), the United States abstained in the vote in the OAS Council. It thereby managed to undo much of the good will its initial reactions to the Peruvian situation had evoked among Latin American liberals.

In trying to recapture some of its image as a champion of democracy, the United States then went back to the OAS Council to seek a compromise resolution expressing the principle that *coups d'état* should be a matter for consideration by Foreign Ministers. The "nonintervention" contingent succeeded, however, in blocking even this mild gesture, and like most compromise moves, the United States proposal wound up pleasing nobody and achieving nothing.

These events of mid-1962 seem further to argue that the inter-

American system, and not the United States alone, should assume the responsibility for decisions on whether diplomatic relations should be maintained and Alliance aid supplied to governments that violate the principles of the program. It is, then, a job for the Conference of Foreign Ministers, the OAS "organ of consultation," or a special standing committee. Under such a procedure, the old ideas of strict nonintervention will have to be shed in order to give the Alliance a modern political meaning.

Aside from the recurrent problem of the *coups d'état* the inter-American system, and the Alliance, must face up to the complex question of how the old dictatorships should be treated. Again, in acting alone, the United States has succeeded only in causing resentment on both sides of the democratic fence. Because Nicaragua and Paraguay have received only limited aid, entrenched interests there have charged that the United States attaches political strings to the Alliance. But because a modicum of aid is still being provided, Washington has been criticized by the liberal opposition in those countries and democratic opinion elsewhere.

In seeking to decide whether such governments should be eligible for aid, both the United States and the inter-American system would have to make the very difficult determination as to whether the chief effect of Alliance assistance would be to help the population or to shore up the regimes in power. The answer in most cases would probably be that it would do both; and it is not necessarily certain that the elimination of all aid, as has been the case with Haiti, would bring down the objectionable regime.

But again, these decisions—each based on the merits of the given situation—should be made jointly by the inter-American system functioning as the political arm of the Alliance.

In a broader political sense, a Hemispheric parliamentary union for the Alliance could serve as the badly needed transmission belt for the program's ideology, and could exert pressure on lagging governments and social groups to accept the reform movements and the concept of the democratic social revolution.

The direct involvement of Latin American democratic political parties in Alliance programs would undoubtedly go far toward making it a living reality on the national, provincial, and municipal levels in each of the republics. The next logical step would be to seek to incorporate the Alliance ideas into the political partisan platforms and to achieve President Kennedy's thus far frustrated dream of Latin American candidates running for office on Alliance platforms. An Alliance parliamentary union could oversee party programs and ideas in annual or biannual meetings throughout the Hemisphere, and a permanent executive coordinating committee could act as a liaison organ and clearinghouse among the individual political parties in Latin America.

In the planning field, recommendations have been made for the establishment in each Latin American capital of a binational Alliance Authority, made up of United States and local economists, engineers, and planners who would jointly elaborate development and investment programs. Each binational group would include a representative of the Alliance's panel of "Nine Wise Men" to enlarge it to a multilateral character.

The precedent for such a mechanism is found in the Brazil–United States Joint Commission that functioned in the late 1940's and early 1950's. It has stood out as one of the most successful examples of cooperation between Washington and a Latin American country. The Commission, whose demise was ordered by the Eisenhower Administration, was sorely missed in subsequent years as the gradual deterioration in United States–Brazilian relations set in.

The primary advantage of a joint Alliance Authority would be to remove the increasing frictions and resentments in the formulation of projects and allocation of financing. It seems unquestionable that joint responsibility for the drafting of the projects *in situ* and joint presentation to the "Wise Men" and the United States Government could go far to remove the complaints, already widely heard, that the Alliance is administered with the same small-town banker's mentality that directed previous United States aid programs to Latin America. Here again, a precedent for such an approach exists, in this case, the studies of broad Colombian and Chilean development plans made by international consortia.

With the creation of the superstructure of a parliamentary body of the Alliance and of binational planning authorities, the next step in realizing the program's concepts would be to form national, provincial, and municipal "citizens' committees" for the Alliance, operating not in the present vacuum but in the context of existing organizations—chambers of commerce; student and labor groups; fraternal associations, like the Rotary or Lions; and professional groups, such as physicians' or lawyers' federations. Such committees could play a large part in giving the Alliance the long-awaited aspect of a democratic social revolution.

This technique, in turn, would further spread the Alliance concepts into the field of community development and stimulate grass-roots participation in the program through self-help projects. International exchange programs, not just between Latin American countries and the United States, but within the continent, would be set up to allow groups from each republic to share in the specific experiences of the others.

This, then, would turn the Alliance for Progress into a true alliance, supply the pageantry and mystique it lacks, equip it to resist antidemocratic pressures, and ultimately, make possible a frontal attack on the ossified economic and social structures in much of Latin America. It would achieve the synthesis of the political and psychological aspects of the Alliance with its economic-development features, making it a comprehensive, multilevel undertaking. Ideology and material progress, which cannot be separated, would then merge to produce at last the democratic social revolution this age demands.

Thus far, however, the Alliance has not entered the stream of Latin America's political life or consciousness as it plods along beset by skepticism in the South and self-consciousness in the North.

The Achievements

Despite its failure to spur Latin America into a democratic revolution, the Alliance for Progress, its by-products, and related activities have nonetheless begun to make a substantial dent in the awesome accumulation of material and human problems.

In broad terms, it has succeeded to an important extent in implanting a serious concept of economic development among Latin Americans who have been demanding it for decades without understanding clearly what it implied in practice.

The Alliance has resulted in the creation of central economic-planning boards in virtually all the Latin American republics, and it has taught the governments to accept, at least in principle, the relationship between economic development and problems of social improvement, health, and education. In a region that lives in a desperate hurry and is, therefore, susceptible to short cuts, the Alliance has spread the notion that capital expansion at the top of the economic structures, such as the building of steel plants, is not sufficient to provide balanced growth. Thus, it has wrought an important change in the traditional Latin American psychology that long favored prestige projects at the expense of an improved economic and human infrastructure. The idea that a steel mill, for example, is a badge of distinction for a developing country has been largely discarded.

Faced by powerful resistance from the entrenched "oligarch" groups and deprived of the mass political support that a social revolution requires, the Alliance has had modest success in starting preliminary work toward land and tax reforms and in persuading many of the governments that fiscal responsibility is a prerequisite for rational development. Measured in relation to the tools it has at its disposal, the Kennedy program has unquestionably started up movement in the right direction where no movement had existed before.

In the three years of its operations, the Alliance has had significant if limited impact on the totality of the Latin American problem, pioneering some programs and aiding and reinforcing others, though it is difficult to avoid the nagging feeling that so much more could have been accomplished if there had been more imagination and drive.

If one thinks in terms of the spectacular, not too much is readily noticeable in Latin America at the end of three years. But preliminary investments have been made in meaningful projects, and their results will become tangible with the passage of time.

These initial investments in resources and techniques run the gamut from international financial arrangements to local school-lunch programs.

In the international field, the Alliance has given strong support to the move toward Latin America's economic integration, presaging the creation, perhaps in five or ten years, of a Latin American Common Market. The Republican Administration had little use for the Common Market ideas propounded at the time by Raúl Prebisch of the United Nations Economic Commission for Latin America. However, under the Alliance concepts, the United States has been sympathetic to these plans and provided some technical assistance.

Latin American economic integration is, of course, an undertaking in which the United States can take very little part for the time being. But the fact that Latin Americans themselves have chalked up accomplishments in partnerships that so markedly advance the notion of the Alliance is a highly encouraging sign. This effort predates the launching of the Alliance, but along with the principle of economic integration in general, it has been absorbed into the Punta del Este Charter. Of the two main existing enterprises, the older is the Central American Common Market, which began with Nicaragua, Honduras, El Salvador, and Guatemala, and now includes Costa Rica. Panama, whose economy is tied to the Canal, has remained outside the Central American group but is to join it as an associate member.

With fairly similar economies, based on coffee, the Central American bloc aims ultimately at a loose political union, like a tiny European Community, to follow the projected customs union in 1965. A system of consultations by Central American Foreign, Finance, Defense, and Interior Ministers has been developed, although there are important historical and political frictions among the isthmus partners.

In recent years, the group's members have unified their tariff procedures after completing the tedious job of unifying the customs nomenclature. Gradual but far-reaching tariff concessions and exemptions have been worked out, and the Central American governments are now beginning to think not only of a free movement of goods within their region but also of complementing their economies in development planning.

To assist the region as a whole, the United States has worked out a system for compensating Central American coffee producers for seasonal price fluctuations through a special fund set up after Punta del Este.

At the conference with Central American Presidents in San José, Costa Rica, in March, 1963, President Kennedy committed the United States to large-scale development-assistance programs for the isthmus countries as a group. Henceforth, aid to Central American industrial and related projects will be channeled through the new Central American Bank, rather than through the individual governments.

In South America, significant steps toward economic integration have been taken through the Latin American Free Trade Association (LAFTA) treaty, which has already attracted most of the continent's republics as well as Mexico. LAFTA has moved far in the direction of tariff concessions to increase the flow of trade in the region and has established efficient central bank arrangements. One of the results of LAFTA is that Brazilian buses and trucks are now being exported to Argentina, and Argentine railroad equipment finds its way into Brazil, free of hard-currency problems and protectionism. The underlying theory is that if new markets are found within Latin America for Latin American producers, trade and the production of manufactured goods will be stimulated. This, in turn, will assist the area's industrial development and enable it to break out of its traditional role as a supplier of raw materials. By the middle of 1963, duties on more than 3,300 products had been eliminated or curtailed in new tariff arrangements.

In another international sphere, and a crucial one for Latin America, the Alliance has brought about the participation of the United States and European countries in the International Coffee Agreement. Prior to the Alliance, the United States had resisted entering into such a pact of producers and consumers, and the Kennedy Administration's move to join in with the Latin Americans was one of those small revolutions in world trade that have been fairly frequent in the postwar years.

The importance of the Coffee Agreement is that it helps to stabilize prices in a world market that for nearly a decade has been suffering from a staggering glut due to serious overproduction. The agreement calls upon the producers to respect export quotas, set on a quarterly basis, in order to keep prices at a reasonable level and avoid fluctuations. The consuming countries, in turn, are committed not to accept coffee in excess of these quotas.

The Coffee Agreement, covering the fifteen Latin American coffee-producing countries and the Africans, is one attempt to help combat the Hemisphere's greatest scourge: the fluctuations in the prices of their basic export commodities. How vitally these fluctuations affect the economies in the Hemisphere is seen from the fact that a 1-cent-per-pound drop in the price of coffee costs Brazil $60 million annually. The Latin Americans assert that through the catastrophic decline in the price of coffee from 1954 to 1959—when it plummeted from about 80 cents a pound to 30 cents —fifteen countries have lost in unearned income more than the Alliance can provide in loans, grants, and private investments. But there is another side to this argument. The price of coffee jumped to the 1954–55 high because of manipulations by Brazilian producers and the government, which extended an "umbrella" over the market and refused to export coffee below an artificially established high price. The resulting bonanza encouraged the African countries to enter the coffee market, and the world market was hit with twice the volume of beans it could consume. Therefore, it may be argued that the Latin American calculation of losses is based on an artificially inflated price level.

The problem of commodities, however, is two-edged. Bolivia, whose fate is tied to tin, another surplus commodity, charged the United States with a violation of the spirit of the Alliance after Washington announced it would sell some of its tin stockpile. Bolivia's anger was motivated by fears that this would make the price of tin drop, though the United States reasoned that maintaining the price at an artificially high level would ultimately hurt the market by making tin users turn to substitute alloys. Despite the fact that the United States has made direct budget grants that have kept Bolivia solvent during the ten years of her social revolution and that it has embarked upon a major project to modernize the Bolivian tin industry in partnership with West German interests and the Inter-American Bank, the reaction in La Paz to the stockpile-sale produced a full-scale political crisis. President Víctor Paz Estenssoro canceled a planned trip to Washington in 1962, and his Cabinet ministers, who subsequently negotiated an $80-million "package deal" loan, joined in anti-American outbursts.

Also in the international field, one of the most successful Alliance activities has been the Inter-American Development Bank. Chartered late in 1960 and beginning operations early in 1961 with capital of $1 billion, the Bank has authorized about $620 million in loans in two years. While the United States contribution to the Bank's capital—$394 million in immediately available money for the Social Progress Fund—was authorized by Congress before the Alliance's birth, the operation was forthwith fitted into the concept of the new program.

The importance of the Bank is that it provides hard- and soft-currency loans to Latin American governments and private entrepreneurs on conditions that cannot be met by private banking institutions in the United States and Europe or by the Export-Import Bank. Unlike traditional lending institutions, the Bank supplies credits from its Social Progress Fund for investment in such non-profit fields as education, sanitation,· and water supply. More than 15 per cent of the authorized loans have already been disbursed—roughly one-half of them to private enterprise in Latin America—financing small industries and infrastructure projects. So successful has the Bank been that a bond issue offered in the New York money market was fully subscribed even before public notices appeared.

An additional attraction of the Inter-American Bank is that it is managed almost entirely by Latin Americans. Like all the participating governments, the United States has a seat on the board of governors, and there is a smattering of American officials in responsible positions. But the Bank is run by Felipe Herrera, a forty-two-year-old Chilean lawyer, economist, and his country's former Finance Minister, and the decisions made by the institution are strictly Latin American. Having developed what is probably the best staff of international economists in the Hemisphere, the Bank is a hardheaded and professional enterprise. But being operated by Latin Americans, it is free from the accusations of niggardliness so frequently hurled against United States lending institutions.

The Inter-American Bank, with the Agency for International Development and the World Bank, forms the trinity that is underwriting Latin America's financial development. These three institutions work in close association, and all of them, along with official and private European interests, will contribute to the long-range development consortia in Colombia and Chile and, later, in other countries.

In direct contributions, the Alliance's efforts are spread the length and the breadth of the Hemisphere, though they are often unsung and not always apparent. In the Peruvian Andes and the Brazilian Northeast, United States surplus food distributed by the Alliance provides emergency relief. School lunches for Peruvian children are credited with increasing attendance in schools by 50 per cent.

In the immense, drought-parched Brazilian Northeast, $131 million in Alliance funds has been committed to basic development projects, complementing the efforts by the Inter-American Bank and the Brazilian Government, working through the Superintendency for the Development of the Northeast (SUDENE). There, the main target is water supply and agricultural development. Irrigation projects may come later, after the United States and Brazil have resolved their difficulties in long-range economic cooperation. When this point is reached, the two plagues of the Northeast, the climate and the "industrials of the drought"—the landlords who control the available water—may finally be overcome, thus ending the politically explosive misery of generations of *Nordestinos*.

Alliance funds have supported land reform in Venezuela, low-cost housing in the slums of a dozen republics, road building from the Bolivian mountains to the lowlands of Central America, schools and universities almost everywhere, and health and sanitation throughout the Hemisphere. Funds for surveys and research and for loans to small farmers are also among the Alliance projects that will someday bear fruit.

In the first two years after its launching, the Alliance was directly responsible for the erection of 140,000 homes or dwelling units; the construction of 8,200 classrooms and 900 hospitals and health centers; the installation of 700 community water systems; the supply of 160,000 agricultural loans; and the printing of 4,000,000 textbooks. All this, to be sure, has not changed the face of Latin America, but it has acted as a significant initial investment.

As the Alliance Charter recognizes, private capital has an essential role in Latin America's economic development. Despite the demands for public-sector investments made by Latin Americans, especially the converts to the new nationalism, the more sober officials and politicians are eager for private industrial capital as a source of jobs and economic activity.

But the attitude toward foreign investments has changed markedly in Latin America, and both capitalists and governments must recognize this. The new political realities of the Hemisphere militate against the presence of foreign investments in the so-called sensitive areas of the economy, principally public utilities. The trend is toward encouragement of investments in manufacturing industries, and recently, big United States companies, such as Standard Oil of New Jersey and the American and Foreign Power Company, have begun diversifying their interests in Latin America.

It is reasonably assumed both in Washington and in Latin America that public funds provided under the Alliance and foreign and domestic private capital should complement each other in the mixed economies now emerging as a pattern in Latin America. But this balance cannot be achieved if some groups in the United States return to the old idea that the *sine qua non* for economic development in Latin America is the creation of a climate favorable to private investments. A report by a group of United States businessmen associated with the Alliance—the Department of Commerce Committee for the Alliance (COMAP)—suggested early in 1963 that public-sector aid be conditioned upon the establishment of such a climate, reflecting the regressive trend that is re-emerging in this country's thinking. To elevate such an approach to the level of an official United States policy in Latin America could destroy the tenuous hold that the Alliance has thus far been able to establish in the Hemisphere. A more rational approach seems to lie in meshing public and private capital investments according to the existing needs, and in encouraging the formation of domestic capital in Latin America. An essential part of this approach would be to bring back to the region the billions of dollars invested abroad by Latin American capitalists who apparently have no faith in the future of their own countries.

However, more crucial than all the considerations of an economic and financial nature about Latin America's development under the Alliance is the human factor. The relationship of the political element to the "revolution of rising expectations" has been discussed, but one must also consider the direct human contacts in terms of the Alliance for Progress. Standing out importantly in this context are the growing activities of the Peace Corps in Latin America. Although they are not organizationally related to the Alliance, the Peace Corps volunteers serve the essential function of encouraging community development, without which the over-all program can have no foundation.

The Peace Corps has become, within a short time, the single most successful United States program in Latin America. Unlike the loans, which take years to show results, the volunteers are visible to the people in the fields and villages, and their work is tangible. Unlike the remote officials of the Alliance, the volunteers are right on the spot, their value measured in immediate, human terms. If the concepts of the Alliance for Progress can be personalized, the Peace Corps volunteers are the means to do it, on the most elementary of levels—that of human contact.

The acceptance of the volunteers in most of the Latin American areas represents a psychological and political acceptance of the United States contribution to the development of the village, the province, the country, and the continent. It inevitably means the acceptance of the Alliance for Progress as a practical idea, rather than as a vague slogan.

However, it is neither practical nor possible to flood Latin America with the young people of the Peace Corps. They fulfill an important role, but the entirety of the program depends upon the whole range of tangible and intangible political, psychological, and material factors that should constitute the positive impact of a democratic social revolution. The Alliance for Progress, to make its mark on history, must become a program that attracts and enlists those who are to be its beneficiaries. It is not that yet.

7.   The Outlook

The Synthesis

ONE OF THE FIRST RULES a reporter needs to learn in Latin America is that he must never be swayed by reason or logic in trying to gauge future events. This precept should apply as well to the contemporary historian or to the foreign-policy maker observing the Latin American scene, who must realize that neither short- nor long-range predictions are possible and that, in all wisdom, none should be attempted. The scene is too crowded, the actors move too fast, propelled by visible and invisible forces of formidable magnitude.

The outlines of the Latin American future are thus hidden from view by the continuing ferment the length and the width of the Hemisphere. Only basic trends and generalities can be discerned in this flux of revolutionary cross currents. Political, social, ideological, historical, human, emotional, psychological, racial, economic, and cultural influences and allegiances clash with each other in each of the twenty republics. A violent reassessment of the old values is under way, as the new Latin American generations, which no longer have any use for the past, are moving into positions of intellectual, economic, and political leadership.

The one constant in all these equations—their common denominator, in fact—is that revolutionary winds are blowing more strongly each day in Latin America. Their nature and direction and intensity do vary, of course. In one place, they take the shape of episodes of violence. In another, they are the gradual but inexorable shift from traditional ideas of politics, economics, and foreign policy to an experimentation in new forms and relationships.

If one general statement about Latin America's future can be made at this point, it is that in the opening period of the decade of the 1960's, her character has undergone a change perhaps greater than in all of the previous decades and that this transformation will go on in the coming years until it reaches the final stage of crystallization.

The unpredictable element is what the nature of that crystallization will be. The best guess that can be ventured, as these words are written late in 1964, is that it is most likely to be a synthesis of the principal trends evident today. This means that probably neither of the two extreme alternatives in the picture will prevail: that Latin America will not "go Communist" or assume the explosive features of the Castro revolution or tie itself to the Communist bloc, nor will it follow a uniformly peaceful path of evolution, incorporating the classic features of the middle-of-the-road Western democracy and international foreign policies fully committed to the West.

Cold realism leads one to accept the likelihood that, in a sense, these two gravitational pulls may neutralize each other. In fact, whatever little perspective is available today on this first phase of the Latin American revolution, it would seem that both the Cuban revolution and the parallel impact of the Alliance for Progress have been digested, or taken in stride, by the Hemisphere.

The initial, almost mystical attraction of the Cuban revolution has already lost much of its novelty and magnetism. The Alliance for Progress is still advancing at a slow pace, particularly in the political and psychological realms, and it has thus far failed to evoke the emotional response required to turn it into the democratic social revolution that President Kennedy had visualized.

After nearly six years of the Cuban experiment, neither Fidelismo nor Communism, as an ideology or a way of life, has won mass support, and there are no hard reasons to think that they will command overwhelming backing anywhere at this late stage. Traditional Western democracy, however, has also brought disenchantment, and Latin American youth has begun to lose faith in it. The new generation, particularly the emerging managerial class, is increasingly attracted to a "technocratic" philosophy—preferring to concentrate on economic development and turn its back on politics, including the practice of democracy—and there are emerging trends toward an authoritarian military control of national development, perhaps on the model of Nasserism in the Near East. There are also powerful practical considerations that have entered on the scene: While Latin America evidently needs the Alliance—or the United States—for sheer economic survival, let alone significant development, she believes she can derive some material profit and some bargaining power from economic relations with the Communist bloc.

What does appear to be taking shape, therefore, is a Latin America that experiences an increasing desire to become uncommitted in the East-West conflict so that her own resources and, if possible, those of both competing blocs can be channeled into her development. The 1963 thaw in the Cold War was greeted hopefully in Latin America, and the extent of Latin American concentration on economic development was illustrated by the joint stand of most of the governments in Brasília and Alta Gracia early in 1964 in preparing a unified position for the United Nations Conference on Trade and Development. There, the Latin American voice raised demands that the industrialized nations of the world, from the United States to the Soviet Union, grant the Hemisphere preferential trade treatment.

This whole approach, of course, also finds expression in a form of political neutralism of various degrees and nuances. The neutralist tendencies were particularly marked in the case of Brazil prior to the April, 1964, revolution that ousted President Goulart. The new regime of President Castelo Branco has edged away from the full-time practice of neutralism—it started out by breaking diplomatic ties with Cuba—but some basic policies, such as the continuation of diplomatic and trade relations with the Soviet bloc, have not been reversed.

Similar trends exist in depth in some other countries, notably in Mexico and increasingly in Chile. In the case of Cuba, most governments are prepared to side with the United States in any effort to liquidate the Castro regime, but even if this goal should ever be achieved, their gravitation toward a broadly uncommitted position is probable. Their interest in seeing Castro vanish is motivated principally by fear that Havana's influence may someday shatter their tenuous political structures and hurl them toward an extremism they do not welcome.

What seems to loom ahead, then, is a Latin America that has been disappointed by both the great world currents, but that, in varying degrees, needs their different contributions, political as well as economic. This is especially true in the realm of economic development and efforts to define the proper roles of the state and of private enterprise in it. But, as matters now stand, the Hemisphere is still suffering in many ways from a kind of schizophrenia, still unable to choose the precise course her destiny should take. But while there may be some merit in this form of diagnosis, it appears more accurate to think of Latin America's future as representing a new synthesis and a new way emerging from the sum of the disappointments in the two great world forces, the sum of the hopes that both Cuba and the Alliance have aroused, and the sum of her needs from the East and West.

It is also probably a fair assumption that Latin America's political development will increasingly veer toward a pronounced left-of-center position—as the modern semantics of politics goes—and that this trend will be reflected in a growing reliance on economic nationalism and statism as the formula for the solution of her great ills. A possible new ingredient in the developing Latin American synthesis may well be a variety of Nasserism—the expression is used loosely, for lack of a better one—in which authoritarian military or military-backed regimes might take in hand the attempts at imposing social reforms.

There have been significant hints of such a trend in the recent past, ranging from the activities of the military governments in Guatemala and Ecuador to the pressures being brought to bear in Brazil by nationalist but anti-Communist officers who found themselves in a commanding position following their revolution in April, 1964, which ousted the left-leaning regime of João Goulart.

This trend is, of course, a reflection of the vast structural and human changes that have occurred in the last generation in the make-up of the Latin American officer class. Traditionally, the Latin American military were regarded as a caste apart from the mainstream of their societies—often they were considered an aristocratic class—and their role in most cases was to protect the established economic order and the social *status quo*. Thus, historically, military *coups d'état* were carried out for fairly reactionary reasons, in opposition to progressive forces, such as APRA in Peru or Acción Democrática in Venezuela in the 1940's.

In the last ten years or so, however, the dominant element in the Latin American military has gradually become the middle class, and a sense of identity has now sprung up between the armed forces and the civilian society. This new generation of middle-class officers is inevitably attuned to the needs and anxieties of the civilian groups in the corresponding strata, their desires for economic development and social improvement. Clearly, the implications of this change for the whole future political picture of Latin America are immense.

This transformation of the military character and mentality has not, to be sure, proceeded with equal effectiveness in every country. It has hardly touched the armed forces of countries like Argentina, Paraguay, or the Dominican Republic, where the caste system still operates strongly, for reasons of tradition as well as of immediate personal interest. But the new military mentality is greatly in evidence in Brazil, which has perhaps the best professional military establishment in Latin America (aside from the Soviet-directed Cuban armed forces), and to an increasing degree in Peru, Ecuador, Bolivia, Guatemala, and El Salvador.

Again, it may be Brazil that will provide some of the leadership in that direction. Marshal Humberto Castelo Branco, who succeeded Goulart as President, rose from the rank of Army private to become one of the outstanding intellectuals among Brazil's general officers. Born in the poverty-stricken Northeast, he has been always aware of the need for basic reforms, and in his first six months in office, he has devoted himself to bringing them about as rapidly as possible.

From the very outset, however, President Castelo Branco and his civilian associates, notably the new Minister of Economic Planning, Roberto de Oliveira Campos, have run into powerful opposition from some of the very same economic groups that only months earlier spearheaded the anti-Goulart revolution. These groups originally argued that Goulart was attempting to use the problem of reforms to set up a leftist, or even pro-Communist, dictatorship, and there was much truth in these charges. But once Goulart was ousted by the lightning action of the military, who finally agreed to join the rebellion, Brazil's powerful vested economic interests began to oppose the democratic reforms that Castelo Branco and Campos were propounding.

If this deadlock persists, a situation may ultimately develop in which the military will take matters over completely and, in so doing, bury Brazil's democratic system for a long time to come. There have already been reports of Army commanders in the Northeast who have forced landlords to pay the minimum legal salaries to their rural workers, ending the tradition of evading cash payments. The more radical of the military revolutionaries, who are demanding "real purges" and a "real revolution," may thus enforce a social revolution in their own way. Should this occur, President Castelo Branco may become the General Naguib of Brazil—a development that is surely not in the country's or the Hemisphere's long-range interest.

In the field of foreign policy, Latin America may likewise lean increasingly toward a form of quiet neutralism such as Brazil had practiced under Goulart and may practice again in a situation of greater military ascendancy, and which Mexico is still vigorously advocating.

The Mexicans in 1963 and 1964 have exchanged Presidential-level visits with Poland, played host to Marshal Tito, President Kennedy, and General de Gaulle of France, sent their President Alberto López Mateos to meet with President Johnson, and played a key neutralist role at the Geneva Disarmament Conference. Most recently, in July and August, 1964, Mexico chose to defy the decision of the American Foreign Ministers calling for a Hemisphere-wide break in diplomatic relations with Cuba, and demanded, instead, a ruling by the International Court of Justice.

There are neutralist leanings elsewhere in Latin America, with the emphasis, fundamentally, on protecting her middle position in the world and remaining as uncommitted as possible in the contest of the giants so that she can be free to concentrate on her material progress. President de Gaulle's tour of South America in September and October, 1964—following his earlier visit to Mexico —was frankly aimed at encouraging these trends as the General kept speaking out against big-power "hegemonies." However, and this was an interesting insight into the peculiar Latin American reactions to the notion of neutralism, President de Gaulle won both applause and delicately couched reminders that uncommitted as the region may wish to remain, it has no intention of forsaking its friendship with the United States.

This whole anticipated process of synthesis and emergence of new forms will not develop uniformly and simultaneously. The conditions and the pressures vary considerably in each of the republics, and each has its special group of immediate problems, traditions, and proposed solutions to digest and absorb into its political stream. In some of the countries—notably Brazil under the post-Goulart regime, Mexico, Peru, and Chile—the governments and the dominant political forces actively advocate change and the movement toward the new synthesis. In others, such as Argentina, Paraguay, and some of the Central American republics, while the establishments seek to prolong the *status quo,* opposing forces are gaining strength.

In still others, particularly Venezuela, there is a spontaneous and somewhat unplanned movement toward change, with the participation of the most diverse national forces, ranging from the government to the leftist and rightist moderates. Venezuela's greatest modern milestone—and possibly one of Latin America's great milestones in recent history—was the events of late 1963 and early 1964, when the attack by the pro-Communist terrorists was defeated by the action of the whole society—not only soldiers and policemen—and Venezuela held a free election leading to the inauguration of Raúl Leoni as the new constitutional President.

While rejecting the revolutionary pressures from Cuba and from domestic terrorists and guerrillas, the Venezuelans also succeeded in bolstering their economy, impressively increasing their food production, and arriving at a truly spectacular rise in national income—this time spread more evenly throughout the nation than had been the case in the past when only the ruling groups benefited from petroleum revenues.

The victory of Eduardo Frei in the Chilean elections in September, 1964, offered the country the promise of rational and speedy economic development and social reform within the democratic framework. By the end of 1964, four important South American countries—Chile, Colombia, Peru, and Venezuela—were ruled by freely elected and socially progressive regimes, prepared to push ahead with the democratic social revolution, and hopefully representing a solid backbone for this trend.

It is one of the great misfortunes of Latin America in this age of instant communications that so little is known in one country of the events in other Hemisphere countries, and it is thus regrettable that the full story of Venezuela's political victory has not become better known elsewhere. As it is, the example of one republic may in time accelerate developments in another one, but by and large, the process is uneven in scope and pace.

As these events unfold, both Latin America as a whole and her individual national components are inevitably caught in the cross winds of external influences competing for the Hemisphere. In this sense, Cuba is being reduced to just another instrument of pressure and influence. The great prize is still the rest of Latin America, and the efforts and policies of the two main world camps—and their subdivisions—emphasize this truth.

From the West comes the effort represented by the United States and the Alliance for Progress. From the East comes the two-pronged and increasingly contradictory effort of the split Communist world. We have seen the limitations and the potential promise of this Western effort. But the efforts of the giants of the East have already acquired distinctly separate characteristics, and this dichotomy between Peking and Moscow may hold the promise of an ultimate failure of the Marxist-Leninist thrust.

The Soviet thrust, which originally profited so greatly from the Cuban revolution and its aftermath, is today of a more sophisticated, gradual, and cautious nature. The Soviet Union seems to favor a step-by-step movement toward socialist states, respecting the Marxist concept of "objective conditions" that may exist in one country but not in another, and hoping to reach its goals through peaceful processes, such as "popular fronts." It prefers infiltration to the abrupt takeover, because of its global interests and its stand vis-à-vis the United States. It realizes that violent revolution and Communization of Latin America before the continent has increased her structural and economic strength would saddle Moscow with the full responsibility for sustaining the region. In the shaping of this conclusion, the lesson of Cuba has undoubtedly played a large and sobering role. If the enormous Soviet economic investment in Cuba, which by 1963 exceeded $1 billion, could not thus far improve the Cuban economy and stabilize the island, then clearly the task of trying similarly to support the rest of Latin America would be well beyond Soviet resources and capabilities. The Soviets' consequent and inevitable failure to solve Latin America's problems, combined with an equally inevitable deterioration of her present standards, would be a blow from which world Communism might never recover.

These considerations have obviously led the Soviet Union to follow a careful and measured course in its Latin American policy. It has encouraged the development of diplomatic, cultural, and trade relations. It is encouraging extreme nationalism, neutralism, and anti-Americanism because these attitudes favor both its immediate and long-range objectives. But for the time being at least, the Soviet Union prefers to let the United States shoulder the burden of bringing Latin America into the twentieth century, on the hopeful theory that later it can pluck the fruit for itself.

The other Communist thrust into Latin America is represented today by Chinese and Cuban strategy. This is the strategy of fomenting immediate and violent revolutions. But while Peking and Havana agree on the objective, they pursue it for different reasons. The Chinese interest is principally ideological in character, relating to Peking's stance in relation to Moscow in terms of the

Communist schism. It forms part of the larger doctrine of the inevitability of the anti-imperialist war and of the desirability of launching revolutions whenever and wherever possible. Since China cannot for obvious reasons even begin to think of assisting Latin America economically, she prefers to try to produce a *fait accompli,* after which Moscow would have no choice—in its role as Communism's affluent partner—but to attempt to foot the bill for the results of the revolutions that the Chinese and the Cubans set off. If such a situation should develop, then the Soviet Union would have to espouse the Chinese version of Marxist truths or risk smashing the Communist alliances once and for all.

Castro, on the other hand, has revived again his doctrine of Latin American revolutions—and his dormant Bolivarian complex —for several reasons, including his own survival. He had drawn back from this incendiary stand in 1961 and 1962 under the influence of the Soviet Union, which believed it vital to convince Latin America that coexistence with Cuba was both possible and desirable. But following the missile crisis of 1962, and the consequent deterioration of his position both in Latin America and in relation to the Soviets, Castro realized that his future depended to an immense degree on the creation of a revolutionary Latin America around his own revolutionary state.

True to his character, he has thrown himself into new acts of defiance and aggressiveness as a means of restoring his position in the Hemisphere, and even in Cuba. Since the mere example of the Cuban revolution has not been enough after four years to lead any other Latin American country into imitating his undertaking, Castro has chosen, with a touch of desperation, to attempt to win it by force.

Part and parcel of his renewed policy of clamoring for revolutions was Castro's complicated relationship with the Soviets in the wake of the missile affair. Forced by Moscow to relinquish the missiles and bombers and subjected to the "humiliating"—Castro's word—Soviet offer to permit inspections on Cuban territory, Castro directed much of his wrath against his Kremlin allies, though realism and Communist solidarity needs have kept it in a reasonably low key as far as the public is concerned. The apparent restrictions and conditions of control that Moscow subsequently placed on its economic aid further cooled Soviet-Cuban relations, though both sides went through rather transparent motions of assuring the world that all was well in their friendship.

It was typical of Castro that he then reacted by making overtures to the Chinese, presumably on the theory that a little family black-mail would be useful. A few obvious gestures toward Albania were the first step in this direction. In his speech on January 1, 1963, celebrating the fifth anniversary of his revolution, the Premier announced that Cuba would remain neutral in the intra-Communist dispute and would, in fact, try to help settle it by presenting an example of Communist solidarity. Pretentious as this offer appeared to be—coming from a man who just a year earlier had admitted that he had not even finished reading *Das Kapital*—it also meant that Cuba was serving notice on Moscow that it would no longer loyally follow the Soviet line, as it had in the past.

Two weeks later, Castro repeated his announcement of neutrality in the Communist controversy, coupling it with an invitation to Latin America to rise in revolution, which, he said, Havana stood ready to aid. The Chinese and Cuban policy lines thus converged, though their motivations differed vastly. When Premier Khrushchev called the international Communist congress in East Berlin, in January, 1963, Castro dispatched only a Cabinet minister, a young revolutionary of the "Chinese" persuasion. The previous year, the Cuban delegation had included the top leaders from both the "old line" Communist and the Fidelista groups. But Cuba's entry into the Communist schism paralleled the internal split between the "old Communists" and the much more radical Fidelistas. It was a split that broke into the open in March, 1962, over the Escalante affair, but was subsequently papered over. It erupted again during the missile crisis, and it has carried over into Cuban domestic as well as international politics.

The dispute between the Soviet and the Cuban-Chinese approaches has likewise been reflected within the Latin American Communist parties, deepening fissures that had been in evidence for several years throughout the Hemisphere. As in Cuba, the dispute among Latin American Communists has been between the policy of immediate violent action, advocated by the younger elements inspired by the Chinese and the Cuban examples, and that of gradual action, including bourgeois alliances, defended by the older Communists, who are responsive to the Moscow line.

This growing divergence has resulted in a series of crippling splits within Latin American Communist parties, the emergence of rival Communist movements, and widespread purges. The pro-Chinese groups have scored some important points, but the total effect is still to weaken the Communist activity as a whole.

The powerful Brazilian Party actually split as far back as 1958

292 · THE WINDS OF REVOLUTION

into "revolutionary" and "moderate" segments, and, indeed, Brazilian Communists take pride in the fact that their own feud preceded the Soviet-Chinese break. The Moscow Party, led by Luiz Carlos Prestes, still retains dominance, at least in membership, but the pro-Chinese group had developed into a cohesive, hard-hitting force, and during the Goulart regime, it established important contacts with Cuban agents, the Julião Peasant Leagues, and other revolutionary "negative left" elements in and out of government.

Both groups published newspapers and periodicals until the 1964 revolution, and the importance then given by Moscow and Peking to the editorials and statements issuing from the two movements was seen in the fact that the Soviet and Chinese radio stations devoted hours of their precious overseas programs to quotations *in extenso* from the proclamations of their respective followers in Brazil. One of the most striking examples in this rivalry occurred late in 1963, when the Soviet Ambassador in Rio called on the Brazilian Foreign Minister to warn him of the dangers of "Chinese infiltration and propaganda."

While it had always been assumed that the pro-Moscow party was financed, at least in part, by the Soviets, the Soviet Embassy indignantly protested in 1963 that the Chinese were "illegally" introducing funds into Brazil to finance *their* Communist followers.

Though it was never formalized, the split in the Venezuelan Party acquired major proportions late in 1963 and early in 1964, as a result of the Communist failure to oust the Betancourt regime and prevent the December elections. The older, pro-Moscow leaders of the Venezuelan Party had earlier allowed themselves to be won over by the younger revolutionary elements to support of the terrorist struggle on the erroneous theory that conditions were "objectively" favorable to a major rebellion, and even Moscow gave its blessings to the whole enterprise. But with the collapse of the revolutionary movement, the leaders of the two groups found themselves at each other's throats.

In Peru, where the land invasions and the whole problem of Indian populations had provided promising conditions for agitation, the pro-Chinese faction captured the whole apparatus of the Communist Party late in 1963. There, the "Chinese" worked with the extreme revolutionary movements outside the Communist Party and with the old Trotskyite splinter groups.

In the Chilean Party, Chinese adherents won important positions in 1963 and 1964, but the over-all control remained in pro-

Moscow hands. In Mexico, the Party had been split *three* ways since early 1963.

Inter-Party dissension grew sharply during 1963 as Soviet-Chinese antagonism reached politically violent proportions, and it became almost impossible for Castro to continue improvising his free-lance policies within the Communist world. In May, Castro went to the Soviet Union for a month's visit that alternated between grandiose acts of welcome for him—including a Red Square reception such as no foreigner had ever before been granted—and secret talks with Premier Khrushchev that had an element of Dutch-uncle persuasion.

Castro returned to Havana with assurances of continued Soviet economic and military support, but the price Khrushchev had exacted from him was Cuba's firm commitment to the Soviet line of peaceful coexistence. The talks must have been a memorable exercise in intra-Communist bargaining, and in the end, Castro had no choice but to bow to Khrushchev's pressure. The overwhelming fact of life is that Cuba cannot exist for even one week without outside aid, and Castro knows as well as anyone else that China is in no position to provide such aid. For the Soviets, lining up Cuba on their side was one of the most important preparations for the July ideological confrontation with the Chinese, for Castro remains Communism's greatest triumph in fifteen years.

But if this tactical concession was possible for Castro in May, the turn of world events in effect canceled it two months later. His political isolation in the wake of the Soviet-American *détente* in July forced Castro to return openly to his aggressive revolutionary line, and by September, it appeared that he might be jeopardizing his entire political future. The deepening split in the Latin American Communist parties, resulting from the Moscow-Peking split, was reflected in their attitudes toward Castro: He was becoming anathema to the pro-Moscow orthodox factions and a hero to the weaker "Chinese line" splinter groups and the modern Trotskyites. After serving for more than four years as the great inspiring symbol for the Hemisphere's Communist parties, Castro was suddenly becoming an embarrassing liability. These developments intensified the conflicts within Communism, creating new problems for the local parties and their allies.

Castro's ideological vagaries between Moscow and Peking continued later in 1963 and again in 1964, following the ebb and flow of larger world events. Castro worked hard to maneuver along the increasingly difficult line of neutrality between Moscow and Peking, striking out in different directions, then pulling back again. Late in 1963, he committed Cuba to all-out support of Venezuelan guerrillas, then seeking to overthrow the Betancourt government and prevent the elections scheduled for December. In a desperate attempt to make the revolutionary strategy succeed, the Castro regime shipped three tons of arms and munitions—including bazookas—to the "Liberation Army." The cache, carried from Cuba aboard a motor launch, was landed secretly at a deserted point on Paraguaná Peninsula late in October, but it was promptly discovered by a fisherman who called in the Army.

According to the Venezuelan Government, whose information was corroborated in February, 1964, by the report of a special investigating commission of the OAS, the Cuban arms were to be used by the "Liberation Army" in conjunction with its "Plan Caracas," which called for capturing Venezuela's capital through a series of synchronized maneuvers involving several thousand men, the full strength of the terrorist movement.

"Plan Caracas" failed when the Cuban arms were seized and key members of the conspiracy arrested. The activities of the "Liberation Army" came to a standstill after the December elections, but the movement was reorganized to some degree in the spring of 1964, and terrorist raids resumed subsequently, though with less frequency and intensity than before. It was the first known case of Cuban arms being shipped in bulk anywhere in Latin America, and it was for this act that the OAS ordered sanctions against Castro in July, 1964.

In this instance, Castro was clearly championing the Chinese line of "instant revolution," which had been espoused by the more radical leadership of the Venezuelan Communist Party and forced upon the older, Moscow-lining elements there. Though final judgments are obviously premature, this Cuban involvement in Venezuela may well have been the high-water mark of Castro's influence in Latin America. The failure of the guerrilla movement—it came chiefly because Venezuelan peasants and workers refused to support it—loomed as the most dramatic defeat of Communism in Latin America since the Castro takeover in Cuba.

The Venezuelan events carried domestic as well as international implications, and in January, 1964, just as the United States– Panama crisis erupted in full, Castro suddenly made another trip to Moscow, as if to emphasize his adherence to the Khrushchev line in the rapidly widening rift with Red China. Additional economic aid was apparently promised Castro in Moscow, although once more Khrushchev insisted that Castro bring some order to his chaotic economy so that Soviet help could be better used, and the "Maximum Leader" returned to Havana full of praise for the Kremlin.

Shortly after his return to Havana, however, Castro embarked upon one of his bizarre political enterprises. For reasons known only to himself, he suddenly unearthed an unsavory seven-year-old scandal involving a young Communist named Marcos Rodríguez, a member of the old-guard Party, who had allegedly betrayed a group of revolutionary students to the Batista police. The students had been killed as a result of this information.

Rodríguez was tried and sentenced to death in secret proceedings in Havana early in 1964, but in March, Castro ordered a new public trial, and was himself the star witness. It never became completely clear what Castro's objective had been in staging the second trial—Rodríguez was again sentenced and ultimately executed—but he succeeded in tainting once more the old Communists along with the Students' Revolutionary Directorate, an anti-Batista group that came to blows with the "Maximum Leader" at the time of his 1959 victory. The trial embarrassed some of the key old-line Communists, who were identified with Rodríguez, as well as Fauré Chomón, the Directorate's leader, who had served as Castro's first Ambassador to Moscow and later as Communications Minister.

Internationally, Castro went on alternating between Soviet and Chinese lines, while his controlled press and radio maintained a studied neutrality in the Moscow-Peking feud. In May, 1964, *Pravda,* the official newspaper of the Soviet Communist Party, published a list of world Communist parties supporting Moscow against Peking, but Cuba was conspicuously absent. A month later, another list appeared in *Pravda,* and here the United Party of the Cuban Socialist Revolution was included.

About the same time, Castro began threatening the United States with the use of his surface-to-air guided missiles against the high-flying U-2's that have been continuing aerial surveillance over Cuba since the 1962 crisis. These threats were timed with indications that the Soviets, phasing out their troops from Cuba, were turning over control of the missiles to Cuban crews. The budding crisis concerning the overflights died down, and Castro, seemingly under

Soviet pressure, struck out in a new direction, making broad overtures to the Johnson Administration.

There are sound reasons to believe that the steadily deteriorating economy, growing internal problems, and Soviet pressure were behind these overtures. During the month of May, Castro had shown his nervousness when he mobilized his entire military establishment in the face of threats by a tiny exile group in Miami to infiltrate their leaders into Cuba and launch a new underground operation against him.

When the United States failed, however, to respond to his overtures and, instead, helped to lead the OAS Foreign Ministers to a condemnation of Cuba for smuggling arms into Venezuela, Castro went back to policies of defiance. In a speech on July 26, celebrating the eleventh anniversary of his revolutionary movement, the Premier again promised that Cuba would help all other Latin American revolutionaries.

All these Communist thrusts and counterthrusts are a part of the developing Latin American realities, and they are mirrored in the Hemisphere's quest for new solutions. They may ultimately contribute to a stabilization of Hemispheric affairs because of the growing duality of the Marxist strategy. But at the same time, they are important ingredients of the convulsions rocking the region.

The Subversion

Communist attempts to win greater ascendancy, if not control, in Latin America through direct revolutionary action are often reflected in visible manifestations. The more veiled aspects of convulsion—of a more profound Latin American revolution—are revealed in the emerging and potential changes in political, social, and economic thought and trends. These changes add up to an intellectual revolution and are, in fact, a new dimension in revolutionary developments. This process includes, of course, the reactions to the problem of Communism in its many forms and levels, as well as the question of relationships with the Communist world, inasmuch as both factors enter into the realities of contemporary Latin American life.

Before probing the phenomenon of the intellectual revolution and of the subsurface or potential convulsions, it will be well to examine the visible convulsions, emanating principally from Communist direct action, that attract public attention because of their frequently spectacular character.

Communist agitation and related acts of violence have appeared in recent years, with growing intensity and frequency. They have occurred chiefly in Venezuela, but also in Brazil, Peru, Bolivia, Mexico, Ecuador, Colombia, and the Dominican Republic, though isolated incidents of this type have taken place almost everywhere in the Hemisphere.

One tends easily to blame Cuban- or Soviet-directed conspiracies for all these outbreaks. But, even if Cuba still serves as an inspiration or arsenal for these movements, and if the Soviets help them up to a point, there is much spontaneous combustion involved in these situations. As often as not, Communism, in one of its manifestations, takes advantage of local explosions rather than setting them in motion. The realization of the various forces that cause violence in Latin America should lead to the understanding that the "export of revolution," in the current Washington cliché, cannot occur where there is no market for it.

One of the most spectacular instances of these extreme leftist convulsions occurred in Venezuela, in February, 1963, with the capture on the high seas of the freighter *Anzoategui* by terrorists who called themselves the "Armed Forces of National Liberation." Many of the leaders of this terrorist "army" were trained in Cuba.

Violent convulsions, in which the Communists and Fidelistas have participated and offered leadership, also occurred in Peru in 1962 and 1963. It was significant that they increased after the July, 1962, military coup, and seemed to lessen after the ruling junta provided a political safety valve by permitting free elections in June, 1963. A failure to hold elections and a continuation of military rule would surely have provided the Communists and their allies with a ready-made "second stage" situation in which opposition to military government could become the required classic rallying point for a revolution or civil war.

But even with the election of President Belaúnde Terry, a left-of-center reformist, the past failures to launch programs of economic and social improvement keep alive the threat of new convulsions in Peru. With the majority of the Peruvian population scratching a miserable living out of poor mountain or desert land—often as virtual slaves of the absentee landowners—and the excess populations migrating to the cities, with their slums and unemployment, the country faces built-in revolutionary conditions. Unlike Venezuela, where an important land-reform program is under way, Peru still looms as the textbook case of a country that is asking

for an extremist revolution. To lead Peru toward a change is, of
course, President Belaúnde's gigantic task.

The recurrent highland violence against landlords and United
States mining interests was undeniably led by Communists. One
of the principal rebel leaders was a Trotskyite named Hugo Blanco,
who operated from the Communist strongholds in the Andean
departments of Cuzco and Puno, where Peru's misery has historically been at its worst, stemming from both the terrible mountain droughts and medieval systems of land tenure. Hugo Blanco
and some of his companions were actually arrested just before
the elections. But the fundamental conditions that gave rise to
Blanco and to the wars between the peasant squatters and the landlords will not be eradicated by sheer force. Peru, therefore, is a
dramatic example of a country whose failures thus far in political
democracy and economic and social justice are an invitation to
disaster.

Violence has occurred in Brazil and, as in Peru, its roots were
in Communist and extreme-leftist agitation taking advantage of
social injustice in land distribution. In the drought-parched Northeast where the "industrials of the drought" control land and water,
the Communist-led Peasant Leagues of Francisco Julião slowly
gained strength and spread their influence to the central plateau of
Goiaz and other parts of the country.

Julião, who followed Castro late in 1961 in declaring himself
a "Marxist-Leninist," visited Moscow and Peking on numerous
occasions and was a frequent guest of Premier Castro in Havana.
His activities, which at one time enjoyed the active support of the
Cubans and the more quiet blessings of the Soviet Embassy in
Brazil, were beginning to create serious prerevolutionary conditions
in the vast Northeast area and to attract sympathy in the more
affluent South-Central region of the country. However, Julião's—
and his Leagues'—operations came to an end, at least temporarily,
with the 1964 civilian-military revolution. After hiding for a few
weeks, he was flushed out by the Army and imprisoned along with
many of his associates. But perhaps more than the anti-leftist
revolution, what had really hobbled Julião was his lack of leadership qualities and of revolutionary charisma. Though he had begun
organizing his League four years before Castro triumphed in Cuba,
Julião never became more than a secondary regional leader, and
therein lay the luck of Brazil.

However, the arrest of Julião or even the ultimate disappearance of his League does not, to be sure, eliminate the underlying explosiveness of the Northeastern problem. Former President Goulart, much as he paid lip service to social justice, never undertook any meaningful corrective measures in the Northeast, failing notably to make any headway in land-tenure problems. Not unlike his predecessors, Goulart advocated nationalism and "Brazilian solutions"—and more than any of his predecessors, he used it for his own political aggrandizement—but until his ouster he had done virtually nothing about the urgent agrarian problems in the Northeast and elsewhere. A wealthy landowner—it is a peculiarity of Brazilian politics that a rich man many function as a pro-labor and leftist demagogue—Goulart had made no serious effort to push his Congress, in which other landowners were and are powerfully represented, to legislate in the area of land reform. He had proposed that the constitution be bypassed to provide for land reform without compensation, but in all his years in power, he made no effort to carry out the many fundamental measures that could have been instituted under the existing laws.

SUDENE, the government's agency for the Northeast's development, had begun to make headway in setting up irrigation, road-building, and other infrastructure works—operating with the assistance of the Alliance for Progress—and, in a most encouraging development, began attracting private enterprise to the area. However, the April revolution ousted SUDENE's managing director, Celso Furtado, and then deprived him—along with several hundred other persons, including former Presidents Quadros and Kubitschek—of political rights for ten years. The crucial question now looming in the Northeast is whether the new regime, committed as it is to reforms, will be able to carry on Furtado's work in the face of all the rising new tensions.

As the Northeastern misery continues—SUDENE's first achievements were hardly a dent in the totality of the problem—migrants from this region keep crowding the labor markets of the big cities, like Rio de Janeiro, creating new social problems and adding to the revolutionary pressures that the new regime may have temporarily allayed, but has not yet permanently solved.

Convulsions of this type have been occurring in a less sustained and less spectacular way in other countries of Latin America. In Colombia, where backlands violence has been going on for fifteen years—first as a political contest between Liberals and Conservatives and, later, as just pure banditry—extremist agitators are working overtime to capture a situation that is potentially ideal for their aims. And recent indications are that they may be beginning to have some success.

It is not likely, at least at this stage, that these activities—what we have called the visible convulsions—will result directly in the breakdown of established regimes or lead by themselves to great revolutions. But they are an important part of the over-all Latin American scene at this time of great change, and they may help to influence the long-range trends in a region that has such an enormous revolutionary potential—physically as well as intellectually.

The Intellectual Rebellion

In trying to assess the present Latin American situation in broad historical terms—and it is as difficult to arrive at an accurate appreciation as it is to snap a photograph of a surging crowd—the temptation is to see it in terms of a future synthesis of the multifarious influences now concentrating on the Hemisphere. Such a synthesis may ultimately take the dominant coloration of the influence that will make itself felt most strongly in the course of the present ideological contest. If the Western democratic ideology finds a new inspiration, its influence may finally assert itself and the new form of Latin America may well lie within the context of the democratic social revolution that the United States says it champions. It is certain, on the other hand, that a continuing failure of the democratic ideology will open the doors to solutions that will be greatly colored by extreme radicalism and the rejection of Western values.

The intellectual revolutionary potential is mounting rapidly in Latin America, against the backdrop of the concrete convulsions, and the great changes seem to be just around the corner in many of the key Latin American countries. It is a new dimension of revolution, and just as it had to seek to adapt itself to the Cuban dimension of revolution, the West will now have to try to fit itself to this latest pattern of change. Being more sophisticated in many ways than the Cuban explosion, this new revolutionary dimension may even be more difficult to accept and understand.

Again, it is Brazil that seems to be the anchor country in this new process. Aside from Cuba, which has concentrated on its peculiar form of political development in conjunction with world

Communism, Brazil has unquestionably gone furthest in the direction of the "new solutions."

The 1960 election of Jânio Quadros was described at the time as the "white revolution"—the revolution by the vote—because his immense pluralities seemed to signify the desire to break away from the political and emotional traditions and patterns of the past. The new nationalism and the "independence" in foreign policy launched by Quadros during his brief tenure in office were inherited by the Goulart regime and, to a great extent, have become a part of the stream of Brazilian political consciousness.

The unabating political crisis between Quadros' resignation in 1961 and Goulart's ouster in 1964 has in its own way accentuated this trend toward a new Brazilian identity. The civilian-military revolution of 1964, which set the stage for a new crisis period, has somewhat blurred the outlines of this identity in the rush of events that changed the country from a chaotic democracy into a still unpredictable form of semidemocracy. But it is safe to assume that regardless of the politics of the moment, Brazilians increasingly demand for themselves a special role in the international sphere and a new destiny in terms of their internal political life.

Economic nationalism at home, particularly in relation to government control of the basic means of production and in relation to foreign investments, appears to have settled into a permanent trend. Though the 1964 revolution halted the tendency Goulart had shown to put the government in control of virtually every important segment of national economy, there is no reason to think that the already considerable area of production under state management will ever revert to private hands. Thus, Volta Redonda, Brazil's main steel plant, was set up as a government operation as far back as 1944, and Petrobrás, the oil monopoly, was founded in 1954—long before Goulart appeared on the stage.

A tradition, therefore, is involved in the structure of Brazil's economy, and the country seems to be moving in the direction of a synthesis in its economic life, with the government and private enterprise sharing in the controls. But the success of this road, like anything else in Brazil, will depend entirely on the ability of the new regime to put the economy in order, curtail the awesome inflation, and begin to solve the tremendous basic problems, such as the plight of the Northeast and the growing nightmare of urban slums.

The young Brazilian generation—including notably the Catholic youth movements that fight Communism with one hand and what they call "imperialism" with the other—would like to see a peaceful, or intellectual, solution to the great revolution that is now being wrought in Brazil. Brazil's tradition of bloodless political change favors a peaceful shift away from the old patterns of yesterday and toward the new patterns of tomorrow. Chances are relatively good that events will happen that way, but even under the best of circumstances, Brazil is already emerging as a changed country. And any changes in this largest of Latin American countries will unquestionably stimulate changes elsewhere.

A revolutionary potential, in its own way vastly more dangerous than that of Brazil, is rapidly mounting in Argentina, perhaps the most advanced socially and economically of the big Latin American countries. There, a political deadlock whose consequences are unpredictable has arisen between the country's two principal forces: the military and the great political mass loyal to what is vaguely and generically known as Peronismo. Born from the ideological hopes and confusions created by the demagoguery of Juan Perón almost a decade ago, Peronismo has survived the ouster of its dictator-founder and the political convulsions of the ensuing eight years to emerge in 1963, as one of the country's strongest single political forces.

Rejected by the military governments that saw in Perón primarily the totalitarian and corrupt dictator that he undoubtedly was, Peronismo—which represented itself as a social protest force—was banned in 1955 from political life. Growing in the political and social vacuum of Argentina, however, it helped elect Frondizi to the Presidency in 1958 and scored in 1962 its first great open victory in congressional and gubernatorial elections.

This victory led the military to carry out the *coup d'état* that ousted Frondizi—who was blamed for having allowed the Peronistas to run—and established the Army-backed regime, which promptly dissolved Congress. Though the military had promised elections, the regime announced early in 1963 that, for all practical purposes, Peronistas would not be allowed to campaign or run for office. The Peronista voters, whose strength increased appreciably after the anti-Frondizi coup, were thus faced with the choice of not voting at all or supporting the least objectionable of other available candidates. However, when elections were held on July 7, 1963, less than 20 per cent of the electorate obeyed Perón's orders, sent from his exile in Spain, to cast blank ballots. With the nation tired of upheavals, the victory went to the moderate but intensely nationalistic Dr. Arturo Illia. Obviously, this alone did not solve Argentina's social-political problem.

It is thus pertinent to stress that in creating Peronismo in the shadow of his bizarre *"Justicialismo"* ideas, Perón did spawn what has ultimately developed into an articulate, well-organized leftist party.

The elections indicated that the ex-dictator's party has lost some of its strength, but the Argentine masses remain inclined toward social protest and radicalism. The question now is how they will be absorbed into a new formula. Both Cubans and local Communists are concentrating on the Peronistas—and it may be worthwhile to recall that "Che" Guevara is an Argentine with some following in the "old country"—and it should not be surprising if they meet with some success. Thus the Argentine political situation, the mounting protest pressures, and the stagnating economy combine into a dangerous revolutionary potential. While the ferment grows, new ideas and new long-range solutions are being contemplated by the younger Argentine generation, dissatisfied as it has been with the sterile policies of the military and of the economically dominant right-wing groups. The seeds have been planted in Argentina for an inevitable "intellectual revolution," part of the emerging Latin American process of the synthesis in political development. The foretaste of this trend was present in the Frondizi Administration, as it was in neighboring Brazil under Quadros and then Goulart, and its continuation can hardly be prevented—even if it can be delayed by those who now control Argentina. After nearly one year in office, President Illia has failed to lead Argentina out of the morass of economic problems and political frustrations, and the ferment that now continues in that wealthy country runs the full gamut from unabating Peronista agitation to a new surge of anti-Semitism, a phenomenon that thrived once before, under Perón's rule. In a twisted sort of way, all these elements, too, are the ingredients of the revolution.

A potential for such an intellectual revolution is also growing in Chile, one of Latin America's politically most sophisticated countries. Even the victory of Christian Democrat Eduardo Frei in the 1964 general elections will inevitably lead Chile to a new political, economic, and social future, probably emphasizing some statism at home and an independent foreign policy. In the latter field, even ex-President Alessandri, basically a rightist, long refused to join the United States in pressures on Cuba, in itself a new departure in foreign policy. But late in the summer of 1964, Chile, along with Uruguay and Bolivia, bowed to the decision of the OAS Foreign Ministers' Conference and broke relations with Cuba.

In Bolivia, an independent trend in foreign policy, particularly toward Cuba, had been in evidence for a number of years. Having gone through its own social revolution in 1952, Bolivia has in a way developed many of its solutions in terms of its own political structure, formally a democracy, but one in which the ruling revolutionary party, the Movimiento Nacionalista Revolucionario (MNR), is assured of permanent control of the national life. It is a political framework similar to that existing in Mexico since the 1910 revolution and its subsequent stabilization, in which political intercourse is so heavily weighted in favor of the ruling group that no possibility is left for the emergence of meaningful opposition parties. Until the ouster of President Paz Estenssoro, in November, 1964, Bolivia had been undergoing a quiet but important process of radicalization at the upper levels of the MNR and of the government. With the newly installed military junta being pressured by both left- and right-wing forces, the outlook is for continued unrest.

In neighboring Paraguay, the Stroessner dictatorship was again confirmed in power in the February, 1963, elections. The President, running against a hand-picked opponent, won easily. But extreme-left-wing agitation by the opposition groups inside the country and in exile is gaining momentum, and in time, revolutionary forces are certain to gather strength in that small, landlocked country.

In Colombia, the backlands violence is a steady counterpoint to efforts to stabilize the country through the continuation of the bipartisan rule of the Liberals and the Conservatives. This system of the "National Front" survived the 1962 elections and the choice of a Conservative for the 1962–66 Presidential period, but it came close to a break-up, and it is questionable whether the bipartisanship will withstand another election. While extremist agitation is increasing, notwithstanding some notable successes of the Alliance for Progress, the central political fact of Colombian life is that there is no democratic leftist party—such as Venezuela's Acción Democrática or Peru's APRA—and political life as a whole revolves around the Conservative and Liberal parties, both basically of rightist persuasion. This is, obviously, a situation that, combined with other factors of instability, presents a long-range revolutionary potential.

In the Dominican Republic, a leftist democratic candidate was overwhelmingly elected to the Presidency in December, 1962, climaxing the process that had begun with Trujillo's assassination eighteen months earlier. His regime and the Dominican Revolutionary Party had initially served as a lightning rod between the rightist and leftist extremes, but this precarious balance collapsed within seven months as the military and the rightists overthrew Bosch, allegedly to save the country from Communism.

Bosch and his efforts at democratic reform—politically inept though they turned out to be—might have offered the Hemisphere another example of an intellectual revolution, but the establishment on September 25, 1963, of the new "rightist state" set the Dominican Republic back many years. What loomed ahead was a period of predatory and selfish rule, liable to be marked by unrest and violence. Although the weaknesses in the national fabric that permitted the 1963 coup stemmed chiefly from deep-seated Dominican problems, it could also be argued that because of overcaution, limited imagination, and an excess of bureaucracy, the Alliance for Progress lost its opportunity to help turn this Caribbean nation into a functioning social democracy.

If the Alliance had done better in this context, then perhaps constitutional government would have survived in the Dominican Republic. As it was, it succumbed to the vicious circle of Latin American politics. The fall of Bosch, coming on the heels of the military coups in Guatemala and Ecuador and followed by a coup in Honduras, made the political score in 1963 a painfully negative one for democracy. Four new military regimes were born, while two countries—Argentina and Peru—returned to democratic rule. In 1964, it was the turn of Brazil and Bolivia to witness military coups, and no matter what the reasons in either case, they represented failures for the democratic ideology and practice.

In Haiti, the situation has verged for so long on the brink of a revolutionary explosion against the extraordinarily cruel and venal dictatorship of President François Duvalier that convulsions of a major scope could occur almost any time. The regime's failure to undertake any meaningful effort to improve its living standards—the lowest in the Hemisphere—has combined with political oppression to create a classic revolutionary situation. There, too, powerful leftist forces are at work—the proximity to Cuba increases the attraction—and pro-Castro sympathies are spreading even among Duvalier's closest associates. The racial problem, based on the President's emphasis of Haiti as a Negro republic rediscovering its African heritage, aggravates the pressures there.

In British Guiana, the political situation has been frozen by Britain's refusal to grant the country her long-awaited independence because of the explosive quarrel between the two main political parties. Cheddi B. Jagan, the elected Prime Minister and an avowed Marxist, controls the East Indian rural populations through his People's Progressive Party, while the anti-Communist groups control the urban African population. Jagan and some of his associates are extremely close to the Castro regime, and Britain's fears are that a grant of independence under the circumstances would result either in a civil war or—if Jagan were successful in controlling the situation—in a Cuban-Guianan alliance. The strikes and riots in the summer of 1963 seem, however, to have postponed independence indefinitely.

In Central America, revolutionary potentials continue to exist. In Guatemala, the new military regime has clamped down on most political activities, but the question is how long they can be suppressed.

In Nicaragua, a hand-picked candidate of the ruling Somoza dynasty was elected to the Presidency early in February, 1963. The refusal of a liberal opposition candidate to run for office—a move criticized by many Central American friends of Nicaraguan democracy—made the election a walk-over for René Schick, the new President. But the outlook is for continued anti-Somoza agitation in the country, a situation from which the extreme left is certain to profit, unless a way is found to encourage the pro-democratic elements.

This, then, is the landscape of the revolutionary potential in Latin America in 1963. Not monolithic, it is a highly varied landscape in which the prospects of violent revolutions and peaceful "intellectual revolutions" stand side by side. It is, to be sure, impossible to blueprint how and how soon these revolutionary situations will reach their maximum intensity, and ultimately, what direction they will take. Predictions are useless because even if certain trends can be discerned, too much is still unpredictable and subject to unforeseeable events. But the fundamental and unquestionable fact is that Latin America, sometimes silently and sometimes in explosions of violent change, is undergoing her greatest revolution since the beginning of her history as a conglomeration of independent states.

The United States

The question that arises again, after surveying the present revolutionary state of Latin America is, of course, how the United States —as a power and as an embodiment of Western concepts of democracy—can influence this march of events. Its presence in Latin America is, to be sure, a part of the Cold War contest with the Soviet bloc and with Communism in its many forms that is being fought all over the world. Latin America has become in the 1960's perhaps the most crucial Cold War battlefield, and the unfolding events in the Hemisphere constitute one of history's great ideological combats.

It has been suggested here that the trends that have already set in in Latin America point toward long-range solutions taking the shape and character of a synthesis of the great forces that are now converging on the region. The possibility of such a synthesis is, in itself, evidence of a great revolution, for old patterns and traditions are being shattered and new formulas and solutions are being produced in the vast, heaving crucible that is Latin America. These trends are, in all likelihood, irreversible in the sense that history and men's ideas do not go backwards, even if occasional regression occurs here or there.

The problem thus facing the United States and the West is to persuade this immense process of synthesis toward the democratic ideology, rather than to seek the impossible and the self-defeating objective of returning Latin America to where she stood when the great revolutionary period emerged after World War Two and found its latest point of reference in the Cuban revolution.

From a pragmatic point of view, the United States clearly must continue to aid the social revolution by mobilizing its own resources and its know-how to help the region to make the material breakthrough into the twentieth century. The disappointments and the obstacles that appear daily in the execution of this task must not be allowed to deflect the United States from the path of the Alliance for Progress. It is a measure of maturity and sophistication not to be impatient too soon or discouraged too easily in participating in what is one of the great historical revolutions of our time.

But to succeed in influencing the Latin American revolution toward the democratic ideology, the dollars and cents of the Alliance for Progress are not enough. President Kennedy stressed this point two years before he took office, and Fidel Castro repeated it when he was told of the Alliance's birth. Both men were, of course, right. Revolutions deal primarily with ideas, and in the final analysis, the battle for Latin America must be fought in the field of ideas.

Thus far, the United States has allowed itself to be placed on the defensive in this ideological struggle by relying on defensive anti-Communist attitudes instead of spreading its own brand of ideological gospel. This is why the importance of the Alliance for Progress in the great democratic revolution has failed to elicit the response it truly deserves. To be successful, then, the United States must somehow reconcile the old Yankee pragmatic approach to Latin America—the view that the Hemisphere poses a merely technical problem of social and economic improvement—with that elusive sentiment of political appeal and excitement that men require in their lives as much as they require better living standards.

Despite the disenchantments and disappointments, a great reservoir of good will toward the United States, and what it stands for, still exists. The *rapport* has not been altogether broken, nor need it be, if imagination and a true understanding of the revolutionary process are permitted to replace bureaucratic timidity. Perhaps the time has come to let our poets help a little in the policy of the Alliance, rather than leaving it exclusively in the lifeless hands of functionaries and technicians. The great strength of the United States in Latin America is its tradition of liberalism, the tradition that seemed to have returned with Kennedy's election. Spreading to the grass-roots level the image of the United States as a liberal nation in its dealings with the world and with Latin America could go far to destroy the apathy and the lack of faith toward the ideology that the United States represents but somehow cannot communicate.

A new challenge to America's ability to communicate its ideological message to the southern part of the Hemisphere came abruptly and dramatically on November 22, 1963, when the news of John F. Kennedy's assassination hit Latin America with the force of a body blow. There have been few Americans in history—and Franklin D. Roosevelt was probably one of them—who have excited the hopes and imagination of Latin Americans as President Kennedy had succeeded in doing in the less than three years of his tenure.

To an extraordinary extent, Kennedy had become identified in Latin American minds with all that was positive and hopeful about the United States image. He achieved this not only because he launched the Alliance—and the Alliance did subsequently bring disenchantment to some—but, more important, because he managed to establish a *rapport* between his own ideas for the United States and the Latin American revolution. His death, therefore, shocked Latin America as it did his own country. The question that was instantly heard everywhere in Latin America was, "What will now happen to us?"

President Johnson wasted no time in offering the answer that nothing would change, that the Alliance would go on, and that the United States dedication to the Hemisphere would continue to be as complete as before. But the image and symbol had vanished forever, and doubts and suspicions set in at once, despite the reassuring words from the White House. A series of unrelated events unhappily and immediately complicated the relationship and rendered the new challenge to the United States and to the untried Johnson Administration even more difficult than it might have otherwise been.

The first difficulty was that, rightly or wrongly, the impression spread in Latin America that President Johnson was more conservative than President Kennedy and that, therefore, the liberal approach to the Hemisphere would now disappear. One of the causes of this impression was the fact that President Johnson's first major foreign-policy move was to name Thomas C. Mann, then serving as Ambassador to Mexico, to take over as the Administration's "one voice" in the conduct of its policies in Latin America.

Again, myths and realities became confused. Mann was immediately depicted as retrogressive in his approach to Latin America and as a throwback to the Eisenhower Administration, which he had served as Assistant Secretary of State for Inter-American Affairs. Though it was true that Mann had spent almost the entire period of the Kennedy Administration in Mexico, and thus had not participated in the formulation of the Alliance concepts and philosophies, he had actually played a major part in the historical process that led to the launching of the Kennedy program. He had been one of the moving forces behind the creation of the Social Development Fund at the 1960 Bogotá Conference, which was a forerunner of the Alliance, but unhappily, he seemed to have little use for the political and ideological notions that had inspired the Kennedy team. This was immediately felt in Latin America, and probably quite unfairly, Mann began his career in the Johnson Administration under something of a cloud.

The concern over this situation became so pronounced in Washington that when Mann was considered for this new post, Senator Hubert H. Humphrey, one of a tiny group of men consulted, handed the President a private memorandum warning that nothing should be done to create the impression that the United States was going back to Republican days in its relations with Latin America.

Mann had served hardly one week in his new job when the Panama crisis, the Johnson Administration's first major encounter with the passions of Latin America, suddenly exploded, with a series of Canal Zone riots. The riots had their roots in the long-standing difficulties between the United States and Panama over the flying of Panamanian flags in the Canal Zone. This time, because of the irresponsible action of American high-school students in the Zone and the American Governor's failure to act appropriately, matters got completely out of hand. Panamanians invaded the Zone without much interference from the Panama National Guard, and United States soldiers firing at the invaders killed several persons.

This was a signal for Panama's President, Roberto F. Chiari, to announce that the United States had committed "aggression" against his country, that he was breaking diplomatic relations with Washington, and that he would not resume them until the Johnson Administration agreed to revise the 1903 Canal treaty. To complicate matters, or perhaps to help set them in motion, Panama was facing Presidential elections in four months, and domestic politics on both sides instantly became involved in the international crisis.

There had been a long history of Panamanian grievances against the United States for what Panama regarded as unjust treatment under an obsolete agreement, including the vesting in perpetuity of United States control over the Canal Zone. The treaty had been revised twice since 1903, and when President Chiari visited Washington in 1962, he and President Kennedy agreed to appoint a commission to negotiate some of these grievances, though the United States refused then, as it does now, to give up the perpetuity clause in the treaty.

The commission was created, but as often happens, it bogged down in details, and the whole problem no longer commanded much White House attention. In time, the group went out of business. But the January, 1964, riots revived the whole subject in the most dramatic possible manner, thrusting upon the United States the onus for shooting Latin Americans, even if it acted in defending the Zone from rioters.

Mann flew at once to Panama for a meeting with President

Chiari, but he returned with the strong conviction that the Pana-manians were attempting to high-pressure the United States into an a priori agreement to renegotiate the treaty. This President Johnson, himself facing an election, would not consent to, and the dispute was taken over by OAS mediators for what turned out to be nearly three months of patient, desultory, and frustrating negotiations. At least three times, the two governments stood at the verge of an accord—after more than twenty different formulas had been pro-posed—but each time, the agreement broke down at the last mo-ment.

President Johnson and Secretary Mann were determined to stand fast against any agreement to a formula that committed this country to renegotiate the treaty without knowing toward what end it would be renegotiating. Right as they may have been, the impact of the whole affair on Latin America was highly regrettable, to say the least. The United States was viewed as tough and inflexible, and it was accused of trying to starve Panama into submission because all economic aid had been interrupted following President Chiari's break in relations. Tourist and other business in Panama had come to a virtual standstill, and in time pressures arose for a settlement.

This was one of the most discouraging periods for the Johnson Administration in its dealings with Latin America, and again, seemingly unrelated events occurred to make it even worse. Be-cause form and style are so important in Latin America, President Johnson was caught, perhaps inadvertently, in a situation that did more damage to the Administration's prestige in the Hemisphere than the whole Panamanian crisis, about which many Latin Amer-icans were already beginning to have second thoughts. This second incident involved Mr. Johnson's speech before the OAS Council on the occasion of the inauguration of the new Inter-American Committee for the Alliance for Progress (CIAP).

For reasons unknown, the President chose to insert in his pre-pared text about the Alliance the statement that no settlement had been reached in the Panamanian dispute, contrary to an OAS announcement the night before. The Johnson statement had a para-lyzing effect on the assembled Latin Americans and a similar impact on Hemisphere public opinion. This may have been the lowest point in the whole relationship, and Latin America began to question with profound seriousness whether the Johnson Ad-ministration really proposed to carry on with the old dedication to the Alliance.

About two weeks later, another unhappy event occurred, again sending shivers through Latin America. This time, it was Secretary Mann who was reported to have told a closed meeting of United States Ambassadors to Latin America, then conferring with him in Washington, that the Johnson Administration would be more "pragmatic" than the Kennedy Administration in judging military coups in the Hemisphere.

This meant, Mann explained, that the United States would not *necessarily* react automatically against the new military regimes with suspension of diplomatic relations, suspension of economic aid, and other coercive measures. The Kennedy Administration had done this in every case in 1963, but Mann argued that inflexible standards should not be applied indiscriminately and that the United States should make its decisions "pragmatically," depending on the circumstances. He went on to say that history had demonstrated that past U.S. efforts aimed at establishing democracy in Latin American countries had had adverse effects—though this was demonstrably inaccurate in the Argentine and Peruvian situations in 1963—and that, therefore, such policies should not be pursued as an automatic response.

The report on the Secretary's admonition to the Ambassadors was obtained by this writer and published in *The New York Times*. Because of the immense Latin American sensitivity to the whole question of *coups d'état,* the report had an electrifying impact. However, as often occurs, it became oversimplified in the process of being conveyed throughout Latin America, with the result that a wholly erroneous impression was created that the United States would now look with favor, or at least indifference, on military takeovers.

Because the regime of President Goulart was ousted by a civilian-military revolution about three weeks after the report on Mann's talk was published—and because the Administration rushed within forty-eight hours to recognize the new government—it was assumed that this, too, fitted into the new policy. Charges were made, in fact, that the United States had been involved directly in the Brazilian coup through the Pentagon or the CIA, though there is no evidence whatsoever of this.

From then on, however, the relationships between the Johnson Administration and Latin America began to improve rapidly. The Panama dispute was finally settled on April 3, diplomatic relations were resumed, and high-level representatives were appointed to "discuss" the whole treaty problem.

On May 11, President Johnson summoned the Latin American Ambassadors to the White House to deliver a speech that, in the view of many Latin Americans and North Americans, should have been made five months earlier, when it might have avoided much misunderstanding. The central passage in that speech, which was music to Latin American ears, restated for the first time since the advent of the Johnson Administration the concepts of democratic social revolution and of democratic ideology in the context of the Alliance for Progress. The President put it this way:

> Our charter charges each American country to seek and to strengthen representative democracy. Without that democracy and without the freedom that it nourishes, material progress is an aimless enterprise, destroying the dignity of the spirit that it is really meant to liberate. So we will continue to join with you to encourage democracy until we build a Hemisphere of free nations from the Tierra del Fuego to the Arctic Circle. . . . But the charter of the Alliance is not confined to political democracy. It commands a peaceful, democratic, social revolution across the Hemisphere. . . .

This speech was probably the turning point in relations with Latin America, restoring them almost to the point they had reached when President Kennedy was assassinated. President Johnson may lack the personal appeal that John Kennedy exercised in Latin America, but since May 11, he has made an extraordinary effort to win the confidence of Latin America. This effort has not gone unappreciated.

Secretary Mann, with political pressure on him diminishing, has reorganized and streamlined the administrative structure of his division, and contrary to earlier fears, the United States has given all-out support to CIAP, the new Alliance steering committee, and its Chairman, Carlos Sanz de Santamaría.

As all these relationships finally seemed to fall into place, CIAP's first business meeting in Mexico, in July, 1964, provided probably the greatest encouragement for the future of the Alliance since its launching in 1961. It was the first time that top-level Latin American and United States representatives had an opportunity to conduct a rational review of the whole program in the light of the experiences of its first three years. An unspectacular but vital program of specific steps was drawn up at the meeting, and while no miracles were being promised, the expectations were for sound results stemming from a kind of cooperation that had not existed before.

Despite all the initial difficulties in the new era of United States relations with Latin America, beginning with the creation of the Alliance by President Kennedy in 1961 and continuing with President Johnson's own problems three years later, a long-range perspective finally began to emerge in mid-1964.

In terms of this perspective, United States relations with a Latin America swept by the winds of revolution must not be judged by the attitude of one country or another toward Castro, even if these attitudes are occasionally irritating or frustrating. They must not be judged in terms of what is good or bad for United States investments in the immediate sense. They must not be judged by the petulance and the irritations that are bound to arise in our daily dealings with Latin American nationalism or exaggerated leftism. They must be judged, rather, in the historical perspective of a great revolution with which, in the real meaning of history, the United States and the West must come to terms.

If this occurs, then Communism may have to face the devastating truth that, after all, Marx and Lenin were not so infallible in predicting a "socialist" future for Latin America and the rest of the underdeveloped world.

Washington
November, 1964

Index

López Mateos, Alberto, 287
Lott, Henrique Teixeira, 32
Luque, Cardinal Crisanto, 93

Machado, Gerardo, 79
Machado, Gustavo, 125
Magloire, Paul, 80
Mann, Thomas C., 126, 183, 234, 253, 310–14
Manuilsky, Dimitri, 40
Mao Tse-tung, 19, 20, 25, 26
Marinello, Juan, 146, 157
Mars, Louis, 217
Martí, José, 78
Matos, Huber, 142
Mexico: economic planning, 244; economy, 68, 72, 76; political patterns, 15, 78, 81, 103, 104, 211, 212, 214; slums, 53; water, 60, 61
Mikoyan, Anastas I., 143, 169
MIR (Revolutionary Movement of the Left), Venezuela, 22
MNR (National Revolutionary Movement), Bolivia, 304
Montiel Argüello, Alejandro, 217
Mora, José A., 251, 254
Mortality rate, 48, 61
Moscoso, Teodoro, 253
Muñoz Marín, Luis, 36
Mussolini, Benito, 28

Nasserism, 45, 266–67, 283, 285
National Institute of Agrarian Reform, Cuba, 152, 157
Nationalism, 37, 84–85, 102–5
Neruda, Pablo, 33
Neutralism, 4, 12, 13, 44–45, 185, 284
Nicaragua: Castro attacks on, 122, 124; economic integration, 276; political patterns, 79, 80, 95, 213, 266, 306
Niemeyer, Oscar, 33
Nixon, Richard M., 52, 89, 106–15, 116, 125, 218

OAS (Organization of American States), 12, 44, 79, 156, 174, 212, 217, 225; and Dominican Republic, 220–22, 268; role in Alliance for Progress, 258–73.

See also Special Consultative Committee on Security; Conferences of Foreign Ministers
Ochoa Gómez, Delio, 124
Odría, Manuel A., 28, 80, 82, 89–92, 107, 215
Ojeda, Fabricio, 129
"Operation Pan American," 42, 115–17, 125, 126, 177, 179, 234, 259–60
ORI (Integrated Revolutionary Organizations), Cuba, 150, 151, 152, 153–57, 159–62, 164, 170

Pan American Health Organization, 59–60, 61, 62, 63
Panama: Cuban aggression, 122–23; economic integration, 276; economy, 73; education, 66; political patterns, 213; slums, 53; U.S. relations with, 2, 310; water, 60
Panama Canal Zone, riots in, 2, 310–11
Paraguay: economy, 73, 76; land tenure, 55; political patterns, 78, 98, 108–9, 210, 213, 304; water, 60, 61
Parties, political, 78–80. See also Democracy; individual countries
Paz Estenssoro, Víctor, 2, 210, 214, 278
Peace Corps, U.S., 251, 281
Peasant Leagues, Brazil, 20, 33, 57, 248, 298–99
Peña, Lázaro, 157
People's Progressive Party, British Guiana, 81, 307
Pérez Jiménez, Marcos, 28, 64, 71–72, 82, 90, 95–97, 215, 228, 297
Perón, Eva: Foundation, 87–88
Perón, Juan D., 9, 16, 69, 80, 82, 86–88, 90, 104, 213, 214, 215, 302, 303
Peru: economy, 68, 76; land reform, 29, 182–83, 248; land tenure, 55, 56; leftist agitation, 20, 291–92; political patterns, 9, 79, 80, 89–92, 94, 104, 109–11, 209, 211, 213, 224–25, 231, 270–71; slums, 52–53; U.S.–Fund dispute, 180

United States: aid, 175, 208, 242; and Argentine coup (*1962*), 223–24; condemnation of Dominican Republic, 219–23; counterrevolutionary measures, 20–21; Cuban policy, 129–36, 165–68; foreign policy, 33, 82–85, 175–77; Guatemalan incident, 81–82, 103; intervention policy, 103; investment capital policy, 84–85; Nixon tour, 106–14; and Peru coup (*1962*), 224–25; recognition policy toward dictators, 82–85; revolutionary challenge to, 4–5. *See also* Alliance for Progress; OAS

United States Caribbean Command, 21

Urbanization: growth of, 17; and migration, 48, 51; and social conditions, 49–54. *See also* Economy

Uriburu, José, 79

Urrutia Lleó, Manuel, 120

Uruguay: education, 66; health, 62; political patterns, 218; water, 60

Valdés, Ramiro, 151

Valencia, Guillermo León, 93, 94, 221

Vargas, Getúlio, 16, 28, 32, 78, 79, 90, 103, 194, 195

Vega, César, 122

Velasco Ibarra, José María, 10, 78, 79, 129

Venezuela: economic planning, 244; economy, 68, 71–72, 76; education, 64, 66; land reform, 29, 245; leftist uprisings, 19, 294, 297; political patterns, 16, 78, 80, 95–98, 101, 104, 113–14, 209, 213, 216, 231; population, 17; slums, 53; water, 60

Warsaw Pact, 148, 156

Water, 48, 58–63. *See also* individual countries

White, Thomas D., 21

World Bank, 264, 279

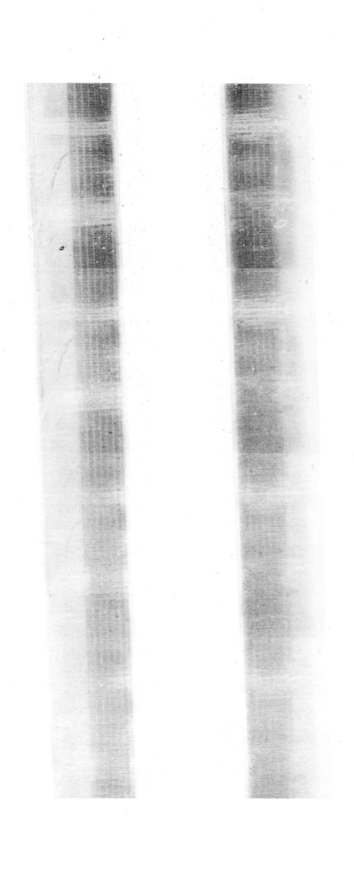